Feminist New Testament Studies

RELIGION/CULTURE/CRITIQUE
Series editor: Elizabeth A. Castelli

Feminist New Testament Studies

Global and Future Perspectives

Edited by

Kathleen O'Brien Wicker,
Althea Spencer Miller,
AND
Musa W. Dube

For Zayn —
With love and
thanks for all
your support!
Love, Kathleen

TO: Zayn
You are the embodiment
of all the hopes and aspirations
these contest dreams.
Exemplar of the highest ideals
of love, justice + the egalitarian
spirit. Bless you always!
love,
Althea Spencer Miller
Christmas '05

palgrave
macmillan

First published in 2005 by
PALGRAVE MACMILLAN™
175 Fifth Avenue, New York, N.Y. 10010 and
Houndmills, Basingstoke, Hampshire, England RG21 6XS
Companies and representatives throughout the world.

PALGRAVE MACMILLAN is the global academic imprint of the Palgrave Macmillan division of St. Martin's Press, LLC and of Palgrave Macmillan Ltd. Macmillan® is a registered trademark in the United States, United Kingdom and other countries. Palgrave is a registered trademark in the European Union and other countries.

ISBN 1–4039–6870–5
ISBN 1–4039–6871–3

Library of Congress Cataloging-in-Publication Data

Feminist New Testament studies : global and future perspectives / edited by Kathleen O'Brien Wicker, Musa W. Dube, Althea Spencer Miller.
p. cm.—(Religion/culture/critique)
Includes bibliographical references and index.
ISBN 1–4039–6870–5—ISBN 1–4039–6871–3 (pbk.)
1. Bible. N.T.—Feminist criticism—Congresses. 2. Globalization—Religious aspects—Christianity—Congresses. 3. Globalization—Social aspects—Congresses. I. Wicker, Kathleen O'Brien. II. Dube Shomanah, Musa W., 1964– III. Spencer Miller, Althea, 1955– IV. Series.

BS2379.F46 2005
225.6'082—dc22   2005043176

A catalogue record for this book is available from the British Library.

Design by Newgen Imaging Systems (P) Ltd., Chennai, India.

First edition: November 2005

10 9 8 7 6 5 4 3 2 1

Printed in the United States of America.

Dedicated to

Mary Wig Johnson
(1913–2003)
Scripps College Alumna and Trustee
and
The Women and The Community of Scripps College

Contents

Conversation Two: Asia and Latin America   113

Conversation Three: Africa and the Diaspora   175

Series Editor's Foreword

RELIGION/CULTURE/CRITIQUE is a series devoted to publishing work that addresses religion's centrality in a wide range of settings and debates, both contemporary and historical, and that critically engages the category of "religion" itself. This series is conceived as a place where readers will be invited to explore how "religion"—whether embodied in texts, practices, communities, and ideologies—intersects with social and political interests, institutions, and identities.

The study of scriptures has long been central to the academic study of religion. *Feminist New Testament Studies: Global and Future Perspectives* invites its readers to undertake a political remapping of this enterprise both in light of more than a generation of critical feminist engagement with scriptural interpretation and in response to many postcolonial challenges to the historical construction of Christianity as primarily a European and North American phenomenon. This volume maps a counterintuitive terrain and records an array of feminist voices from around the globe, opening up a new critical geography for the study of the religious texts of the Christian tradition. The contributors to this volume struggle with the ambivalent implications of globalism and globalization. They explore the tensions embedded in the notion of "scripture" itself, a notion that is as tied up with questions of canon, authority, normativity, and constraint as it is with practices of critical rereading, productive and countercultural resistance, and liberation. The contributors to this volume do not ask, "What does scripture mean?" but rather, "How does scripture work in the service of various political, social, and theological ends?" Writing from a range of subject positions and social locations, the scholars whose work appears in this collection raise a substantive challenge to the field of the academic study of religious texts. Their work therefore makes an important contribution to the conversations that this series hopes to stage.

New York City
February 2005

Elizabeth A. Castelli
RELIGION/CULTURE/CRITIQUE Series Editor

Foreword

Scripps College entered the twenty-first century as a small liberal arts college for women at the edge of a great metropolis. Virtually all of the fundamental values of the College are both challenged by, and find opportunities in, this new century. Women around the world are the objects of attention, research, exploitation, solicitation, and enlistment, but luckily they are also increasingly the subjects of their own development, the heroines of their own lives, in Dickens's phrase. The liberal arts tradition is challenged intellectually by its internal dynamics and challenged historically from without and within by its association throughout Western history with the dominant culture, gender, race, and class.

Scripps College finds in its heritage the seeds of its own intellectual growth and liberation—as represented in the college seal of the woman sowing seeds of wisdom. This heritage was reinforced when the College welcomed scholars, students, concerned laity, and others from around the world to the campus for the conference "The Global Future of Feminist New Testament Studies." The College's heritage is honored in this volume, the memorial of those conversations that took place at Scripps College in the spring of 2003, all centered on the issues of globalization and interpretation of the New Testament.

This volume of academic reflections on a set of critical texts at the heart of Western culture is a product of the best kind of scholarship to emerge from the liberal arts tradition and the interdisciplinary understanding of that enterprise at Scripps College. Here in this volume, as at the conference from which it arises, we find explorations of the texts from different historical, cultural, ethnic, theological, liturgical, racial, and class perspectives. Because these texts, like the other constitutive texts of different religious traditions, have often defined gender roles and set cultural norms, they are critical to women's self-concepts, roles, possibilities, and experience. They have been used, and are used today, to justify attitudes toward, and limitations of, women not only within religious institutions, but also in some secular and civic institutions as well. Yet we know that these texts have been and are being read anew millions of times every day, and some of those readings are liberating and even revolutionary. And those readings are increasingly overlapping and informing one another as the modes of communication among peoples multiply and reify, as claims to universalism are tested daily through congresses, conferences, telecommunications, web publishing, and other interactions of a kind and number that were unthinkable even a decade or so ago.

The scholars who gathered at Scripps College to discuss the effects, possibilities, threats, and dynamics of globalization met together—as have scholars for thousands of years—to review their ideas and receive comment and criticism, to hear others' views and therefore possibly revise their own, to determine whether their incipient ideas about a direction or a new idea find resonance and stir interest. In short, these scholars constitute a community of learners and teachers, stretched around the world, who are making meaning for future generations of scholars, students, members of faith communities, and others.

It was wholly appropriate that the conference and this volume honored the career and contributions of Professor Kathleen O'Brien Wicker, a valued scholar, faculty colleague, and community leader at Scripps College. Kathleen's own intellectual career mirrored the increasing recognition in North American New Testament scholarship of the validity and vitality of other approaches, particularly the traditions of the formerly colonized areas of the world, where Christianity is finding much of its growth and power. In circumstances, landscapes, cultural and religious traditions far removed from Western Europe, Kathleen's scholarship found a new direction and energy. From that renewal came fresh scholarship and intellectual passion that carried all before it. This volume, like the conference, is a tribute to the power of intellectual passion to inspire new insights, new productions, and new students. All of Professor Wicker's colleagues, students, friends, and admirers join me in celebrating this volume as a fitting tribute to her decades of teaching and research that has benefited generations of students in Claremont and legions of admirers and scholars around the world.

January 15, 2005   Nancy Y. Bekavac
Claremont, California   President, Scripps College

Preface and Acknowledgments

This volume is a collection of the papers, responses, and reflections presented at a conference, or as we preferred to call it, a series of "Conversations" held at Scripps College in Claremont, CA in the spring of 2003. The conference theme and title, *The Global Future of Feminist New Testament Studies*, was inspired by our growing awareness that the shift in Christianity from the global north to the global south would have important implications for feminist New Testament studies and for the role of women in Christianity.

The structure of this volume retains the structure of the conference that was organized into three geopolitical areas: North America and Europe, Asia and Latin America, and Africa and the Diaspora. This organizational format has political implications, we realize, but the organization was dictated by logistical rather than political considerations. We are also aware and regret that only a limited number of global perspectives are represented in this volume, particularly those from the global south.

We resisted the impulse to add additional papers and responses to this volume, however, because we felt that each "Conversation" had an internal cohesion that would be lost if we added essays not written specifically for this context. This volume should be regarded not as the last word but as an invaluable early attempt to address the shape of feminist New Testament studies as a global project in the first half of the twenty-first century. We trust that these essays are only the beginning of a conversation that will evolve as the decades unfold.

We express our sincere thanks to the many people who made the conference and this volume possible. Without the generous support of President Nancy Y. Bekavac and Dean Michael D. Lamkin of Scripps College, the 2003 Conference on *The Global Future of Feminist New Testament Studies* would not have happened. Many other academic colleagues and staff members at Scripps and the other Claremont Colleges also made important contributions to the success of the conference, for which we are grateful. The participating scholars, some of whom traveled thousands of miles to be here, were a pleasure to collaborate with. Without them, neither the conference nor this volume would have come into being.

Scripps College President Bekavac and Dean Lamkin were also enthusiastic in their support for the publication of the conference papers that appear in this volume under the title, *New Testament Studies: Global and Future Perspectives*. We are grateful to President Bekavac for accepting our invitation to write the Foreword to the volume as well.

Amanda Johnson, Religion Editor for Palgrave Macmillan-USA, and her staff in the United States and at Newgen in India and Series Editor Elizabeth Castelli made the process of preparing this book for publication a comfortable one. They were always generous with their time and expertise in assisting us in the publication process. Linda Sullender at Scripps managed all the logistical details for both the conference and the timely preparation of the manuscript for publication. All of us who have been involved in this project have appreciated her ever-gracious and competent assistance. Words alone cannot express our gratitude to Linda.

The editors owe a special word of appreciation to the students who collaborated with us in the conference and in the volume. They shared their ideas in a seminar, responded faithfully to requests for their active assistance during the conference, and provided the updated information needed for the volume. Their perspectives, expressed in the reflection essays written for the seminar, are an important part of this volume and this project.

Kathleen Wicker and Althea Spencer Miller express their special thanks to Musa W. Dube for agreeing to join them as a coeditor of the volume. All three of us also thank each other for the opportunity to sit together weekly over dinner and then to enjoy the dessert of the conversations produced by the editing process that went on into the night. We believe that this editing process has been an important act of feminist engagement that has further shaped our global and future perspectives on feminist New Testament studies and intensified our commitments to this project.

We invite you, as readers, to become collaborators with us in this conversation. Although we have organized the essays according to the original order in which they were presented, you need not read them in this order. Each of the essays stands as a major contribution on its own. Wherever you choose to begin, we trust that you will be challenged by this journey of exploration of *New Testament Studies: Global and Future Perspectives*.

Kathleen O'Brien Wicker, Althea Spencer Miller,
and Musa W. Dube

List of Contributors

Isabel Balseiro is Alexander and Adelaide Hixon Associate Professor of Humanities at Harvey Mudd College. She is the editor of *Running Towards Us: New Writing from South Africa* (Heinemann, 2000) and coeditor of *To Change Reels: Film and Film Culture in South Africa* (Detroit, Michigan: Wayne State University Press, 2003). With a fellowship from the American Council of Learned Societies she spent the academic year 2003/2004 at the University of Cape Town conducting research on African cinema.

Sheila Briggs is Associate Professor of Religion at the University of Southern California. Her research interests lie in feminist theology, nineteenth- and twentieth-century (German) theology, early Christianity, and theories of history and modern liberation movements. Current projects include research on the relation of attitudes toward gender and the Jewish Torah in the writings of Paul, and "The Xena Project," a look at an ancient past that never happened except in the imagination of contemporary popular culture: the television series *Xena Warrior Princess*. She is coeditor (with Mary Fulkerson, Duke University) of the *Oxford Handbook of Feminist Theology*.

Gay L. Byron is Associate Professor of New Testament and Christian Origins in the Baptist Missionary Training School Chair of Biblical Interpretation at Colgate Rochester Crozer Divinity School, Rochester, New York. She is the author of *Symbolic Blackness and Ethnic Difference in Early Christian Literature* (London and New York: Routledge, 2002) and assistant editor of *Asceticism* (ed. Vincent L. Wimbush and Richard Valantasis, New York: Oxford University Press, 1995). She is currently working on a commentary on the book of *James*, which will be included in a forthcoming African American New Testament commentary.

Elizabeth A. Castelli is Associate Professor of Religion and Women's Studies at Barnard College. She is the author of *Imitating Paul: A Discourse of Power* (Louisville: Westminster/John Knox Press, 1991) and *Martyrdom and Memory: Early Christian Culture-Making* (New York: Columbia University Press, 2004). She is the coauthor of *The Postmodern Bible* (New Haven: Yale University Press, 1995). She has edited several volumes and special journal issues, including *Women, Gender, Religion: A Reader* (New York: Palgrave/Macmillan, 2001) and *Interventions: Activists and Academics Respond to Violence* (New York: Palgrave/Macmillan, 2004). She is also the editor of the series, Religion/Culture/Critique, which is published by Palgrave/Macmillan.

Noelle Champagne is a 2005 graduate of Scripps College with a dual major in English Literature and Religious Studies. With an undergraduate emphasis in feminist and contemporary studies, her main areas of interest are feminist New Testament theology and postcolonial studies. She plans to pursue a post-graduate education in folklore and mythology.

Elizabeth Conde-Frazier is Associate Professor of Religious Education at the Claremont School of Theology. She is a religious educator who integrates the discipline of religious education with theology, spirituality, and the social sciences. Her writings include "Hispanic Protestant Spirituality" in *Teología En Conjunto: A Collaborative Protestant Hispanic Theology* (Louisville, KY: Westminster/John Knox Press, 1997); *Multicultural Models of Religious Education*, ed. (Atlanta, GA: SCP/Third World Literature Publishing House, 2001); "Latinas and Religion," *Latinas in the United States: An Historical Encyclopedia* (Scranton, PA: Scranton University Press, forthcoming); and *A Many Colored Kingdom: Multicultural Dynamics for Spiritual Formation*, coauthored (Grand Rapids, MI.: Baker Academic, March 2004).

Musa W. Dube is Associate Professor of Religious Studies at The University of Botswana. Her publications include *Postcolonial Feminist Interpretation of the Bible* (St Louis: Chalice Press, 2000) and with Musimbi Kanyoro, *Grant Me Justice: HIV/AIDS and Gender Readings of the Bible* (Peitermaritzburg/New York: Cluster & Orbis, 2004). She is the editor of *HIV/AIDS & the Curriculum: Methods of Integrating HIV/AIDS in Theological Programs* (Geneva: WCC, 2003); *Other Ways of Reading: African Women and the Bible* (Atlanta and Geneva: Society of Biblical Literature and WCC Publications, 2001); with Gerald O. West, *The Bible in Africa: Transactions, Trajectories, and Trends* (Leiden: Brill, 2000). She is a coeditor of the present volume.

Lincoln E. Galloway is Assistant Professor of Homiletics at Claremont School of Theology. He is from the Caribbean island of Montserrat and the Methodist Church in the Caribbean and the Americas. His interests include socio-rhetorical approaches to biblical texts and critical engagement of liberative theologies for exegetical and homiletical tasks. He is author of *Freedom in the Gospel: Paul's Exemplum in 1 Cor 9 in Conversation with the Discourses of Epictetus and Philo* (Leuven: Peeters, 2004).

Filiberto Nolasco Gomez is a graduate of Pitzer College, class of 2004. He completed a self-designed major in education with an emphasis on Socio Political Pedagogies. Filiberto was awarded a Watson Fellowship for the 2004–2005 academic year, during which he traveled to Guatemala, South Africa, and Northern Ireland, to fulfill his project entitled "Education on the Margins: Pedagogy and Agency in Marginalized Communities." Following this experience he will pursue a master of fine arts degree in film with a focus on documentary film.

Sonya Gravlee is currently a Ph.D. student in Women's Studies and Religion at Claremont Graduate University in California. Her research interests include feminist theology, gender theory, feminism and film studies, peace and justice issues, postcolonialism, religion and culture, constructive theologies, and women and religion. She also teaches part-time at the University of La Verne and works at the Institute for Antiquity and Christianity, both in southern California. A UCC minister who served in Texas before returning to school, Gravlee plans to combine teaching and ministry as a college chaplain when her Ph.D. studies allow.

Holly Hight graduated from Scripps College in 2004 with a B.A. in Religious Studies. Her senior thesis won Best Thesis in Religious Studies from Scripps College. In November of 2004, Holly started working for Bread for the World—a Christian citizen's movement devoted to advocacy for the poor and hungry. She is helping expand awareness about the global AIDS crisis, extreme poverty, and hunger. She lives in Pasadena with fellow Claremont graduates.

Erin Jacklin graduated summa cum laude from Claremont McKenna College in 2003. She majored in Religious Studies with an emphasis on New Testament interpretations. Her Senior Thesis, "Interpretation and Community: Historical Interpretations of the Gospel of Mark" received the Best Thesis in Religion award from Claremont McKenna College. She plans to pursue graduate studies in the fall of 2005.

Hisako Kinukawa is codirector of the Center for Feminist Theology and Ministry in Japan International Christian University, Tokyo, Japan, where she is an adjunct professor. She teaches courses on Biblical Studies, Gender Issues and the Bible, Introduction to Theology and Women's Studies at a number of universities and seminaries in the United States and abroad. Her publications in English include *Women and Jesus in Mark: A Japanese Feminist Perspective* (New York: Orbis Books, 1994), and an essay in *Women Moving Mountains: Feminist Theology in Japan* (2000). She has published four books in Japanese, edited an issue of *In God's Image* (1999) on Japanese feminist theology, and has translated several English works into Japanese, including Antoinette Clark Wire's book *The Corinthian Women Prophets: A Reconstruction through Paul's Rhetoric* (Minneapolis: Fortress, 1990) and *Searching the Scriptures* (2002) edited by Elizabeth Schüssler Fiorenza.

Rosemary Radford Ruether is the Carpenter Professor of Feminist Theology at the Graduate Theological Union and a member of the faculty at the Pacific School of Religion in Berkeley, California. She is the author of numerous books including *Sexism and God-Talk: Toward a Feminist Theology* (Boston: Beacon Press, 1983); *Women and Redemption: A Theological History* (Minneapolis: Fortress Press, 1998); *Gaia and God: Ecofeminist Theology and Earth Healing* (San Francisco: Harper, 1992); *The Wrath of Jonah: The Crisis of Religious Nationalism in the Israeli-Palestinian Conflict* (Minneapolis: Fortress Press, 2nd ed., 2002); editor (with Rosemary Skinner Keller) of *In Our Own Voices: Four Centuries of American Women's Religious Writing* (San Francisco: Harper, 1995). She is currently working on a two-volume encyclopedia on women and religion in North America.

Elizabeth Schüssler Fiorenza is Krister Stendahl Professor at Harvard University Divinity School. Her publications include *In Memory of Her: A Feminist Theological Reconstruction of Christian Origins* (New York: Crossroad Publishing Co., 1983/1992; translated in 12 languages); *Jesus; Miriam's Child, Sophia's Prophet: Critical Issues in Feminist Christology* (New York: Continuum, 1995), *Sharing Her*

Word: Feminist Biblical Interpretation in Context (Boston: Beacon Press, 1998); *Jesus and the Politics of Interpretation* (New York: Continuum, 2000); and *Wisdom's Ways: Introducing Feminist Biblical Interpretation* (Maryknoll: Orbis Books, 2001). She is a cofounder and coeditor of the *Journal of Feminist Studies in Religion* and a coeditor of *Concilium*. She was elected first woman president of the Society of Biblical Literature and has served on editorial boards of major biblical journals and societies.

Lydia Sohn is a 2005 graduate of Scripps College in Claremont, California with a dual major in Asian American Studies and Religious Studies. Ms. Sohn plans to continue her religious education in Divinity School with a focus on Pastoral Care and New Testament studies. Her passions include social justice—particularly for minorities in the United States.

Aída Besançon Spencer is Professor of New Testament at Gordon-Conwell Theological Seminary in South Hamilton, Massachusetts. Born and reared in Santo Domingo, Dominican Republic, Dr. Spencer is the author of a number of writings including *Beyond the Curse: Women Called to Ministry* (Peabody, MA: Hendrickson, 1985); *Paul's Literary Style* (Lanham, MD: University Press of America, 1984); contributions to *Latino Christian Thought at the Dawn of the 21st Century* (Nashville: Abingdon, 2004); and coeditor of *The Latino Heritage Bible* (Iowa Falls, IA: World Bible Publishing, 2002). Dr. Spencer has served as social worker, minister, and educator in a wide variety of urban settings and is an ordained Presbyterian minister (PCUSA).

Althea Spencer Miller from Jamaica is a Doctoral candidate in Biblical Studies at Claremont Graduate University. Her publications include "Ecumenicity, Gender and Ethics: A Biblical Vision," in Tetsunao Yamamori, Bryant L. Myers, and Kenneth Luscombe, eds., *Serving With the Urban Poor* (Monrovia, California: MARC, 1998); and "When the Stones Cry Out," a paper written for the Claremont School of Theology Convocation 2000 on Urban Ministry and pending publication. She was co-convener of the Global Future of Feminist New Testament Studies Conference at Scripps College in the spring of 2003 and is a coeditor of this volume.

Prinny Stephens is a graduate student in Classics with interests in ancient Greek fables, Gnosticism, and early Christianity.

Karen Jo Torjesen is Dean of the School of Religion and Co-director of the Institute for Antiquity and Christianity at the Claremont Graduate University. She is also the Margo L. Goldsmith Professor of Women's Studies in Religion and Director of the Women's Studies in Religion program. Her publications include *Hermeneutical Procedure and Theological Structure in Origen's Exegesis* (Berlin, New York: De Gruyter, 1986, c1985); and *When Women Were Priests: Women's Leadership in the Early Church & the Scandal of their Subordination in the Rise of Christianity* (San Francisco: Harper, 1993).

Katrina Van Heest is currently pursuing a doctoral degree in New Testament at Claremont Graduate University and is an alumna of Scripps College. Ms. Van Heest's academic interest is broadly in the study of the role of sacred text in society. Her current studies focus on Pauline writings—especially from a perspective that seeks to produce responsible feminist analysis with respect to contemporary Jewish–Christian relations—and the effects of technological development and globalization on cultural and social interactivity.

Kathleen O'Brien Wicker is Professor of Religious Studies Emerita at Scripps College and an adjunct professor at Claremont Graduate University. Her publications include "Teaching Feminist Biblical Studies in a Postcolonial Context," in *Searching the Scriptures: A Feminist-Ecumenical Commentary and Translation* (ed. Elizabeth Schüssler Fiorenza, New York: Crossroad Press, 1993); "Sacred World and Sacred Text: The Mehu Healing and Retreat Center in Ghana," with Kofi Asare Opoku in *African Americans and the Bible: Sacred Texts and Social Textures* (ed. Vincent L. Wimbush, New York: Continuum, 2000), and translator/editor *Porphyry the Philosopher To Marcella* (Atlanta: Scholars Press, 1987). She was co-convener of the Global Future of Feminist New Testament Studies Conference at Scripps College in the spring of 2003 and is a coeditor of this volume.

Vincent L. Wimbush is Professor of Religion and the founder of the Institute for Signifying Scriptures at Claremont Graduate University. In addition to numerous scholarly articles, he is the author of *Paul, The Worldly Ascetic: Response to the World and Self-Understanding According to 1 Corinthians 7* (Macon, GA: Mercer University Press, 1987), and the editor of *Rhetorics of Resistance: A Colloquy on Early Christianity as Rhetorical Formation* (*Semeia* 79, 1997 [1999]); *The Bible and the American Myth: A Symposium on the Bible and Constructions of Meaning* (Macon, GA: Mercer University Press, 1999); and *African Americans and the Bible: Sacred Texts and Social Textures* (New York: Continuum, 2000).

Zhiru is Assistant Professor of Religious Studies at Pomona College, Claremont, California. Her publications include "The Ksitigarbha Connection: A Missing Piece in the Chinese History of Pure Land Buddhism," *Studies in Central and East Asian Religions*, 12/13 (2001–02); "The Emergence of the Saha Triad: Iconic Representation and Humanistic Buddhism," *Asia Major* 13.2 (200); and "The Maitreya Connection in the Tang Development of Dizang Worship Buddhist Milieu," forthcoming in *Harvard Journal of Asiatic Studies* 65.1 (2005).

Introduction

Kathleen O'Brien Wicker

Reading the Baobab Tree

An African proverb states: "Truth is like a baobab tree; one person's arms cannot embrace it."[1] The baobab tree is distinctive in its appearance, with its trunk very large in circumference and its branches a root-like intertwined tangle crowning its top. When the proverb makes the baobab tree a metaphor for truth, it suggests that truth is also something massive, not completely graspable, certainly not by one person alone. The baobab's distinctively interlaced branches suggest the complexities of truth as well, not easily defined, categorized, and disentangled.

An alternative reading says that the baobab tree asked to be the best, brightest, and most handsome tree in Africa. The Creator wearied of these demands and finally tore the tree out of the ground and planted it upside down. As a result, the baobab grows leaves only once a year and the rest of the time its roots reach toward the sky.[2]

Both the proverb and the legend about the baobab tree provide useful perspectives on this volume that contains essays, responses, and reflections by women and men from Africa, Asia, the Caribbean, Latin America, and North America on the global future of feminist New Testament studies. The proverb emphasizes the ability and necessity for all people to contribute their perspectives if truth is to be more adequately approximated. The upside-down baobab tree, for its part, images an "upside-down" global map representing the shift in Christianity from the global north to the global south that Philip Jenkins discussed in his 2002 book, *The Next Christendom: The Coming of Global Christianity*,[3] and the challenge to the scholarly agenda of New Testament studies in the north that is inevitable in such a global context, whether "global" is interpreted as a geographical or an analytical category.

The Context and Content of the Discussion

In 2003, Scripps College invited a number of scholars to participate in a conference on *The Global Future of Feminist New Testament Studies*. They were asked to speak about the future of feminist New Testament studies in light of the shift in the locus of Christianity to the global south. The participants in this discussion, who were multifaith, Christian, Buddhist, and nonreligious, spoke from their particular contextual locations about their perceptions of feminist New Testament interpretation, and how it might address the new global realities, both religious and political.

In these essays, which were originally presented at the conference, complex and intertwined questions are addressed: What will global feminist New Testament interpretation look like in the next few decades as a result of the shift in the locus of Christianity that Jenkins has pointed to? Who will participate in these conversations and who will shape the issues for discussion? Who will be excluded from the conversations? What sources, resources, and methods will be used in future feminist New Testament scholarship and praxis? The essays examine a variety of examples and proposals that envision new methods for reading biblical texts and types of "accessible" feminist New Testament scholarship that will enable women globally to struggle more effectively against oppression in all forms and from whatever sources it derives.

Most conference participants focused on the idea of global Christianity and concluded that a number of transformations would be required in the way that feminist New Testament studies has been engaged in, if it is to be responsive to the new global realities. They called for the recognition of the socio-political and economic contexts of the past and present that continue to shape the lives of women and their societies. They emphasized the need to sharpen current feminist theoretical frameworks that are responsive to global, national, institutional, and individual realities. They urged that new and inclusive methodologies for the study of the New Testament, multi-logues with people of other faiths and cultures, and positions of advocacy for women's empowerment, justice, and peace, be developed if feminist New Testament studies is to have a global future.

Two important caveats were issued in these essays by those who were in agreement with this general interpretive framework. Althea Spencer Miller used her Caribbean context to warn of responding to this global transformation with reductionist paradigms that fail to recognize the diversity within and among southern cultures. She states: "For the Caribbean, the historical complexities of class, race, religion, gender, sexual orientation, age, Christian denomination, family, marital status, require a far more nuanced picture of Christianity and inter-religious relationships." Buddhist scholar Zhiru cautioned against letting Christian taxonomies dominate the conversation as they have done in the study of religion since the nineteenth century.

Elizabeth Castelli, however, challenged the assumption that global Christianity should be the major concern of the conference. She argued rather that the Christianity of globalization should be its focus, since "the New Testament can undergird in both structure and content a global politics that promises to generate and sanction global violence and global suffering." Sheila Briggs elaborated this argument in her response to Castelli's essay, saying that ". . . the Christianities of the South are not necessarily religions of the poor and marginalized, and are not necessarily committed to liberative political practices or biblical interpretation. Indeed the church leadership in Africa, Latin America and Asia is often drawn from the same elites as the political rulers. They may pursue interests and agendas which are not directed to the well-being of the majority of their peoples." Castelli, drawing upon the work of Arjun Appadurai, who envisions a "grassroots globalization" with potential for disrupting the globalization agenda, calls for an activist "transnational feminism" with similar disruptive potential.

Recognizing the Sociopolitical and Economic Contexts of the Past and Present

Modernism has challenged reductionist assumptions and paradigms about the commonality of human experience and has destabilized categories such as race and gender. In addition to race and gender, sexual orientation, age, ability, and many other factors are recognized as creating distinctive worldviews that influence interpretation, whether in reading biblical texts or in living. But there are also larger structures at play that affect the lives of both individuals and of societies. This Introduction addresses some of these individual and societal factors, beginning with the larger global forces that have influenced individuals, societies, and cultures.

Imperialism, Colonialism, Neocolonialism, and Globalization

Imperialism, the imposition of foreign systems of power by one political group over others, has been practiced throughout human recorded history. Imperialism is also reflected in religious texts such as the New Testament that both struggle against systems of political domination and impose internal imperialistic controls on dissidents within the community. In modernity, imperialism has taken the form of colonialism, characterized by the exploitation of the human and natural resources of one people for the benefit of the exploiter, and the alteration or destruction of their cultural systems.

Missionary teaching in the colonial context almost always resulted in a painful distancing of people from their cultural traditions, a practice they legitimated by appeal to biblical texts. The language of the missionaries disparaging traditional culture as paganism and devil worship was deeply offensive to most people. Colonized people, of course, recognized both the abuses of power by these imperial systems and the weaknesses of empire, but naming them publicly usually had disastrous consequences. As the African proverb says: "The leopard has only seven whiskers but how dare anyone get close enough to count them."

But, in spite of the intentions of the colonial powers, cultural hybridity was the ultimate outcome of their endeavor. Both the colonized and the colonizers were affected by their mutual interactions, without, however, being totally transformed into the "Other." This applied in the areas of religion as well as in culture. Or as Sheila Briggs states, "Hybridization does not necessarily imply homogenization, but often the opposite . . . globalization does not spell the eradication of the local but its complication and intensification."

Althea Spencer Miller uses Lucy Bailey as an icon that indicates that the complexity and intensity of the Caribbean is a continuing bequest of colonialism. It does not correspond to the dichotomizing rhetoric of north/south discourse. Neither colonialism nor its grandchild, globalization, has produced a homogenized culture.

Globalization is the latest form that structures of power and domination have taken to control the world. Globalization is, according to Elizabeth Castelli and others, an economic and political system of domination and exploitation, no longer under the control of nation-states. This assessment of globalization holds that the "market now has control over social, economic and cultural relationships of people. All other social forces, including the state, which regulated people's needs and priorities, have ceased to operate."[4] Sheila Briggs further observes that "the advance of globalization . . . is the culmination of processes of cultural hybridization of colonizer as well as of colonized that European empires and missions initiated."

Economic and social violence in the era of globalization has been a focus of the work of Mexican theologian Maria Pilar Aquino. Aquino, according to Rosemary Ruether, "analyzes gender oppression in the context of the multi-dimensional aspects of racial, class, cultural and ecological violence wrought by neo-liberal economy, as the framework for her feminist liberation theology." Redemption, in her theology, is the realization of the "fullness of life" that results from overcoming oppressive hierarchies in all areas of life. She argues, according to Ruether, that the "neo-Liberal market economy that claims to have triumphed as the only possible economy and way of life . . . is not only creating poverty and violence for most humans outside this elite, but also rests on an idolatrous claim to universal truth and normative ethics for human fulfillment."

Brazilian theologian Ivone Gebara has "focused in her recent writing on dismantling the patriarchal cosmovision of dualistic hierarchy that sustains ideologies and social systems of domination of some (Christian white male ruling class humans) over others (non-Christians, non-whites, women, the poor and the earth)," according to Rosemary Ruether. Gebara develops a theology of the Trinity that sees "vital interrelationality" as its essence, and describes whatever limits or destroys the possibilities of interrelationality, including economic and other kinds of domination, as "sin."

While advocates of globalization promise a world without borders, a vision that feminists and others regard as a mixed opportunity, Hisako Kinukawa calls for us to be suspicious and to interrogate the much proclaimed fallen boundaries of the globalization era, for, as she holds, new and "higher borders have been produced as the result of breaking down the traditional borders." The following discussion focuses on some of these new and higher borders.

Economic and Cultural Systems of Violence and Domination

Current systems of violence and structures and discourses of domination include racism, classism, heterosexism, anti-Semitism, orientalism, and anti-immigrationism. These forms of domination survive by creating systems of violence against people, particularly the most powerless, the poor, and women and children. The most powerless, globally, are not confined to any one region or continent. Rather, as Elisabeth Schüssler Fiorenza points out, "wo/men as a group are disadvantaged worldwide in and through the processes of globalization. Wo/men still earn only two-thirds of what

One of the rewards of such engagement is the enrichment, both personal and professional, that accompanies it. Aída Besançon Spencer emphasizes the positive values that northern feminists can learn from other cultures, using the values and practices of Hispanic cultures as examples. She calls for solidarity that goes beyond gender to other oppressed groups, since she holds that "Justice for women needs to be related to justice for others." Althea Spencer Miller complements this view by calling for the inclusion of males in these considerations, especially those who have experienced the manipulation of gender in colonial and other power relationships.

The decentering process must also apply to the relationship between women of different statuses and from different classes, whatever the context. Musa Dube's narration of her experiences as a graduate student is only one example of the divisions among women that weaken our ability to act effectively in the world. She calls for a revolutionary feminist New Testament studies that will join in the project of creating solidarity and building capacity. Dube laments the fact that only four women in all of Africa have Ph.D.s in New Testament and proposes that feminist New Testament studies organizations be established that would set the agenda and build its capacity through a programmatic approach to scholarship, training, research, and writing. These strategies, and others like them, are required if feminist New Testament studies is to result in an inclusive scholarship.

Developing New/Inclusive Methodologies for the Study of the New Testament

Critique of the Academy

The essays all call for the implementation of strategies for New Testament interpretation that move beyond the traditional approaches of the academy. In the view of the contributors, the academy has an agenda for biblical studies that is often oppositional to new and inclusive methodologies for the study of the New Testament. Elisabeth Schüssler Fiorenza reminds us that New Testament studies has traditionally not produced knowledge "in the interest of wo/men who by law and custom have been marginalized and exploited as well as excluded from scientific theology and biblical interpretation for centuries." She goes on to observe, "Biblical discourses in the public sphere are advocating either literalist biblicism or academic scientism. As long as this is the case, struggles for justice, radical equality, and the well-being of all will remain marginal in the discourses of the discipline."

Aída Besançon Spencer observes that "academia has historically been an individual, single, serious pursuit. A lot of this perspective that infiltrates academia similarly pervaded the corporate world." Her claim that the academy embodies the same values as the corporate world calls for future global feminist New Testament studies that is self-conscious and critical of its values and contexts of operation.

Vincent Wimbush observes that current biblical scholarship focuses on content and meaning in the texts. He argues that these interpretations, whether done by men or women, including feminists, move within "the circle not of interestedness in general, but religious-confessional investment and apologetics in particular, no matter how masked the positionality may be." He proposes a new approach, which he calls "signifying on scripture," that is concerned "not so much with the meaning *of* or *in* the Bible, but with the Bible *and* meaning, the phenomenology and politics and social psychology of the making and engagements and social functions of, and social practices in connection with, the Bible." For Wimbush, this approach allows more opportunity for "reading darkly" out of the African American experience.

Sheila Briggs adds to the critique of feminist biblical criticism. She states, "Feminist biblical interpretations are not hermetically sealed from others and we can discover that we have strange and in some cases unpleasant bedfellows. This is not a moral argument against engaging in feminist New Testament studies but a warning against a moral naiveté that assumes our good intentions control how our scholarship is configured in the dense systems of communication which are the most prominent feature of globalization."

Musa Dube agrees with Wimbush, Castelli, and Briggs that some feminist New Testament scholars "are possibly doing a scholarship that is largely ancient, theoretically based, socially detached, rather than action oriented towards executing real changes in the communities and structures of the world." By contrast, most biblical interpretation in the global south begins with the recognition that the bible was written for the community in response to their lived experiences. Dube also argues that the academy has created a deep chasm between itself and faith communities. Feminist New Testament studies as a discourse that seeks to change the world must find ways of working with the communities of faith that consume the New Testament. While scholars go about their work with little impact on faith communities, she states, Christian communities proceed in their process of interpretation with confidence, knowing that they are dealing with a "spiritual thing." Thus, a decision by feminist New Testament scholars to ignore faith communities, particularly those of the global south, is in effect a choice for irrelevance and non-engagement with many "ordinary readers" of the bible.

Inclusive Methodologies/Feminist Strategies for Reading the New Testament

Drawing upon the numerous suggestions and critiques offered earlier, the scholars contributing to this volume suggest new inclusive methodologies and feminist strategies for reading the New Testament in the context of globalization. These strategies include multilayered readings as suggested by Hisako Kinukawa, the proposal for a critical global feminist studies by Elisabeth Schüssler Fiorenza, readings based on mestizo/a consciousness used by Aída Besançon Spencer and Elizabeth Conde Frazier, the use of popular symbols, ideas, and methods for interpretation suggested by Lincoln Galloway, the "signifying on Scripture" approach that Vincent Wimbush employs, the disruption of imperialist agendas practiced by Althea Spencer Miller and Gay Byron, the feminist ideological critique that Elizabeth Castelli undertakes, and gender critique in the context of global pluralism called for by Karen Torjesen.

Hisako Kinukawa employs a multilayered reading of biblical texts that includes "1) a global political perspective, 2) a perspective given by the peculiar position of Japan in Asia and the world, and 3) a perspective given as a woman in Asia." The stories of Naomi and Ruth, according to her analysis, show "what it means to accept people of other faiths and to understand ourselves as each coming from different parts of the world with different social locations." She uses the pericope about the Syro-Phoenician woman to expose the power relationships at work in the text that "[produce] dominant and subordinate relationships between the protagonists in the story."

Elisabeth Schüssler Fiorenza's proposal for a new field of critical feminist interpretation in the academy has multiple foci. It resists the "malestream scientific ethos" of most of the biblical scholarship. It works toward institutionalizing emancipatory scholarship. It engages difference in terms of "referentiality to actual experiences of oppression and socio-political struggles" and it creates "solidarity and alliances . . . among feminists of different social locations and . . . among all those in biblical studies who pursue a rhetorics, politics and ethics of emancipation and well-being for everyone."

The scholarship of Aída Besançon Spencer and Elizabeth Conde-Frazier also illustrate how mestizo/a identity provides unique perspectives for interpretation. Aída Besançon Spencer sees new possibilities for feminist biblical scholars from the north to be enriched by the hermeneutical contexts that Latina feminists adopt from their cultures for use in reading biblical texts. These include the themes of God as stranger, fiesta, or hospitality, emphasis on the arts, and a different understanding of time.

Responding to Aída Besançon Spencer, Elizabeth Conde-Frazier states that within the Latino/a community "there are two sacred texts: the biblical text and the text of the everyday, *lo cotidiano*, which is the testimony of where God has entered our lives. Both are an account of God's activity in the world. The two texts mutually release the power of God in each other."

Lincoln Galloway says that in the Caribbean the task is to reclaim the region's "history and culture, music/hymns/songs, dance, literature, sermons, liturgy, poetry, proverbs, and traditions. . . . All of this must take place with greater intentionality about its relevance and meaning in the context of a multicultural, multi-religious, and diverse geographic region." This task is shared by other regions in the global south as well.

Vincent Wimbush's hermeneutical strategy of "signifying" on Scripture mentioned earlier, calls for a wider framework of studying the New Testament by using a critical approach that takes seriously the subaltern uses of the bible in a variety of social contexts. In the African American context, "signifying" involves valorizing in favor of African American instead of Euro-American interpretations of the bible. Wimbush supports this hermeneutical strategy, saying, "To be fully human is to interpret. To interpret is to seek meaning. The truly free individual is the one who seeks meaning through radical readings—open ended readings about the self in the world, necessarily including the past, readings that represent openness to other ways of knowing, readings that expand the boundaries and genres of scripturalizing."

Althea Spencer Miller and Gay Byron model exegetical strategies that analyze the particular power relationships at play within selected texts in order to disrupt their imperialistic agenda. Spencer miller introduces the reader to a poor, elderly Jamaican woman, Lucy Bailey, and imagines her encounter with a feminist biblical scholar, to embody her challenge to dominant paradigms of interpretation. Relating Lucy Bailey's story to that of the Jerusalem widow who gave her two small copper coins as an offering at the Temple (Luke 21:1–4), Spencer Miller's analysis exposes both the politics of the Jerusalem Temple and the social subordination of women, the poor, and the oppressed in the first century.

Gay Byron "explores the imperialist agenda in patristic writings as well as in ancient texts that contain references to Egyptians/Egypt, Ethiopians/Ethiopia and Blacks/blackness." She concludes that language referring to color and ethnicity in early Christian texts is primarily symbolic and that this "ethno-political rhetorics" came to *symbolize* certain theological, ideological, and even political intra-Christian controversies and challenges. She sees the importance of this approach for the continuing development of womanist biblical hermeneutics in which color is a significant hermeneutical category.

Elizabeth Castelli asserts that the "future should be concerned far less with the practice of exegesis than with a sustained interrogation of the work the bible does in contemporary situations and in the service of a wide range of political goals." She regards "the hegemony of Christianity as a potentially deeply troubling feature of thinking about the modern, globalized situation where feminism and the production of knowledge are interrogated." She calls for a transnational feminist and ideological biblical critique, based on "the capacity to build strategic alliances across the traditional boundaries of nation-states," that can both clarify and challenge the rhetorical uses and abuses of political power.

Karen Torjesen believes that "the religious pluralism within Christianity could be an important resource for decentralizing the Western exegetical tradition." She states: "The fact that all of us are members of a global society requires us to move beyond both our national identities and our cultural identities. The demands of this new global citizenship will transform feminist exegesis and teach us to approach sacred texts with the consciousness that the cultural and regional diversity of readers will discover and create multiple new meanings on the surfaces of once familiar texts." She also argues for the continuance of the work of feminist scholarship in "decentering the narrative perspective by critiquing the deployment of the category of generic femaleness by excavating the lives of historical women."

Finally, Hisako Kinukawa calls for a "multi-logue future" in which "reading texts and practicing theology in daily life are intertwined and inseparable." She states:

> If we lose sight of our social locations and the reality of the world, our praxis of reading texts will also tend to be lifeless as we lose sight of the social locations and the reality of the world of the texts . . . [it] implies practicing our multiple dialogues with diverse people or thoughts or texts through activating our plural feelers of communication . . . the second multi-logue . . . ask[s] us to keep our minds as open as possible to other faiths or religionists so that we may learn from them as well, so we may work with them collaboratively for our enterprise to pursue a world of justice and peace. Lastly, the most difficult but most urgent need is to continue our multi-logue with women and men in other countries so that we may keep de-colonizing ourselves and keep becoming postcolonial subjects as we read the texts.

Advocacy for Justice/Peace/
Women's Empowerment

Many of the contributors to this volume join Kinukawa in calling for combining an active praxis of interpretation with new hermeneutical strategies of textual interpretation. Their approaches to active feminist praxis include human rights advocacy, organized response to the global HIV/AIDS epidemic, and justice, peace, and environmental initiatives. Althea Spencer Miller offers additional reflections on feminist pedagogy as a liberative praxis in the next essay in this volume.

A Human Rights Advocacy Approach to Feminist
New Testament Studies

Hisako Kinukawa describes her efforts to help to make retribution for the violation of the rights of Korean "Comfort Women" held in virtual captivity by the Japanese government. She engaged with other Japanese women and men in holding an International Women's Court in December, 2000, that vindicated the honor of the Korean women and condemned those who perpetrated war crimes against women in Asian countries that were committed by the Japanese imperial government and military power from 1931 to 1945.

Musa Dube has promoted efforts to encourage a human-rights based approach to teaching, research, writing, and praxis. She observes that "feminist discourse has been influenced by the Human Rights movement and the United Nations initiated women's empowerment assemblies that set a worldwide empowerment of women in all aspects of life," but regrets that feminist New Testament scholarship has contributed very little to these efforts. She concludes that "feminist New Testament studies and other feminist religious studies are . . . disconnected from the human developmental world that is trying to concretely empower women." Isabel Balseiro, however, observes that "many Two Thirds World activists and scholars remain skeptical of the validity of human rights approaches to Two Thirds World problems," because of the troubling claims of universality implicit in this model.

Feminist New Testament and the HIV/AIDS Crisis

Dube, who served since 2001 as the World Council of Churches theological representative for HIV/AIDS in Africa, calls feminist New Testament scholars to "explore new directions on reading the text within the HIV/AIDS context." She argues that this disease, which has killed so many millions already and will continue to do so into the future, is rooted in systems of social injustice, stigma, and discrimination. It attacks "the less privileged members of society, the poor, women, children, homosexuals, displaced people, immigrants, discriminated races and ethnic groups, who have no power to protect themselves from infection or to get quality care." Dube regards the lack of significant response or impact by the feminist New Testament community as a sign that "there is something drastically amiss in our practice." She invokes the biblical Rahab and the ribbon she hung from her window to call feminist New Testament scholars to find effective ways to engage this and other major injustices of our world.

Justice and Peace Initiatives

In addition to her activist engagement in areas of social injustice against women, Elizabeth Castelli also focuses on violence and suffering. She has joined others in "exploring the ways in which the Bible and religious discourse as a whole lend themselves in deeply ambivalent ways toward the project of a critical theory of those intractable aspects of human social life." She describes her collaborative efforts to organize "a multifaceted initiative called 'Responding to Violence,' that has brought feminist activists and academics together to assess the material, institutional, interpersonal, and ideological conditions that have brought our world into its current peculiar predicament."

Ecological and Environmental Concerns

Ecology and the environment ground the theological work of Althea Spencer Miller and Lincoln Galloway. For both, the sounds, tastes, and textures of their homelands in the Caribbean are an essential aspect of their theologizing. According to Galloway, the environment is also an arena of praxis. He states, "This connection to the land has provided stability to people's lives and contributed to the nurturing of community. . . . Caribbean people's connection to the land provides an opportunity to invite greater stewardship of our land and natural resources, and for advancing theological understandings that reflect care of the earth's resources, ecological concerns, and ultimately, resistance to, and avoidance of all acts of violence, degradation, and devaluing of creation and life."

Ecological and environmental advocacy is also found in the theological and activist work of the Mexican and Latin American feminist theologians Elsa Tamez, Maria Pilar Aquino, and Ivone Gebara as well as in that of Rosemary Ruether. For Gebara, according to Ruether, "Life as inter-relational creativity exists on every level of reality. As earth it shows us the dynamic inter-relational process of life unfolding in the biosphere." Such perspectives lead these women to champion the wise use of natural resources that are so often exploited irresponsibly in a globalized world.

Feminist New Testament Studies: Global and Future Perspectives

There are too many different pointers to future directions to be confident in saying definitively where global feminist New Testament studies will go in the future. It undoubtedly will express itself differently at different times, in different contexts, and in the work of different scholars. However, given the shift that has occurred in global Christianity from the north to the south, it is realistic to assume that the future of feminist New Testament studies will be strongly influenced by Southern readers. It is also likely that global feminist New Testament interpretive methodologies will be much more diverse than they have been in the past and much less determined by the old canons of historical-critical scriptural interpretation. Some tension will probably continue between paradigms and interpretive strategies that have developed in the north and in the global south, as well as between scholars in the academy and readers in the church, and within each of these groups. But it is to be hoped that all sides will recognize that their strength lies in a combination of approaches to global and future challenges.

The participants in these conversations will be pronouncedly more diverse in gender, age, class, culture, religion, sexual orientation, and background. Some academics will concentrate on developing new theoretical models. Other academics and communities of faith will develop collaborative agendas for action. Multi-logues within and outside of the Christian faith communities will also enrich awareness of spiritual values, which will assume more significance than hermeneutical strategies. Popular culture will join historical materials in providing sources for interpretation. Inclusive models of scholarship, often ones that focused on praxis as part of interpretation, will be developed that will enable women to struggle more effectively against global oppression in all forms and from whatever sources it derives.

This volume is an announcement that the baobab tree has been turned upside down. It is also an invitation to join hands as equals with different experiences and insights around the baobab tree, in order to assist in creating a new and global future for feminist New Testament studies. The task is a challenging one, but encouragement is offered to those who respond to the challenge by the African proverb that states, "when spider webs unite, they can tie up a lion!"

Notes

1. Proverbs are part of the oral tradition in Africa. This and the other proverbs cited in the Introduction are familiar proverbs in Ghana, West Africa.
2. This legend is found on the following website http://www.dsctanzania.org/news/baobabbooks.html.
3. Philip Jenkins, *The Next Christendom: The Coming of Global Christianity* (New York: Oxford University Press, 2002).
4. Ecumenical Association of Third World Theologians, EATWOT-ATC 2000: 218–219. Spiritus 174 t. XIV Mass 2004 . . . EATWOT-ATC V Theological Paper "Thou Shall Not Worship Other Gods: Towards a Decolonizing . . . XXIII, N°2, Décembre 2000, pp. 212–231 (mz traduction). . . .

Chapter 1

Feminist Pedagogies: Implications of a Liberative Praxis

Althea Spencer Miller

Introduction

Essayists in this volume launch a call for nothing less than a reconceptualization, retooling, and refitting of biblical studies that feminists do. They launch a frontal assault on a discipline that in its current practice is too mired in antiquity and modernistic analytic methodologies and too "tribal" in its interests and focus. This call resonates with earlier voices that delineated the entrenched tribalism and time-bound focus of Eurocentric biblical criticism.[1] The loci of proponents of change are those of subaltern voices that experienced a kind of cognitive dissonance and dual alienation in their adaptation to Eurocentric biblical studies that sought to do criticism by scientific methodologies, which was focused on theological, soteriological, and Christological issues, and which selectively scoured antiquity for its repository of history and meaning-making.

Our essayists go beyond echoing that call, however. We are seeking the fora, discursive universes, conceptual perspectives, and practical methodologies that can facilitate this pristine engagement of biblical scholarship in a pluralistic and multivalent mode, suitable for a globalized environment. It has been correctly observed that the subaltern voices for change are those of African Americans, Latin American liberation theologians, a group that expanded to include voices from Africa and Asia.[2] The essayists in this volume include those voices and recognize that the broad regional[3] and categorical brush strokes occlude a diversity that is subregional, ethnic, gendered, and interreligious/nonreligious. A significant element in the challenge to change is to a Christian biblical theology that speaks only of Christian voices and ignores the explicit interreligous relationality that is a concomitant of globalization. This self-conscious diversity focuses the intent to contribute to and expand the vision of a liberatory education that is evolutionary, inclusive, and open-ended.

Our essayists and respondents reflect a liberatory paradigm that requires a review of the focus of biblical scholarship, the subjectivity of the scholar, and the teleology of the discipline. Fernando Segovia exposed and critiqued the pedagogical implications of historical, literary, and cultural criticism as requiring in varying degrees a patriarchal stance that reflects "not only the broader Eurocentric character of theological education in general but also the strong Eurocentric control over culture."[4] His solution included a rejection of historical, literary, and cultural criticism and moves instead "within the ambit of the cultural studies paradigm" that emphasizes the diversity of readers, contexts, methods, and readings.[5] Musa Dube poignantly expresses this concern in a metaphor that represents the engagement with Eurocentric biblical criticism from the margins as looking into a mirror. Her description:

> As a black Motswana African woman, I am indeed privileged to be admitted in this hall of magnificent mirrors; I have, nevertheless, struggled to see my image. Its mirrors occasionally give me a piece of what should be my face, and it is usually something undesirable.[6]

Our essayists' visions of subaltern approaches to biblical scholarship are commensurate with this tenor that recognizes the creation of "others," the valorization of Eurocentrism, and a persistent pretense to an apolitical, objective, academic study of the bible. They advance the liberatory paradigm because of the consciousness of religious diversity and contextual loci that they explicate as they experiment with contextual reading methodologies.

Shaping the Vision

The global focus of the conversations necessarily brought the relationship between the bible and politics, multiple supremacies, and imperialisms into relief. The sins of the age are named: imperialism, colonialism, neocolonialism, globalization, sexism, heterosexism, patriarchy, and religious supersessionism. The distance between critical biblical readings and global structures of domination measured by an historical silence[7] on these issues is itself antiquated and now intolerable. An overriding concern of our essayists is that academics engage critical biblical readings in terms of the bible's relationship to contemporary issues. Castelli is concerned about violence, first[8] as a gender-based relationship of dominance in which women are too often the recipients of masculine violence at the personal level and also with women as bearers of the brunt of the consequences of international and civil wars. She exemplified her call to contemporary engagement with the use of biblical texts in the political arena through an examination of the co-optation of the prologue to the Gospel of John by President George W. Bush in his rationalization of the role of the United States in the war against terror. Biblical motifs became subservient to overtly warring intentions as rationales for those motives. Castelli's foray is not based on a concern to determine proper exegesis of the texts. It is, rather, an effort to understand the rhetorical effect of the Christian use of the bible in contemporary political discourse. Castelli addresses the current tabula of political meaning-making in relation to the bible; making overt that which has been tacitly present for centuries of empire—the role of the Bible in the shaping of imperialisms. The sharpened edge of such an approach to criticism is that it unveils the occlusions of the past through which reflective assertions of religious complicity in subjugation and domination were denied a clear and comprehensive evidential basis. The connective tissue that she uncovers depends on an emotive persuasiveness, rather than logic. It connects the religious sensibility to the national politico-mythology thus reducing separate entities into identical twins conjoined at the heart. The latter then bestows its authority on the former creating an undividable and nearly insurmountable unity of heart and purpose. Therein is a development of rhetorical criticism applied to current appropriations of biblical texts that is an innovative and active adaptation of that which Schüssler Fiorenza identifies as the socio-rhetorical discourse of the scriptures with ethical[9] import for the institutionalized practice of biblical criticism. As Schüssler Fiorenza points out, ". . . critical practice rhetoric is able to investigate the dimensions of domination and freedom in a cosmopolitan world."[10] This Castelli demonstrates.

One of the consistent cornerstones of Schüssler Fiorenza's critique of academic biblical criticism is the attribution of positivist rather than rhetorical and discursive approaches to the reconstruction of history. There is a tacit or assumed confidence in her critique that a liberatory approach to historical reconstruction is an essential ingredient in the development of epistemologies that would unmask the collusion of biblical criticism with the powers of domination. The implied understanding is that such an approach has the potential to also liberate biblical studies from such collusion. It, at least, provides biblical readers the analytical tools necessary, through historical analysis based in ideological criticism, to recognize that collusion in its contemporary manifestations. Recognition empowers resistance or redirection of that force. That potential is neither foolproof nor without risk. It is precisely because malestream "scientific methods and theoretical perspectives"[11] (read historical-criticism) have been shaped by kyriarchal institutions that we cannot assume that biblical studies will produce transformative epistemologies. Her call for a process of rhetorical-ethical analysis does not completely escape Segovia's critique of historical criticism as a pedagogy that produces elitist knowledge of mechanical/scientific methods by urging emphases on modes of critical reflection and analysis rather than on the acquisition of technical procedures and rules.[12]

Schüssler Fiorenza's mode of critical reflection does not fully escape Segovia when her recommendations for reading the bible critically are directed toward a specific reading cadre.[13] Her considerable experience in working with Christian women would belie this but it distinguishes the focus of her recommendations, which is directed toward the professional reader. It is the professional reader that she exhorts to position her/himself in the *polis* and the *ekklesia*. Self-reflexive positioning is important. Eurocentrism developed in biblical scholarship because the readers occupied a Eurocentric position. Other ethnicities will also read with their positionalities. The goal is to decenter and dethrone malestream Eurocentrism and to empower hitherto marginalized reading methods and interpretations to enter into the orb of biblical studies.

The orb is a structure with at least two tiers: malestream and subaltern biblical scholars on one layer and ordinary readers on another. Positionalities for Schüssler

Fiorenza means taking one's subjectivity as an agent of interpretation into account thereby becoming cognizant of one's presuppositions. For Byron, Dube, Kinukawa, and Spencer Miller their relationship to Christian institutions is one of their positions and means representative biblical criticism. As Dube and Spencer Miller assiduously maintain, it means reading with the people at the grassroots: "reading with ordinary readers."[14] When Schüssler Fiorenza reconceptualizes biblical studies through the fostering of "an ethos of critical reflexivity, democratic debate, intellectual, multilingual, and multidisciplinary competence,"[15] she is not writing primarily of an ordinary reader. It is here that she does not fully escape the critique of Segovia that the pedagogy of historical criticism creates hierarchies. Yet, if the academy cannot practice Schüssler Fiorenza's reconceptualization and those of the essayists there will be difficulty if not impossibility in negotiating the academy's relationship to the "ordinary" readers. While it is impossible to completely jettison historical criticism in Segovia's terms, Dube's recognition that "the cry against biblical textual violence, its suppression of diversity . . . its alignment with global structures of dominance must finally be addressed by those concerned with reading . . . for liberation, and for both immediate and global social justice"[16] requires methodological responses that incorporate *polis* and *ekklesia* in ways that enhance those articulated by Castelli and Schüssler Fiorenza.

Vincent Wimbush begins his pursuit of alternative creative methodological responses by pondering the impact on the academic guild of biblical scholarship should an interpretive history of African Americans become the focal point of biblical studies. Shaping the propulsive edge of a new adventure in frontier exploration Wimbush questions both the work of African American biblical scholars and feminist scholars. He tests the present boundaries, the two-pronged agenda, of both subsectors of the biblical disciplines. By allusive reference, he questions that agenda that currently drives the study of African Americans and the Bible. Does putting African Americans at the center of the study of the Bible mean identifying African characters in the Bible and focusing upon the African origins of biblical traditions? "What might be the implications and ramifications of construing the study of the Bible—its impetus, methods, orientations, approaches, politics, goals, communications . . . on bases *other* than European cultural presumptions and power, interests and templates?"[17] In his essay in this volume, "Signifying on Scriptures: An African Diaspora Proposal for Radical Readings," Wimbush similarly critiques the double-pronged feminist agenda that "merely" contests content-meaning and approaches and methods. Very simply he raises the question that is at the heart of the issues raised by others such as Dube, Segovia, Schüssler Fiorenza, and Castelli. Is the challenge merely about "equal opportunity to hold forth in this way, the way of the male old guard?"[18] Wimbush's proposed new frontier is reflected in the title of his chapter, that is, signifying on scriptures. To signify on Scriptures in relation to biblical literature is to reflect on the questions, "How does the Bible function, what and how does the Bible 'mean?' "[19]

In a polyphonous counterpoint, Wimbush's comments evoke Dube's anguished "mirror" in which her reflection could not appear except in distorted view. To that anguished recognition his base line rises sonorously and awesomely, "For me to read 'darkly' (*en ainimati*) is to attempt now to read . . . through and on the basis of . . . my dark self and my dark world." Because "It is the reading of the *self* (not the

dominance of Asia, severely exploitative relationships with other Asians, a wealthy nation, a colonizing nation. Yet as a Christian she is a member of a minority religion. As a Christian she brings the wealth of Japanese religious history and belief that she cannot ignore in her practice of Christianity. As a woman she shares with other Japanese women the culpability of her compatriots, both military and civilian, in the issue of the use of other-nationaled women as "comfort women." Her personal and national configuration does not fit neatly and fixedly within the categories so readily available to the "Western" postmodernist and to the executors of grand narratives.

Kinukawa incarnates the dilemma that challenges the very concepts of grand narratives or metanarratives should we retain, in any subcategory or species of grand narrative, a binary construction of the historico-political and sociopolitical forces that shaped civilization. This challenge also reminds that the experiences and reactions of subaltern voices are neither homogenous nor necessarily harmonious. The complexity of the multi-logue bespeaks the complexity of the grand narrative schema. Racism, classism, ageism, heterosexism, ableism, nationalism, sexism, rationalism, scientism, as categories of grand narratives seem inadequate for addressing the scope of dysfunctional sociohistorical relationships. For whom do these categories work, why and how? Kinukawa's presence in the multi-logue immediately destabilizes confidence in the extent of the satisfactory functionability of these categories. Is postmodernism destined to be another category of "Western" abstractionism serving an ideational/incarnational imperialism?

Faced with a potentially debilitating imagining of the complexity of the multi-logue, it is easy to reject the effort to realize the idea in practical terms. Kinukawa's use of the story of Ruth may "inspire us in her openness to other faiths and her courage to cross the borders."[26] Her use of the Ruth story might encourage us in two ways. Kinukawa sees more in the story of Ruth and Naomi than "a simple devotion of Ruth for the companionship of Naomi."[27] Though there is more to the story, might the process of overcoming the debilitating aspects of complexity begin with such a "simple" idea?

Elizabeth Conde-Frazier's response is an invitation to academic rigor through co-construction.[28] Co-construction begins with "*Lo cotidiano*"[29] that "allows the voiceless to tell their stories and to cry out to the heavens for justice and peace. It allows us to see how God's grace, justice, presence and love manifest themselves in everyday occurrences."[30] This permits us to recognize experience as the valid incipient locale of our reflections. The sharing of those experiences is an encounter that leads to a sharing of the heart (*corazón*), "a metaphor for the whole of one's conscious, intelligent and free personality."[31] Up to this point Conde-Frazier is describing a conscious, willed, and intentional devotion for companionship that is founded in compassion, meaning to suffer with and to undergo with rather than to pity.[32] Thus Kinukawa and Conde-Frazier humanize the theories and critiques with which we work and place the task of interpretation also in a realm of human interaction and the need for human fellowship. The goal of education then becomes one of processing us toward understandings of shalom rather than to socialization into the present status quo. Shalom as goal would discourage the dominant ethos of competitive meaning-making. It encourages collaboration and values the acknowledgment of reliance in the midst of earnest debate.

The second way of Kinukawa is the invitation to read the Bible along with knowledge of other faiths. This phrasing is not quite true to Kinukawa's self-conscious heritage and embrace of multiple religious faiths. To me, a citizen of the African Diaspora, an heiress of colonialism, her testimony strikes with particular poignancy, because that heritage has thoroughly diluted and desecrated the spirituality of my ancient continental ancestors. I can read my own phrasing as a sterilized "westernization" of Kinukawa's richly pulsating and fulsomely present past. Her invitation requires a stirring in me, and others like me, of that which has been suppressed into invisibility and insentience—a reaching out to the African sisters to say, "Tell me, tell me, or simply show me!" When my sister shows me, is she signifying scripture for me as her memory and her present converge to enable my participation in Kinukawa's invitation? Does Kinukawa's invitation not invite us to participate in the scriptural activity of other religions that we might be better able to understand even our own? Such an understanding of her invitation would contribute to current transformational currents in comparative religious studies and the study of receptivity.

Even the language of reading the Bible along with knowledge of other faiths would require an expansion of scholarly foci. There would be a significant and immediate impact upon biblical studies should there be greater exposure to Jewish and Muslim understanding of both the Hebrew Bible and the Christian scriptures and the Koran. Yet, within the Western tradition, how revolutionary, how troubling, how "awful" might it be to read the Bible through the eyes of the politically and nationalistically subaltern voices? Zhiru envisages the possibility of "the forum of Buddhist-Christian dialogue expanding to include Islam, Judaism, and other religions."[33] Despite this vision she is concerned that interfaith multi-logues may still wind up privileging the Christian tradition. She recognizes and cautions against the "act of reading scripture . . . becoming another form of colonization, where the religion and culture that possesses the economic and political means to initiate the multi-logue ends up dominating the forum of religious exchange through the terms of the discourse."[34] When the converse dialectic is transacted and multivocal polysemy and the dominant of any category look into the mirror, seeing not the self they know, but the self that others know, we experience the distorted self-reflection, or worse a disappearing reflection, would this usher in the liberatory epoch of learning to read as, "seeing through a mirror darkly?"

Our conversation partners have, in different ways, focused on the biblical guild or tribe. Doubtlessly each person has produced readings that are sophisticated by consciously using tools that are additions to the normal act of reading. The average nonprofessional biblical reader is unconcerned about politicized readings of the Bible from various positionalities and with the establishment of peace and justice in our world, broadly defined as concomitant product of their reading act. Somewhere in the professional mind is the idea that we are either reading representatively of such persons or we are reading for their liberation. Can the layperson read for her or himself without acquiring the tools of New Testament scholarship? Is there a place for their readings in the guild? Is there a place for the guild in their readings? Is it desirable to answer these questions in the affirmative?

Dube's response to the last question is a convicted, "Yes!"[35] Any scholarship seeking to empower the marginalized and engage subaltern vocality must be able to recognize the explicit agency of such persons. Otherwise the effort seems to be nothing more than patronage with a globalized conscience and pretensions to liberation.

Dube writes with specific recommendations for the future of Feminist New Testament Scholars that there is a double edge among our essayists. As feminists some such as Schüssler Fiorenza, Castelli, and Wimbush write with a sense of challenge to the guild at large. Others are like Dube who place their frontier among feminist biblical scholars. Among the latter the presumption of a liberatory biblical education rests on the intentions of feminist biblical scholars to empower women through biblical study. Because Feminist New Testament Studies (FNTS) has declared itself to be an interested scholarship that advocates the rights of women and the oppressed, there are at least three things necessary. One is a deliberate connection with the communities of faith. The other is a spiritual language that addresses the faith of women who are the "consumers of religious texts." The third is to explore ways of doing New Testament (NT) studies with and from contemporary faith communities.[36]

The third necessity is potentially fecund in some of its senses. First, this is a stance that may altogether remove the tribal boundaries. The opening of the guild to conversation with biblical laypersons and an increased presence of professional practitioners of faith certainly would spawn a revisiting of the role of specialized tools in biblical study. Second, it would add to the scholarly enterprise dimensions that are based in immediate reality and immediate appropriation and application to the process of interpretation. Third, it would increase the accessible knowledge base for both the scholar and the layperson. Fourth it must not be presupposed that only the laypersons would benefit. Fifth, it would lend integrity to the liberatory discourse of the guild.

On the other hand, Dube identifies two associated problems: the protection of academic freedom and the integrity of the feminist voice. There are five kinds of institutions to which this concern must be addressed. They are churches in the Two-Thirds World, churches in the developed world, seminaries in the Two-Thirds World, seminaries in the developed world, and general universities. The cumbersomeness of such an endeavor may be simplified by an appeal to two kinds of subalterns within the guild who are also representatives of the five kinds of institutions listed earlier. There are subalterns within the American biblical academies who are representatives of minority groups within the United States. There are also subalterns who are international representatives of national categories. These are not represented by American minority groups. There may be representatives of each group found in any biblical institution anywhere in the world. The problems associated with greater communication between faith communities and the academic guild that Dube identifies require carefully developed covenantal terms that recognize the integrity of institutions, create a safe medium for the conversation, and articulate agreed-upon expectations and ways of negotiating the unanticipated subsequences of such communication. This meeting of differing spheres of discourse for interchange and cross-fertilization requires the overcoming of two mutual antagonisms manifested as anti-intellectualism in faith communities and anti-spirituality in the academy. Dube acknowledges that this coworking will be difficult[37] and admittedly there are real problems on either side. The postmodern, post-ecclesiastical academy is more prepared to be an open-ended evolutionary institution, even though within its own terms, than is the dogma-loyal church. Will the church, not only the Two-Thirds World church but also any conservative oriented Christianity, be comfortable to engage a liberatory conversation such as that described by our essayists? Under what terms will the faith community be able to participate?

There is an urgency in the situation on both sides for the engagement to which Dube calls and a need to facilitate that engagement. Dube, herself, points us to a part of the answer: the development of a Society of Feminist New Testament Studies using the Circle of Concerned African Women Theologians as a model. Dube can also offer as a model for the product of this effort *Other Ways of Reading: African Women and the Bible*.[38] Here, a collection of African women, a mixture of "trained" and "ordinary" readers do biblical interpretation using storytelling and divinatory methods. The book then exemplifies readings done by "ordinary" readers and through publication is a means of making this collected knowledge available and accessible beyond the scope of the participants. Technology increases the possibility of availability and accessibility through the development of videos, audio cassettes, CDs and the internet—putting globalization in the service of a worthy liberatory rather than exploitative goal. One may call these countercultural readings only if the academy is the normatizing culture. On the other hand, without the homology of the academy these readings are an example of multivocal polysemy—to be taken seriously by the guild rather than dispensed with as quaint, artefactual, curiosities. There is a need for more publications like this. Concomitantly, there is need for these publications to become standard texts in biblical courses.

Subaltern experiences of the Eurocentric Western-oriented classroom continue to be one of alienation from the religious commitments that spawned their interest in biblical studies as a way of examining and articulating the breadth of the religious life. In such an environment many scholars, including ethnic Euro-Americans, are compelled to relegate their religious faith to the margins of their scholarly expertise in order to succeed in the academy. It is neither necessary nor desirable to insist that biblical scholars associate with a religious community. However, it is neither necessary nor desirable to insist that they disassociate from the religious enterprise in order to be scholars. Some of our essayists are adamant that the religious community be more intimately engaged in the pursuit of biblical knowledge at the levels of textual appropriation for use in religious communities as well as in the appropriation of a more broadly based ancient history. Such an engagement requires a greater openness to more globally divergent approaches to biblical studies and the continuous decentering of interpretation.

The most difficult and intricate aspect of the pedagogical challenge comes from the recognition by Dube and Spencer Miller that a truly liberatory biblical study ought to engage the agency in reading of the uncritical reader, that is, the ordinary reader. This is the point at which the gauntlet is laid against trappings and pretensions to instrumental acquisitions for expert readings, even liberatory ones. Will there ever be a sufficiency of knowledge if the understandings and methodologies of the "ordinary, non-critical reader" are not included? The implicit and explicit challenges are twofold. Castelli and Wimbush shape new frontiers that are less concerned about the "ordinary reader." Castelli declares herself to be religiously disinterested. Not all critical biblical readers are interested in the Bible as a religious book and certainly not all are interested in reading with the faith communities. It has to be clearly stated also that not all faith communities are Christian and not all Christian faith communities read the Bible in the same way. Who is the "ordinary reader" of Dube and Spencer Miller? As a collection of peoples, they appear to have features similar to the complex Hisako Kinukawa and Lucy Bailey.

The dilemma revealed by the effort to integrate critical and ordinary readers evolves from the heart of the beginnings of this essay. This is not the dilemma of a carefully controlled classroom atmosphere where Eurocentrism functions as the unifying and dominant cultural perspective and hermeneutical mode. Daniel Patte reflecting on *Semeia*: *"Reading With" African Overtures*, writes, "By its very existence, this volume calls me and any other European–American biblical scholars to acknowledge that our own critical work originates in quite different cultural, social, and political contexts."[39] The differing contexts mean that the identities of the "ordinary readers" are myriad but nonetheless excluded from the repositories of knowledge necessary to the acquisition of vista of critical biblical study. What this means is that the standard text book that introduces European and Euro-American students to the history of biblical studies proceeds as if the colonial missionary enterprise never occurred. It assumes the only serious and worthwhile study of the Bible occurred on the European continent, in England and, now, in the United States. The subaltern student is required to study the same trajectory. What happened when the Bible was received in the countries of Africa, Asia, the Caribbean, Latin America, the Pacific? Students from American minority groups and other countries must study this Europeanized history of biblical interpretation as if it were the only kind that occurred. They (we) must return to our own with the "Good News" that the history, culture, and message of the Bible is best known when done the Eurocentric way! Is the history of biblical studies tainted by colonialism?![40]

Kathleen O'Brien Wicker identified as colonial biblical interpretations that assumed the divine legitimization of patriarchy, the unique validity of Christianity, that justified exclusions, and universalize the particular.[41] "Feminist biblical interpretations," Wicker declares, "question these major hermeneutical principles of colonial biblical interpretation."[42] Already in 1993, Wicker focused on biblical education as the mechanism of colonialism and as colonial in its practices. In 2005 we begin to go further. A further sobering recognition is that Eurocentrism holds no monopoly on colonial attitudes. Kinukawa exposed the Japanese practice of colonialism. A history of colonialist practices may be uncovered should one look carefully at the past and present of any group. This is the angst that Byron seeks to escape when she situates herself in a theoretical framework "that emphasizes indigenous understandings of Christianity" rather than the "Christian discovery of indigenous societies."[43] In a move reminiscent of the womanist critique of Eurocentric feminism, Byron writes:

> Although I appealed to womanist hermeneutics in my study of Egyptians, Ethiopians, Blacks, and blackness, I must admit that this interpretive lens did not enable me to critically assess the discursive role of the Ethiopian or Black woman in early Christian writings, nor did it enable me to articulate a *global* [Byron's emphasis] understanding of such readings not only for African American women, but for women of African descent living here in the United States and throughout the world.

In similar vein, the use of African American categories, or any other ethno-American category for meta- or textual analysis does not necessarily suffice for the complexity of the international scene. It is that complexity that disorders the definition of the "ordinary reader." It is that complexity that confounds attempts to organize conversations that constantly omit components that ought to be present. It is the will to remove the taint of colonialism that Byron seeks to correct when she says, ". . . it is imperative that feminist and womanist biblical critics rearticulate the meaning of global feminist New Testament interpretation by listening more carefully to the marginal voices of women *from the South* . . ."[44]

The postmodern tendency toward using binary oppositional categories is stymied by Byron's statements, Kinukawa's presence, and Spencer Miller's "Lucy Bailey." The world resists reduction to dominant/dominated, textual/oral, theoreticians/realists, and north/south. We occupy multiple and contradictory categories. This, too, is partially the residue of Christian aided and validated colonialisms. Jamaican women from Jamaica, Japanese women from Japan, Hispanic women from a Hispanic country, are not minorities in relation to their own countries. However, in relation to the guild they are all subaltern voices. Although Dube quotes Osiek on the incorporation of minority voices, it is clear that she values the hybridity of *Southern* women as products of imperialism rather than as a category defined by not being a contemporary citizen of the current empire.[45] However victimized Euro-American women may have been, they have been and also are the beneficiaries and at times the victimizers. The decolonization of the heritage of biblical education is two-pronged in its concerns. Can the master's/mistress' tools dismantle their house?[46] Wicker supports "acts of subversion in the hope of preserving and developing liberating visions for a redefined and reconstructed future which includes all people . . ."[47] Dube takes the next step in this intricately woven fabric of our international relationships and invites a treasonable transgression of boundaries by the One-Third World readers with the words, *Our life for yours.*[48]

Feminist biblical studies constitutes a high vision of consciously ethical methodologies and outputs. The experience of marginalization first felt within the guild by white feminists resulted in a clamor for inclusion. The resultant domino effect occurred in a world where minority ethno-Americans in the context of the civil rights struggles and the "Black is Beautiful"[49] era sought self-definition within the guild. Womanist thought began to blossom. In the world at large former colonies of former empires fought for and won independence and the political boundaries of the world were being redrawn around nationalities. Off stage, the missionaries effectively conducted their enterprise to the Two-Thirds World where the future of Christianity lies.[50] There is no self-evident or necessarily logical connector that makes this an essential reason to be inclusive in biblical studies. Globalization is one such reason. The impact of global interconnectedness requires an ability to recognize that useful knowledge is widely available and ought to be accessed. It may provide another response to Rebecca Chopp's question, "How do we teach persons to develop/build community that is both attentive to local situation and in dialogue with global context?"[51] It surpasses the incorporation of minorities into the mainstream of the biblical academy in the United States. It requires in more developed countries, where there is an influx of international students (good pragmatic reasons for opening the embrace to include ethical readings that are liberatory in intent and inclusive in presuppositions), that there be an incorporation of multiple and diverse sources of histories of biblical reception, autochthonous interpretations, hermeneutics, and methodologies along with the recognition that these too constitute the reservoir of human knowledge and accomplishment. Pedagogically, it also means the development of new understandings of the classroom, the encouragement of wider international exposure, and the development of new biblical studies curricula and areas of expertise. These indicate a need for profound and far-reaching institutional changes.

Segovia's insightful critique of historical, literary, and cultural criticisms is a threshold exposé when he recognizes the pedagogical implications in those critical tools. They do imply the educator as repository of specialist knowledge, the student as passive recipient who is enculturated into a disciplinary sociolect and responsive to an external authority. A liberatory pedagogy engages a more interactive and dynamic sphere of knowledge-sharing than those implications offer. There is nothing implicitly erroneous about teaching the use of tools. The tool, itself, is not therefore a pedagogical problem except where the selection of tools is unnecessarily and superciliously exclusionary of other valid tools.

Segovia identified attitudes accompanying the teaching of tools that are universalizing and claiming a false monopoly upon ways of reading. It is not self-evident that cultural criticism[52] is innately free of those attitudes and attributes even though it be an improvement upon the traditional fare. The tools and the goals of their impartation only partially determine the learning environment. The learning environment is a conglomerate of institutional vision, institutional policy, classroom ethos, curricula and syllabi choices, human constituents, and aesthetics. The countries that have had a long history of providing theological education can no longer assume that students from around the globe who come for accreditation enter devoid of useful histories and knowledge. Rather, the assumption should be that it is worthwhile, not only to themselves but also to the providing institutions to have their histories and their lores integrated into the learning environment. What then is the vision of this change?

The Way Forward

The hope of our age is identified by hermeneutical, methodological, pedagogical, and teleological categories that are founded on a liberatory paradigm that is oriented toward praxis. A necessary companion in this hope is the development of pedagogical principles that guide an ethos of praxis in the classroom. This Greek term was redefined by Karl Marx and appropriated for religious actions by Latin American liberation theologians. Praxis is the unifying of theory and action so that the development and modification of theory occurs in the content of action. The importation of this conundrum occurs within the classroom experience and for reflections upon that experience by both students and teachers.

Feminist biblical scholars who are also critically interested in pedagogy are not alone in seeking a framework of understanding for a liberatory education. In this regard, as they move through the theology of pedagogy to consider the practical outworkings, they join concerns with a wider group within the United States and Canada that is already giving considerable thought to theories and experiences of multicultural and liberatory pedagogies, some doing so in postcolonial terms.[53] Multicultural pedagogy has preuniversity education as its focus and liberatory peda- gogies have been theorized and experienced primarily within undergraduate courses in Women's Studies (WS). The development and growth of WS was fruitful ground for new pedagogical thought. As feminism expanded to include multiple areas of dis- crimination and oppression its connection to multicultural pedagogy along the lines of race, class, and gender inequities resulted in cross-fertilization and an emphasis on the politically liberatory or emancipatory function of the classroom. With this con- nection, the feminist classroom was poised for conceptual dismantling from WS to becoming a pedagogy usable in any classroom, virtually in any subject area, inclusive of the physical sciences.

Women's Studies in Religion (WSR) is the locale of feminist pedagogies in the religious studies disciplines. WSR developed almost concurrently with WS. Religious History (with special focus on Early, Medieval, and Reformation periods) and Philosophy were some of the earliest sectors to develop and sustain feminist interests in religion. Biblical Studies were not exempt. The early works of women such as Phyllis Bird, Antoinette Clark Wire, Elisabeth Schüssler Fiorenza, Phyllis Trible, Renita Weems became milestones in biblical study from women's and American minority perspectives. The product of their work is best known as the uncovering of biblical canonical women's stories as foci of attention. They wrote as women, asking the questions that were of interest to women. They did textual interpretation in ways that related to historical-critical scholarship while maintaining and prioritizing a responsiveness to women's issues in this application. In this venture the canon for biblical study of ancient women was purposefully expanded to include extra- canonical literature.[54] The recovered stories might have occluded the subtle ideologi- cal perspective shared in general with WS: that women's experiences and intuitions constitute a particularistic episteme that can function as hermeneutic and heuristic positionalities. In this our essayists would emphasize the inclusion of international women's experiences and intuitions.

The aforementioned women scholars and others of their time legitimized the foregrounding of women's stories as providing data and information about the world and experiences of the ancient woman. Previously, stories about women had been under-attended and were quite circumscribed in appropriation and application. Appropriation and application focused on establishing and legitimizing the subordi- nate roles of women in relation to men and as mothers and caretakers, defining the parameters of women's functioning and competence, characterizing the sexuality of women, and confirming women's predilection to go astray, and to take others with her. Women's history was important insofar as it served to support men's histories and concepts. The feminist biblical focus on women's history served to uncover a great diversity in women's lives along with characteristics of heroism, wisdom, cultic and prophetic participation, and their relationships to each other. It also identified the exploitable vulnerability of the ancient woman. Most vitally, within the study of reli- gion, it established the validity of women's religious history as a disciplinary entity. Castelli recognized that women's lives and thoughts could also be used to analyze and construct theology.[55] This was a quiet revolution, that challenged and destabilized patriarchal entrenchment in the interpretation of women's canonical and eventually extra-canonical stories.

The new frontier requires an ethical, liberatory paradigm that corresponds to that of feminists. The unfolding of this ethic in the classroom will devolve differently depending on the location of the classroom, that is, whether in a superpower, old power, or Two-Thirds World situation.[56] The North American classroom is now a microcosm comprising of the multiple ethnicities and classes of North America. Additionally, persons from other nations add international culture, class, and ethnicity to the classroom, increasing the complexity. A presumption that North American representatives are co-terminal with their autochthonous peoples will not suffice for understanding of this complexity. The implications for curricula, broadly speaking, and syllabi in the institutions these persons attend, especially for educating countries that have a ruling relationship to issues of empire, was discussed earlier.

Within an international context the postcolonial interest adds to the dimensions of liberatory interest. Reading the Bible for liberation or transformation involves perspectival readings that value alternate voices. The multi-logue affects the understanding of liberation as well as the nature of transformation and the extent to which they can be applicable in a given time and place. In relation to the dominance of Europe and North America in the doctrinal and historical critical study of the Bible the voices that emerge outside of these continents are practically subaltern.

Multivocal polysemy offers alternative cultural, political, and economic perspectives from which to read the Bible. Some of those voices will bring an alternate dominant cultural narrative to bear on interpretations. That subaltern voices either are challenged or challenge themselves to provide radically contrastive interpretations in order to establish their viability through alterity is a tenuous practice but perhaps a necessary phase. Subaltern voices may offer readings that uncover the power dynamics operative in the portrayal of women in the Bible or offer readings that analyze the role of class and ethnicity in the determination of choice and way in which biblical stories are told and in the history of interpretation. Such deconstructive critical activity shuffles between entrenched positivistic historicizing that is prescriptive on the one hand, and a dialogical, socially conscious analytic process on the other. In other words there is both method and meaning in the subaltern perspective. But these perspectives remain marginal to the core or elective courses in the biblical studies curriculum. A transformation in the ethics of biblical criticism to a liberatory curriculum would require that such perspectives and the history of biblical transmission and reception in the historical missionary field become substantive subjects in the biblical curriculum. A feminist pedagogy means a movement to a liberatory curriculum that includes courses and ideas generated outside the Eurocentric, malestream history of criticism and dogmatic interpretation. How then would we speak of this kind of approach to biblical interpretation?

Schüssler Fiorenza rejects ideological, postcolonial, and cultural criticism in favor of a paradigm of emancipatory rhetoric[57] because the former failed to make "*wo/men* subjects of interpretation, connected intellectuals, or historical agents central to their theoretical frameworks . . . nor takes wo/men's experience into account when analyzing social location and the operations of power within discourse."[58] Ironically, her rejection indicates the very kind of dialectic necessary in and for the liberatory classroom. The language of ideology, the history of postcolonialism, the reality of culture, are the most pertinent issues for many Two-Thirds World femininst biblical scholars and students in the classroom.[59]

For them, emancipation is not only a liberatory concept but a historical moment that preceded and catapulted ideology, culture, and history's schema to the forefront of consciousness. One would think that this should make a very good argument for the use of "emancipatory rhetoric" as the paradigmatic discourse for biblical studies. But for many Two-Thirds World women the balance is between that of the liberation of themselves as *wo/men* within their postcolonial cultural contexts and the liberation of their people as a whole who know that gender is but one aspect of the oppression they experience; hence the need to foreground culture, era, and ideology as an undergirding aspect of international power. Perhaps, then, we should not be seeking a universal paradigm. Instead we need a cross-cultural conversation about pedagogy that creates and elucidates ways of producing, teaching, and experiencing the paradigms that work for a variety of women in a variety of situations.

This is an example of the conversation that can occur in the feminist classroom. The feminist biblical studies classroom, as a liberatory environment, can be prepared for the dialectical problems by the experience of predecessors who persevere in the worthy experiments of the WS and multicultural classrooms. In the 1970s, second wave feminism took a courageous leap forward with the development of WS as an academic discipline. The aims were clear: (a) to correct gender based imbalances in historiography; (b) recover women's history as an integral entity thus redressing egregious exclusions in the general study of history; and (c) extricate women's herstory (history) from its encapsulation in and subordination to masculinist histories. In its political aspect, WS sought to conscientize women students to the historical and contemporary oppression, subordination, and marginalization of women in the home, the workplace, and in civil society. With these goals and intentions WS developed feminist pedagogy as a gendered perspective that repudiates masculinist methods of reasoning and teaching, thus countering linear logic by elevating intuition, narrativity, personal experience, group, and experiential learning. Women's ways of knowing through caring, intuition, and experience were the particularistic episteme that critiqued traditional repositories of knowledge, knowledge transmission, and analytical methods. Within WS the feminist episteme enjoyed a monopolistic and supraordinated hermeneutical and heuristic position.

Simultaneously, there was much experimentation to find democratic methods of teaching that would utilize the students' own knowledge bases, create safe place and equal ground for the vocalization of marginalized perspectives, expose nontraditional sources of knowledge, valorize oppressed minorities, enable students to first identify and then theorize themselves and their experiences as subjective agents in the learning environment, and develop students committed to extend the process of transformation beyond the classroom. The classroom would be one prototype of a just society. Methods that fit this kind of pedagogical aim include group work and small group discussions, and the seminar format prevailing over straightforward lectures. Classroom discussions were developed from student questions, the primary approach to social issues was experience-based so anecdotal evidence was encouraged, sometimes even the syllabus would be based on the demographic configuration and expressed interests of the students and classroom design preferenced seats in circles rather than rows. Many WS courses and departments required a component of service-based learning for successful completion of course or graduation requirements.[60] The feminist classroom was a place of advocacy in which the work of the activist informed theoretical reflections. Feminist teachers broke with traditional notions of the professor as the repository of expert knowledge but this too had its inherent challenges.

Early experiences in homogeneous classrooms were more felicitous than later ones. As feminist courses were cross-listed homogeneity changed into intra-race, interrace, and gender heterogeneity. Some kinds of marginalization such as ageism, heterosexism, and classism crossed the lines of race and gender. Additionally, in any of the above categories there could be international students coming from democracies, totalitarian governments, traditional, religious, and hierarchical, societies. The potential configurations were manifold. The early assumptions of WS could not readily accommodate such a fluid mix. The overall experience was not easily manageable and required additional skills in understanding deeply emotional, psychological processes and managing classroom dynamics as they presented themselves. For many feminist pedagogues these were developments that stretched their analytical and reflexive capabilities in new and promising directions and proved to be far more complex than originally imagined. This suggests that pedagogy should be a requisite course for graduate students to enable the understanding and management of classroom complexities.

The promise and problematics of managing positionalities required a reconceptualization of identity. The rise of cultural constructivism within feminist thought as a counter-concept to essentialism gave new direction. Cultural constructivism militated against essentialist ideas of biological determinacy especially in its contribution to determinations of women's roles with respect to reproductive rights. Additionally, essentialist notions of identity posed psychological and epistemological problems. Stable essentialist concepts of identity fed stereotyping. Other problems with the essentialist approach to identity were psychological and epistemological. Minority students were required to be authorities on their particular minority group. They bore the burden of representation to the liberatory classroom. The ideal of finding voice meant that minority students had to posture as repositories of knowledge based on their particular experiences as minorities. This was a failure to recognize the diversity within apparently homogeneous groups. Whereas it was assumed that ethnic, class, and gender categories provided homogeneity, the classroom experience showed that minority students did not always agree with each other in understandings of their political or status positionings even when they occupied the same general categories. The experience-based episteme also asserted the unassailability of experience. This emphasis created hierarchies and polarities in redressing the silence and under-representation of minorities. The oppressed can speak more authoritatively about the effects of oppression on the oppressed than can the oppressor. This both silenced those from the dominant groups and denied them access to engagement with the experience of oppression. Perhaps more far-reaching, it made it difficult to process students beyond personal experience to theorizing about that experience.

Anti-essentialism became a buzzword in feminist thought. Yet this conceptual development also held both promise and problem. Anti-essentialism proved unsatisfactory for heiresses of colonialism for whom the construction of identity and the establishment of solidarities requires the ability to recognize canons of historical and experiential similarities. Construction of identity is critical for many postcolonial peoples. Also, politics of the body differ among the multiple cultures that constitute our world and that represent themselves in the microcosmic kaleidoscope of the classroom. Without a graspable and nuanced articulation of cultural essentialism as a subaltern tool the task of identity construction for the classroom and for sociopolitical discourse will be partial and unilateral. Yet maintaining essentialism as a fixed category lends itself to the ongoing attribution of pejorative stereotypes and encourages the imposition of social strictures. A helpful direction lies in the application of positivistic realism to the question of identity.

How then was the liberatory classroom to function? The intent of WS to transform women into politically and socially critical positions in terms of feminist critique met a reasonable measure of success that was limited by the variables in identity. A challenge to feminist pedagogy concerned a proselytizing intent that conflicted with freedom of choice as to outcome. Is the freedom of critique not a basic tenet of a liberatory framework? Ought feminist pedagogy to be open to the possibility of critique even of its own positioning? The obvious answer is, "Yes." However, at a deeper level of intent is the idea that students in a liberatory classroom are not regurgitators. A constructive outcome requires: (a) the association of academic study in the humanities, sciences, and technology with sociocultural issues; (b) personal involvement in the processing of course material, experiential learning, and the classroom dynamics; and (c) eventually taking a position on the relationship described in (a) and on particular social issues based on an understanding formed by that involvement described in (b).

Feminist educators such as Frances A. Maher and Mary Kay Thompson Tetreault suggest the democratization of definitions of "mastery," "voice," and "authority." In the liberatory classroom and curriculum "mastery" would be "an interactive construction of meaning" in which students and teacher search for "complex connections to the material rather than find the right answer."[61] The idea of voice countered traditional authority in its goal that the student find her own voice. Finding voice meant that the student engaged the topics and themes of the class from a gendered perspective, with an increasing awareness of the multiplicity of positionalities that she occupied. In the heterogeneous classroom the process of finding one's voice often began with recognition of the individual's contradictory position in relation to privilege and disadvantages. "Authority" in its democratic form resides in the class as a community of learners that included the teacher.

This is a radical conceptualization of the classroom's dynamics and it elicited responses that feminist and multicultural educators categorize as "resistance," "nonengagement," and "engagement." Resistance is negative engagement that dissents against the liberatory philosophy. Non-engagement can be of two kinds. Either a student is unengaged because the process is not of interest and perceived to be irrelevant or because it is too alien to a preferred, more comfortable learning style. In both, the student might also perceive the classroom as too invasive of personal privacy. Engagement is the desired response. The engaged student manifests an involvement in the classroom activity through spoken participation, group participation journaling, or conversations with the professor among other means. That involvement may be marked at a deeper level by self-assessing reflexivity, recognitions of connectedness, and the movement from personal experience to theorizing, a form of praxis. The first two present particular points of tension with the hoped-for outcome. At stake is the attainment of a transformational position without the use of coercive strategies. The student who leaves the feminist classroom should have an active consciousness of the relationship between the study of various theories, her/his personal stake in and experience of society, and the ability to critique her/his world.

The experiences of WS and multicultural educators are models that suggest some of the possibilities that the feminist biblical classroom (FBC) may experience. The diversity of the FBC is further complicated by the presence of self-conscious religious diversity. Within undergraduate and graduate institutions, religious diversity includes multifaith backgrounds, for instance, Christians, Jews, Muslims, Hindus, Wiccans; different approaches to faith practice, for example, conservative, liberal, mystic, New Age spiritualities; agnostics, atheists, religious renegades, and the irreligious. These differences constitute a web of approaches toward biblical studies. It is necessary to build bridges to nondogmatic biblical criticism as practiced in many tertiary educational institutions.

Within seminaries the range of approaches to biblical criticism is less varied. A liberatory critical feminist pedagogy is more likely to encounter a relatively sympathetic reception in a seminary that traditionally embraced historical criticism rather than biblical literalism and tends toward a more radical critical stance to Christian activism. This is a different kind of teaching experience than that of the undergraduate or secular graduate school. Nonetheless, we must note that within the United States and Canada the profile of the seminary student is increasingly that of a second career adult. In many other parts of the world the seminarian(a) is a first career person, often entering seminary immediately following high school or university graduation. Within the United States there are many international seminarians and Americans who enter seminaries under the heavier influence of a conservative orientation to Christian faith. There is, then, greater purchase into the idea of the Bible as the normative, prescriptive, word from God to humankind. This is also true in other countries where missionaries laid the foundations for Christianity. One import of the essays in this volume is as signs of the need to engage conversation at the international level with the proponents of a liberal approach to biblical studies and with those of a more conservative viewpoint wherever they may be.

For many seminarians the encounter with historical criticism is a jarring experience that is met with a range of responses from delight and relief to dismay and disdain. The idea of liberatory perspectival biblical readings may be welcomed or rejected depending on a student's location within that range. The location of the introduction of perspectival readings within the trajectory of the overall biblical studies curriculum may require strategic thinking in such a case. Additionally, it cannot be imagined that the international student is going to share the same liberatory concerns as the American students. Further, the problematics encountered in the development of feminist pedagogy in WS are pertinent to the seminary context because of diversity of American international identities that are usually present in the classroom. The concerns about Mastery, Authority, Voice, and the response schema of Resistance, Non-engagement and Engagement will need ongoing praxis and methodical experimentation within the seminary classroom perhaps even more so than in the secular classroom.

The Global Future of Feminist New Studies Conference was accompanied by a seminar class, with the same title, held at Scripps College in Claremont, California. It was a small class that emphasized classroom discussion and group work. The papers from this collective effort are included in this publication. In significant ways this class was a feminist classroom. The diversity included one male student from a Two-Thirds World country, a Jewish student, Christians of different backgrounds, as well as persons without religious commitment. The circle-centered classroom and professorial facilitation, receptivity, and guidance made the classroom a safe place where students had the freedom to debate with each other, express dissent, collaborate to find the places of consensus, and face disagreement with respect. Through this class students were given a fuller opportunity to prepare through the writings of the conference presenters thus shaping a prepared confidence as they attended the conversations. Their inclusion in this book attests the value of decentering authority and recognizing the capacity of the student to also be teacher.

Whereas pedagogical considerations focused on the classroom, it is not the only sphere in which learning occurs. We have given some thought to conversations between the academy and various faith communities. It is possible to envisage learning centers that are built on retreat models. It is also possible to conceive of learning sites that are nontraditional. Service learning as advocated by feminist teachers can be extended to biblical studies. It could be an exciting prospect for the biblical scholar to actually test theories and interpretations in the places where plain common sense makes sense—for that scholar to sit with the "ordinary reader" in the actual *cotidian* of life. Their research tools, critical inquiry, actual research may be influenced by the quotidian. What then might biblical scholarship learn?

Conclusion

Feminist pedagogy is concerned both with the ideology of teaching and the methods. It introduces into the classroom a plethora of possibilities that resist easy answers and disallow the maintenance of homogeneous neatness. It shows the insufficiency of pedagogical considerations that analyze the tools of a discipline without an examination of practical pedagogy. The feminist tendency to alliances invites that biblical scholars and teachers take a more careful look at critical theoretical developments in the field of education as a way of understanding the practical challenges to a liberatory pedagogy.

The experience of these conversations and the conversation partners reveal the complexity of the undertaking. Rhetoricity may provide a discursive universe for biblical studies, yet the accompanying tendency to dehistoricize can prove inadequate for the needs of the subaltern voice. Rhetoric and positivism may need to engage in dialogue and with the company of Two-Thirds World hermeneutics in order to forge a new and meaningful way forward. There is not a liberatory paradigm that will succeed without the practice of praxis and an openness to the disorder of multivocal polysemy both in theory and in practice. In that spirit I will not determine the parameters of the vision of a feminist pedagogy. That is a conversation waiting to happen.

Notes

1. One of the most sustained and diverse discussions of the need for pedagogical change in biblical studies is in Fernando F. Segovia and Mary Ann Tolbert, eds., *Teaching the Bible: The Discoursed and Politics of Biblical Pedagogy* (New York: Orbis Books, 1998). The *Semeia Journal* also devoted two issues to this need: one addressing interpretation in a general way, Katie Geneva Cannon, Guest Editor and Elisabeth Schüssler Fiorenza, ed., *Interpretation for Liberation* (Atlanta, Georgia: Scholars Press, 1989), 47 and another with a specialized focus on Africa, Gerald West and Musa W. Dube, eds., *"Reading With": An Exploration of the Interface Between Critical and Ordinary Readings of the Bible. African Overtures* (Atlanta, Georgia: Scholars Press, 1996), 73. One of the earliest recognitions of the need for feminist *postcolonial* hermeneutics came from Kathleen O'Brien Wicker, "Teaching Feminist Biblical Studies in a Postcolonial Context," in Elisabeth Schüssler Fiorenza, ed., *Searching the Scriptures. Vol. I: A Feminist Introduction* (New York: The Crossroad Publishing Company, 1993), 367–380. Yet the first fledgling effort at a dialogue between Two-Thirds and One-Third World theologians was sponsored by the Society of Biblical Literature in 1990. Jonathan A. Draper's summary account of the history of its development may be found at http://www.hs.unp.ac.za/theology/afas.htm. Since that first effort, a number of theoretical and interpretive works have appeared: Cain Hope Felder, ed., *Stony the Road We Trod: African American Biblical Interpretation* (Minneapolis: Fortress Press, 1991); Brian K. Blount, *Cultural Interpretation: Reorienting New Testament Criticism* (Minneapolis: Fortress Press, 1995); Elisabeth Schüssler Fiorenza, *Rhetoric and Ethic: The Politics of Biblical Studies* (Minneapolis: Fortress Press, 1999); Vincent L. Wimbush, ed., *African Americans and the Bible: Sacred Texts and Social Textures* (New York: Continuum, 2000); Randall C. Bailey, ed., *Yet With a Steady Beat: Contemporary U.S. Afrocentric Biblical Interpretation* (Atlanta, Georgia: Society of Biblical Literature, Semeia Studies, 2003), 42; Musa W. Dube, *Postcolonial Feminist Interpretation of the Bible* (St. Louis, Missouri: Chalice Press, 2000). A handful of books from Christian faith traditions indicates an even earlier beginning to publications and ongoing projects for subaltern voices. See, John S. Pobee and Barbel von Wartenberg Potter, *New Eyes for Reading: Biblical and Theological Reflections by Women from the Third World* (Geneva, Switzerland: World Council of Churches, 1986); Barbel von Wartenberg Potter and Fred Kaan, *We Will Not Hang our Harps on the Willows: Global Sisterhood and God's Song* (US Ed., New York, NY: Meyer Stone Books, 1998); Lois Miriam Wilson, *Telling Her Story: Theology out of Women's Struggles* (Toronto, Ontario: The United Church Publishing House, 1992), Margaret Warren, Trans. and ed., *Women Moving Mountains: Feminist Theology in Japan* (Kuala Lumpur, Malaysia: Asian Women's Resource Centre for Culture and Theology, 2000). In the Caribbean as early as 1984 there was a brave little publication, Marjorie Lewis Cooper and Althea Spencer-Miller, ed., *News Eyes for Seeing: Report on the First Caribbean Clergywomen's Consultation* (Kingston, Jamaica: Gooden Printers, 1984).

2. Joseph C. Hough, Jr., "Globalization in Theological Education," in Fernando F. Segovia and Mary Ann Tolbert, eds., *Teaching the Bible: The Discourses and Politics of Biblical Pedagogy* (New York: Orbis Books, 1998) 61–63.

3. Regional here refers to international groupings of countries, e.g., Asia, the Pacific, Latin America, the Caribbean.

4. Fernando F. Segovia, "Pedagogical Discourse and Practices," in Segovia and Tolbert, eds., *Teaching the Bible: The Discourses and Politics of Biblical Pedagogy* (New York: Orbis Books, 1998), 19.

5. Segovia, "Pedagogical Discourse," 20.

6. First written in Mosala: 50–51. Cited here from Gerald O. West and Musa Dube, "Introduction," in Gerald O. West and Musa Dube, eds., *The Bible in Africa: Transactions, Trajectories, and Trends* (Boston: Brill Academic Publishers, 2001) 10.

7. West and Dube, "Introduction," 13.

8. This is a chronological "first." The political import is now her priority.

9. Ethics is not to be confused with moral(s). "Ethics thematizes moral actions on a metalevel of reflection as it asks for moral principles, norms, and criteria for judging an action as moral." See her discussion in Elisabeth Schüssler Fiorenza, *Rhetoric and Ethics: The Politics of Biblical Studies* (Minneapolis: Fortress Press, 1999) 65.

10. Schüssler Fiorenza, *Rhetoric and Ethics*, 80.

11. Schüssler Fiorenza, *Rhetoric and Ethics*, 68.

12. For a fuller discussion of these issues, see Schüssler Fiorenza, *Rhetoric and Ethics*.

13. An exception to this is Elisabeth Schüssler Fiorenza, *Wisdom Ways: Introducing Feminist Biblical Interpretation* (New York: Orbis Books, 2001), which is directed toward the non-professional reader.

14. West and Dube, "Introduction," 10, Althea Spencer Miller, "Lucy Bailey Meets the Feminists" (essay in this volume).

15. Schüssler Fiorenza, *Rhetoric and Ethics*, 198.

16. West and Dube, "Introduction," 15.

17. Vincent L. Wimbush. "Introduction: Reading Darkness, Reading Scriptures," in *African Americans and the Bible: Sacred Texts and Social Textures* (New York: Continuum, 2000) 3.

18. Vincent L. Wimbush, "Signifying on Scriptures: An African Diaspora Proposal for Radical Readings" (essay in this volume).

19. Wimbush, "Introduction: Reading Darkness," 27.

20. Wimbush, "Introduction: Reading Darkness," 29.

21. Wimbush, "Signifying on Scripture" (essay in this volume).

22. "Jea" is described in Wimbush, "Signifying Scripture" as an eighteenth/nineteenth-century narrator of slave experience. (See essay in this volume.)

23. Wimbush, "Signifying on Scripture" (essay in this volume).

24. Wimbush, "Introduction," 21.

25. Hisako Kinukawa, "Biblical Studies in the 21st Century: A Japanese/Asian Feminist Glimpse" (essay in this volume).

26. Kinukawa, "Biblical Studies" (essay in this volume).

27. Kinukawa, "Biblical Studies" (essay in this volume).

28. Elizabeth Conde-Frazier, "A Framework Toward Solidarity and Justice: Response to Aída Besançon Spencer" (essay in this volume).

29. English translation may be "quotidian" or that which pertains to the everyday.

30. Elizabeth Conde-Frazier, "A Framework" (essay in this volume), quoting from Loida I. Martell, "*Lo Cotidiano*: Finding God in the Spaces of the Everyday," unpublished paper.

31. Elizabeth Conde-Frazier, "A Framework" (essay in this volume).

32. Elizabeth Conde-Frazier, "A Framework" (response paper in this volume).

33. Zhiru, "An Asian Buddhist's Response to a Japanese Feminist Glimpse of Biblical Studies in the 21st Century" (response paper in this volume).

34. Zhiru, "An Asian Buddhist's Response" (response paper in this volume).

35. Musa W. Dube, "Rahab is Hanging out a Red Ribbon: One African Woman's Perspective on the Future of Feminist New Testament Scholarship" (essay in this volume).

36. Dube has a fuller discussion of this in "Rahab is Hanging out a Red Ribbon" (essay in this volume).

37. Dube, "Rahab is Hanging out a Red Ribbon" (essay in this volume).

38. Musa W. Dube, ed., *Other Ways of Reading: African Women and the Bible* (Atlanta: Society of Biblical Literature/Geneva: WCC Publications, 2001).

39. Daniel Patte, "Biblical Scholars at the Interface Between Critical and Ordinary Readings: A Response," in *Semeia: An Experimental Journal for Biblical Criticism: "Reading With" African Overtures*, 73: 1996: 263–276 esp. 263.

40. Daniel Patte, "Biblical Scholars at the Interface," 263.

41. For a fuller discussion see Kathleen O'Brien Wicker, "Teaching Feminist Biblical Studies in a Postcolonial Context," in Elisabeth Schüssler Fiorenza, ed., *Searching the Scriptures* (New York: Crossroad Publishing Company, 1993) 372.

42. Kathleen Wicker, "Teaching Feminist Biblical Studies," 372.

43. Gay Byron, "The Challenge of 'Blackness' for Rearticulating the Meaning of Global Feminist New Testament Interpretation" (essay in this volume).

44. Gay Byron, "The Challenge of 'Blackness' " (essay in this volume).

45. Musa W. Dube, "Rahab is Hanging Out a Red Ribbon" (essay in this volume).

46. Reflections on Audre Lorde's question as adopted by Wicker in "Teaching Feminist Biblical Studies," 370, where she cites Audre Lorde. "The Master's Tools Will Never Dismantle the Master's House," in *Sister Outsider: Essays and Speeches* (Trumansburg, NY: Crossing Press, 1984) 110–123.

47. Kathleen Wicker, "Teaching Feminist Biblical Studies," 370.

48. Musa W. Dube, "Rahab is Hanging Out a Red Ribbon" (essay in this volume).

49. James Cone, *A Black Theology of Liberation* (Philadelphia: Lippincott, 1970) is the generative work.

50. Philip Jenkins, *The Next Christendom: The Coming of Global Christianity* (New York: Oxford University Press, 2000).

51. Rebecca Chopp, "A Rhetorical Paradigm for Pedagogy," in Segovia and Tolbert, *Teaching the Bible*, 301.

52. Segovia, "Pedagogical Discourse," 19.

53. See bell hooks, *Teaching to Transgress* (New York: Routledge, 1994), M. Jacqui Alexander and Chandra Talpade Mohanty, *Feminist Genealogies, Colonial Legacies, Democratic Futures* (New York: Routledge, 1997); Gail E. Cohee, Elisabeth Däumer et al., eds., *The Feminist Teacher Anthology: Pedagogies and Classroom Strategies* (New York: Teachers College Press, Columbia University, 1998); Maralee Mayberry and Ellen Cronan Rose, eds., *Meeting the Challenge: Innovative Feminist Pedagogies in Action* (New York and London: Routledge; 1999); Amanda Coffey and Sara Delamont, *Feminism and the Classroom Teacher: Research, Praxis, and Pedagogy* (London: RoutledgeFalmer, 2000); Frances A. Maher and Mary Kay Thompson Tetreault, *The Feminist Classroom: Dynamics of Gender, Race and Privilege* (Maryland: Rowland and Littlefield Publishers, 2001 Expanded Edition); Daphne Patai and Noretta Koertge, *Professing Feminism: Education and Indoctrination in Women's Studies* (New York: Lexington Books, 2003) to name a few of hundreds of publications.

54. Elisabeth Schüssler Fiorenza, "Transgressing Canonical Boundaries," in Elisabeth Schüssler Fiorenza, ed., *Searching the Scriptures* Vol. 2: *A Feminist Commentary* (New York: Crossroad Publishing Company, 1994) 1–16.

55. Elizabeth A. Castelli, "Romans" in Elisabeth Schüssler Fiorenza, ed., *Searching the Scriptures* Vol. 2: *A Feminist Commentary* (New York: Crossroad Publishing Company, 1994) 272–300 esp. 280–292.
56. These delineations are determined to some extent by geography and history. That you can find Two-Thirds World situations in a superpower country and dominant groups in Two-Thirds World countries complicates the divides. Therefore, the liberatory pedagogue must be interested in local demographics in order to identify an applicable liberatory perspective.
57. Schüssler Fiorenza, *Wisdom Ways*, 5.
58. Schüssler Fiorenza, *Wisdom Ways*, 5.
59. Alexander and Mohanty give a fuller discussion of this in M. Jacqui Alexander and Chandra Mohanty, eds., *Feminist Genealogies, Colonial Legacies*, xvii.
60. Many institutions have increased opportunites for community service with a clear regard for the value of such opportunities in the development of a well-rounded student.
61. Frances A. Maher and Mary Kay Thompson Tetreault, *The Feminist Classroom: Dynamics of Gender, Race, and Privilege* (Boston: Rowman & Littlefield Publisher, Inc., Expanded Ed. 2001) 19.

Conversation One: Europe and North America

Chapter 2

The Power of the Word: Charting Critical Global Feminist Biblical Studies

Elisabeth Schüssler Fiorenza

With this contribution, I want to honor the work of Professor Kathleen O'Brien Wicker that this conference celebrates, and I will do so by exploring the future possibilities of critical global feminist Christian Testament (CT) Studies.[1] Our present and future are always shaped by the past and our hopes, and visions are rooted in memory. In order to move into the future, it is very important to understand from where and how far we have come.

I am often asked: "With whom did you study feminist biblical criticism?" I usually reply: "Feminist biblical studies as an academic area of inquiry did not exist when I was a student. Therefore, we had to invent it." This question does not just bespeak historical forgetfulness. It also reveals how far we have come in the past 30 years. Since publications and courses on feminist biblical interpretation or biblical women's or gender studies abound today,[2] many students no longer remember a time when feminist biblical studies in religion and feminist theology did not exist in the academy.

Now that feminist biblical studies have come of age and move toward the future it is timely to assess this field of study and its prospects in a global context. Such a global context bespeaks at one and the same time the exploitation of wo/men around the world and the feminist affirmation of cultural particularities and wo/men's networking in solidarity to bring about change and transformation. I will therefore first discuss my understanding of critical global feminist biblical studies, then go on to sketch their genealogy. I then look at the danger of the academization and scientification of feminist biblical studies and finally argue that feminist biblical interpretation needs to be constantly reshaped in the interest of "dissident"[3] global solidarity.

I understand feminist biblical studies as an important scientific area of research that seeks to produce knowledge in the interest of wo/men,[4] who by law and custom have been marginalized and exploited as well as excluded from scientific theology and biblical interpretation for centuries. Although wo/men have interpreted scriptures and shaped religion throughout the centuries,[5] their work has been marginalized and forgotten. Consequently, a feminist biblical interpretation has to adopt a critical feminist hermeneutics and theological ethos of liberation as its theoretical framework and approach of inquiry.

While throughout Christian history wo/men have interpreted the bible, feminist biblical studies in their academic incarnation are of very recent vintage. Moreover, their ethos is always in danger of being co-opted by the reigning academic paradigm of interpretation. Such academic incorporation raises difficult questions. By theological ethos, I do not mean a dogmatic or ecclesiastical worldview, but the disciplined critical reflection on how discourses about the Divine and religion interrupt globalizing discourses of dehumanization or inspire discourses of well-being. In addition, I would insist that even studies that call themselves *feminist*, must be analyzed as to whether their goals are emancipatory and their theoretical assumptions interrupt global discourses of domination.[6] In the face of globalization, I argue, feminist scholars should not subscribe to a "so-called" value-detached, neutral, objectivist scientific investigation because scientific interpretation and knowledge are always already enmeshed in structures of domination and exploitation. Such structures of domination and subordination engender kyriarchal domination and kyriocentric[7] discourses of dehumanization.

A Critical Global Feminist Analytic

Structures of domination and subordination throw into question the dualistic conceptualization of women's studies in terms of gender as the basic feminist category of analysis. Alice Duer Miller's witty jingle expresses the understanding of feminism in terms of gender dualism well:

Mother, what is a feminist?
A feminist, my daughter
Is any woman now who cares
To think about her own affairs
As men don't think she oughter.[8]

In this understanding, feminism is the rejection of male control and the affirmation of female independence. Such a conceptualization of domination in terms of gender or patriarchy/androcentrism, however, does not suffice in a global context. In such a context, the analytic category of gender/patriarchy/androcentrism understood as men's domination over women must be inflected in and through an analytic that can articulate the intersecting structures of domination and prejudice. Women are not just defined by gender, but also by race, class, nationality, age, sexuality, and imperialism. Hence, the obfuscating ideological character of androcentric language must become conscious.

To make conscious the power of kyriocentric language and discourse in general and biblical language[9] in particular, I use the expression *wo/men* always in an inclusive way and invite readers to engage in a spiritual-intellectual exercise that reverses the usual linguistic practice. In a Western androcentric, grammatically male-determined language system such as English, masculine terms like *men, he*, and *mankind* are used as generic terms for human beings and are therefore presumed to include wo/men. Simply by learning how to speak, men experience themselves as central and important whereas wo/men learn that we are not directly addressed but are subsumed under male terms.

In a grammatically androcentric (i.e., male centered) language system wo/men always have to think twice and to deliberate whether we are meant or not when we are told, for example, that "all men are created equal" or that we are "sons of G*d." To lift these noxious language mechanisms into consciousness, I am using wo/men as inclusive of men, s/he as inclusive of he, and fe/male as inclusive of male. Thereby I invite male readers to deliberate and adjudicate whether they are also meant when I refer, for instance, to *globalized wo/men*. Since the limits of our language are the limits of our world, I recommend this "thinking twice" approach as a good spiritual exercise for the next 100 years or more.

Religious and biblical language tells us that we are made in the image of G*d,[10] who is generally understood as male. Wo/men thereby internalize that the Divine is male and not female. Simply by learning to speak or to pray, wo/men learn that we are marginal, insignificant, "second class citizens" in society and religion. It seems to me, therefore, that only those Two-Third World feminist scholars who have not been socialized into a Western androcentric language system, because the languages of their native country is not gendered, can break this power of male centered language over us. Scholars who have grown up in a language system that, for instance, is a *status system*, are able to make significant contribution to feminist translation, thought, and theology although feminist research in this area is still very much lacking.[11]

At the same time by problematizing *woman* through my writing, I want wo/men to pause and ask which wo/men are meant since not all wo/men are the same and the differences between wo/men are as great or often even greater than those between wo/men and men of the same race, class, or ethnic group. Wo/men are not a unitary group and do not have a feminine nature and essence in common. Wo/men are not a different human species from men nor are we all the same. Rather, wo/men come in all sizes, shapes, and colors. What it means to be a *woman* is different in Europe, Africa, or Asia. It means something different when you are black or white, young or old. It means something different if you have grown up in a pueblo or in an academic environment. It means something different if you are a beauty queen or differently abled, a girl or a mother; it means something different if you are a student or a teacher, the lady of the house or her slave.

Wo/man or wo/men is an unstable fragmented category and one cannot assume that all wo/men are similar in their hopes and desires. Hence it becomes important to ask which wo/men come to mind when one speaks of *woman's perspective*. Are they right-wing or feminist, black or white, native or foreign? Wo/men as much as men are socialized into the mindsets and worldviews of the dominant culture. We are not better human beings or able to envision a different future just because we are *wo/men.* Changing language patterns is a very important step toward the realization of a new consciousness. Not femininity or *woman* but wo/men's rich diversity must constitute the feminist perspective and theoretical framework of a "global reading" of the bible.

Such a critical understanding of language requires that we conceptualize feminist biblical studies as a critical rhetoric of inquiry[12] that treats biblical texts and scholarly interpretations as arguments rather than as descriptive statements or theological doctrines. It investigates both how biblical texts and interpretations *mean* and what *they do.* Such an understanding of biblical texts as "rhetorical" overlaps with Edward Said's view that "Texts are worldly, to some degree they are events, and even when they appear to deny it, they are nevertheless a part of the social world, human life, and of course the historical moments in which they are located and interpreted"[13] but it accentuates this insight in a critical feminist mode. I understand, therefore, feminist biblical studies as an important scientific area of research that seeks to produce knowledge in the interest of wo/men who by law and custom have been marginalized and exploited as well as excluded from scientific theology and biblical interpretation for centuries.

Although some strains of postmodernism and post-feminism are adamant in their rejection of speaking about "social structures of domination" and focus on ideology instead,[14] I maintain that a critical feminist hermeneutics cannot relinquish the analysis of structures of domination. Rather than abandon such a systemic analysis, I have suggested that we replace the dualistic notions of *patriarchy* and *androcentrism* with the intersectional analytic of kyriarchy that is, *emperor, lord, slave-master, father, husband, elite educated male structures of* domination and focus on its ideological kyriocentric discursive formations. Such a complex structural analytic can critically evaluate gender and other dualisms and articulate the variegated facets of domination and subordination.

In the face of wo/men's globalized inequality a strong feminist movement is called for that does not understand wo/men's oppression just in terms of gender dualism or the domination of all wo/men by all men but in terms of intersecting structures and discourses of domination: racism, heterosexism, poverty, imperialism, ethnocentrism, and ageism and insists on the revalorization of *differences* and not just of *gender difference.*

My preferred definition of feminism is expressed by a well-known bumper sticker that asserts, tongue in cheek, "feminism is the radical notion that wo/men are people." This definition accentuates that feminism is a radical notion and at the same time ironically underscores that at the beginning of the twenty-first century, feminism should be a common sense view. Wo/men are not just ladies, wives, handmaids, seductresses, or "beasts of burden," but wo/men are full decision-making citizen-subjects. This definition alludes to the democratic assertion "We, the people" and positions feminism within radical democratic discourses, which argue for the rights of all the people. It evokes memories of struggles for equal citizenship and decision-making powers in society and religion. According to this political definition of feminism, men can advocate feminism just as wo/men can be antifeminist.

Theologically, feminism understands wo/men as the people of G*d and indicts the death-dealing powers of oppression as structural sin and life-destroying evil. Hence, feminist theologies and studies in religion have the goal not only to fundamentally alter the nature of malestream knowledge about G*d, the self, and the world, but also to change institutionalized religions that have excluded wo/men from leadership positions. Feminism is thus best understood as a theoretical perspective and historical movement for changing sociocultural and communal-religious structures of domination and exploitation. Therefore, it becomes necessary to focus specifically on the struggles of multiple oppressed wo/men for self-determination and justice in society and religion that leads to a different self-understanding and vision of the world.

Such a critical feminist liberationist approach engages a "doubled" analysis of power, one that conceptualizes power as structural—pyramidal, or more precisely as kyriarchal relations of domination, and one that understands power horizontally as an ideological network of relations of domination. Both modes of power, the vertical and the horizontal, are at work in capitalist globalization. The kyriarchal (i.e., imperial) pyramid of domination is structured by race, gender, sexuality, class, empire, age, and religion, which are intersecting systems that have multiplicative effects of dehumanizing exploitation and othering subordination.

In working with a social analytic of domination and liberation I prefer a *status* rather than an *identity* model of inquiry that is able to examine the institutionalized structures and value patterns of domination for their effects on the relative status of social actors both in a given society and in a text. If such status inscriptions constitute persons as peers, capable of participating on a par with each other, then we can speak of status equality or grassroots democracy. If they do not do so, then we speak of domination and subordination. Wo/men's struggles for radical democratic equality seek to abolish relations of domination and to establish those of subordinated status as full partners and peers with equal rights and responsibilities.

In the days of post-feminism and the "war on feminism" (New York Times) by the Christian Right and the Bush administration it is often argued that wo/men are not discriminated against or oppressed, that feminist rhetoric and not discriminatory structures turn wo/men into victims. I am frequently told by young wo/men that they cannot connect with a critical feminist interpretation for liberation because they do not feel disadvantaged and have not experienced discrimination.[15] They are convinced that feminist struggles were won by their mothers or grandmothers.

I generally respond to such interlocutors that if they come from a middle-class, white, racially and nationally privileged background, it is quite understandable that they have not yet experienced oppression or even discrimination. Yet, anyone who knows how to read the newspapers or gets involved in religious or university politics[16] soon will learn that feminist struggles are not yet over. Feminist theology and biblical studies are still very controversial and far from being accepted by leaders in religion and academy.

A glance at statistical data on wo/men's situation in the United States and around the world can easily document that wo/men as a group are disadvantaged worldwide in and through the processes of globalization. Wo/men still earn only two-thirds of what men in similar situations earn; the majority of people living in poverty are wo/men; violence against wo/men and gynecide, that is the killing of wo/men, is on the increase; sexual trafficking, various forms of forced labor, illiteracy, migration, and refugee camps spell out globally wo/men's increasing exploitation.

Economic globalization was created with the specific goal, to give primacy to corporate profits and values and to install and codify such market values all over the world. It was designed to amalgamate and merge all economic activities around the world within a single model of global monoculture. In many respects wo/men are suffering not only from the globalization of market capitalism but also from their sexual exploitation instigated by such market capitalism.

The Human Rights Watch World Report extensively documents the systemic inequality, abuse, violence, discrimination, starvation, poverty, neglect, and denial of wo/men's rights that afflict the lives of wo/men around the globe.[17] Hence, the experience of white middle- or upper-class U.S. wo/men is not typical and does not adequately comprehend the extent of wo/men's oppression worldwide. A global feminist biblical hermeneutics, therefore, must critically look at its politics of location. While it is important that we recognize our social location and celebrate our particular cultural-religious differences, we also need to be wary of the global-capitalist ethos of fragmentation and competition that prevents our solidarity.

In and through cultural, political, and religious discourses the social structures in which we are positioned are interpreted. Since we cannot stand outside of the interpretive frameworks available in our society and time, we "make sense" out of life with their help. For instance, one wo/man might be influenced by neoconservatism and believe that her social position results from the fact that she worked harder in life than the wo/man on welfare who lives down the street. Another wo/man influenced by right-wing religious fundamentalism might make sense of her situation by believing that she is blessed by G*d because of her virtuous life, whereas the unmarried mother on welfare has gravely sinned and therefore is punished. Again, another wo/man might think that her success as a wife and mother is due to her feminine attractiveness and selfless dedication to her husband and children, and that the fate of the wo/man on welfare is due to her lack thereof.

If we always have to resort to existing interpretive discourses and frameworks for making sense of our lives or of biblical texts, then the importance of social movements for justice becomes obvious. Since malestream hegemonic discourses provide the frameworks in which we "make meaning" in oppressive situations, feminist discourses must provide interpretive frameworks that illuminate not only the choreography of oppression but also the possibilities for a radical democratic society and religion.[18] We are able to articulate an emancipatory self- and world-understanding only within the context of radical democratic movements, which shape theories that help us to exploit the contradictions existing between diverse socio-hegemonic discourses.

Here the distinction between a wo/man's *structural position* and her *subject position* becomes important. Every individual is *structurally* positioned by birth within social, cultural, economic, political, and religious structures of domination. No one chooses to be born white, black, Asian, European, mixed race, poor, healthy, male, or female. We always find ourselves already positioned by and within structures of domination and the chances we get in life are limited by them. For example, wo/men are not poor or homeless because we have low motivation, faulty self-esteem, or poor work habits. Rather wo/men are poor or homeless because of our *structural position* within relations of domination.

Unlike a *structural position* a *subject position* is variable, open to intervention and changeable but also limited by hegemonic structures of domination. According to the theorists Ernest Laclau and Chantal Mouffe,

> A "subject position" refers to the ensemble of beliefs through which an individual interprets and responds to her structural positions within a social formation. In this sense an individual becomes a social agent insofar as she lives her structural positions through an ensemble of subject positions.[19]

The relationship between a *subject position* and a *structural position* is quite complex since our self-understandings are always already determined by our *structural position* with its rewards and pressures. Thus, a person might be theoretically able to live her structural position through a wide range of subject positions, but practically might be restricted to a rigidly defined and closed set of available interpretive frameworks. Hence, the importance of emancipatory movements and the different interpretive frameworks they articulate.

Feminist critical theory has made a range of such interpretive frameworks and categories available to wo/men for shaping our *subject positions*.[20] It has provided various social analytics for diagnosing and changing wo/men's structural positions in and through the articulation of different *subject positions*. Key analytic concepts and categories with which to read in a feminist fashion have been developed either as reverse discourse to the binary intellectual framework of systemic dualisms or in a critical liberationist frame. Feminist biblical studies also has shared in this intellectual process.

Genealogy of Feminist Biblical Studies

While academic feminist biblical studies are of recent vintage, the study of *wo/men* in the bible was already flourishing when I started to study theology in the late 1950s. Just as according to Virginia Woolf the library shelves were filled with books written by men about wo/men,[21] so also the religious libraries had a great array of tracts on "women in the bible." These were either moralistic tales to inculcate the standards of Christian femininity with the help of biblical wo/men characters and saints, or they were written to legitimate wo/men's exclusion from or admission to ordination. Others again were apologetic in tone arguing that Jesus and Christian religion has liberated wo/men. Such portrayals of Jesus and his liberation of wo/men were often used for missionary purposes or served antifeminist and anti-Jewish interests.

Like the study *about women*, so also wo/men's biblical studies in which wo/men are not just objects but also subjects of interpretation, have a long history starting with antiquity and continuing throughout the Middle Ages and modernity. In the nineteenth century Sojourner Truth, Anna Maria Stewart, and the Grimkè sisters, for instance, claimed such authority of interpretation in the struggle for the abolition of slavery, Elizabeth Cady Stanton edited the Woman's Bible[22] and Antoinette Blackwell wrote a scientific paper on 1 Corinthians. However, the wo/men scholars of the time were, according to Cady Stanton, not willing to collaborate in the project of the *Woman's Bible*.[23]

Many feminists were and still are convinced that the bible and religion are anti-wo/men and hence must be rejected as hopelessly patriarchal. Biblical interpretation is the domain of believers but not the task of feminists. Yet, already in the nineteenth century Elizabeth Cady Stanton pointed to the pitfalls of such a feminist attitude. She maintained that feminists must concern themselves with the bible and religion because many women still believe in them. She also pointed out that one cannot reform one segment of patriarchal society without reforming the whole. If feminists are concerned with the liberation of women, then they must take account of the fact that many women not only consult the bible as an inspiring authority but also value and transmit it as a source of strength and hope. Feminists, whether believers or not, must concern themselves with the bible and its interpretation because it still has great power in the lives of many women.

In addition, it needs to be pointed out, feminists who have left biblical religions but have grown up in Western cultures have also internalized many biblical patterns and stereotypes. Western cultures are still permeated with the symbolism and values of the Christian Scriptures. In order to understand Western art, music, and literature one needs a certain amount of biblical literacy. Cultural ideologies and media stereotypes are still based on and derived from the bible. Biblical texts and images fund the cultural language of hate against wo/men, against blacks, against homosexuals, against Jews, or against pagans.

The *biblical women's studies* scholarship emerging in the 1970s saw wo/men both as subjects and objects of interpretation. However, the *women's studies* approach also has been in danger of continuing the objectifying "women in the bible" genre or the Christian apologetic approach that in the face of feminist criticism proclaims either the bible or Jesus as the liberator of woman.[24] This approach places the biblical text or Jesus in the center of attention rather than reflecting on the subjectivity and agency of wo/men. A radical feminist Post–Christian or Post–Jewish approach in turn has rejected the bible as totally patriarchal and indicted those who still claim it as their heritage as "reformist," self-alienated, and co-opted by patriarchal religions.

These feminist hermeneutical debates of the late 1970s and early 1980s presented challenges to articulate more fully a hermeneutical framework that was both critical and liberationist rather than apologetic and neoorthodox. My own work therefore thought to elaborate a different feminist model of critical interpretation.[25] Such a different feminist model, I argued, has first to place wo/men as citizen-subjects, as the *ekklēsia of wo/men*,[26] into the center of attention. In order to become feminist studies, I maintained, studies on *women in the bible* must recognize wo/men in religion as historical, cultural, theological, and scientific subjects and agents.

Second, biblical research and scholarship must be done in the interest of *all* wo/men and engender a radical democratic societal, cultural, religious, and personal transformation. Theologically such an approach seeks to assess whether a biblical text reveals G*d as a G*d of domination and oppression or as a G*d of liberation and well-being and in what context the text receives its meaning. It understands "revelation" as what is put into Scripture by G*d "for the sake of 'our' that is wo/men's salvation."

Utilizing an ancient Jewish hermeneutical insight it seeks for the Divine in "the white spaces" between the letters and words of Scripture.[27]

Third, such a research focus on wo/men as producers of critical knowledge requires a *double paradigm shift* in the ethos of biblical studies. A paradigm shift from a positivist scientist, allegedly interest-free and value-neutral objectivist ethos of scholarship to a scientific feminist one on the one hand and a shift from an androcentric or better kyriocentric linguistically based cultural ethos to a critical feminist one on the other hand. It is a shift from a scientific positivist to a scientific feminist interpretation. Such a reconceptualization of biblical studies must finally be interdisciplinary or transdisciplinary. It must not only integrate the insights of philology, classics, archeology, sociology, anthropology, ethnography, epistemology, and historiography but also recognize the fundamental feminist criticism of these academic disciplines and their feminist reconceptualizations.[28]

The Academic Field of Feminist Biblical Studies

Such a reconceptualization of biblical studies in critical feminist terms is necessary because the self-understanding of biblical studies as a positivist science cannot address the challenges raised by globalization. Central to the self-understanding of biblical studies, whether practiced in the academy, public discourse, or in religiously affiliated institutions, is the insistence on the scientific character of its research. By identifying as a scientific practice, biblical studies are determined by the theoretical assumptions that have shaped and governed positivist scientific discourse.

Positivist scientific discourse seeks to produce objectivist and disinterested research in terms of quantitative methods, refinement of the technology of exegesis, archeological research, production of factual knowledge, anti-theological rhetoric, and the deployment of social-scientific models that are derived from cultural anthropology or quantitative sociology. The theological form of such a positivist attitude claims to be handing down the word of G*d as once and for all given, revealed truth. Both discourses, the positivist scientific and the positivist theological one, insist on such disinterested authoritative knowledge in order to maintain their public credibility and authority.

The discipline thus continues to socialize future scholars into a reifying methodological allegedly value-free positivism and future ministers into biblicist literalism and theological positivism. Biblical discourses in the public sphere are advocating either literalist biblicism or academic scientism. As long as this is the case, struggles for justice, radical equality, and the well-being of all will remain marginal in the discourses of the discipline.

It is well known that biblical studies emerged on the scene together with other disciplines in the humanities that sought to articulate their discourses as scientific practices in analogy to the natural sciences. The feminist theorist Sandra Harding has pointed to a three-stage process in the emergence of modern science shaping and determining scholarly discourses, their presuppositions, and intellectual frameworks.

The first stage, according to Harding, consisted in the breakdown of feudal labor divisions and slave relations.[29] The second stage is exemplified in the New Science

Movement of the seventeenth century that flourished in Puritan England and brought forth a new political self-consciousness with radical social goals.[30] Scientific knowledge was to serve the people and to be used for redistributing knowledge and wealth.[31] The third stage produced the notion of purely technical and value-neutral science. The progress that science represents is based entirely on scientific method. The institutionalization of science meant the separation of science's cognitive and political aims and the restriction of true science and scientists to the former.

Pure science, according to Harding, was characterized by atomism, the claim that nature's fundamental units are separate with no intrinsic connection. This model goes hand in hand with the political assertion that individual males are not bound to the group in which they are born but are autonomous individuals who form alliances by contract. It also goes hand in hand with *value-neutrality*, which captures what is real through impersonal, quantitative language; and *method*, understood as norms, rules, procedures, and scientific technologies. Scientific values are transhistorical human values; they are not particularistic, local, partial, or political. Historically and culturally specific values, emotions, and interests must be kept separated from depoliticized transcendental scientific practices.

Biblical studies as a discipline is located at this third scientific stage that constructs a sharp dualism between science and theology, or scientific discourse and ideology, in order to prove itself as free from ideology. A series of structuring dualisms[32] and dichotomies between science and politics, history and theology, knowledge and fiction, past and present, rationality and faith, male and female, white and black, Caucasian and Asian, and so on, determine the Western scientific worldview. As a scientific discourse biblical studies thus participates in the discourses of domination, which were produced by science.

For it is also at this third stage of the development of academic scientific disciplines that the discourses of domination—racism, heterosexism, colonialism, class privilege, ageism—were articulated as "scientific" discourses.[33] While previously discourses of colonization were developed on the grounds of Christian religion, now positivist science takes the place of religion and continues its work of hegemonic legitimization. The discourses of domination were formed as elite discourses that justified relations of ruling. Hence, "soft" academic disciplines such as history, sociology, and anthropology, in their formative stage, had to develop discourses of domination in order to prove that they also belonged to the "hard" sciences. Thereby academic social-science disciplines supported European colonialism and capitalist industrial development.

For instance, the nineteenth-century professionalization of history fostered scientific practices advocating commitment to an objectivity above the critical scrutiny of such categories as class and gender, along with strict use of evidence, less rhetorical style, the development of archives, libraries, peer reviews, and professional education. Scientific historical discourses created an intellectual space inhabited by an "invisible and neutered I" that was considered as a "gender- and race-free" community of scholars. At the same time, science was producing discourses of exclusion such as racism, heterosexism, and colonialism barring all wo/men and disenfranchised men from the professions and turning them into objects of research. As Bonnie G. Smith puts it:

> Using women as the sign both of gender in its entirety (i.e., women as the gendered other to the neutral man) and of all that was outside of history, the new scholars created

a fantasy world of the Real, that is, of history. It was a world purged of gender (as well as class [and race]), sufficient unto itself in charting and defining significant human experience in the past, and redolent of the power such claims generated.[34]

American sociology in its formative years exhibits the same symptoms as scientific historiography. It was influenced by European anthropological discourses that emerged with imperialism, and understood colonized peoples as "primitives" who were considered to be more natural, sexual, untouched by civilization, and inferior because of their innate biological differences—for instance, their allegedly smaller brains. In the United States, Indian Americans and African Americans were those who represented the "primitive" in sociological and anthropological scientific discourses. They were construed to be either violent or childlike or both. People who were Not-white and Not-male were praised as "noble savages" or feared as "blood-thirsty cannibals" on biological and cultural grounds.

Asians, Africans, native peoples, and white women were viewed as childlike, a factor used to explain their supposedly inferior intelligence.

> White women and Blacks were also seen as more embodied, "natural," and controlled by their physical, biological essences. Both were viewed as having an inherent "nature" of some sort—for Blacks violence, for White women passivity. Collectively, these comparisons generated a situation in which race and gender gained meaning from another, situated within economic class hierarchies that drew upon these ideas . . . Remaining in the private sphere of home and caring for the family would protect middle-class White women from the dangers of the public sphere that, with urbanization and industrialization, was increasingly populated by poor people, immigrants, Black people, and "fallen" women . . . Thus social processes that created these categories in the first place, namely, restricting wo/men to the private sphere and racially segregating African-Americans, could largely be taken for granted.[35]

To give an example from the use of biblical discourse: in an article entitled "The Use of the New Testament in the American Slave Controversy: A Case History in the Hermeneutical Tension between Biblical Criticism and Christian Moral Debate," J. Albert Harrill[36] has convincingly shown that the discourse on slavery has decisively shaped the development of historical-critical biblical studies. He argues that the abolitionist arguments during the American slave controversy pushed the field toward a critical hermeneutics and a more critical reading of the text in terms of an ethics of interpretation. The pro-slavery arguments in contrast "fostered a move to lit-eralism emboldened by the findings of biblical criticism that the New Testament writers did not condemn slavery."[37] According to the plain literal sense of the biblical text Jesus and Paul did not attack slavery but only its abuse. Hence, the pro-slavery argument required a positivist literal reading of the bible that was done in the name of biblical science. Moreover, the study of Shawn Kelley on *Racializing Jesus* also has shown how biblical scholarship through the reception of the ideological frameworks of the Tübingen School and the philosophy of Heidegger via Bultmann has become racialized, whereas the work of postcolonial biblical interpretation[38] has underscored how such racialization has served colonial interests.

Consequently, critical global feminist CT studies have to critically investigate the theoretical frameworks and scientific methods that we adopt from malestream biblical studies. While some have argued that feminist biblical studies does not need to develop its own method, I would maintain that we not only should scrutinize traditional methods and their frameworks as to their emancipatory or concealing functions but also articulate feminist critical approaches and methods.

Rather than reinscribing the disciplinary divisions between theological and scientific interpretation, between literary and historical methods, between sociopolitical and religious approaches or between sociological—and ideological—religious criticism, critical feminist biblical studies, I have argued, must work for a paradigm shift that can overcome these dualisms by conceptualizing biblical studies as a rhetorics and ethics of inquiry and transformation. To reconceptualize biblical studies as a rhetorics and ethics of inquiry and transformation would engender research the following areas:

1. Global experience and sociopolitical-religious location of the subjects of biblical knowledge.
2. Systemic structural sociopolitical analysis of the rhetorical and historical situation.
3. A hermeneutics of suspicion, which includes ideology—and language—critique, a critique of method and epistemology, cultural and literary criticism, as well as a critique of religion and theology.
4. Ethical and theological evaluation of texts and interpretations as to how they serve global domination or equality and well-being.
5. A cultivation of the interpretive scholarly imagination and ritualization of texts and traditions to create the "other worlds" that we desire and strive for.
6. A rewriting of biblical history as emancipatory historical reconstruction, as memory and heritage in the struggle for liberation and well-being.
7. A critical praxis of change and transformation in a global world of domination.

These seven hermeneutical areas of research could facilitate conscientization and cultural, social, religious, and disciplinary transformation by providing intellectual and spiritual resources to individuals be they scholars or citizen-readers of the bible for engaging in the emancipatory "hermeneutical dance" of feminist critical interpretation.[39] Such emancipatory scholarship could provide the rhetorical methods and ethics of inquiry for emancipatory feminist practices of a "dissident globalization."

Critical Areas of Debate in Global Feminist Biblical Studies

The "new field" of critical feminist interpretation is positioned *in-between* globalization and localization, universality and particularity, isolationism and networking, disinterested academy and social movement, difference and differences, modernism and postmodernism. Hence, it is always dangerous to dissolve these tensions of the "in-between" and struggles against global oppression and dehumanization by succumbing to competitive infighting and aggressive behavior against each other.[40] How we resolve the debates and disagreements in the following areas seems to me crucial for the future of global CT studies.[41]

First: insofar as feminist biblical studies have been accepted by the Western academy, they are in danger of becoming co-opted by its malestream scientific ethos. This has various ramifications but the most important one in my view is the co-optation of feminist biblical studies through professionalization. Feminist students continue to be socialized into the hegemonic kyriocentric paradigm of the discipline while feminist faculty are forced to prove their academic excellence and good citizenship in terms of positivistic scientific standards.[42] For instance, I have met many young doctoral students across the world who were told by their advisors that if they want to do a feminist dissertation they needed first to critically deconstruct the allegedly intellectually naïve work of the first generation of feminist scholars. Then with the help of malestream theory a la Barth, Foucault, Bordieu, Derrida, Lacan, or Rahner and other hegemonic scholarship in the field (e.g., archeological finds, form and redaction criticism, the method of the Jesus Seminar or Social Scientific research on the Mediterranean) they must reconceptualize the problem of their research so that they can produce acceptable "new" scholarship. It is therefore not surprising that many students do not seriously study feminist works and that young feminist scholars either repeat work that has been done without quoting it and even being aware of it or of misconstruing it in such a fashion that the results of such previous feminist work are now claimed as their very own but in a kyriocentric key.

Second: according to Thomas Kuhn a new scientific paradigm can only emerge and rival the existing paradigms if it produces not only new knowledge but also new institutions.[43] If the rhetorical—emancipatory feminist paradigm of biblical studies should gain the strength to change the discourses of the discipline we need to search for ways of institutionalizing such emancipatory scholarship in the interest of dissident globalization. The present institutional locations of feminist biblical discourses in the academy, the church, and the media are not able to promote justice, equality, and well-being for all as long as they remain beholden to the third stage in the development of science. The separation of academic feminists from feminist social movements and their problems and questions conforms feminist biblical studies more and more to the interests of the academy rather than keep us responsible to global movements for change.

The Australian feminist Dale Spender has shown a long time ago, that in the past 400 years (and I would maintain throughout history) feminist ideas have been trivialized, silenced, and forgotten.[44] Consequently, the next feminist generation cannot learn from the thought of their predecessors but is compelled so to speak to reinvent the intellectual wheel again and again. As the historian Barbara Caine has shown, it is not just the dominant kyriarchal society and academy that fosters the forgetting of feminist knowledge. It is also every new generation of feminists themselves who finds it hard to recognize the work of their forerunners and therefore is compelled to distance themselves from the ideas of their predecessors in order to prove the novelty and creativity of their own ideas:

> At the same time historians have to recognize that the frequent rejection of the term "feminism"—and of any sense of connection with earlier feminists—by women who have embraced the notion of female emancipation indicates that women find it hard to

establish trans-generational links or to set themselves up as legitimating or authoritative figures for each other or for future generations.[45]

Third: another reason why a feminist paradigm shift from a positivist scientist to a critical-emancipatory scientific one has not yet been effective is the continuing reduction of feminist biblical studies to wo/men's or gender studies that work with an essentialized understanding of wo/man or retrace the dualistic Western sex-gender system but neglect to see racism, colonialism, class exploitation, and poverty, ageism, nationalism, war, imperialism, and other forms of domination as crucial elements of wo/men's oppression. Insofar as feminist studies remain focused on sexual difference, wo/man, the feminine, and patriarchy as gender domination, on what I have called the ideology of the white Lady, we are not able to articulate and research the pyramidal intersectionality of domination that continues to reproduce ancient kyriarchal structures, that is, the dominations of the Emperor, Lord, Master, Father, Husband, the privileged white educated male that still shape our lives and make women and subordinated men to second-class citizen.

Moreover, what Rey Chow calls "the differences revolution" has taken hold especially also in avant-garde feminist biblical studies. As long as difference is conceptualized, however, only in positivist, post-structural, linguistic terms that eschew all referentiality to actual experiences of oppression and sociopolitical struggles, difference is seen solely as positive and not also understood as an indicator of domination. As long as power is understood only as circulating horizontally and not also vertically in its oppressive force, the differences of kyriarchal oppression will either be positively romanticized or result in resentment and infighting among those on the margins of biblical studies.

Fourth: structural change in biblical studies in my opinion is only possible if and when we create solidarity and alliances on the one hand among feminists of different social locations and on the other among all those in biblical studies who pursue a rhetorics, politics, and ethics of emancipation and well-being for everyone. Religious communities and persons face a theo-ethical choice: either they spiritually sustain the exploitation of global capitalism or they engage the possibilities for greater freedom, justice, and solidarity engendered by the technological market forces of globalization. World-religions either inspire individuals and groups to support the forces of economic and cultural global dehumanization or to abandon their exclusivist tendencies and together envision and work for a feminist spiritual ethos of global dimensions; either they advocate radical democratic spiritual values and visions that celebrate diversity, multiplicity, tolerance, equality, justice, and well-being for all or they foster fundamentalism, exclusivism, and the exploitation of a totalitarian global monoculture. This ethical choice does not reinscribe the dualisms created by structures of domination but struggles to overcome and abolish them.[46]

Since nation-states are no longer in control of globalization, social political theorists such as Hardt and Negri have pointed out that it may be more appropriate to understand globalization in terms of empire. Insofar as the nation-state is replaced by multinational corporations its globalizing economic, cultural, and political forces form a polycentric empire.[47] The danger of this shift from nation-state to international corporation is that democratic government no longer can be exercised and the system of global capitalism is not held democratically accountable. However such globalization also presents possibilities for more radical democratization worldwide. It also makes possible the interconnectedness of all being and the possibility of communication and solidaric organization across national borders on the basis of human rights and justice for all.

Insofar as transnational capitalism crosses all borders, exploits all peoples, and colonizes all citizens it requires a counter-vision and dissident strategy that Chela Sandoval has called "democratics," a strategy and vision that has affinities with my own attempt to articulate the space of the *ekklēsia of wo/men*[48] as a critical radical democratic space of interpretation. Since *ekklēsia*, understood as radical democratic congress of fully entitled, responsible decision-making citizens, has never been fully realized either in Christian history or in Western democracy, the expression *ekklēsia gynaikōn, the ekklēsia of wo/men*, functions as a linguistic means of conscientization. Since the signifier "wo/man" is increasingly used by right-wing religions to draw exclusive boundaries, it is important to mark linguistically the difference between religion as kyriarchal institution and as *ekklēsia*, the decision-making assembly of the people.

Qualifying *ekklēsia* = radical democratic congress with *wo/men*, seeks to lift into consciousness that academy, society, and religion are still governed by elite powerful men who have been exclusive of wo/men and other servant-peoples for centuries. It seeks to communicate a vision that connects struggles for a more democratic and just religion with global, societal, and political democratic movements for justice, freedom, and equality. These movements have emerged again and again throughout the centuries because of the disparity between the professed vision of radical democratic equality and the actual reality of domination and subordination in society and religion that they experience daily.

This is the case because neither the French nor the American democratic revolutions fought for *wo/men* and disenfranchised men to become fully empowered decision-making citizens. Instead they developed scientific theories that sought to legitimize colonialism and the exclusion of wo/men and subaltern men from democratic rights and government. The struggles of the subordinated others for full citizenship and civil rights, radical equality and justice have sought to correct this situation and to realize the vision of radical democratic equality and rights.

Sandoval explains "democratics" as one of the methods of the oppressed in the following way:

> With the transnationalization of capitalism when elected officials are no longer leaders of singular nation-states but nexuses for multinational interests, it also becomes possible for citizen-subjects to become activists for a new decolonizing global terrain, a psychic terrain that can unite them with similarly positioned citizen-subjects within and across national borders into new, post-Western-empire alliances. . . . Love as social movement is enacted by revolutionary, mobile, and global coalitions of citizen-activists who are allied through the apparatus of emancipation.[49]

However, I am somewhat hesitant to claim "love" as the sole revolutionary force or to reduce "oppositional social action to a mode of 'love' in the postmodern world."

Although I am well aware that numerous U.S. Third World feminists have eloquently written about the power of love in struggles for justice,[50] I cannot forget the function of "romantic love" in the oppression of wo/men nor the anti-Jewish valorization of the "New" Testament *God of love* over the "Old" Testament *God of Justice.* "Democratics," in my view, must be equally informed by justice as Patricia Hill Collins has argued:

> Justice transcends Western notions of equality grounded in sameness and uniformity . . . In making their quilts Black women weave together scraps of fabric from all sorts of places. Nothing is wasted, and every piece of fabric has a function and a place in a given quilt. . . .[T]hose who conceptualize community via notions of uniformity and sameness have difficulty imagining a social quilt that is simultaneously heterogeneous, driven toward excellence, and just.[51]

In this image of quilt and quilting for the making of justice, the decolonizing practices of a global democratics, of the *ekklēsia of wo/men,* and a critical feminist dissident global interpretation converge. To conceptualize feminist interpretation as such a critical quilting of meaning in different sociopolitical locations will enable us to articulate biblical visions of justice and well-being for all.

Notes

1. I use "feminist" as an umbrella term to signify an intellectual and social movement. Such a formal category needs to be contentually specified with, e.g., womanist, mujerista, Latina, queer, Western, global, critical, liberationist, etc., since there are numerous articulations of feminist theory and practice. Such a political use of "feminism" as an umbrella term seeks to avoid the fragmentation and splintering of feminist power that is still marginal in societies and religions around the globe. Since the expressions *New Testament* and *Old Testament* carry supersessionist overtones vis-à-vis Judaism, I prefer to speak of *Christian* rather than *New Testament* studies.
2. Cf., e.g., Janice Capel Anderson, "Mapping Feminist Biblical Criticism," *Critical Review of Books in Religion* 2 (1991): 21–44; Elizabeth Castelli, "Heteroglossia, Hermeneutics and History: A Review Essay of Recent Feminist Studies of Early Christianity," *The Journal of Feminist Studies in Religion* 10/2 (1994): 73–78. For Jewish feminist interpretations, see the work of Esther Fuchs, Ilana Pardes, Adele Reinhartz, Tal Ilan, Amy Jill Levine, Cynthia Baker or Alicia Suskin Ostriker, and many others. See also Esther Fuchs, "Points of Resonance," in Jane Schaberg, Alice Bach, and Esther Fuchs, eds., *On the Cutting Edge, The Study of Women in Biblical Worlds* (New York: Continuum International, 2003) 1–20; For Muslim feminist hermeneutics see, e.g., Amina Wadud, *Quran and Woman. Rereading the Sacred Text from a Woman's Perspective* (Oxford: Oxford University Press, 1999); Barbara F. Stowasser, *Women in the Qur'an: Traditions and Interpretations* (New York: Oxford University Press, 1994); Asma Barlas, *"Believing Women" in Islam. Unreading Patriarchal Interpretations of the Qur'an* (Austin: University of Texas Press, 2002).
3. Chela Sandoval, *Methodology of the Oppressed* (Minneapolis: University of Minnesota Press, 2000).
4. For the problematic meaning of the term *woman/women* see Denise Riley, *"Am I That Name" Feminism and the Category of Women in History* (Minneapolis: University of Minnesota Press, 1988); Judith Butler, *Gender Trouble. Feminism and the Subversion of*

Identity (New York: Routledge, 1990). My way of writing *wo/men* seeks to underscore not only the ambiguous character of the term *wo/man or wo/men* but also to retain the expression *wo/men* as a political category. Since this designation is often read as referring to white women only, my unorthodox writing of the word seeks to draw to the attention of readers that those kyriarchal structures that determine wo/men's lives and status also impact that of men of subordinated race, classes, countries, and religions, albeit in different ways. The expression *wo/men* must therefore be understood as inclusive rather than as an exclusive universalized gender term.

5. See Patricia Demers, *Wo/men Interpreters of the Bible* (New York: Paulist Press, 1992); Marla Selvidge, *Notorious Voices. Feminist Biblical Interpretation 1500–1920* (New York: Continuum, 1996); Gerda Lerner, *The Creation of Feminist Consciousness. From the Middle Ages to the Eighteenseventy* (New York: Oxford University Press, 1993) and especially the work of Elisabeth Gössmann. Cf. her biography *Geburtsfehler weiblich: Lebenserinnerungen einer katholischen Theologin* (München: iudicium Verlag, 2003).

6. In her book *Postcolonial Feminist Interpretation of the Bible* (St. Louis: Chalice Press, 2000) and other writings, Musa W. Dube has pointed to the shortcomings of my writings when read from an anti-imperialist perspective. While I readily concede that my work like all other work is limited by my social location, it was difficult for me to understand, why I have been singled out for such harsh criticisms. This was puzzling because Musa is well aware of the multiple possible readings of texts and concedes that the "theoretical articulations of *kyriarchy* and *ekklesia of women* do go a long way toward counteracting imperialism, if followed" (p. 37). Reading the story of Musa's grandmother about the beautiful princess who was killed by the other girls of the village because they realized: "As long as Utentelazandlane is alive, no one will ever notice us," has shed light on this predicament. [Cf. Musa W. Dube, "Jumping the Fire With Judith. Postcolonial Feminist Hermeneutics of Liberation," in Silvia Schroer and Sophia Bietenhard, eds., *Feminist Interpretation of the Bible and the Hermeneutics of Liberation* (New York: Sheffield Academic Press, 2003) 60.] I want to thank Musa for helping me to understand the power dynamics that were operating at this and other feminist academic conferences.

7. I coined the neologism *kyriarchy* derived from the Greek words for "lord" or "master" (*kyrios*) and "to rule or dominate" (*archein*) in order to redefine the analytic category of *patriarchy* in terms of multiplicative intersecting structures of domination. *Kyriarchy* is a sociopolitical system of domination in which elite, educated, propertied men hold power over wo/men and other men. *Kyriarchy* is best theorized as a complex pyramidal system of intersecting multiplicative social structures of supremacy and subordination, of ruling and oppression. *Kyriocentrism* is a name for the linguistic—cultural-religious ideological systems and intersecting discourses of race, gender, heterosexuality, class, imperialism, and other dehumanizing discourses that legitimate, inculcate, and sustain *kyriarchy*, i.e., multiplicative structures of domination.

8. Alice Duer Miller, *Are Women People? A Book of Rhymes for Suffrage Times* (New York: George H. Doran, 1915).

9. Cf. Christina Hendricks and Kelly Oliver, eds., *Language and Liberation. Feminism, Philosophy and Language* (Albany: SUNY, 1999).

10. In order to mark the inadequacy of our language about G*d, I had adopted the Jewish orthodox way of writing the name of *G-d* in my books *Discipleship of Equals* and *But She Said*. However, Jewish feminists have pointed out to me that such a spelling is offensive to many of them because it suggests a very conservative, if not reactionary, theological frame of reference. Hence I have began to write the word *G*d* in this fashion in order to visibly destabilize our way of thinking and speaking about the Divine.

11. See now, however, the very interesting article of Satoko Yamaguchi, "Father Image of G*d and Inclusive Language. A Reflection in Japan," in Fernando F. Segovia, ed., *Toward a New Heaven and a New Earth. Essays in Honor of Elisabeth Schüssler Fiorenza* (Maryknoll: Orbis Books, 2003) 199–224. I hope that this article will engender more research on biblical translation and interpretation in non-androcentric language contexts.

12. For the development of this argument, see my book *Rhetoric and Ethic. The Politics of Biblical Interpretation* (Minneapolis: Fortress, 1999).

13. Edward Said, *The World, the Text and the Critic* (Cambridge: Harvard University Press, 1983) 4.

14. Ann Brooks, *Postfeminisms. Feminism, Cultural Theory and Cultural Forms* (New York, Routledge, 1997).

15. See e.g., Elizabeth A. Richman, "Separate *and* Equal?" *Lilith. The Independent Jewish Women's Magazine* 29/1 (2004) 28–29, who confronts her mother's experience of discrimination with those of her own generation that allegedly has not lived through such experiences of inequality. However, I am doubtful that one can speak for a whole generation.

16. See the very significant article by María Pilar Aquino, "The Dynamics of Globalization and the University. Toward a Radical Democratic-Emancipatory Transformation," in Segovia, ed., *Toward a New Heaven and a New Earth*, 385–406.

17. See Christa Wichterich, *The Globalized Wo/man. Reports from a Future of Inequality* (New York: Zed Books, 2000); Ann-Cathrin Jarl, *In Justice. Women and Global Economics* (Minneapolis: Fortress, 2003); Marjori Agosin, *Women, Gender, and Human Rights. A Global Perspective* (New Brunswick: Rutgers University Press, 2001).

18. The expression *malestream* articulates the fact that history, tradition, theology, church, culture, and society have been defined by elite men and have excluded wo/men. Frameworks of scholarship, texts, traditions, language, standards, paradigms of knowledge, and so on, have been and are elite male-centered and elite male-dominated. See the contributions of Gabriele Dietrich, "People's Movements, the Strength of Wisdom and the Twisted Path of Civilization," Bonna Devora Haberman, " 'Let My Gender Go!' Jewish Textual Activism," Marsha Aileen Hewitt, "Dialectic of Hope," and Marjorie Procter Smith, "Feminist Ritual Strategies: The Ekklēsia Gynaikon at Work," in Segovia, ed., *Toward a New Heaven and a New Earth*.

19. Anna Marie Smith, *Laclau and Mouffé: The Radical Democratic Imagination* (New York: London, 1998) 58–59.

20. See e.g., Musa W. Dube, ed., *Other Ways of Reading. African Women and the Bible* (Atlanta: SBL, 2001); María Pilar Aquino, Daisy L. Machado, and Jeanette Rodriguez, *A Reader in Latina Feminist Theology. Religion and Justice* (Austin: University of Texas Press, 2002); Rosemary Radford Ruether, ed., *Gender, Ethnicity and Religion. Views from the Other Side* (Minneapolis: Fortress Press, 2002) and the articles by Vincent Wimbush, "In Search of a Usable Past: Reorienting Biblical Studies," and Ivone Gebara, "A Feminist Theology of Liberation: A Latin American Perspective with a View toward the Future," in Segovia, ed., *Toward a New Heaven and a New Earth* 179–198 and 249–269; *cf.* also the significant work by Vincent Wimbush, ed., *African Americans and the Bible: Sacred Texts and Social Textures* (New York: Continuum, 2000).

21. Virginia Woolf, *Three Guineas* (New York: Harcourt, Brace, Jovanovich, 1966).

22. See my book *Sharing her Word. Feminist Biblical Interpretation in Context* (Boston: Beacon, 1998) 50–74; and Kathi Kern, *Mrs. Stanton's Bible* (Ithaca: Cornell University Press, 2001).

23. The first *wo/man* who joined the SBL in 1894 was Anna Ely Rhoads but the Society elected its first *wo/man* president only in 1987. In 1970 *wo/men*'s membership in the SBL was only 3.5%. of the overall membership according to Saunders, p. 103, with reference to Dorothy C. Bass.

24. For a critical discussion, see my books, *Jesus. Miriam's Child and Sophia's Prophet* (New York: Continuum, 1994) and *Jesus and the Politics of Interpretation* (New York: Continuum, 2000).

25. See also my article "Method in Wo/men's Studies in Religion: A Critical Feminist Hermeneutics," in *Methodology in Religious Studies: The Interface with Women's Studies*, ed. Arvind Sharma (Albany: State University of New York Press, 2002) 207–241.

26. For a very perceptive contextualization of this feminist articulation, see Elizabeth Castelli, "The Ekklēsia of Women and/as Utopian Space: Locating the Work of Elisabeth Schüssler Fiorenza in Feminist Utopian Thought," in Jane Schaberg, Alice Bach, and Esther Fuchs, eds., *On the Cutting Edge*, 36–52; In *Feminist Biblical Interpretation in Theological Context. Restless Readings* (Burlington: Ashgate Publ. Co., 2002) 32–59 and 142–162; Jánnine Jobling discusses the concept of the ekklēsia of wo/men but chooses *ekklēsia* without the qualification with *wo/men* as her hermeneutical key concept, in order to restrict the concept to the Christian feminist movement (143). In so doing she reinscribes the division between the Christian and the so-called secular women's movements, which I thought to overcome with this radical democratic, *counter-kyriarchal* image.

27. Cf., e.g., Naomi M. Hyman, *Biblical Wo/men in the Midrash: A Sourcebook* (Northvale, NJ: Jason Aronson Inc., 1997).

28. See, e.g., Nancy Sorkin Rabinowitz and Amy Richlin, *Feminist Theory and the Classics* (New York: Routledge, 1993).

29. Sandra Harding, *The Science Question in Feminism* (Ithaca: Cornell University Press, 1986) 218, with reference to Edgar Zilsel, "The Sociological Roots of Science," *American Journal of Sociology* 47 (1942).

30. Harding, *Science Question*, 219.

31. Wolfgang van den Daele, "The Social Construction of Science," in *The Social Production of Scientific Knowledge*, ed. Everett Mendelsohn, Peter Weingart, Richard Whitley (Dordrecht: Reidel, 1977) 38.

32. For such structuring dualisms in Q research see the forthcoming dissertation of Melanie Johnson-DeBaufre and her article "Bridging the Gap to 'This Generation': A Feminist Critical Reading of the Rhetoric of Q 7:31–35," in Shelly Matthews, Cynthia Briggs Kittredge, and Melanie Johnson-DeBaufre, eds., *Walk in the Ways of Wisdom. Essays in Honor of Elisabeth Schüssler Fiorenza* (New York: Trinity Press, 2003) 214–233. For a comprehensive interpretation of Q scholarship see e.g., Richard Horsley, *Whoever Hears You Hears Me: Prophets, Performance and Tradition in Q* (Harrisburg: Trinity Press International, 1999) and Burton L. Mack, *The Lost Gospel: The Book of Q and Christian Origins* (San Francisco: HarperCollins, 1993).

33. See Ronald T. Takaki, "Aesclepius Was a White Man: Race and the Cult of True Womanhood," in *The Racial Economy of Science: Toward a Democratic Future*, ed. Sandra Harding (Indianapolis: Indiana University Press, 1993) 201–209; Nancy Leys Stepan and Sander L. Gilman, "Appropriating the Idioms of Science: The Rejection of Scientific Racism," 170–193, and Nancy Leys Stepan, "Race and Gender: The Role of Analogy in Science," 369–376.

34. Bonnie G. Smith, "Gender, Objectivity, and the Rise of Scientific History," in *Objectivity and its Other*, ed. Wolfgang Natter, Theodore R. Schatzki, and John Paul Jones III (New York: The Guilford Press, 1995) 59.

35. Patricia Hill Collins, *Fighting Words: Black Women and the Search For Justice* (Minneapolis: University of Minnesota Press, 1998) 100–101.

36. J. Albert Harrill, "The Use of the New Testament in the American Slave Controversy: A Case History in the Hermeneutical Tension between Biblical Criticism and Christian Moral Debate," *Religion and American Culture* 10/2 (2000): 149–186.

37. J. Albert Harrill, "The Use of the New Testament," 174.

38. Shawn Kelley, *Racializing Jesus. Race, Ideology and the Formation of Modern Biblical Scholarship* (New York: Routledge, 2002). For the rhetoric of blackness in antiquity and Early Christianity see Gay L. Byron, *Symbolic Blackness and Ethnic Difference in Early Christian Literature* (New York: Routledge, 2002). For pathbreaking work in postcolonial biblical studies, see the work of Kwok Pui Lan, Laura Donaldson, Musa W. Dube, Fernando Segovia, and R. S. Sugirtharajah. See also the contributions of Musa W. Dube, "Ahab Says Hello to Judith. A Decolonizing Feminist Reading," Kwok Pui Lan, "Engendering Christ," Fernando Segovia, "Liberation Hermeneutics. Revisiting the Foundations in Latin America," R. S. Sugirtharajah, "The End of Biblical Studies?" and Richard A. Horsley, "Subverting Disciplines: The Possibilities and Limitations of Postcolonial Theory for New Testament Studies," in Segovia, *Toward a New Heaven and a New Earth*.

39. For the translation of these research areas into practical strategies of interpretation that can be used by all wo/men engaging in biblical interpretation, see my book *Wisdom Ways. Introducing Feminist Biblical Interpretation* (Maryknoll: Orbis, 2001).

40. I do not want to be misunderstood. I do not want to stifle such critical debate but draw attention to its political location that must be taken into account.

41. The feminist academic rhetoric of difference and particularity, for instance, is no longer directed against elite white male and female scholars, not against "gender" or "white Lady" feminists but against liberationist feminists and subaltern male scholars.

42. See my article "Rethinking the Educational Practices of Biblical Doctoral Studies," *Teaching Theology and Religion* 6 (April 2003): 65–75.

43. Thomas Kuhn, *The Structure of Scientific Revolutions* (Chicago: University of Chicago Press, 1962).

44. Dale Spender, *Women of Ideas (And What Men Have Done to Them)* (Boston: ARK Paperbacks, 1983).

45. Barbara Caine, "Women's Studies, Feminist Traditions and the Problem of History," in Barbara Caine, Rosemary Pringle, eds., *Transitions. New Australian Feminisms* (Sydney: Allen & Unwin, 1995) 3.

46. I want to thank the anonymous reviewer of this article for her/his careful and perceptive reading and especially for drawing my attention to the possibility of such a misreading of such an ethical choice in terms of dualism.

47. Michael Hardt and Antonio Negri, *Empire: A New Vision of Social Order* (Cambridge, MA: Harvard University Press, 2001).

48. For an excellent critical discussion of this concept see Jánnine Jobling, *Feminist Biblical Interpretation in Theological Context. Restless Readings* (Burlington, VT: Ashgate Publishing Co., 2002) 32–60, 142–163.

49. Chela Sandoval, *Methodology of the Oppressed* (Minneapolis: University of Minnesota Press, 2000) 183.

50. Audre Lorde, bell hooks, Toni Morrison, Cornel West, June Jordan, Gloria Anzaldúa, Maria Lugones, Merle Woo, Alice Walker—to name just a few.

51. Patricia Hill Collins, *Fighting Words. Black Wo/men & the Search for Justice* (Minnesota: University of Minnesota Press, 1998) 248–249.

Chapter 3

Globalization, Transnational Feminisms, and the Future of Biblical Critique

Elizabeth A. Castelli

The paper I wrote for this conference was a preliminary attempt to take theoretical stock of the terms of our engagement. I wrote it during a period when I was also working in an ongoing collaboration with Janet Jakobsen who directs the Center for Research on Women at Barnard College where I teach. Our efforts were organized around a multifaceted initiative called, "Responding to Violence," that has brought feminist activists and academics together to assess the material, institutional, inter-personal, and ideological conditions that have brought our world into its current peculiar predicament.[1] The thinking I've begun to do around the places where transnationalism, globalization, religion, and violence intersect has been thoroughly influenced by the insights and deep commitments of the participants in our ongoing work together. I can't name all of these people, but I do want to acknowledge the help that Janet Jakobsen, Erin Runions, Neta Crawford, Laura Donaldson, and Minoo Moallem have given me in thinking about these matters.

The invitation I received to participate in this conversation included the following assignment: "We are interested in having you describe the nature of your own work in the area of feminist New Testament studies. We also want to engage with you in a dialogue about your perspectives on global and Christian transformation in the next half century from your cultural context, and [we want you to] speak to the implica-tions of these developments for the future of feminist New Testament studies and for the lives of women." In the initial letter of invitation, the conference was called, "The Future of Global Feminist New Testament Studies." The conference is now called "The Global Future of Feminist New Testament Studies." I, for one, am particularly interested in the matter of the traveling adjective here, since its mobility may have something to tell us about the vexing theoretical questions that are embedded in our assignments for today. That said, I have tried to do my assignment as best I could, and found that I could do it best by trying to think about the terms that frame the conversation as a whole and then by considering a particular example where a feminist intervention in the global deployment of a New Testament text might help us understand the stakes involved.

Having said that I have tried to do my assignment, I do not plan to expend much time at all on my past work. I have spent a good bit of energy participating in feminist and cognate political conversations with and about the letters of Paul. I have also contributed to various conversations about the place(s) of feminist theory in the project of biblical critique as a whole. But since today's papers inaugurate a look toward the future, I don't want to spend time looking backward and inward. Nevertheless, I do think, that I should probably begin by saying something about the sources and institutional locations of my feminism.

The feminism I now claim has its roots in a lot of different places: it has roots in my family and in the mid-1960s' elementary school classrooms where my teachers were politically radical Roman Catholic nuns who offered a compelling model of the committed life and who demanded academic excellence, intellectual rigor, and ethical conviction from their students and from themselves. It has roots in the university classroom, in the living rooms of the various feminist collectives where I lived as a college student, in the battered women's shelter where I worked after college, in the offices of state legislators from whom I sought to extract funding for the shelters and legislation for the women, and in the streets. It has been focused in a fairly consistent way on the problem of violence—interpersonal violence, institutional violence, state violence. It continues to be shaped now in feminist coalitions and collaborations that are intentionally transnational in their focus. But the feminism I claim was not, by and large, formed in the church (the formative influence of the Sisters of Loretta notwithstanding), nor do I see my project as necessarily relevant to the church or to the global future of Christianity. I mention this particularity because I seem to be in a bit of a minority on the program for this series of conversations, among a majority of *Christian* feminists. I teach Religion and Women's Studies in a liberal arts college for women where the majority of students are not Christians and do not study the New Testament from an insider's point of view. And so my feminist engagements with matters of biblical critique are situated in a distinct institutional location, more in the interdisciplinary academic study of religion and feminist theory than in Christian theological contexts. These realms are not, of course, necessarily incommensurate. But they do initiate different conversations, start from different premises, tend in different directions, and emphasize different things. That said, let me turn to the categories I've undertaken to interrogate.

Feminism. Globalization. Christianity. The Bible. How do we begin to initiate a conversation that pays attention to the complex dynamics characterizing the relationships between and among these big categories? And since I've been invited here to occupy the position of Euro-American/North American—a category I will want to trouble a bit, to be sure—how do I initiate such a conversation *in relation to* the fact that U.S. political, economic, and military power currently casts such a long shadow across the rest of the world? What has the fact of that power to do with feminism and with the future of biblical critique?

All of these terms—feminism, globalization, Christianity, and the Bible—should be appearing in your minds right now in shimmering italics and with neon quotation marks setting them off from one another. None of these terms is, of course, a simple or neutral signifier. Each word is a node in a theoretical network reaching outward to other terms, problematics, histories, and conflicts. In my title, I have already modified one term by speaking not of feminism (unmarked and in the singular) but of transnational feminisms. There's a rhetorical strategy embedded in that modifier, one aimed at reconfiguring the story of feminism that we might be trying to tell here.

In attempting to reconfigure that story, there are many resources at one's disposal, especially the scholarship and writing by feminists traveling under the category of the postcolonial and the transnational.[2] "Transnational" has an often pejorative connotation, given its use so often to modify "capitalism." But it need not, so when I use it here, I intend to suggest the capacity to build strategic alliances across the traditional boundaries of nation-states. I have been especially influenced by the critical work of Minoo Moallem, a feminist scholar from Iran who did her graduate work in Canada and now works in the United States. (Her personal transnational biography reminds us that linking identity to geography might serve as an under-theorized obfuscation or an over-simplification.) Moallem's analysis of the intersections of religious and feminist discourses is both provocative and clarifying of the many political stakes involved in the postmodern, globalized situation that frames our intellectual activity— especially intellectual activity at the intersections of politics and religion. In her recent essay, "Transnationalism, Feminism, and Fundamentalism," Moallem has argued that, "Feminisms and fundamentalisms are now competing global forces, both attempting to find means to control the mechanisms of cultural representation. Both feminism and fundamentalism are major factors responsible for and responding to the 'crisis of rationality' as well as the crisis of 'masculinity' and 'femininity.' Both arose inside the problematic of modernity as it deals with relations between men and women with respect to the universal and the particular, public and private, family and state, and individual and community."[3]

Moallem's essay goes on to deconstruct the binarism that has characterized many discussions of the relations between feminism and fundamentalism, especially in their stereotypic manifestations as "western egalitarian feminism" and "Islamic fundamentalism." As Moallem points out, this particular binary then comes to be replicated endlessly in other oppositions: "good and evil, freedom and unfreedom, civilization and fanaticism, modernity and tradition."[4] Moallem's analysis points out many places where feminism and fundamentalism, as competing strategies of cultural representation and competing regimes of truth, both begin from positions of critique but produce different accounts of the "problem" that is to be solved through a turn to one or the other as a "solution." Ultimately, Moallem worries about the tendency of these two figures to become mirror images of one another. As she puts it: "Feminism and fundamentalism cannot avoid mirroring each other. A separation between the ontological as a site of fundamentalist recognition of the feminine self and the epistemological as a site of feminist consciousness has culminated in exclusive forms of subjectivity. . . . [F]undamentalism has become contagious to its feminist counterpart because it takes pleasure in what is prohibited to feminism."[5] I will come back to this figuration of "feminism" and "fundamentalism" later.

Moallem's essay is challenging and provocative on a number of points, and I want to pull two especially relevant threads out of her discussion. The first involves the insistence on the "modernity" of feminisms. This insistence is, in part, a recognition of feminism's roots in the intellectual and political effects of the Enlightenment. But feminism's relationship to and engagement with the Enlightenment have, from the start, embodied both the practice of critique and the critical supplement (in Derrida's sense of the term). That is, feminism may have emerged, in part, out of the Enlightenment critique of religious dogmatism but it also immediately served as a critique of the Enlightenment's humanism, which put "rational man" at its core. As Laura Mandell put it recently, "feminism is both antidote to and child of Enlightenment thought, sometimes hampered by the very philosophy that prompted its 'birth.' "[6] Different feminist theorists will trace the relationship of feminism to the Enlightenment and to modernity variously, but the fact of the existence of the relationship is indisputable. This observation does not mean that feminism belongs only to the cultures that inherit the Enlightenment's ambivalent legacies, nor that feminism bears in any simple way a monolithic or indelible stamp of its modern genealogy. For exploring the question of feminism's relationship to biblical critique, this observation means that we need to take seriously the question of how to pay attention to the role of "the modern" in any interrogation of feminism and the Bible.

The second point I want to pull out of Moallem's discussion is the concern over the category of "religion" in the binarism that haunts "feminism" and "fundamentalism." Moallem reminds us both that the category of "fundamentalism" implies the presence of "religion"—and since "feminism" is pitched as the opposite of "fundamentalism," it must also imply the absence of "religion." In trying to complicate the picture, Moallem suggests the necessity of disrupting a definition of "fundamentalism" that closes off the possibility of secular manifestations. As she puts it,

> In this context, I intend to situate fundamentalism as a modern discursive formation (no less modern than "progress" or "development") with a genealogy and a history of representation. Fundamentalism may be defined as follows: a regime of truth based on discourses identified with, or ordained by, God (taken metaphorically or literally) and binding its observants. This definition of fundamentalism is, I know, problematic to the extent that it remains tied to religion, and to the history of Christianity in particular. . . . I believe, therefore, that any religion-based construal of fundamentalism must be challenged and replaced by an analytical definition that enables critical intervention in both religious and secularist forms of fundamentalism.[7]

One might also argue alongside Moallem that feminism needs to be interrogated and explored in terms of its overlap with the field of "religion" and not simply assumed to be situated against it. This latter observation may seem to be self-evident in a conversation about feminist biblical studies, but my point isn't only that "feminism" has something to say about "religion," but that "feminism" bears some of the stamp *of* "religion." Consider this recent characterization of feminism: ". . . feminism—in this respect strongly resembling the phenomena signaled by the word *nationalism*—is at once a varying set of historical practices and *an ideal 'returning' at various historical times and places, as certain religious ideals return,* and therefore requiring critique and reinterpretation. . . ."[8] This observation has a number of implications for thinking about the intersections of feminism and the analytical category of "religion" in general as well as the particular social formations that travel the globe as "religions" in particular. As we proceed, we'll see how these two elements—the role of "the modern" and the intersections of "feminism"/"fundamentalism" and the categories of "secular" and "religious" are important for reconceptualizing biblical critique.

The "transnational" modifier that I have placed in front of "feminisms" in my title is linked to the second analytical category I have evoked in my title: "globalization"— a term that also has, at best, a politically ambivalent charge. Since our conference is devoted to the "global future" of a feminist critical practice, some theory of "globalization" is necessary. Of course, globalization is ubiquitous as both an analytical category and as a social and institutional practice across a wide swath of terrains and endeavors: economics, more notably perhaps, but also politics, cultural expressions of all sorts, and of course "religion." I confess to only a very partial understanding of all the dimensions of the "fact" of globalization, and I am dependent on the insights of colleagues working in fields such as anthropology, geography, economics, political science, media studies, and women's and gender studies to help make sense of the term. For the preparation of this paper, I have been helped in particular by the work of anthropologist Arjun Appadurai. In the introductory essay to a special issue of the journal *Public Culture* that appeared in 2000, Appadurai sketches a portrait of the current situation in which different interests seek to stake out their positions vis-à-vis globalization. After a brief discussion of the particular investments of Northern and Western academics, Appadurai points out that there are different economic, cultural, and religious questions animating the anxieties of vast numbers of other people. As he summarizes matters with concision and characteristic wit:

> Social scientists . . . worry about whether markets and deregulation produce greater wealth at the price of increased inequality. Political scientists worry that their field might vanish along with their favorite object, the nation-state. . . . Cultural theorists . . . worry that in spite of its conformity with everything they already knew about capital, there may be some embarrassing new possibilities for equity hidden in its workings. Historians, ever worried about the problem of the new, realize that globalization may not be a member of the familiar archive of large-scale historical shifts. And everyone in the academy is anxious to avoid seeming to be a mere publicist of the gigantic corporate machineries that celebrate globalization. Product differentiation is as important for (and within) the academy as it is for the corporations academics love to hate.
>
> Outside the academy there are quite different worries about globalization that include such questions as: What does globalization mean for labor markets and fair wages? How will it affect chances for real jobs and reliable rewards? What does it mean for the ability of nations to determine the economic futures of their populations? What is the hidden dowry of globalization? Christianity? Cyber-proletarianization? New forms of structural adjustment? Americanization disguised as human rights or as MTV?[9]

For our purposes here, I am especially interested in this last set of questions concerning "the hidden dowry of globalization." One could spend considerable time fruitfully exploring the links that might bind the different items included in this series: what, indeed, do Christianity, cyber-proletarianization, structural adjustment, and Americanization (human rights/MTV) have to do with one another? Is the ghost of

Max Weber being ironically revived somehow, the Protestant ethic and the spirit of capitalism winning the day 100 years after Weber's stark analysis of European economic and political domination?

But my assignment is to reflect upon the global, the future, the feminist, and the biblical here. Hence, I can only focus on one aspect of Appadurai's suggestive provocation that Christianity may constitute globalization's dowry. What might feminist New Testament critics make of this formulation? I have several thoughts: first of all, the very image that Appadurai deploys reminds us, unwittingly perhaps, to keep always in our thinking the question, asked by anthropologist Catherine Lutz: *does theory have a gender?*[10] In this context, what does it mean for a theory of globalization to use the figure of "the dowry" as a metaphor? Dowries, as we all know, are collections of property and money that constitute a form of venture capital in a marriage. They remind us that marriage, for whatever its sentimentalized reconfiguration in the early twenty-first century, is about property and therefore about property law and therefore about the state. Moreover, the dowry is specifically the property or money brought by a *bride* to her *husband* on their marriage. Why might the exchange represented by "globalization" be construed or expressed in or as a dowry, and how would "Christianity" function as globalization's dowry? Who is being married to whom here? Who is the bride and who is the groom? If Christianity is configured here as the property brought *by the bride to the husband on their marriage*, what geopolitical or economic relationship *figured as marriage* is implied here? Perhaps we are to understand this observation in terms of Philip Jenkins's recent argument about "the next Christianity," whereby the "future" of Christianity resides outside the economically developed North and West, and "globalized Christianity" takes on new political meanings and raises particular challenges to the understanding of "the church" historically and in the present.[11] Perhaps we are to think of the economic marriage metaphor in relation to another metaphor that appears elsewhere in the essay, where globalization is described as "this chaotic, high velocity, *promiscuous* movement of financial (especially speculative) capital."[12] I must admit to sharing the general view expressed here about the "worrisome implications" of the movements of globalized capital, but what does it mean to characterize this movement as an example of "promiscuity"? If marriage is about regulated exchange of property, represented as the dowry, which is Christianity, what are the rhetorical effects of speaking of capital's indiscriminate gadding-about as unregulated sexualized behavior? Is global capital a fallen woman who needs to be domesticated through a good Christian marriage? And marriage, precisely, to whom? *Wives, be submissive to your husbands as to the lord.*

I am, of course, being purposefully provocative in zeroing in on this passing metaphor in Appadurai's essay. After all, his main objective in this essay is most certainly *not* to articulate a theory that depends so centrally upon gendered, sexualized, and moralistic metaphors. Rather, his objective is to promote efforts to develop and support new research trajectories into the circumstances of globalization, trajectories that are characterized by democracy and autonomy and by their contribution to the interests of the poor. He sees these trajectories as enabled by "strategies, visions, and horizons for globalization on behalf of the poor that can be characterized as 'grassroots globalization' or . . .'globalization from below.' "[13] Moreover, the main direction of his argument involves the practice of academic and intellectual labor.

Indeed, he entitles his essay, "Grassroots Globalization and the Research Imagination." He grounds his critique in the observation that, for scholars working within the institutions of privilege in the West and the North, the research imagination has too easily naturalized its own "protocols of inquiry," rendering the practices of knowledge formation in other contexts illegible or unintelligible. But I raise *both* his main objective *and* his most likely unconscious rhetorical flourishes as *equally* important elements to be considered in a discussion such as ours. A significant part of the future of any intellectual project is to take account of the increasingly interconnected global situation and the challenges that those interconnections raise to the assumptions that underlie the production of knowledge, and Appadurai focuses our attention on the institutional and ideological transformations that such an account-taking demands. But I want to suggest that part of the process of theorizing and implementing such transformations must involve denaturalizing the gendered/sexualized/moralistic metaphors that routinely ground the critique as a whole. We see all the time how the figure of "woman" is deployed metonymically to represent cultural difference *tout court*. How many photographs of veiled or burka-wearing Muslim women have we seen since September 2001? How are sexual difference and cultural-difference-represented-as-sexual-difference used in the context of theorizing the current global situation—not only by academics but also by policy makers, journalists, and ordinary consumers of global media? (Cynical efforts of the current administration's attempt to rationalize military intervention on the basis of "our" respect for women come to mind.[14])

Transnational feminisms can help us out here as they have frequently called our attention to the role that naturalized and apparently unconscious gender metaphors have played in the theorization of globalization, and also to the often absent place accorded to gender in the theory of globalization. Feminist anthropologist Carla Freeman, for example, has put the latter question in this way in a recent essay: "What are the implications of a divide between masculinist grand theories of globalization that ignore gender as an analytical lens and local empirical studies of globalization in which gender takes center stage?"[15] Put differently, what does it mean to make gender the vocabulary but not the grammar of a discourse about globalization? (Erin Runions has pointed out to me that the focus on the local in antiglobalization activism has been strategic in an attempt to resist grand narratives, which are generally masculinist in character. This is a point I will want to clarify as I continue to work on this question.)

Related to this concern over the place of gender in globalization theory is the tendency in some quarters to subsume feminist knowledge under the logic of area studies. This problem is multilayered and complex, and it is part of the broader problem of the role of "the multicultural" in the university and in political organizing inside and beyond the walls of academe. Ella Shohat has been an especially articulate critic of the area studies model as it has been mobilized in the service of creating geographically based identities as "fictive unities" in the exploration of women's lives around the globe. She points out that "area studies" itself as an intellectual field of inquiry has its roots planted firmly in cold-war policies and initiatives that served particular political projects and were invested in forms of cultural reductionism. Transnational feminist studies, Shohat argues, must "begin from the premise that genders, sexualities, races, classes, nations, and even continents exist not as hermeti-cally sealed entities but rather as part of a permeable interwoven relationality."[16] She goes on: "Our challenge, I think, is precisely to avoid a facile additive operation of merely piling up increasingly differentiated groups of women from different regions and ethnicities—all of whom are projected as presumably forming a coherent yet easily demarcated entity. . . . an additive approach, which has women of the globe neatly neighbored and stocked, paraded in a United Nations-style 'Family of Nations' pageant where each ethnically marked feminist speaks in her turn, dressed in national costume."[17] For our shared project here, Shohat's critique cautions against mapping politics and identities geographically or culturally. It recalls Chandra Talpade Mohanty's crucial observation that categories such as "Western" and "Third World" are not "embodied, geographically or spatially defined categories" but are rather ideologically constituted "political and analytic sites and methodologies."[18]

I am interested in bringing Shohat's critique into our conversation, and I am also interested in noticing the metaphors she uses to articulate her feminist cautions. Whereas Appadurai used metaphors of promiscuity, marriage, and dowry provocatively (and probably unconsciously) and the specter of Christianity as the embodiment of that dowry to make a point about globalization, Shohat makes a different but related rhetorical move. In order to caution against the dangers of universalizing feminism, she invokes the metaphor of Christian missionizing. She writes: "It is fundamental to deploy a multiperspectival approach to the movement of feminist ideas across borders. We must worry about globalist feminism that spreads its programs around the world as the universal gospel, just as we have to be concerned about localist fem-inism that surrenders all dialogue to the dead end of an overpowering relativism."[19] Now, of course, Shohat's project is not *about* the Christian gospel any more than Appadurai's project is *about* unbounded sexuality or marriage or Christianity per se. But both theorists are fundamentally concerned about the effects of imposing certain naturalized framings of the global situation (Appadurai) or of feminism (Shohat) on processes of knowledge production. In both cases, Christianity emerges as the figure *par excellence* for the unwanted (if also) unintended consequence or, indeed, the danger embedded in any globalist enterprise. As Walter Mignolo continually reminds us, Christianity is deeply implicated in the modern conceptualization and imple-mentation of globalization, especially in the Americas where the process of globaliza-tion was staged and enacted through a universalizing Christian mission and the colonial impulse toward "civilization."[20] As we think together about "feminist New Testament studies"—itself a form of knowledge production—it would behoove us to consider how a project so inextricably intertwined with Christianity can turn some of its tools of critique upon that intertwined relationship.

Moallem, Appadurai, and Shohat have each in her or his own way lent some helpful categories and frameworks to considering the global future of feminist New Testament studies. Moallem's work reminds us to keep in mind the question of "the modern" in thinking about feminism and to remain conscious of the binarisms that shadow theorizations of feminism and its purported "other," fundamentalism. Appadurai urges what he calls a "grassroots globalization," one that urges "academics from the privileged institutions of the West (and the North) . . . to reconsider . . . their conventions about world knowledge and about the protocols of inquiry ('research') that they too often take for granted."[21] Meanwhile, in urging a critical engagement between feminism and area studies, Shohat argues for different narratives of history and current circumstances, narratives "in which variegated pasts and presents parallel and intersect, overlap and contradict, analogize and allegorize one another."[22]

For feminist New Testament critique, the programs outlined by these different theorists have—in my view—profound implications. Moallem's argument that feminism and fundamentalism are competing global regimes of truth that are deeply modern can be brought fruitfully to bear on the reception history of the New Testament (and the Bible more generally) in specific locations and under a wide range of ideological conditions. Appadurai's optimistic rendering of the potential for a sort of grassroots globalization that shifts the terrain of knowledge production in significant ways echoes efforts in postcolonial and contextual biblical studies to challenge the very protocols of inquiry that have framed work in the field for the last two centuries at least. Shohat's critique of the area studies model for feminist inquiry reminds us of the political embeddedness of the model itself *and* the need for any "global" project to be, in fact, "transnational."

That all three of these theorists in different ways worry about the hegemony of Christianity as a potentially deeply troubling feature of thinking about the modern, globalized situation where feminism and the production of knowledge are interrogated invites—perhaps demands—some of our sustained attention in this conversation. The worry cannot simply be dismissed, it seems to me, by gesturing vaguely at the suspicion so often directed against religion as a whole in activist and academic circles alike. Nor can it be neutralized by a dispassionate turn toward a narrative such as that of Philip Jenkins, which reads the next 50 years of Christianity in world-historical terms. Christianity's complicity in the European colonialist projects in Asia, Africa, and Latin America has been well documented by historians as one feature of the bigger story. (David Chidester's work on southern Africa and Nicholas Dirks's work on colonial India immediately come to mind here.[23]) The postcolonial appropriation of Christianity is an unfolding story, and one whose legacy will most certainly not be monolithic politically, institutionally, or theologically. (One example of its complexity, however, can be seen in the example of the recent debates within the global Anglican church that have pitted institutional authorities in Europe and North America, on the one hand, and institutional authorities in Africa, Asia, and Latin America, on the other, against one another.[24]) It will be very surprising, indeed, if this unfolding story does not establish its fault lines on issues of gender and sexuality, both because such fault lines are the fault lines of modernity itself and because sexual difference seems to operate as the interpretive analogy for cultural difference, as I've already argued. It seems to me that a conversation about feminist New Testament studies' global future, constituted as it is here in terms of Christianity's global future, will have to take up these kinds of difficult questions in a serious and sustained fashion.

I want to spend the remainder of my time addressing myself to the question of feminist biblical critique—New Testament studies more specifically—in light of some of these theoretical issues to which I have only had time to gesture briefly and citationally.

Feminist New Testament studies in the last two decades has, like feminist studies in religion *tout court*, been devoted to several different strands of intervention and critique: historical recovery and reconstruction; imaginative reconstitution of traditions and practices; and ideological critique.[25] These different strategies and approaches are not organized in a teleological or evolutionary line. Each one has a slightly different history, set of participants, and trajectory. Each one responds to a particular institutional history and set of constraints. That I will now argue for the central importance of feminist ideological critique as one leading edge in imagining a feminist future for biblical critique does not reflect any intention to diminish the other available strategies. Insofar as I teach, write, and speak from a particular institutional, national, and political location, I see feminist ideological critique as the best voice in which I can articulate a position. That there are other positions being articulated seems to me to be a sign of strength and not weakness.

At the beginning of my presentation, I noted that I had been asked to occupy the slot in this program that has been assigned to the Euro-American/North American and that, despite my misgivings of this "area studies" assignment, I needed to ask the question: How do I initiate a conversation about the *global* future of feminist New Testament studies *in relation to* the fact that U.S. political, economic, and military power currently casts such a long shadow across the rest of the world? What has the fact of that power to do with feminism and with the future of biblical critique? And now, a more specific question: how can feminist biblical critique provide a critique of *both* the Bible *and* the political, economic, and military position of the United States at the current moment? These are far more sweeping questions than can be answered in a single talk, but let me try out one particular example.

I have watched with great interest and alarm since the fall of 2001 as the Bible and certain strands of modern, American-born biblicism have performed complicated ideological work in the political scene in the United States and in the American imaginary. There's of course a longer historical trajectory here: remember back in 1981 when Reagan used a verse from the Gospel of Luke to rationalize his military build-up? In any case, it seems to me that the political work to which the Bible has been put in the current situation urgently invites feminist attention and critique. I will spend the remainder of my time exploring one example from the public rhetoric of the U.S. biblicist-in-chief, George W. Bush. In exploring this example, I do not intend to save the Bible from its politicization, as some interpreters have sought to do. I operate from the position that the Bible, for better or worse, already possesses ample cultural and political capital and already has plenty of people looking out for its reputation and its well-being. Therefore, I am interested in exploring the work that the Bible is doing in political contexts, but not because I want to defend its integrity or its "real meaning" from purported distortion or perversion. (In any case, I don't put much stock in notions like "textual integrity" or "real meaning.") I am interested in the work that the Bible is doing in political contexts because I want to interrogate its assumed capacity and suitability to perform that work. I am willing to concede that I am more comfortable when the Bible does work in the service of liberation or progressive sorts of justice than I am when the Bible is invoked by the political right wing. But that said, it's the very function of the Bible at all in these contexts that I want to question. That I focus on George Bush's use of the Bible and biblical imagery as more problematic reflects specifically on the current arrangement of power in this society, an arrangement that doesn't (at the moment, at least) place the power to coerce or to kill in the hands of people or groups who read the Bible with liberationist lenses on.

And so, to Bush and the Bible.[26]

As you most certainly already know, on the first anniversary of the September 11 terrorist attacks, George W. Bush made a series of carefully orchestrated, choreographed, and scripted public appearances that culminated in his address to the nation that evening from Ellis Island. In this speech, Bush repeatedly invoked a range of Christian theological categories, the American myth of a nation chosen by God, and images of biblical temporality and utopian eschatology. But perhaps the most striking evocation of the Bible echoed through the closing paragraph of this address, for Bush ended his speech with these words: "Tomorrow is September the 12th. A milestone is passed, and a mission goes on. Be confident. Our country is strong. And our cause is even larger than our country. Ours is the cause of human dignity: freedom guided by conscience, and guarded by peace. This ideal of America is the hope of all mankind. That hope drew millions to this harbor. That hope still lights our way. And the light shines in the darkness. And the darkness will not overcome it. May God bless America."[27]

I suspect that everyone reading this book will recognize that the last image—the light shining in darkness and the darkness not overcoming it—comes directly from the prologue of the Gospel of John (John 1:5). The logic—if we may generously call it that—of the Bush speech creates a series of analogies or parallelisms between a series of abstract nouns: *the ideal of America* equals *the hope of all mankind* equals *the light that shines in the darkness*. According to this logic, in short, the ideal of America *is* the light that shines in the darkness. Now, if we go back to the prologue of the Gospel of John, we see that it is structured similarly and it, too, presents a series of analogies and parallelisms: the logos was with God and was God and was part of creation and had life within itself and the life within the logos was the light of humanity, the light that shines in the darkness. If we go a step further and map these two sets of claims onto one another, we encounter this extraordinary claim: "the ideal of America" is the light of humanity that was the life within the logos that was with God "in the beginning" and was God. So, we have a rather astonishing intertextual assertion that "the ideal of America" is the same thing as the light/life that is present within the logos (the organizing principle of all of creation), the logos itself being both with God and God itself.

But as astonishing as this theological assertion might be, it is not the end of the story. For the prologue of John goes on to describe the alienation of the light from the world. "The true light that enlightens every person was coming onto the world. It was in the world, and the world was made through it, but the world knew it not. It came to its own home, and its own people did not receive it. But to all who received it, who believed in its name, it gave power to become children of God" (John 1:9–12). If we come back to the Bush speech, which claims that the ideal of America *is* the light shining in the darkness, and substitute "the ideal of America" for "the light" in the prologue of John, we come up with this set of implied theological claims: "The true **ideal of America** that enlightens every person was coming onto the world.

The ideal of America was in the world, and the world was made through **the ideal of America**, but the world knew **the ideal of America** not. **The ideal of America** came to its own home, and its own people did not receive it. But to all who received **the ideal of America**, who believed in its name, it gave power to become children of God."

When these sets of cosmic claims are situated alongside the utopian and eschatological claims about the providential character of history, we encounter a dizzying and unsettling juxtaposition of nationalism and theological determinism. "I believe there is a reason that history has matched this nation with this time," Bush confessed, and soon afterward, he asserted, "We do know that God has placed us together in this moment, to grieve together, to stand together, to serve each other and our country." History and God converge here, and the temporality of the current situation is, again in the context of the logic of the prologue of John that will be invoked in the next paragraph, but a moment in the unfolding of creation in which "the ideal of America" plays a definitive and cosmic role as "the light shining in the darkness."

A critical feminist engagement with this rhetoric and with this reading of the prologue of John might well as a first step notice the effacement of the feminine and the maternal in both the biblical text and in the speech itself. The speech opens with an evocation of the terrible losses that September 11 represent, speaking mostly in generalities until coming to a single specific example: "it's been a year of sorrow, of empty places, of *newborn children who will never know their fathers here on earth,*" (but, the implication seems to be, will know their Father in heaven?). The prologue of John meanwhile makes it clear that the genealogical relationship that matters is that which exists between God and his children, children who are not born of blood or carnal will or human desire but of God (1:13). In more cosmic, theological terms slightly later on, the *monogenês huios*, the one in the bosom of the Father is invoked as the exception, the conduit through which the invisible God becomes known. We are in a world of fathers and their children, the Father and the Son, linked by seeing (or not seeing) and knowing (or not knowing), a world of patrilineage and effaced (or veiled?) mothers. (It is perhaps not incidental that the efforts of Bush-the-son since September 11 have had a decidedly Oedipal cast. One doesn't need to be Freud or Fellini to understand Bush-the-Son's assertion that *his* war will be bigger and longer than his father's.)

But a critical feminist reading of the interplay of these two texts—a commemorative, nationalist speech and a Christological hymn—can also ask what work the Bible (both as thematic resource and as citational symptom) is doing as an authoritative intertext in the midst of a nationalist commemoration. To pose this question is not to argue about Bush's hermeneutical assumptions—whether he has read the text correctly or not—but about the ideological assumptions that govern the citational gesture. (One should note that others undertake the strategy of arguing with Bush's hermeneutic, often to very salutary effect. See, for example, the *New Yorker* magazine's "Talk of the Town" on January 20, 2003, where the writer observes that the Bush administration seems to be reading the "Heavily Revised Non-standard Version" of the Bible, which promises salvation to the rich.[28]) In exploring the citational gesture at work in Bush's discourse, one can see how this speech creates a biblically inflected "we" against whom "the enemy" is menacingly poised. "Our deepest national conviction is that every life is precious, because every life is the gift of a creator who intended us to live in liberty and equality. More than anything else, this separates us from the enemy we fight. We value every life; our enemies value none. . . ." Here, we have moved from one Johannine textual world to another, from the prologue of the Gospel of John to the Johannine apocalypse, traveling from the beginning of time to its culmination. This move is itself not a uniquely modern move, but it has particular modern ramifications when the ideological gesture can be enforced through the military apparatus of the most heavily armed nation in the history of the world. When the story of the light that shines in the darkness (aka the ideal of America) incorporates the story of the light's alienation from the world and the story of the special status of those who believe in the name of the light (aka the name of America), we arrive at a chilling realization. When you tell the story this way, any refusal to link one's fate with that of the light shining in the darkness/the ideal of America is both a refusal to be counted among the children of God *and* an abdication of the cosmic facts of the matter. If one were to enter into the field of foreign policy and international relations with these stories in one's head, it would not be a surprise to see them authorizing a political unilateralism. Indeed, in this dualistic framing of the matter, unilateralism is all there is.

A transnational feminist biblical critique can serve in an engagement with this example by pointing out the religious and secular fundamentalisms embedded in this Christian configuration and conflation of cosmic light and America, by interrogating the gendered character of this characterization and its apocalypticism, by denaturalizing the metaphors, logics, and claims to authority that are part of its rhetoric. A transnational feminist biblical critique can remember that this framing of "the ideal of America" as "the light shining in the darkness" overlaps with the interests of American economic institutions and its globalizing impulses—and a transnational feminist biblical critique can remember the anxieties expressed about the role of Christianity in establishing and sustaining relationships coded by globalization. A transnational feminist biblical critique can participate in a broader project of reconfiguring the Bible as a *modern* text so that it can also participate in the destabilization of facile if persistent claims about the Bible as a mystifying, ancient, and self-evident authority. And a transnational feminist biblical critique can turn its critical precision tools back onto itself, interrogating and even challenging the globalizing impulse embedded in the Christian biblical tradition itself.

Such a transnational feminist engagement with the New Testament will likely not only look for those places in texts and their deployments where "women" or "the feminine" figure. Where there are claims being made about power or violence, gender is inevitably part of the configuration—to say nothing of the reality that women around the globe so often bear the brunt of power's workings and the impact of violence.

What I have presented here is a series of provisional reflections on some of the theoretical elements that I believe are central to an engagement with the global future of feminist New Testament studies. From my point of view, that future should be concerned far less with the practice of exegesis than with a sustained interrogation of the work the Bible does in contemporary situations and in the service of a wide range of political goals. Feminist New Testament studies needs to attend to the anxiety about the function of "Christianity" that is routinely expressed by theorists of transnational feminism and globalization—and by "attend to the anxiety," I do not mean simply explain it away. I mean, rather, that historical and contemporary complicity of "Christianity" with colonialisms and fundamentalisms needs to be addressed in a sustained and critical fashion, and not only because we have seen in the example of Bush's nationalist/commemorative speech how the New Testament can undergird in both structure and content a global politics that promises to generate and sanction global violence and global suffering.

For my own work, attending to such concerns means turning attention to the very problems of violence and suffering, and exploring the ways in which the Bible and religious discourse as a whole lend themselves in deeply ambivalent ways toward the project of a critical theory of these intractable aspects of human social life. I do not really know yet what such an exploration will look like. This chapter represents some preliminary steps in trying to think that through.

Notes

1. This work came to public expression in two conferences: "Responding to Violence," a colloquium with Jody Williams, held at Barnard College in October 2002; and "Feminist Responses/Alternatives to Violence in a Transnational Context," held at San Francisco State University in November 2003. The "Responding to Violence" website can be found at: http://www.barnard.edu/bcrw/respondingtoviolence/index.htm. Some of the papers from that conference have been published in *Reverberations: On Violence*, ed. Elizabeth A. Castelli (a special issue of the *Scholar and Feminist Online* 2.2 [Winter 2004]), at http://www.barnard.edu/sfonline/reverb/, and a more extended archive of the conference appears in *Interventions: Activists and Academics Respond to Violence*, ed. Elizabeth A. Castelli and Janet R. Jakobsen (New York: Palgrave Macmillan, 2004).
2. The literature here is far reaching. A groundbreaking essay for many feminist theorists was Chandra Talpade Mohanty, "Under Western Eyes: Feminist Scholarship and Colonial Discourses," *Boundary 2* 12 (1986): 333–358. See Mohanty's recent return to these issues in " 'Under Western Eyes' Revisited: Feminist Solidarity through Anticapitalist Struggles," *Signs* 28 (2002): 499–535. Other important anthologies include Inderpal Grewal and Caren Kaplan, eds., *Scattered Hegemonies: Postmodernity and Transnational Feminist Practices* (Minneapolis: University of Minnesota Press, 1994) and Caren Kaplan, Norma Alarcón, and Minoo Moallem, eds., *Between Woman and Nation: Nationalisms, Transnational Feminisms, and the State* (Durham: Duke University Press, 1999). For an excellent anthology that integrates feminist theory, postcolonialism, and the study of religion, see Laura E. Donaldson and Kwok Pui-Lan, eds., *Postcolonialism, Feminism and Religious Discourse* (New York: Routledge, 2001).
3. Minoo Moallem, "Transnationalism, Feminism, and Fundamentalism," in *Women, Gender, Religion: A Reader*, ed. Elizabeth A. Castelli with Rosamond C. Rodman (New York: Palgrave, 2001) 119–145, quotation at 120.
4. Moallem, "Transnationalism, Feminism," in Castelli and Rodman, eds., *Women, Gender* 120.
5. Moallem, "Transnationalism, Feminism," in Castelli and Rodman, eds., *Women, Gender* 135.
6. Laura Mandell, "The First Women (Psycho)analysts; or, The Friends of Feminist History," *Modern Language Quarterly* 65 (2004): 69–92, at 70.

7. Moallem, "Transnationalism, Feminism," in Castelli and Rodman, eds. *Women, Gender* 121–122.

8. Margaret Ferguson, "Feminism in Time," *Modern Language Quarterly* 65 (2004): 7–27, at 21 (emphasis added).

9. Arjun Appadurai, "Grassroots Globalization and the Research Imagination," *Public Culture* (2000): 1–19, quotation at 1–2.

10. See, e.g., Catherine Lutz, "The Gender of Theory," in *Women Writing Culture*, ed. Ruth Behar and Deborah A. Gordon (Berkeley: University of California Press, 1995), 249–266.

11. Philip Jenkins, *The Next Christendom: The Rise of Global Christianity* (New York: Oxford University Press, 2002). Jenkins's book certainly invites a reading for gender.

12. Appadurai, "Grassroots Globalization," 4 (emphasis mine).

13. Appadurai, "Grassroots Globalization," 3.

14. Karen Beckman, "Feminism in the Time of Violence," *Scholar and Feminist Online* 2.2 (Winter 2004): http://www.barnard.edu/sfonline/reverb/beckman1.html

15. Carla Freeman, "Is Local : Global as Feminine : Masculine? Rethinking the Gender of Globalization," *Signs* 26 (2001): 1007–1037, quotation at 1008. (This issue of *Signs* was a special issue, guest edited by Amrita Basu, Caren Kaplan, Inderpal Grewal, and Liisa Malkki devoted to the theme, "Globalization and Gender.")

16. Ella Shohat, "Area Studies, Gender Studies, and the Cartographies of Knowledge," *Social Text* 72 (Fall 2002): 67–78, quotation at 68.

17. Shohat, "Area Studies," 68.

18. Mohanty, " 'Under Western Eyes' Revisited," 502, n. 4.

19. Shohat, "Area Studies," 70.

20. Walter D. Mignolo, "Globalization/Mundialización: Civilizing Processes and the Relocation of Languages and Knowledges," in *Local Histories/Global Designs: Coloniality, Subaltern Knowledges, and Border Thinking* (Princeton: Princeton University Press, 2000), 278–311. See also his *The Darker Side of the Renaissance: Literacy, Territoriality, and Colonization*, 2nd ed. (Ann Arbor: University of Michigan Press, 2003).

21. Appadurai, "Grassroots Globalization," 18.

22. Shohat, "Area Studies," 78.

23. David Chidester, *Savage Systems: Colonialism and Comparative Religion in Southern Africa* (Charlottesville: University Press of Virginia, 1996); Nicholas B. Dirks, *Castes of Mind: Colonialism and the Making of Modern India* (Princeton: Princeton University Press, 2001).

24. See Mary-Jane Rubenstein, "An Anglican Crisis of Comparison: Questions of Gender, Sex, and Religious Authority, with Particular Reference to the Church of Nigeria," *Journal of the American Academy of Religion* 72 (2004): 341–365.

25. See my "Women, Gender, Religion: Troubling Categories and Transforming Knowledge," in *Women, Gender, Religion: A Reader*, ed. Elizabeth A. Castelli with Rosamond C. Rodman (New York: Palgrave, 2001) 3–25, esp. 4.

26. I am by no means alone in analyzing Bush's use of the Bible. See also Erin Runions, "Biblical Promise and Threat in U.S. Imperialist Rhetoric before and after 9/11," *Scholar and Feminist Online* 2.2 (Winter 2004): http://www.barnard.edu/sfonline/reverb/runions1.htm; John M. Murphy, " 'Our Mission and Our Moment': George W. Bush and September 11," *Rhetoric & Public Affairs* 6 (2003): 607–632; John A. Wickham, "September 11 and America's War on Terrorism: A New Manifest Destiny?" *American Indian Quarterly* 26.1 (2002): 116–144; Michael Angrosino, "Civil Religion Redux," *Anthropological Quarterly* 75.2 (Spring 2002): 239–267. See also the special forum on "Evil" in *Rhetoric & Public Affairs* 6.3 (Fall 2003): 509–566, which analyzes the theological roots and rhetorical uses of this category in contemporary American political discourse,

especially that emanating from the Bush White House. George W. Bush's religiosity has been the subject of many journalistic treatments; see, e.g., Ben Tripp, "Bush's Boss is a Jewish Carpenter: Of Jesus and George," *CounterPunch*, September 5, 2002: http://www.counterpunch.org/tripp0905.html; "George W.'s Personal Jesus," *Gentlemen's Quarterly* (September 2003): 330–335, 394–397; Jack Beatty, "In the Name of God," *Atlantic Monthly*, March 5, 2003: http://www.theatlantic.com/unbound/polipro/ pp2003-03-05.htm; Ira Chernus, "Did Bush Say God Told Him to Go to War?" *Common Dreams.org*, June 30, 2003: http://www.commondreams.org/views03/0630-04.htm; among many other stories.

27. "Vigilance and Memory: Transcript of President Bush's Address to the Nation on Sept. 11 Anniversary," *New York Times*, September 12, 2002, Late Edition, B8.

28. Hendrik Hertzberg, "Dividends," *New Yorker*, January 20, 2003, 29–30.

Chapter 4

Response: Globalization, Transnational Feminisms, and the Future of Biblical Critique

Sheila Briggs

Elizabeth Castelli has chosen to explore the theme of the global future of feminist New Testament studies in terms of globalization. Now this may seem obvious but think for a moment of alternative approaches. After all, biblical studies have a global future because they are linked to the spread of Christianity throughout our planet. But how do we describe Christianity as a global phenomenon? What is at stake when we decide between two possible phrases to describe it? Do we want to talk about global Christianity or the Christianity of globalization? These two terms carry very different connotations.

The phrase "global Christianity" indicates a shift in the axis of gravity away from Europe and North America to Latin America, Asia, and Africa. It also implies an ecclesiastical process that accompanied the political independence of Third World countries from their former colonial masters. It suggests that the institutional control and cultural hegemony of the Western churches, which were exercised through the missions of the colonial period, have been broken. Therefore, the majority of the Christians of the future will not only reside in the South but will also produce their readings of the bible under indigenous leadership and cultural norms.

If one, however, prefers the term "Christianity of globalization" then the global spread of Christianity is placed in more ambiguous and potentially negative terms. Castelli is intrigued by Arjun Appadurai's phrase "the hidden dowry of globalization." When Appadurai inquires about "the hidden dowry of globalization" he may be employing a gendered and sexualized metaphor but when he suggests various candidates for this role he is speaking of actual historical formations that mold our material and ideological world. He lists Christianity because it has become commonplace to see this as a critical component of the cultural transactions that shaped the relationships between colonizer and colonized and thus made the stuff out of which the contemporary cultural currency of globalization has been minted.

Are global Christianity and the Christianity of globalization identical? I do not think that theorists like Arjun Appadurai make a distinction between the two. "The hidden dowry of globalization" could refer to the Christianity of Gustavo Guttierez or that of George Bush or that of Elizabeth Schüssler Fiorenza or to all of them. The Christianity of globalization removes the narrative of emancipation that is contained within the phrase global Christianity. It awakens us to the fact that the Christianities of the South are not necessarily religions of the poor and marginalized, and are not necessarily committed to liberative political practices or biblical interpretation. Indeed the church leadership in Africa, Latin America, and Asia is often drawn from the same elites as the political rulers. They may pursue interests and agendas that are not directed to the well-being of the majority of their peoples. One has only to think of the appalling policies on AIDS, adopted by several African governments and advocated by local church leaders. Nor is it only church leaders within denominations of Western origin that are drawn from and allied with local elites. Pentecostal churches in Latin America and independent churches in Africa may recruit among the poor but their leadership in many cases remains in the hands of the elite who have ties to conservative Christians in the West.

The phrase "hidden dowry of globalization" emphasizes that Christianity, like MTV, are situated not only in the culture of globalization but also in its political economy. A dowry is an economic transaction. Christianity as a global network is integrated into the flows of capital and labor. Money and personnel are circulated not only between North and South but also between regions of the South. Migration and large diaspora communities make religious organizations and institutions part of the complex global system of economic exchange. Korean and Nigerian Christians bring their own forms of Christianity with them and maintain an active circulation of funds and personnel between the once home country and often many geographically dispersed centers of migration. Mosques, Hindu, Sikh, and Buddhist temples are to be found in European and North American cities with the sort of frequency in which missions of the colonial era planted churches in countries where Christianity had not existed. The old colonial map of the political economy in which resources flowed from the colonized periphery to the colonial metropolis has been thoroughly revised.

The contemporary global capitalist economy has been indigenized, that is, its centers are no longer exclusively in Europe and North America but local metropoles are emerging in what was once the colonized periphery. This is most obvious in Asian countries like India and South Korea (the latter has also seen a dramatic increase in its Christian population). This pattern that is highly visible in Bangalore and Seoul is already incipient in Sao Paolo and Lagos. Again, religious patterns of exchange and interaction simulate economic ones. Conservative Episcopalians in Orange County, California or Maryland, upset over homosexual ordination in the United States, appeal not to Canterbury but to Lagos for the exercise of ecclesiastical authority.

Globalization, whether we think of it in terms of culture or political economy, is not synonymous with Westernization, although the greatest beneficiaries of the global capitalist economy are the elites of the North. Elizabeth Castelli does well to remind us of Chandra Talpade Mohanty's crucial observation that categories such as

"Western" and "Third World" are not "embodied, geographically or spatially defined categories" but are rather ideologically constituted "political and analytic sites and methodologies."[1]

Elizabeth Castelli renews Ella Shohat's criticism of area studies and the notion of geographically based identities and the reifications of culture and cultural identities that accompany it. The dichotomy between Western and non-Western has been rendered obsolete by the advance of globalization, which in itself is the culmination of processes of cultural hybridization of colonizer as well as of colonized that European empires and missions initiated.[2] Hybridization does not necessarily imply homogenization, but often the opposite. It is important to remember that globalization does not spell the eradication of the local but its complication and intensification. That dense system of communications allows people to inhabit simultaneously multiple locations.

Transnational professionals who live in the metropolitan centers of the global economy take advantage on an everyday basis of the integration of local cultures in the global communications infrastructure. I am a Briton who has lived in the United States for most of the last 20 years. Yet, cheap airfares and phone calls allow me frequently to be physically present in Britain or to have direct contact with people there. I read British newspapers on the Internet and watch the BBC via satellite television. My experience of migration is different from that of earlier generations because I have never had to leave in any irrevocable or absolute sense my country of origin. Yet, even those migrant workers who do not share my socioeconomic privileges are able on a less frequent and extensive basis to have access to at least many of the same features of the global communications system.

Multiculturalism is not limited to the economic magnets of migration in the North, such as the United States, western Europe, or Japan. Yet, there is no single pattern of multiculturalism to be found everywhere. My British local culture of origin and the local Californian culture in which I currently reside are multicultural, but how multiculturalism is inflected in Britain is different than in southern California. I expect a computer engineer from Bangalore currently living and working in Silicon Valley would make a very similar observation to mine. Globalization does not lead necessarily to homogenization of local cultures but to more complex and more differently complex local cultures. To ask about the global future of feminist New Testament studies is also to enquire about how we thematize and analyze these transformed local cultures where transnational feminisms and transnational feminist biblical interpretations take place.

Castelli herself would seem to prefer Christianity of globalization to global Christianity. For her the fact that the theorists she discusses "in different ways worry about the hegemony of Christianity as a potentially deeply troubling feature of thinking about the modern, globalized situation where feminism and the production of knowledge are interrogated invites—perhaps demands—some of our sustained attention in this conversation." She explicitly refuses to turn to the narrative of global Christianity and the breaking of Western hegemony in Christianity to be found in the work of Philip Jenkins. Yet, her main example of the Christianity of globalization is the violent biblicism of George Bush. That she chooses this particular example may be motivated by the dire historical moment in which our original conversation took place. In February 2003, George Bush had the world poised on the brink of a biblical Armageddon. It may also be explained by her assigned task of speaking from the context of North America and Europe. However, in the hybridization of cultures and identities, which globalization promotes, and since Christianity is a major vehicle of hybridization, George Bush's biblical rhetoric may not be our only worry if we survive it. Feminist New Testament studies, whether they are engaged in by Christians or by others who recognize Christianity's global effects, will act as a capillary mechanism through which Christianity and the Christian bible permeates/penetrates every region of our world. Even radical biblical critique is a compliment to Christianity's ideological power. Breaking the hegemony of Western models of biblical studies does not ensure liberative practices. We need to critically interrogate all forms of biblical criticism, wherever they are situated geographically, whether they are traditional or innovative, and even when they are practiced by feminists as to what are their political consequences. Feminist biblical interpretations are not hermetically sealed from others and we can discover that we have strange and in some cases unpleasant bedfellows. This is not a moral argument against engaging in feminist New Testament studies but a warning against a moral naiveté that assumes our good intentions control how our scholarship is configured in the dense systems of communication, which are the most prominent feature of globalization.

Biblical criticism is very much a product of modernity. This is obvious in the sense that much biblical criticism in the last two centuries has self-consciously seen itself as a modernization of understanding the bible and of Christianity in general. But there is here no simple antithesis of modern biblical criticism and traditional precritical biblical interpretation. Castelli refers at length to Minoo Moallem's discussion of the competition of fundamentalism and feminism and stresses the point that both arise inside modernity and its regimes for the representation of gender.[3] Both feminism and fundamentalism may vehemently criticize modernity and view themselves as breaking out of its political and intellectual frameworks. But Castelli, following Moallem, argues they offer very different critiques of modernity, defining its problems and proposing solutions in opposing ways. Tradition is as much a modern category as progress and emancipation and appeals to tradition within a religious or secular framework in engagement of a modern rhetoric and the pursuit of modern politics.

Does feminism's and biblical criticism's inextricable involvement with the problematic of modernity suggest that ideology should be the primary concern and ideology critique the primary task for the future of feminist New Testament studies in a globalized world? Toward the end of her chapter Castelli remarks, "From my point of view, that future should be concerned far less with the practice of exegesis than with a sustained interrogation of the work the Bible does in contemporary situations and in the service of a wide range of political goals." I am concerned by the implications of Castelli's downplaying of exegesis for the future of historical reconstruction in feminist New Testament studies wherever they are practiced. I would agree that where New Testament exegesis narrows its focus to what Castelli earlier characterizes as questions of "textual integrity and real meaning" we have a discipline blind to its own ideological operations. Historical scholarship of any kind can never be ideology-free and uncovering the ideological work of history writing is a significant aim of feminist biblical criticism. The underlying issue here is whether we accept or not certain postmodern claims about knowledge being always and only strategic. There is a practical political problem with this claim since conservative and reactionary strategic knowledges seem at this historical moment to be more successful than progressive and liberative ones. This is the case not only in the post–September 11 United States but also in the Christianities of the South—one thinks of recent African intervention in the Anglican debate over homosexual ordination.

Apart from questions of the political effectiveness of a feminist biblical criticism that sees itself as a strategic knowledge engaged in ideology critique, there are strong theoretical grounds for a broader approach than ideological criticism in feminist New Testament studies, however important it may be. Truth-claims are never free from ideology, and this is especially the case in history and theology, the two modes of enquiry that most influence feminist biblical criticism. Yet truth claims even as ideology are trying to make sense of a material world, which is not solely constituted by the use of language in competing politics and forms of knowledge. Such an argument could be taken as coming dangerously close to positivism. Historical methods and questions can reflect a positivist agenda and they have done so. Yet, I am not proposing here that material reality can be known through history as a scientific form of enquiry. We are living in a world where positivist science has long been questioned and non-positivist paradigms of science developed. Arkady Plotnitsky writing about the role of real numbers in mathematical idealization wrote about an approach to mathematics that might also be appropriate to feminist New Testament studies in the context of globalization. Having insisted on radical alterity as part of any conception of reality, he concludes, "We may be entering, indeed already inhabiting, increasingly complex landscapes that enlarge the space of the known and the unknown alike, which is perhaps the only sense of progress one can still think of."[4] The radical alterity of the material world arises out of its double constitution by both the ideological truth-claims of any form of knowledge and by the fact that it always exceeds these, the unknown exceeds the known. Historical reconstruction in feminist New Testament studies began as the attempt to understand the interplay of the material conditions of early Christian women's lives with the competing ideologies of gender in their sociocultural context. By self-critically examining its own ideological impulse and by allowing post-structuralist theory to destabilize its categories of women and gender as fixed identities, such feminist work can avoid the illusion that it has overcome the radical alterity of material reality to give us a full and accurate account of the gendered past of early Christianity. The surplus of material reality beyond ideological construction renders it unknown and constitutes its radical alterity. Yet, at the same time the space of feminist historical reconstruction has been enlarged because the resistance of this surplus to our modes of enquiry constantly demands new models, new strategies, new practices of knowledge. Facing the increasingly rapid and invisible transformations of material reality under the impact of globalization that outpace all production of knowledge, perhaps this is the only sense of emancipation that we can still think of.

Notes

1. Chandra Talpade Mohanty, " 'Under Western Eyes' Revisited: Feminist Solidarity through Anticapitalist Struggles," *Signs* 28 (2002): 502, n. 4, quoted in Castelli, "Globalization," 16.

2. The concept of hybridity has been developed in postcolonial theory. In the early and canonical formulation of cultural hybridization in Homi K. Bhaba's work, colonial Christian missions were already identified as its vehicle, see *The Location of Culture* (London: Routledge, 1994) 102–122.

3. Minoo Moallem, "Transnationalism, Feminism and Fundamentalism," in *Women, Gender, Religion: A Reader*, ed. Elizabeth A. Castelli with Rosamond C. Rodman (New York: Palgrave, 2001) 119–145.

4. Arkady Plotnitsky, "Complementarity, Idealization and the Limits of Classical Conceptions of Reality," *South Atlantic Quarterly* 94 (1995): 566.

Chapter 5

The Challenge of "Blackness" for Rearticulating the Meaning of Global Feminist New Testament Interpretation

Gay L. Byron

Introduction: Situating the Task in the Midst of Multiple Realities

My task, as I see it, is extremely complex. I have been asked to discuss a number of topics that should press us to consider the impact of global and Christian transformations upon the future of feminist New Testament studies. The list of topics include the following: discuss my perspective on global and Christian transformations in the next half century from my cultural context; address how my scholarship has been local and how it has been influenced by an awareness of global concerns of and about women; envision the future direction of African American Christianity; assess the connections that African American Christianity will have or further develop with the churches of the southern hemisphere, especially Africa and other areas of the diaspora; identify the challenges feminist scholarship will face over the next 50 years in the face of projected global transformations; and consider how it will continue to have a positive impact on the lives of women globally. In addition, I have been asked to describe the nature of my own work in feminist New Testament studies by discussing some of the findings from my research dealing with motifs about "blackness" and ethnic difference in early Christian writings. Clearly, each of these topics could easily comprise an essay of its own; but the task of weaving them together for the purpose of assessing the future of global feminist New Testament studies, though complex, is a very welcome task.

I must admit at the outset that speaking about globalization, feminist biblical criticism, and African American Christianity is filled with many potential pitfalls. I stand in a particular sociocultural, scholarly professional, and geopolitical location that in many respects informs—for better or for worse—how I view these broad topics. First, as an African American clergywoman, I serve in a predominately white denomination—the Presbyterian Church (USA). Although I was raised in a southern Black baptist church tradition and have pastored and served in mainly African American or Caribbean American Presbyterian churches, my actual experience with the varieties of African American Christianit(ies) is quite limited.

Second, as a New Testament scholar, I consider myself a relative newcomer to this level of critical dialogue and inquiry with respect to feminist biblical interpretation. Of course, I have benefited immensely from the groundbreaking reconstructionist project of Elisabeth Schüssler Fiorenza with respect to understanding the roles and functions of women in early Christian communities and her more recent attempts at understanding the politics of biblical interpretation, as well as the many other engaging projects of feminists scholars such as Antoinette Clark Wire, Mary Ann Tolbert, and Amy-Jill Levine, just to name a few.[1] I also had the wonderful opportunity to work with Elizabeth A. Castelli while researching and writing my dissertation at Union Seminary. Her keen theoretical insights and eloquent way of articulating the feminist critique and clarifying the value of gender criticism for understanding the New Testament enabled me to sharpen my own understanding of women in early Christian writings.[2] Furthermore, I have utilized the critical hermeneutical insights of womanist theologians and biblical scholars in various graduate school projects as a strategy for bringing to the foreground perspectives and questions that are particular to experiences of African American women.[3] In addition to all of this, I now teach at an institution where questions about women and gender are central to every aspect of our curriculum.[4] But, I have not had the opportunity to articulate in a systematic fashion my understanding of the benefits, limitations, and future challenges of both feminist and womanist criticisms and their utility for the lives of women of African descent. Nor have I had the opportunity to extend my understanding of feminist and womanist biblical interpretation beyond the European and North American scholars who have defined the field in the United States.

Finally, as an African American woman constantly contending with the complex "matrix of domination" that informs the ethos of this country, and with loyalties to those from what is considered the "Third" or "Two Thirds" World, I am for the first time attempting to analyze my own understanding of the impact of globalization for my scholarship about women in early Christian writings, and to assess the challenges that stem from the acknowledgment that I am now deeply rooted in a transnational context that calls me to cultivate new conversation partners who extend beyond my comfortable and privileged geopolitical position in the United States.[5] In this regard, my understanding of globalization must be situated in a theoretical framework that emphasizes indigenous understandings of Christianity rather than "the Christian discovery of indigenous societies."[6]

After briefly discussing the global and Christian transformations that are challenging and redefining our assumptions about the "global North" and the "global South," I will summarize the thesis of my recent book, *Symbolic Blackness and Ethnic Difference in*

Early Christian Literature, and provide two examples of symbolic representations of Ethiopian and Black women.[7] I will use this material as a springboard for summarizing the challenges facing future generations of feminist and womanist scholars and African American Christians in the wake of expansive global and Christian transformations. I will also share the theoretical challenges that I face with respect to this topic, and then conclude with an appeal to my European and North American colleagues to work toward conversations and coalitions that will shift the foundations upon which we envision the future direction of global feminist New Testament studies.

"To the South": Global and Christian Transformations

Philip Jenkins, in his book entitled, *The Next Christendom*, analyzes the impact of globalization on world Christianities and documents how "the center of gravity in the Christian world has shifted inexorably *southward*, to Africa, Asia, and Latin America."[8] He further describes how "the era of Western Christianity—or Christianity of the global North—has passed within our lifetimes, and the day of Southern Christianity is dawning."[9] In the face of this transforming moment in the history of religion, no longer will it be realistic or viable to think of Christianity as a European faith or "the White man's religion." Neither will it be realistic to think of Christianity in Africa, Asia, or Latin America as solely the by-product of Western missionary activities. Thus, the implications of this shift "to the South" are widespread not only for demographers and political analysts, but also for biblical scholars, theologians, and historians of religion who are seeking to rearticulate the meaning of ancient scriptures, Christian traditions, and global realities.

Jenkins provides useful demographic summaries and population projections in order to emphasize the "Southern Boom" that is fueling the "next Christendom" of the twenty-first century.[10] In sub-Saharan Africa, for example, several nations are expected to double their population in the next quarter-century, even after allowing for the effects of AIDS. The eight largest nations in this region (Nigeria, Ethiopia, Democratic Republic of Congo, South Africa, Sudan, Tanzania, Kenya, and Uganda) had a combined population of about 400 million at the end of the twentieth century, and by 2050, according to Jenkins, the population of these nations could rise to over a billion.[11] Moreover, the world's youngest nations—Uganda, Niger, and the Congo—are African, while the oldest countries are all in Europe or Japan.[12]

With respect to the United States, population trends indicate that the ethnic character of the country will become less European and less White as the nation continues to grow.[13] Recent census statistics indicate that Latin Americans and Hispanics are now the largest minority group in the United States at 37 million, with African Americans ranking a close second at 36.2 million.[14] As many demographic experts had predicted more than a decade ago, U.S. society is steadily moving away from a "Black and White affair to a multicolored reality."[15]

The rise of Christianity in the global South raises all types of questions about the use of the Bible.[16] Jenkins claims that "only newer churches (i.e., those from the global South) can read the Bible with any authenticity and immediacy, and that the Old Christendom must give priority to Southern voices," yet he does not appeal to any examples of "Southern voices" in his analysis.[17] Scholars, such as Lamin Sanneh, Professor of Missions and World Christianity at Yale Divinity School, offer poignant critiques of Jenkins's Western conceptual framework that emphasizes Christianity as a new world religion in the global South.[18] Sanneh calls into question the assumptions that undergird discussions about global Christianity, which focus on "the Christian discovery of indigenous societies," and suggests a new framework that emphasizes "the indigenous discovery of Christianity."

> The Christian discovery of indigenous societies describes the process of missionaries from the West coming to Africa or Asia and converting people, often with political incentives and material inducements. The indigenous discovery of Christianity, by contrast, describes local people encountering the religion through mother tongue discernment and in the light of the people's own needs and experiences. The indigenous discovery places the emphasis on unintended local consequences, leaving the way open for indigenous agency and leadership.[19]

Thus, I would suggest that this "global Christian revolution," to borrow Jenkins's phrase, that is taking place before our very eyes should lead to a focus upon the reading strategies of those from the global South and the "Southern voices" that are embedded in early Christian writings. At this point, I would like to introduce my research dealing with the symbolic representations of Egyptians, Ethiopians, Blacks, and blackness in early Christian literature as a means for considering how representations of ethnic groups *from the South* might aid in discussing the challenges and the possibilities facing feminist New Testament studies.

"Blackened by Their Sins": Symbolic Blackness and Ethnic Difference in Early Christian Literature

The church father Jerome in his homily on Psalm 86 says the following:

> At one time we were Ethiopians in our vices and sins. How so? *Because our sins had blackened us.* But afterwards we heard the words: "Wash yourselves clean!" And we said: "Wash me, and I shall be whiter than snow. We are Ethiopians, therefore, who have been transformed from blackness into whiteness." (Jerome, *Homily 18 on Psalm 86*)

In *Symbolic Blackness and Ethnic Difference in Early Christian Literature*, I classify and examine the symbolic usages of Egyptians, Ethiopians, Blacks, and blackness in early Christian literature as a means for understanding the ideological basis of how early Christians shaped their conceptions of vices and sins, sexual threats, and "heretical" movements in their communities. As the quote by Jerome indicates, early Christians used these ethnic groups and color symbols as strategic pedagogical and homiletical devices.[20]

Because of the many, diverse representations of these ethnic groups in Christian writings, I found it necessary to develop a classification or taxonomy of what I call "ethno-political rhetorics." Ethno-political rhetorics are discursive elements within texts that refer to "ethnic" identities or geographical locations and function as political invective.[21] Although there are many different interpretations of ethnicity, I view it as a social construct that draws attention to the differences that exist within communities. By drawing attention to symbolic representations of ethnicity in early Christian writings, I was able to identify one of the ways in which group boundaries were construed within early Christianity that led to "insiders" and "outsiders."[22]

The taxonomy demonstrates how the most remote people ("beyond the rivers of Ethiopia") symbolized the moral and political extremes to which Christianity could extend. Ancient Christian authors used Egyptians/Egypt, Ethiopians/Ethiopia, Blacks/blackness as polemical devices to respond to their intra-Christian opponents. At times, their ethno-political rhetorics also responded to external persecutors of their communities. By focusing on the ethno-political rhetorics related to Egyptians/ Egypt, Ethiopians/Ethiopia, and Blacks/blackness, I was able to isolate some of the major threats that challenged the early Christians and, more importantly, I was able to explore how Christian writers developed discourses that were derived from assumptions about ethnic difference and color symbolism operative within the ancient world.

Symbolic Blackness systematically documents how New Testament texts, apocryphal writings, patristic commentaries and homilies, theological treatises, and monastic teachings included ethno-political rhetorics about Egyptians/Egypt, Ethiopians/ Ethiopia, and Blacks/blackness as forms of political invective and cultural signifiers that addressed the problems of sinful beliefs and practices, sexual temptations and bodily passions, and heretical movements within early Christianity. Such discourses developed within early Christian writings as a response to the political situations, social conditions, ethnic differentiations, and gender orientations of the ancient world. Early Christians developed discursive strategies based on the othering of marginal ethnic groups—and, as I will discuss later, marginal ethnic women. While most of the texts selected for analysis are from extra-canonical sources, the implications for New Testament studies are significant.

First of all, this study challenges the general reader and interpreter of ancient Christian sources to consider the power of symbolic language related to color and ethnicity in shaping attitudes, values, worldviews, and practices of early Christians. This symbolic language is steeped in ethnic and color perceptions within the ancient world. Although scholars have generated many studies on rhetorical criticism and the New Testament, none to my knowledge have undertaken a study examining how Egyptians/Egypt, Ethiopians/Ethiopia, and Blacks/blackness have functioned as polemical devices within ancient Christian writings. Second, this study identifies and classifies some of the diverse representations of these ethnic groups, geographical locations, and color symbols through a *historical* taxonomy of ethno-political rhetorics. Now, for the first time, it is possible for scholars from various disciplines to compare and analyze the ubiquitous usages of these ethnic groups in ancient Greco-Roman writings. Third, this study proposes a theoretical framework for understanding the intersection of ethnicity, gender, and politics within ancient Christian writings.

From the evidence examined in this book, it is clear that assumptions about ethnic and color differences in antiquity influenced the way Christians shaped their stories about the theological, ecclesiological, and political developments within early Christian communities. As a result, Egyptians, Ethiopians, Blacks, and blackness invariably became associated with the threats and dangers that could potentially destroy the development of a certain "orthodox" brand of Christianity. In spite of the basic contention that Christianity was to extend to all peoples—even the remote Ethiopians—from the review of the different types of ethno-political rhetorics expressed in early Christian writings it appears that certain groups of Christians were marginalized and rendered invisible and silent. They were in the words of Jerome "blackened by their sins."[23]

These groups of Christians were not solely or simply marginalized because of the color of their skin or their ethnic identity, although on the surface the narratives sound as if this is the case. In other words, the ethno-political rhetorics, which include both pejorative and idealized representations of Egyptians, Ethiopians, Blacks, and blackness, are not necessarily directed against these actual ethnic groups, but rather they refer to those within different Christian communities who were falling away from the "orthodox" teachings and moral standards that were being established by the dominant voices of the respective communities. Ethnic and color difference came to symbolize certain theological, ideological, and even political intra-Christian controversies and challenges. Ethno-political rhetorics in early Christian writings call attention to the power of ethnic and color-coded symbolic language to create the religious, political, social, and cultural reality of ancient Christians.[24]

Of particular significance for feminist and womanist scholarship is the section of the book in which I analyze the depictions of Ethiopian or Black women in monastic writings, mainly from Upper Egypt, from the fourth through sixth centuries CE.[25] Ethiopian women in the stories of the desert fathers and other monastic writers symbolized the multifaceted threats that both gender and ethnic difference represented to those constructing the religious and ideological boundaries within late antique Christian literature. These women symbolized the dangerous sexual vices that challenged the piety and self-control of the monks. While the references to Ethiopian women in monastic literature are sparse compared to the references to women in general, I argue that their use by Christian authors of late antiquity was part of a sophisticated discursive strategy of vituperation—a type of ethno-political rhetoric—that signaled a complex web of power relationships among a circle of Christians in Roman Egypt. Ethiopian women functioned in the texts as markers of difference that symbolized the acceptable standards, social roles, and norms within certain types of monastic culture.

Evidence about the real experiences of Ethiopian women within the desert is virtually nonexistent. Clearly, these women must have been considered attractive and seductive to the monks. This extreme attraction, coupled with a sense of danger and fear, led to the striking ambivalence that is evident throughout the stories that depict Ethiopian women. The ethno-political rhetorics about Ethiopian women are focused on physical descriptions that effectively turned the presumably attractive and sexually seductive Ethiopian woman into a repugnant and invisible object. I will now turn to one example from the Sayings of the Desert Fathers to emphasize this point.

Anonymous, *Apophthegmata Patrum* 5.5

The *Sayings of the Desert Fathers* (*Apophthegmata Patrum*) is one of the most significant texts from late antique monastic culture that provides evidence for the threats symbolized by the Ethiopian woman. The Latin version of the *Sayings*, known as the *Verba Seniorum*, includes the following story under the rubric of fornication. In this text, the devil appears as an ugly, evil-smelling *Ethiopian woman* who distracts a young monk from his ascetic life:

> A certain man went into the desert of Scete to become a monk. He took with him his infant son. When the boy became a young man the demons [*daemones*] began to wage their war against him. The young man told his father, "I must go into the world because I am not able to bear the *desire of lust* [*carnales concupiscentias*]." His father consoled him. But the young man said, "I do not want to bear this burden any longer. Allow me to return to the world." His father said to him, "listen to me, son, take with you forty days worth of bread and work one more time and spend forty days in the inner desert." The young man obeyed his father and lived a life of seclusion and hard work in the remote desert. Twenty days passed when, suddenly, he saw the work of the devil appear before him, "and it stood before him in the form of an *Ethiopian woman [mulier Aethiopissa], smelly and disgusting in appearance [fetida et turpis aspectu],* so much so that he could not bear her smell. She then said to him, 'I am she who appears sweet [*dulcis*] in the hearts of men, but because of your obedience and your labor, God does not permit me to seduce you, but I have let you know my *foul odor [fetorem].*' " [The Ethiopian woman] left him, and he thanked God. He came to his father and said: "Father, I no longer wish to go into the world, for I have seen the work of the *devil [diabolos]* and have smelled her foul odor." The young man's father replied, "if you had stayed another forty days deep in the desert, you would have seen a greater vision."[26]

The Ethiopian woman in this *Saying* is used as a polemical device to indicate the threat of fornication. The author highlights this threat by drawing attention to the woman's smelly and disgusting appearance. The desert fathers often linked fornication to foul odors or stench, but when the foul odor is associated with an ethnic other, such as the Ethiopian woman, I would argue that the authors are trying to communicate the importance of maintaining boundaries or keeping a safe distance from those who would present a threat within the desert.[27]

Long before the monastic material from the fourth and fifth centuries, we find evidence of ethno-political rhetorics about Ethiopian women in apocryphal literature from the second century. For example, in the *Acts of Peter*, Marcellus recounts to Peter a dream that featured an Ethiopian woman who was described in the following manner:

> a most evil-looking woman, who looked like an Ethiopian (*Ethiopissimam*), not an Egyptian (*Aegyptiam*), but was all black (*nigram*), clothed in filthy rags. She was dancing with an iron collar about her neck and chains on her hands and feet.

Marcellus continued his narration of the dream by demonizing the Ethiopian woman:

> "When you [Peter] saw her you said aloud to me, 'Marcellus, the whole power of Simon and of his god is this dancer; take off her head!' But I said to you 'Brother Peter, I am

a senator of noble family, and I have never stained my hands, nor killed even a sparrow at any time.' And when you heard this you began to cry out even louder, 'Come, our true sword, Jesus Christ, and do not only cut off the head of this demon (*daemonis*), but cut in pieces all her limbs in the sight of all these whom I have approved in thy service.' And immediately a man who looked like yourself, Peter, with sword in hand, cut her all to pieces, so that I gazed upon you both, both on you and on the one who was cutting up the demon, whose likeness caused me great amazement. And now I have awakened and told you these signs of Christ (*signa Christi*)." And when Peter heard this he was the more encouraged, because Marcellus had seen these things; for the Lord is always careful for his own. So cheered (*gratulatus*) and refreshed (*recreates*) by these words he stood up to go to the forum. (*Acts of Peter* 22)[28]

The Ethiopian woman in the *Acts of Peter*, as well as the numerous Ethiopian women who appear throughout monastic writings challenged me to clarify the theoretical foundation of the "womanist biblical hermeneutic" I so anxiously wanted to apply to these texts. Womanist interpreters focus upon the experiences of Black women and use these experiences as central in the articulation and interrogation of ancient biblical writings. Womanist biblical scholars in particular examine how Black (namely, African American) women interpret and utilize biblical texts for their survival and explore the intersection of race, class, and gender in biblical writings.

New Testament scholar Clarice J. Martin claims that a womanist Biblical hermeneutic "has a four-fold interest where gender, race, class, and language issues are all at the forefront of translation and interpretation."[29] Womanist biblical interpreters take seriously the sociohistorical context in which Black women have found themselves as moral agents. They identify ways in which the plurality of experiences of African American women is both consistent with and in contradistinction to mainstream American sociopolitical and theological culture.[30]

Hebrew Bible scholar Renita J. Weems further develops a womanist hermeneutic by describing the reading strategies of African American women. In her essay entitled "Reading Her Way Through the Struggle," Weems points out that "what is considered the appropriate way to read or interpret literature is dependent upon what the dominant reading conventions are at any given time within a culture. . . . One's sociocultural and economic context exerts enormous influence upon not only how one reads, but what one reads, why one reads, and [for] what one reads."[31] Thus, Weems encourages African American women to "use whatever means necessary to recover the voice of the oppressed within biblical texts."[32] In her article entitled "The Hebrew Women are Not Like the Egyptian Women," Weems explores how gender, race, and ideology work together in the text about the Egyptian midwives in Exodus 1:8–22.[33] Here, she identifies an "ideology of difference" operating in this text through which the narrator exploits the assumptions about the differences between Egyptians and Hebrews.

As much as these scholars and others who have contributed to womanist biblical criticism have enabled me to claim a sense of authority as a biblical interpreter, to integrate some of the concerns of African American women in my interpretation of biblical texts, and to understand the ideological import of gender, race, and class in biblical writings and their interpretive traditions, I still find womanist biblical hermeneutics theoretically limited by its heavy emphasis on canonical texts, its sweeping assumptions about the reading strategies of Black women and their participation in the "black church tradition," and its lack of engagement with postcolonial and transnational readings of ancient Christian writings. Although I appealed to womanist hermeneutics in my study of Egyptians, Ethiopians, Blacks, and blackness,[34] I must admit that this interpretive lens did not enable me to critically assess the discursive role of the Ethiopian or Black woman in early Christian writings, nor did it enable me to articulate a *global* understanding of such readings not only for African American women, but also for women of African descent living here in the United States and throughout the world.

The Black woman *from the South*—that is, the Ethiopian woman—presents a wonderful challenge for feminist and womanist biblical critics who are grappling with strategies and methods for responding to the global transformations in Christianity. My own research about the Ethiopian or Black woman shifts the focus to the marginalized and silent position she has maintained throughout European and North American interpretations of early Christian writings. As cultural critic bell hooks has noted, the margin has an important place in the discourse of blackness. hooks describes the margin as "a central location for the production of counterhegemonic discourse" and "*a site one stays in, clings to even, because it nourishes one's capacity to resist.*"[35] hooks asserts that blackness derives strength from its position at the margins and thus marginality actually becomes a space of power.

It is in this vein that I want to suggest that "blackness" in early Christian writings, and stories about "Black women" in particular, problematizes the entire endeavor of global feminist New Testament interpretation, especially for European and North American feminist and womanist scholars engaged in this level of interpretation. "Blackness" presents a gripping challenge to my European and U.S. colleagues who have been on the forefront of defining the discourses and conceptual paradigms for understanding feminist and womanist biblical criticism. With the radical global and Christian transformations taking place in this nation and beyond, it is imperative that feminist and womanist biblical critics rearticulate the meaning of global feminist New Testament interpretation by listening more carefully to the marginal voices of women *from the South* embedded in early Christian writings.

The Challenge of "Blackness" for Understanding the Future of Global Feminist New Testament Studies

For the remainder of this chapter I want to explore some of the challenges of "blackness" for understanding the future of global feminist New Testament studies. I will do this by (1) examining the challenges posed to future generations of feminist and womanist scholars; (2) assessing the challenges for those seeking to envision the future direction of African American Christianity; and (3) sharing some of the theoretical challenges I have encountered in my efforts to formulate a hermeneutical perspective in light of the transnational considerations that influence New Testament studies.

Challenges Facing Future Generations of Feminist and Womanist Biblical Scholars

As noted earlier, "blackness" calls attention to the intra-Christian controversies and threats that challenge certain "orthodox" views of early Christianity. Despite a trenchant critique of patriarchy, imaginative and illuminative reconstructions of early Christianity, and good intentions, feminist biblical critics are still by and large locked into a Western paradigm that accepts uncritically the imperialist framework of most New Testament scholarship. In order to become more relevant for the lives of women, feminist critics must continue to heed the voices of biblical interpreters from the global South.

Scholars such as Musa Dube have already begun to lodge a potent challenge to feminist critics to consider the Western imperialist rhetoric that still permeates most feminist critiques of the Bible.[36] In *Postcolonial Feminist Interpretation of the Bible*, Dube challenges biblical interpreters to critique the imperialist agenda inscribed in biblical writings. She especially critiques Schüssler Fiorenza's reconstruction of early Christian origins, which downplays the imperial setting of the Greco-Roman world and ignores the ideological strategies of imperialism inscribed in New Testament texts.[37] Her incisive critique of Western biblical scholarship (both White Western male and female readers) with respect to interpretations of the Canaanite woman in Matthew 15:21–28, as well as her inclusion of the reading strategies of African Independent Church (AIC) women from her own country, Botswana, render her postcolonial feminist critique extremely valuable.[38]

Feminist critics, therefore, are challenged to take into account the indigenous "feminist" approaches that are emerging throughout the world. Because of the many different understandings of "feminism," it is imperative that multiple perspectives are included, especially those from the global South, in conversations such as the one for which this chapter was written. For example, in one collection of essays dealing with women in sub-Saharan African nations, an "African-feminist approach," which differs radically from Western forms of feminism, is suggested:

> This newly emerging African-feminist approach has been the direct outcome of women's responses to political leaders who have attempted to partially manage recent crises by further limiting and exploiting women. . . . [African-feminism] has largely been shaped by African women's resistance to Western hegemony and its legacy within African culture.[39]

With respect to womanist scholars, it is imperative that we continue to define the meaning of womanist biblical hermeneutics. The works of Martin and Weems are important starting points, but they were intended to open the dialogue and outline the tasks that await future generations of biblical scholars. As noted earlier, some African women adhere to feminist criticism, while African American women tend to be far more cautious (even suspicious) of its relevance for Black women in the United States. Literary critic Clenora Hudson-Weems argues that Black women should move away from the term feminism altogether as this keeps White women at the center and invariably in power even in global discussions of Black women's concerns. She contends that "africana womanism" is a more apt description of Black diasporic feminism.[40]

Even Dube, who has clearly found some merit in feminist critiques of the Bible, challenges Schüssler Fiorenza's notion of the *ekklesia* of women as the hermeneutical center of feminist biblical interpretation. Although the *ekklesia* of women holds out hope to all feminists struggling for liberation, according to Dube, its imperialist discourse "undercuts its liberational intentions and alienates Two-Thirds World and non-Christian women—to the extent that the *ekklesia* of women is almost equivalent to the *ekklesia* of White, middle-class Christian feminists."[41]

This alienation of Two-Thirds World or non-Christian women is a serious critique in the face of the widespread global shifts articulated earlier in this chapter. Thus, another challenge that feminist scholars must consider as they rearticulate the meaning of global New Testament studies is the development of strategies for engaging the rich pluralist religious fabric of American society and the indigenous religious traditions throughout the global South in the task of biblical interpretation in a manner that moves beyond the binary pitfalls of Christian/non-Christian, Black/White, First World/Third World, and the like. We—that is European and North American scholars of the Bible interested in the global future of feminist New Testament interpretation—must begin to listen to the voices of those who adhere to "different" faiths, hail from "other" cultures, and live in "distant" lands as we reformulate the methodologies that might lead to a more representative form of global feminist biblical interpretation.

Diana Eck in her compelling analysis of pluralism in America indicates that the U.S. is becoming one of the most religiously diverse nations in the world.[42] Through a plethora of examples from years of fieldwork and research, she paints a picture of the religious landscape of America that includes Hindus, Sikhs, Buddhists, Muslims, Jews, and Christians for the purpose of envisioning "a new religious America" that is far more tolerant of difference and change. She ultimately hopes to inspire a greater awareness of some of the major religious traditions represented in America so that the stereotypes, violence, and marginalization that occur to "others" might be eradicated. She invites interested readers to find ways to build bridges among different communities of faith through collaborative projects and dialogue.

This type of dialogue is occurring on a local level in many places throughout the United States. The Fifth Annual Helen Barrett Montgomery Institute, "Women of Faith in the United States: A Dialogue about Diversity," held at Colgate Rochester Crozer Divinity School is a recent example.[43] With a primary focus on Jewish, Christian, and Islamic communities of faith, this conference sought to understand the ways in which women in these communities understand and express their faith. The conference was designed to examine ways in which women speak about God, how women are living amid and thinking about religious diversity, common experiences that make solidarity among women of faith amid diversity uniquely possible, and how women, through their articulation of and witness to their faith, are transforming their faith communities. Central to the success of this conference was the collaborative planning efforts of the women (both clergy and non-clergy, Christian and non-Christian, Black and White, urban and suburban, rich and poor) from the various faith traditions for the selection of the speakers and topics for the conference.

This enabled the participants—Jewish, Muslim, and Christian women—to learn from one another of the challenges, concerns, and victories of their respective faiths, scriptures, and traditions. Jewish, Islamic, and Christian scholars such as Jane Adler, Yvonne Yazbeek Haddad, Kwok Pui Lan, Mercy Oduyoye, and Jane I. Smith sat at the same table and discussed ideas about the interfaith diversity of women in the United States. Such a collaborative model might serve to break down the walls that continue to divide feminist and womanist biblical interpreters from the global North and global South.

Global feminist New Testament studies should empower women to forge strategic bonds with other women—not just with women who share their same demographic profile, but women of differing religious, ethnic, political, class, and geographical identities and locations. The point is to develop a type of "accessible" scholarship that might help women across the globe to struggle efficaciously against multiple systems of global oppression. That is, systems that keep women in subjugated positions in society and prohibit them from fighting oppressive political regimes or religious traditions.

Before sharing my personal theoretical challenges as I grapple with the future meaning of global New Testament studies, I want to discuss the future direction of African American Christianity in light of the Christian and global transformations evolving before our very eyes.

The Challenges for the Future Direction of African American Christianity

One of the chief challenges facing those seeking to envision the future direction of African American Christianit(ies) in the wake of expansive global and Christian transformations is the basic recognition that there are "varieties of African American religious experience." Anthony Pinn in his book bearing this title argues quite convincingly that it will become irresponsible of religious scholars—even "tragic"—to assume that Christianity is the only brand of religion for African Americans.[44] He states:

> It is my contention that African American religious experience extends beyond the formation and practice of black Christianity. That is to say, historically African Americans have participated in a variety of traditions, such as Yoruba religious practices, Voodoo, Islam, and humanism. . . . The narrow agenda and resource base of contemporary African American theological reflection troubles me because it limits itself to Christianity in ways that establish Christian doctrine and concerns as normative. It has considered the church its sole conversation partner.[45]

As more and more attention is directed toward the global South it will become imperative for biblical interpreters, who are seeking to elucidate a deeper understanding of the complexities of African American Christianity, to engage the religious traditions that are considered non-Christian and explore the possibilities for "extrachurch" conversations.[46]

My Personal Theoretical Challenges with Respect to the Global Future of Feminist New Testament Studies

My own theoretical challenges with respect to this important topic deal with the points that I raised at the beginning of this chapter, which include coming to terms with where I stand in the midst of all of the competing realities that inform my understanding of global feminist New Testament interpretation. Thus, my first theoretical challenge involves outlining the direction for my own brand of womanist biblical hermeneutics, which takes the transnational context in which I conduct my research much more seriously.

Sociologist and Black feminist critic Patricia Hill Collins argues that "placing African-American women's experiences in a transnational context simultaneously provides a new angle of vision on U.S. Black feminism as a social justice project and *decenters the White/Black binary that has long plagued U.S. feminism* [emphasis mine]."[47] She further states that focusing on a transnational context shifts the understanding of U.S. Black feminism from "being White feminism in black-face" to a more sustained focus on the common themes that U.S. Black feminists share with women of African descent throughout the world. Thus issues of great concern to U.S. Black women (including myself!)—such as "work and family, negative controlling images, struggles for self-definition in cultural contexts that deny Black women agency, sexual politics that make Black women vulnerable to sex work, rape, and media objectification, and understandings of motherwork within Black women's politics—find different meanings in a transnational context."[48] I am excited about the possibilities that exist for my future research projects in light of this additional hermeneutical perspective.

My second theoretical challenge involves refining my understanding of the definitions and assumptions related to globalization and global Christianity that are implicitly utilized throughout this chapter. In this regard, I need to clarify and even problematize the use of the term "global" that has been used to frame the conversations for this conference. According to Lamin Sanneh, global Christianity is the "faithful replication of Christian forms and patterns developed in Europe."[49] Global Christianity presumes an imperialist framework wherein global structures of power and economics are not critiqued or eradicated. Sanneh suggests that it is more appropriate to focus upon "world Christianity," which turns attention to the indigenous discovery of Christianity. He defines world Christianity as follows:

> "World Christianity" is the movement of Christianity as it takes form and shape in societies that previously were not Christian, societies that had no bureaucratic tradition with which to domesticate the gospel. In these societies Christianity was received and expressed through the cultures, customs, and traditions of the people affected. World Christianity is not one thing, but a variety of indigenous responses through more or less effective local idioms, but in any case without necessarily the European Enlightenment frame.[50]

This shift in perspective from a "global" to a "world(ly)" frame of reference might enable feminist and womanist New Testament critics to overcome the textual, ideological, and geopolitical biases that subtly influence our interpretations of scripture.

A third theoretical challenge has to do with my analysis of ethno-political rhetorics discussed earlier. My research actually left me with a number of unresolved questions about the symbolic representations of Ethiopian and Black women as well as the reconstructionist projects about women in early Christian communities that neglect to consider the possibility that Black women were part of the *ekklesia* of women. For the most part, feminist critics focus upon canonical sources. Had I done this, I would have missed the Ethiopian or Black women that are a very present part of early Christian discourses and traditions, and I would have missed the opportunity to refine my own understanding of feminist and womanist hermeneutics. Related to this is the fact that there are many sources *from the South*—both ancient and modern—that have not been included or deemed appropriate for the study of the New Testament. I hope to pluck away at this imbalance through my local scholarship that is becoming far more grounded in global concerns.

Conclusion: Conversations and Coalitions

When I think of the challenge of "blackness" for rearticulating the meaning of global feminist New Testament interpretation, I must admit that I find it hard to imagine feminist New Testament interpretation looking much different than it has in the past. Invariably, the conversations among feminists (presumably White Western feminists) remain defined by imperialist discourses, which tend to undermine the potential for strategic coalitions that go beyond narrow identity politics.[51] Although we have European and North American scholars leading the way—once again—for this series of conversations, I remain hopeful that in some way this tripartite conversation or dialogue among European, North American, Latin American, Caribbean, Asian, and African scholars might inspire us to stretch beyond the "pseudo-maternalism" that creeps into coalitions among First and Third World women.[52]

Though situated in this North American context, I view myself as a voice *from the South*, as one who, from my marginal perspective, can identify some challenges and possibilities for our dialogue. The challenge of "blackness" therefore is to focus upon the ambiguities, the problematics, the threats, even the *intra-feminist* controversies in new and imaginative ways so that future generations of biblical interpreters might come to a more complete understanding of the meanings, roles, and functions of *all* women discussed in early Christian writings.

Notes

1. See, e.g., Elisabeth Schüssler Fiorenza, *In Memory of Her: A Feminist Theological Reconstruction of Christian Origins* (New York: Crossroad, 1983); *Searching the Scriptures*, ed. E. Schüssler Fiorenza, 2 vols. (New York: Crossroad, 1993–1994); *Wisdom Ways: Introducing Feminist Biblical Interpretation* (Maryknoll: Orbis Books, 2001); and *Rhetoric and Ethic: The Politics of Biblical Studies* (Minneapolis: Fortress Press, 1999). Antoinette

Clark Wire, *The Corinthian Women Prophets: A Reconstruction through Paul's Rhetoric* (Minneapolis: Fortress, 1990); Mary Ann Tolbert, "Defining the Problem: The Bible and Feminist Hermeneutics," *Semeia* 28 (1983): 113–126; Amy-Jill Levine, ed., *"Women Like This": New Perspectives on Jewish Women in the Greco-Roman World* (Atlanta: Scholars Press, 1991).

2. See, e.g., Elizabeth A. Castelli, "Heteroglossia, Hermeneutics, and History: A Review Essay of Recent Feminist Studies of Early Christianity," *Journal of Feminist Studies in Religion* 10 (1994): 73–98; "Paul on Women & Gender," in *Women and Christian Origins*, ed. Ross Shepard Kraemer and Mary Rose D'Angelo (New York: Oxford University Press, 1999) 221–235, and *Women, Gender, Religion: A Reader*, ed. Elizabeth A. Castelli (New York: Palgrave, 2001).

3. See, e.g., the writings of Clarice J. Martin and Renita J. Weems, which will be discussed later in this chapter.

4. The Program of Women & Gender Studies was established at Colgate Rochester Crozer Divinity School in 1990. All M.Div. students are required to take at least one Women & Gender Studies course.

5. For a critical discussion about the "matrix of domination" and the challenges facing Black feminist critics, see Patricia Hill Collins, "U.S. Black Feminism in Transnational Context," in *Black Feminist Thought: Knowledge, Consciousness, and the Politics of Empowerment*, Second Edition (New York and London: Routledge, 2000) 227–250.

6. Lamin Sanneh, *Whose Religion is Christianity? The Gospel beyond the West* (Grand Rapids: Eerdmams Publishing Co., 2003) 10. I will discuss Sanneh's work later in this chapter.

7. Gay L. Byron, *Symbolic Blackness and Ethnic Difference in Early Christian Literature* (London and New York: Routledge, 2002).

8. Philip Jenkins, *The Next Christendom: The Coming of Global Christianity* (New York: Oxford University Press, 2002) 2.

9. Jenkins, *Next Christendom*, 3.

10. Jenkins, *Next Christendom*, 83–85.

11. Jenkins, *Next Christendom*, 83. For more recent projections, see Todd M. Johnson and Sun Young Chung, "Tracking Global Christianity's Statistical Centre of Gravity, AD 33–AD 2100," *International Review of Mission* 93/369 (2004): 166–181.

12. Jenkins, *Next Christendom*, 84.

13. Jenkins, *Next Christendom*, 99–103.

14. See Lynette Clemetson, "Hispanics Now Largest Minority, Census Shows," *New York Times*, January 22, 2003, Al, column 4.

15. See William A. Henry III, "Beyond the Melting Pot," *Time Magazine* (cover page title *America's Changing Colors: What will the U.S. be like when Whites are no longer the majority?* April 9, 1990): 28–31.

16. See Jenkins, *Next Christendom*, 131–132, 217–220. Jenkins only briefly addresses this topic by highlighting some sweeping generalizations about what he considers are the major interpretive differences between biblical readers in the global North and the global South.

17. Jenkins, *Next Christendom*, 217.

18. Sanneh, *Gospel beyond the West*, 13–93.

19. Sanneh, *Gospel beyond the West*, 55.

20. Byron, *Symbolic Blackness*, 55–58.

21. Byron, *Symbolic Blackness*, 2.

22. Byron, *Symbolic Blackness*, 2.

23. Jerome, *Homily 18 on Psalm*, 86.

24. Byron, *Symbolic Blackness*, 12–13.

25. Byron, *Symbolic Blackness*, 77–82, 94–103.

26. PL 73, col. 879. See Byron, *Symbolic Blackness*, 97–98. See also Benedicta Ward, *The Wisdom of the Desert Fathers: The Apophthegmata Patrum—The Anonymous Series* (Oxford: SLG Press, 1975), 10.

27. Byron, *Symbolic Blackness*, 99–100.

28. *Acts of Peter* 22. Text in *Acta Apostolorum Apocrypha*, ed. Ricardus A. Lipsius and Maximilianus Bonnet, 2 vols. (Hildesheim: Georg Olms, 1959) 1: 69–70. English translation in *New Testament Apocrypha*, trans. E. Hennecke, 2 vols. (London: Lutterworth, 1992) 2: 305. See also Byron, *Symbolic Blackness*, 17.

29. Clarice J. Martin, "Womanist Interpretation of the New Testament," *Journal of Feminist Studies in Religion* 6/2 (1990): 41–61, quotation at 42.

30. Clarice J. Martin, "The *Hausafeln* (Household Codes) in African American Biblical Interpretation," in *Stony the Road We Trod*, ed. Cain Hope Felder (Minneapolis: Fortress, 1991) 228.

31. Renita J. Weems, "Reading Her Way Through the Struggle: African American Women and the Bible," in Hope Felder, *Stony the Road We Trod*, 57–77, quotation at 64.

32. Weems, "Reading Her Way," in Hope Felder, *Stony the Road*, 73.

33. Renita J. Weems, "The Hebrew Women Are Not Like the Egyptian Women: The Ideology of Race, Gender and Sexual Reproduction in Exodus 1," *Semeia* 59 (1992): 25–34.

34. Byron, *Symbolic Blackness*, 25–27.

35. See bell hooks, "Marginality as a Site of Resistance," in *Out There: Marginalization and Contemporary Cultures*, ed. Russell Ferguson et al. (New York: Museum of Contemporary Art, 1990) 341–343, quotation at 341(emphasis mine).

36. See Musa W. Dube, *Postcolonial Feminist Interpretation of the Bible* (St. Louis: Chalice Press, 2000).

37. Dube, *Feminist Interpretation*, 27–30.

38. For her discussion of the reading strategies of AIC women, see Dube, *Feminist Interpretation*, 39–42, 184–195. Dube is not alone in her critique of imperialist readings of New Testament texts. See, e.g., Richard A. Horsley, *Jesus and Empire: The Kingdom of God and the New World Disorder* (Minneapolis: Fortress Press, 2003).

39. Gwendolyn Mikell, ed., *African Feminism: The Politics of Survival in Sub-Saharan Africa* (Philadelphia: University of Pennsylvania Press, 1997) 3–4.

40. See Clenora Hudson-Weems, "Africana Womanism," in *Sisterhood, Feminisms, and Power: From Africa to the Diaspora*, ed. Obioma Nnaemeka (Trenton: Africa World Press, 1998) 149–162, cited in Collins, "U.S. Black Feminism," 236. For a full analysis of Africana Womanism, see Hudson-Weems, *Africana Womanist Literary Theory* (Trenton: Africa World Press, 2004).

41. Dube, *Feminist Interpretation*, 31.

42. Diana L. Eck, *A New Religious America: How a "Christian Country" Has Become the World's Most Religiously Diverse Nation* (San Francisco: HarperCollins, 2001). For a different perspective on this topic, see William R. Hutchison, *Religious Pluralism in America: The Contentious History of a Founding Ideal* (New Haven: Yale University Press, 2003). I am grateful to my colleague Melanie A. May who recommended Hutchison's book and offered several critical suggestions for improving this chapter.

43. The Dialogue was held from November 4 to 6, 1999.

44. Anthony B. Pinn, *Varieties of African American Religious Experience* (Minneapolis: Fortress Press, 1998).

45. Pinn, *Varieties*, 1.

46. Pinn, *Varieties*, 6–7.

47. Collins, "U.S. Black Feminism," 233.

48. Collins, "U.S. Black Feminism," 233.

49. Sanneh, *Gospel beyond the West*, 22.

50. Sanneh, *Gospel beyond the West*, 22. For a comprehensive account of Christianity as a world religion, see Dale T. Irvin and Scott W. Sunquist, *History of the World Christian Movement*, Vol. 1: Earliest Christianity to 1453 (Maryknoll: Orbis Books, 2001).

51. Dube, *Feminist Interpretations*, 26; Collins, 234. See also, Oyeronke Oyewumi, *The Invention of Women: Making African Sense of Western Gender Discourse* (Minneapolis: University of Minnesota Press, 1997).

52. See Collins, "U.S. Black Feminism," 234–235, for a discussion about pseudo-maternalism among White Western feminists and Third World women.

Chapter 6

Response: Paradoxes of Positionality as the Key to Feminist New Testament Studies

Karen Jo Torjesen

For I am the first and the last.
I am the honored and the scorned.
I am the whore and the holy.
I am the wife and the virgin.
I am <the mother> and the daughter.
I am the limbs of my mother.
I am a barren woman
who has many children.
I have had many weddings
and have taken no husband.

For I am knowledge and ignorance.
I am shy and bold.
I am shameless, I am ashamed.
I am tough and I am terror.
I am war and peace.

I, I am sinless,
And the root of sin comes from me.
I am desire outwardly,
And within me is self-control.
I am hearing adequate for everyone
And speaking that cannot be repressed.
I cannot talk or speak,
And plentiful are my words.

Hear me in gentleness,
And learn from me in roughness.

I am the woman crying out,
And I am cast upon the face of the earth.

I am present in all fears,
and I am strength in agitation.
I am a weak woman,
and I am well in a pleasant locale.
I am foolish and I am wise.

Why have you hated me in your counsels?
Because I shall be silent among the silent
and I shall appear and speak? [16]
Why have you hated me, you Greeks?
Because I am a barbarian among barbarians?
For I am the wisdom [of the] Greeks
and the knowledge of the barbarians.
I am the judgment of Greeks and barbarians.
I am the one whose image is great in Egypt
and who has no image among the barbarians.

"Thunder, Perfect Mind," *Nag Hammadi Codices* VI, 2. Translation © Marvin W.
Meyer. *For private use only, quoted with permission of the translator*

This anonymous writing from early Christianity, now referred to as "Thunder,
Perfect Mind," probably comes from an African woman who uses the paradoxes of
her multiple gendered and political identities to create a discourse on the nature of
ultimate realities.

The organizers of this conference have created a powerful congruence between the
questions they have posed and the scholars they have invited. The questions—about
the impact on New Testament studies of globalization as a political phenomena and
the shift of Christianity to the Southern hemisphere as a social phenomena—are
illustrated in the lives and experiences of the presenters. We are positioned to learn a
great deal both from the presentations and the presenters.

The paradoxes of positionality, when fully explored, will establish the context for
feminist New Testament studies. In Gay Byron's opening statements she introduces
us to the questions and to the paradoxes of her own positionality—a woman bearing
the authority of a faith community, and a New Testament scholar critiquing the
foundational texts of her tradition; an African American clergy woman in a predominantly white denomination, a scholar trained in Euro-American feminist critiques
whose loyalties lie with two-thirds of the world; a citizen of America deeply troubled
by its growing structures of colonialism.

She, like our author of "Thunder, Perfect Mind" uses the paradoxes of her positionality to point to the wider cultures to which feminist New Testament studies must
address themselves. In her identities as cleric and scholar, she inhabits two distinct cultural communities. I choose to designate these professional identities as cultural because

they require participating in a distinctive "nomos"—the Greek term used to denote the distinctive values, norms, customs, and traditions that regulate the life of a social group.

New Testament studies must pay attention to differing strategies, methodologies, and interests as they function in these two distinct cultures. In the academy, the power of knowledge is understood as its study, appropriation, and production; while within the church the power of knowledge is measured in its appropriation and incorporation into a social context.

Gay Byron's position as African American clergywoman in a predominantly white denomination highlights both the paradox of ethnic identity and dominant culture and the paradox of local cultures and nationalities.

It is precisely Gay Byron's position as an African American within American culture that points up several generative paradoxes. Her religious identity is located in a distinctive ethnic community, one that results from a creative, vital synthesis of African and American cultures. An appreciation for the dynamics of cultural hybridity and its reshaping of religious traditions will be critical for future feminist New Testament studies.

As a descendant of an African diaspora she is aware of the influence of African traditional religions on African American Christianity. Early Christianity as well was shaped by the traditional religions of the Mediterranean, African among them. Knowledge of that influence has been repressed historically by a methodical polemic against "paganism." Despite Christianity's overtly expressed hostility, there has been and continues to be a fascinating and dynamic relationship between Christianity and traditional religions. Through giving serious attention to the historical and contemporary relationships between Christianity and traditional religions, feminist New Testament studies is in a position to make connections with feminists in Africa and Latin America who are drawing on the presence of traditional religions to shape feminist discourses.

As an African American, Gay Byron's hyphenated identity straddles the relationships between nations and continents, between the colonizer and the colonized. It is the paradox of her positionality that gives her the critical insight into the "the matrix of domination" that eludes most of the white feminist scholarship. Perhaps the most difficult task facing feminist New Testament scholarship is that of coming to terms with the positionality of the oppressor, the colonizer, and learning to see how that skews the hermeneutical field. In this context, I am writing specifically of American feminists whose own cultural formation occurs within a society that has exercised cultural dominance in a variety of forms in Latin America, Asia, and the Middle East. Just as African American feminist and womanist scholars have urged white feminists to pay closer attention to the social construction of whiteness and the privilege that it invisibly confers, so American engagement with global New Testament scholarship will require that we give attention to ways in which the power relations between colonizer and the colonized are ignored or obscured by the hermeneutical methodologies most often taught in the academy. It will be the hermeneutical task of the North American feminist to "see ourselves as others see us." Future feminist New Testament scholarship will benefit from serious engagement with postcolonial theory.

The paradox of positionality is that not only do we speak and think and write from particular positions, but also that the phenomena that we study (Christianity, New Testament interpretation, feminism) itself exist only in particularized forms. We are learning a hermeneutics of suspicion about totalizing discourses. "World Religions" evolve a universalizing strategy through which their claims to universal, transcultural validity are created by suppressing their cultural embeddedness and particularities. Cultural particularities are either assimilated and universalized, or demonized and suppressed. In their self-representations they are dislocated and abstracted from the cultural contexts in which they were formed and reformed and formed again. It is precisely to these particular cultural contexts that we must return for a global approach to feminist New Testament studies.

How do we privilege cultural particularity? In what ways can local and regional cultures become a matrix for feminist New Testament studies? What would it mean for feminist New Testament studies to insist on the importance of local and regional cultures for the hermeneutical project? I would first like to answer the question historically, following the lead of Gay Byron's expansion of our "canon" to include the literature of early Christianity. Let me start by saying these are the writers among whom I am most at home. My own scholarly migrations began with the study of the theology of early Christianity and my research focused on the exegetical practices of the day. I began my career as a student of Patristics, the fathers of the church, and fully assimilated their universalizing discourses, heretical constructions of the "other," and the creation of the category of "pagan." After years of engagement with feminist scholarship and the critical questions honed in that community, I have returned to the study of early Christianity with new eyes and new questions.

The Roman empire, which functions symbolically as the ancestor of Western cultural hegemony, in fact, operated like a military dictatorship. Cultural assimilation was minimal and the kingdoms and territories annexed maintained to a large extent their own customs, traditions, languages, social and political institutions. Christianity throughout this period of empire was forged in regional and ethnic cultures as multiple local theological, liturgical, and exegetical traditions. Furthermore, these local and regional theologies were also shaped by the rivalries between ethnic groups and the relentless competition between regional and imperial interests. Christians who created theologies within the matrix of their own cultural context and in rivalry with other contexts found language and meanings within scripture that they believed justified extending their cultural vision. In doing so they created their own exegetical traditions and hermeneutical practices that articulated a distinctive cultural vision.

Latin Christianity with its highly centralized organizational structure positioned itself as the authoritative voice of Christianity, an attitude that Western Christianity has inherited and extended. However, since antiquity, these regional Christianities have survived and thrived, just beyond the boundaries of the world of Western Christianity. In Africa, Egyptian and Ethiopian Christian communities trace their origins back to the first century, see themselves as independent Christian churches, and celebrate their unique versions of Christianity as a treasured cultural heritage. In western Asia, Byzantine, Syriac, and Arabic Christianities have also formed distinctive theologies, liturgies, and exegetical traditions. There is a vast body of literature available for the study of how these communities appropriated and transformed scriptural meanings. Commentaries, homilies, florilegia, and *questiones* have been preserved in these language traditions and offer new opportunities for scholars. The possibilities of feminist analysis have been barely touched and would be quite fruitful. We should also remember the entire theological and literary production of these Christianities was created by "persons of color."

Let us return to the most important challenge of Gay Byron's work, "The Challenge of Blackness," in early Christian writings. By identifying these deeply troubling stories about "black" women in early Christian writings as a discursive strategy, Gay Byron situates this punishing rhetoric in a larger sociopolitical context. In her "taxonomy of ethno-political rhetoric" she shows how—whatever the social relations were between Egypt, Ethiopia, and Greco-Roman Christianity—a set of derogatory meanings have been imposed on "blackness," which gets carried forward in the tradition as a powerful symbolic cipher of sinfulness, lust, and sexuality.

In response to Gay Byron's challenge, future feminist New Testament scholarship will need to be alert to the derogatory references to blackness that occur throughout the entire theological tradition in the discourse of sin, sexuality, and the heretical "other." Just as feminist scholarship has exposed and subverted the derogatory use of femaleness in the discourse on sin, sexuality, and the heretical "other," we will need to take a similar tack with respect to the issue of "blackness" and to Ethiopian and Egyptian ethnicity.

Feminist scholarship has begun the work of decentering the narrative perspective by critiquing the deployment of the category of generic femaleness and by subverting the category of generic femaleness by excavating the lives of historical women. Does Gay Byron's call for "transnational readings" also direct us to explore the ancient roles of Egyptian and Ethiopian kingdoms as rivals to a fledgling Roman empire? Do the modern notions of Egypt and Ethiopia become important for our reflections?

There is also important diversity work for the historian of religions. There are regional Christianities—Egyptian, Ethiopian, Syrian, Arabic, and Greek—beyond the boundaries of Latin or Western Christianities. The religious pluralism within Christianity could be an important resource for decentralizing the Western exegetical tradition. There are new sources to be found in the history of exegesis and the history of reception of biblical texts in these diverse communities who have created meanings for their particular cultural context through the interpretation of scriptural texts. These other exegetical traditions could well be the subject of the "rhetoric and ethics of inquiry and transformation." The fact that all of us are members of a global society requires us to move beyond both our national identities and our cultural identities. The demands of this new global citizenship will transform feminist exegesis and teach us to approach sacred texts with the consciousness that the cultural and regional diversity of readers will discover and create multiple new meanings on the surfaces of once familiar texts.

Chapter 7

Reflections on Conversation One
Sonya Gravlee, Erin Jacklin, and Prinny Stephens

Part One of the Tripartite Conversation on the Global Future of feminist New Testament studies highlights a number of tensions in feminist New Testament studies in North America and Europe today. These areas include the struggle between the universal and the particular, the primacy of written text versus cultural milieu, and the place of feminist critique in religious studies. Presenters Elisabeth Schüssler Fiorenza, Elizabeth Castelli, and Gay Byron—as well as respondents Sheila Briggs and Karen Torjesen—each address these areas of tension. In the conference's inaugural paper, Schüssler Fiorenza provides a useful metaphor to discuss the field of Feminist New Testament Studies (FNTS): the "social quilt." If imagined as an intricate and vivid patchwork design, this "social quilt" allows space for multiple voices of biblical interpreters from diverse global perspectives. Patches of different colors, shapes, and sizes work together to create something both useful and aesthetic. The "social quilt" called FNTS implies a whole that is more than the sum of its parts.

Likewise, the three presenters in the conversation and their respondents all bring to FNTS different positionalities and raise diverse issues, yet their conversation taken as a whole poses important questions about the "global future" of FNTS. As Castelli notes, envisioning such a reality demands that the framing of the conversation about FNTS be questioned at the outset, as she demonstrates by problematizing the title of this conference and the goals it seems to espouse.

Included in the fabric of the "social quilt" of FNTS is the tension between the universal and the particular, a struggle most clearly depicted in Schüssler Fiorenza's body of work. In *Jesus: Miriam's Child, Sophia's Prophet* she declares,

> If feminist theologies relinquish the claim that their critiques and insights have universal validity, they are in danger of feeding into postcolonial attempts of crisis management that operate through the particularization, fragmentation, and regionalization of the disenfranchised and oppressed.

While the desire to critique oppressive power structures in order to change them (and one assumes, change them for the better) is understandable, it is also problematic. In her work, Schüssler Fiorenza calls for an ethic of scholarship, an ethic that moves toward justice, liberty, and hope. Though such an ethic may be deeply needed and valuable, the other participants question the assumptions of universality underlying Schüssler Fiorenza's bold call for change. Isolating and defining the idea of "justice," for instance, raises many questions: justice for whom, at whose expense, and by what standard? Should justice be rooted in a Christian ethic or in an ideal of justice that transcends all religious barriers? As a whole, however, the conference did call for the pursuit of justice, hope, and liberty in biblical interpretation, with both contemporary and ancient mis/uses of the Bible cited as evidence of the necessity of some kind of guiding ethic lest the Bible continue to be used as a tool of domination by the ruling elite.

Byron demonstrates the necessity for FNTS to problematize assumptions. Her critique of the white, Western feminist biblical critics focuses primarily on the blindness of such critics to their own entrapment by imperialist structures. For instance, she cites third-conversation presenter Musa Dube's criticism of reconstructions of early Christianity that neglect the impact of the Greco-Roman political, social, and cultural structure upon those early Christian origins. This neglect translates into the contemporary scene as the "universal" that Schüssler Fiorenza desires, which reflects assumptions only possible for those who exercise some control in the power structures. As such, Schüssler Fiorenza's *ekklesia* of women may be read by many as an "*ekklesia* of White, middle-class, Christian feminists."

Castelli also addresses the problem of the imperialism inherent in a "Euro-American" feminist critique because "U.S. political, economic, and military power currently casts such a long shadow across the rest of the world." Keeping in mind the power base of the North in the world scene today, the truths, universals, assumptions, and so forth of feminist criticism need a dose of post-structuralist deconstruction as much as the hegemonic, positivist discourses they engage. Schüssler Fiorenza too quickly dismisses the merit of post-structuralist critique in her worthy quest for justice in a world of injustice. Nonelite " fe/male" voices, however, repeatedly ask, "Justice for whom?" As Briggs notes, in spite of the good intentions of elite feminists, one can no longer assume that what Euro-American feminists call "just" translates as justice for peoples in the rest of the world. Torjesen describes this as a "paradox of positionality" and calls for a feminist biblical criticism that addresses itself to ever-widening audiences.

This "paradox of positionality" also describes the second tension highlighted by the chapters in this section: the struggle between the primacy of the written text and the cultural milieu in which that text is interpreted. Again, Schüssler Fiorenza reveals the dangers inherent in a positivist reading of sacred texts. But while she reveals those dangers, she too, focuses primarily on those texts, searching for a "truth" or value within them that transcends the culture in which they were written, as well as the cultures in which they are read. As such, in spite of her challenge to positivist readings of scripture, she falls prey to the same trap.

On the other hand, Byron and Castelli—while concerned with the written text—critique it in terms of how it is used politically and religiously and socially in a cultural context. Byron examines a scene from the apocryphal *Acts of Peter* in antiquity; Castelli explores speeches from 2002 by U.S. President George W. Bush. Each looks at how leaders use "Christian" texts to support the eradication of the enemy. For Byron, Marcellus's story from the *Acts of Peter* illuminates the dangers inherent in blackness, femaleness, and ethnic-otherness for monks in the fourth and fifth century. To protect themselves from this danger, the "true sword, Jesus Christ . . ." is used to "cut off the head of this demon . . . [and to] cut in pieces all her limbs. . . . ," proving that "the Lord is always careful for his own." God's word, Jesus, functions as the protector of the chosen, as well as the destroyer of the enemy.

In like manner, Bush's rhetoric a year after September 11 appropriates allusions from Christian scriptures to assure the American people (and warn the world?) that the ideal of America will protect the chosen (Americans) and destroy the enemy (anyone who might harm America/ns). His rhetoric uses the Word of God rooted in biblical imagery: ". . . The ideal of America is the hope of all mankind. That hope drew millions to this harbor. That hope still lights our way. And the light shines in the darkness. And the darkness will not overcome it. May God bless America." The interplay of light and darkness used by Bush comes directly from the prologue to John's Gospel, as Castelli notes. Such use leads one to the assumption that the "ideal of America" equals "the light" in John's prologue so that the ideal of America comes directly from God for the enlightenment of all *man*kind. Earlier in the same speech, Bush clearly delineates the differences between (good) America and the (evil) enemy: America values every life; America's enemies value none. Hence, America is superior to her enemies, just as those who receive the light of God are superior to those who do not.

While a positivist approach to the biblical text will insist that the text does not speak to contemporary America, a global feminist critique cannot ignore and, in fact, must criticize the way the text is used to justify oppressive structures and behavior. Textual scholars may insist that the early church sought inclusiveness of difference; however, their assurances pale in comparison to the use of Christian scriptures to eradicate difference of any sort—regardless of the cultural setting.

As important as it is to study the written text, its use in cultural contexts cannot be ignored by FNTS. Through a kind of cultural criticism, the conference presenters and respondents look to the issues of the "Two-Thirds World," as well as to their own contexts. By deconstructing the language of the power-elites, they create space to facilitate alternative constructs. While framing the beginning of the conference with voices from the United States and Europe may seem problematic, such a beginning with the "powerful north" in the global conversation presses the issues of positionality and experiential voice. Positionality must be both confessed and addressed for the "social quilt" to have integrity. After all, finding ways to navigate the multiple positionalities in hopes of creating a unique and useful structure of the "social quilt" is in a sense the goal of this conference. The project of decentering biblical studies moves the power of biblical interpretation out into the margins of the global community. It is in the margins that one can achieve a "double-vision" capable of seeing the world both from within and without the systems of power and domination. This position can be one of great insight and is vital to any useful conversation about the global future of FNTS. Without such decentering of the power locales within biblical studies, the conversation inevitably remains rooted in its imperialistic, positivist trappings.

Finally, the first conversation of the conference questions the overall place of feminist criticism in religious (particularly biblical) studies: does it live at the margins, move to the center, decenter the whole endeavor, or find still other options? The two main power structures that currently legitimate and create biblical interpretation are the academy and faith communities. But can the goals of creating global feminist New Testament criticism successfully be reached exclusively within either or even both of these institutions? What about the insights and experiences of those outside of or on the margins of the academy and the faith communities? What space remains for those voices in biblical studies? What can be learned from the "black Ethiopian woman" or others proclaimed "enemy" or outside the power structures of orthodoxy? For FNTS to seriously consider its global future, it must continue to question the legitimating principles of knowledge and problematize the questions used to frame its critiques, recognizing that the power structures that lend legitimacy also inform scholarship. In other words, FNTS must consider that the questions asked determine the answers found. Therefore, FNTS must continue to question the questions, seeking space for new areas of conversation.

So while the struggle continues between the universal and the particular, and between the importance of the written text versus its interpretation and use in a cultural context, the struggle consists of more than those simplistic oppositions. For instance, the struggle of feminists to create a more just world is admirable and even noble; however, it cannot be accomplished by retreating to a white, Western, elitist particularity that has been proclaimed a universal truth or value or standard by which all efforts can and should be judged. Similarly, study of the biblical texts themselves raises hopes for a faith and a tradition based on justice; however, the use of those same texts to justify oppressive structures and practices cannot be ignored in any serious examination of sacred Christian texts. In order to examine these texts seriously and thoughtfully, it is imperative that feminist scholars address biblical, cultural and academic use and misuse of the biblical texts. Through identifying how the Bible is used and misused in faith communities around the globe, FNTS may be better able to fashion a "social quilt" that is truly reflective of different perspectives, experiences, and modes of religious expression. What is required for a global feminist study of the New Testament is a space where a multiplicity of voices are raised, experiences are valued, and truths are revealed in hopes of understanding not only the texts but also ourselves and one another better.

Conversation Two: Asia and Latin America

Chapter 8

My Journey as a Latin American Feminist New Testament Scholar

Aída Besançon Spencer

When I finished graduate school, I was trying to find a job in New Jersey and I went to an organization that I had heard was looking for a Hispanic person to work with them. The Anglo administrator interviewing me, as he sat, indicated, after a few initial words, "You should consider working on a little accent and wearing a more typical Spanish dress—maybe that might help you get a job."

Similarly, when I told interested people that I was going to write about being a Latin American feminist, some in surprise blurted out—Are you Latin American?—and others—Are you a feminist? To be Latin American must you be a person of olive or creamy brown color with an accent? To be feminist must you appear masculine, have short-cropped hair and be angry? I am Latin American and a feminist and a Christian.

My Journey

I was born in Dominican Republic and spent my first ten formative years there. Each year I return to visit my family. According to Dominican law, I will always be a Dominican citizen. I am also American because of my Puerto Rican mother who is a U.S. citizen and culturally because I have lived in the United States since entering sixth grade. I am Latin-*American*, which is different from Latin only or American only. I am intercultural. My friend and former colleague Robert Pazmiño explains:

A person who is "Hispanic-North American" is conscious of being at a point represented by the position of the hyphen in that term, the position of navigating and balancing the convergence of two cultures which rotate in distinct orbits and require careful coordination and balance.[1]

He adds that Jesus of *Galilee* was in a similar position. Samuel Solivan observes: "When we Hispanics/Latinos visit Puerto Rico to see our families, we are told that we are not true *puertorriqueños*, while back home we are told that we should return to the island where we belong." "We are strangers" for "both sides of our North American Hispanic reality."[2] Normally, Latin Americans may be more like each other than they are like Hispanics brought up in a Hispanic country or like Anglo-Americans who have only been interested in their own perspectives on issues. Patty Lane explains: "Second generation Americans may share common experiences that more closely link them to each other than to a first generation person of their same cultural heritage." They have in common a "third culture by combining the parents' culture with the new culture."[3] To varying degrees, Latin Americans will have more problems with cultural and personal identity than pure Latinas/Latinos. For example, Daniel Rodríguez-Díaz agrees: "In the Latino communities, as in the African-American, Asian, and Native American, the matter of *identity* burns in the heart of all."[4]

I am also a feminist. Webster's *Dictionary* defines "feminism" as "(a) the theory that women should have political, economic, and social rights equal to those of men (b) the movement to win such rights for women."[5] I can't understand how any woman today could agree that women should have *less* than equal political, social, and economic rights than men! Being reared in my early elementary years in a mainline religious setting outside the United States in the Dominican Republic, I was never exposed to Protestant fundamentalism. I confirmed my early Christian education by personally trusting in Jesus to transform my life when I was in college. My Dutch father wanted me to be an ambassador; my Spanish mother wanted me to be a physician. The world was open before me. So I proceeded to become an ambassador for *God* and a physician of the *spirit*. I did not know any better!

When I finished college, I began working as a community organizer among Hispanics in Plainfield, New Jersey. The community organization wanted people who were bilingual and I wanted to use my intercultural background to help others succeed in mainstream Anglo culture. The Hispanics needed translation, employment, and other benefits so they could move from being lower to middle class. But I found that what I did was incomplete. What good would it do if I helped the poor economically and socially but not spiritually? I would be a partial help. That's when my husband-to-be, now the Rev. Dr. William David Spencer, told me about his Master of Divinity studies at Gordon-Conwell Theological Seminary in Philadelphia, and encouraged me to attend. So I asked him, "Do women go to seminary?" This was 1969. He answered enthusiastically, "yes!" because this evangelical school had at least one woman there studying. I joined with several others.

I originally planned to get a two-year Masters degree there and return to social work. When that campus closed, I switched to another seminary, a more liberal one, ironically, where a male student for the first time told me the Bible demands women are to be silent. I remember that moment and the person who said it as if it were yesterday. This was not, however, the policy of the school and my male New Testament professor encouraged me to continue. However, my female advisor did discourage me from learning Greek. I was too ignorant to complain, but my fiancé helped out again—offering to tutor me in Greek. Princeton Theological Seminary only had a two years' Masters in Christian Education and as I slowly came to know my interests (and I believe God's call on my life), I decided to switch to the three years' Master of Divinity program, which prepares students for full time ministry. Wouldn't it be great to be paid to tell people about Jesus, the one who transformed and is yet transforming my life? So I entered New Testament studies through a slight opening in the door, being tutored on the side in New Testament Greek and taking an entrance test.

After an extensive search through the Bible, the Mishnah and early church material, presented publicly in 1973 and published in 1974 as the article "Eve at Ephesus,"[6] I decided women could very much follow God's calling without a ceiling placed on our commitment, and I was ordained by the Presbyterian Church (PC) in 1973, within the first 100 women ordained by the PC(USA). If other women and men had not fought for the equal rights for women as elders (1930) and ministers (in 1956) in the PC, I could not have had this openly acknowledged position. When I finished seminary I worked at the Trenton State maximum security prison teaching English as a second language with the inmate Latin American population and then as a campus minister with Trenton State College, both in New Jersey, while keeping my ties with the inmates as a volunteer minister. I discovered that much of what I did as a minister was educational:

- I organized a worship service where I dealt with the difficult questions people asked of Christians.
- I wrote my first article, for the campus newspaper *Ultimme Umana/La Voz Oculta*, "Won't Get Fooled Again," explaining why I was a Christian *and* a Hispanic. I sent the same article to the inmate production *La Llave*, in a Spanish and English version *No te deje cojer de bobo.*[7]
- I organized classes on Christianity and Judaism taught by the college chaplains.

Thus, by observing my own practice I learned how God had given me teaching and organizational spiritual gifts. To test those spiritual gifts, my husband and I together went to Newark, New Jersey to teach the Bible at New York Theological Seminary. I loved teaching adult students who were preparing to minister and I loved studying the Bible (my literary and historical interests all came together and were helpful as I dwelled more and more on the riches of God's written revelation). After completing my Th.M. at Princeton Theological Seminary and Ph.D. at Southern Baptist Theological Seminary, I was called to teach at Gordon-Conwell Theological Seminary, where I have taught since 1982 both at its suburban and urban campuses.

Briefly, that's my journey as a Latin American feminist and New Testament scholar. Even as Esther learned that her background as a Jew would be helpful to other Jews in the midst of Persian political affairs (Esther 4:14), so too I learned that my background—totally out of my personal control—as a Latin American in the midst of Anglo-American academic affairs could not be ignored because it would still be helpful to other Latin Americans. We need more Latin American feminists in New Testament studies! Every person God has created, being transformed into Jesus' disciple, can add to a more wholistic perspective, representative of God's global transforming movement. God creates us and God can re-create us—both who we are as humans and who we are as Christians can be of benefit to the larger human and ecclesiastical body.

Four Comparable Latin American
and Feminist Perspectives

What are some of the unique, helpful perspectives of Latin Americans? How do these unique, helpful perspectives of Latin Americans intersect with comparable feminist themes? I would like to highlight four of these themes, compare them with four comparable feminist themes and finally conclude with four challenges for the future.

The first theme is God as stranger. Ada María Isasi-Díaz writes: "I am caught between two worlds, neither of which is fully mine, both of which are partially mine. . . . As a foreigner in an alien land, I have not inherited a garden from my mother but rather a bunch of cuttings. Beautiful but rootless flowering plants—that is my inheritance."[8] After extensive study of Hispanics in North America and Puerto Rico, Justo González concludes that:

> The mood and the basic imagery of Hispanics in this country are those of a people in exile. Many are exiles in the literal, everyday sense. For some reason, they have left their native lands and come to this land. Some are political exiles. . . . Others are economic refugees. . . . Others are "ideological refugees." The image projected by this country was such that they became convinced that the values of this society were better than those in their own native societies, and that therefore they would be more at home here. . . .
>
> Then there are many others who are not exiles in the sense that they left the land of their birth to come to this nation. They were born here. And so were their parents and grandparents. But they too are strangers in the deeper sense of living in a land not their own. Although they are U.S. citizens by birth, they are often seen and treated as less than full citizens, and therefore they are strangers living in a native land that remains foreign.[9]

Isasi-Díaz begins *En la Lucha/In the Struggle: A Hispanic Women's Liberation Theology* with a poem by New Yorker Lourdes Casal that declares she "will always remain a marginalized stranger" even when she returns to the city of her birth. The marginality is within.[10] Allan Figueroa Deck, too, describes Hispanics as "Strangers in Their Own Land and Church."[11] "A pilgrim people" is another image used for Hispanics. Hispanics in America, therefore, bring to worship "the painful experience of not quite belonging."[12]

The image of exile is a recurring theme in contemporary Hispanic American Christian literature. Fernando Segovia writes that "an experience of marginalization and oppression" is "the key to the liberating message of the Bible," and emphasizes "diaspora hermeneutics."[13] Isasi-Díaz entitles the conclusion of *Hispanic/Latino Theology* "Strangers No Longer" and describes Latino/Hispanic communities as "marginalized and oppressed people in the United States."[14]

To illustrate this truth biblically I anchored this anomie in the concept of God the stranger. As Jesus said, I was a stranger and you did or did not gather me in (you welcomed me or did not welcome me, you received or did not receive me as a guest) (Matthew 25:35,43), and, again, "The foxes have dens and the birds of the heaven places to encamp but the Heir of humanity does not have where he may lay down his head" (Luke 9:58).[15] Focusing on the theme of the stranger as a part of the redemptive community reminds the larger church of this biblical paradigm. It reminds us of the need for justice for the stranger. It reminds us of the God who is impartial:

> For the Lord your God is the one who is God of the gods and Lord of the lords, the Mighty, the Great, the Strong, and the Wonderful, who is not partial and does not take bribes, executing justice for the orphan and widow and loving every stranger, giving each one food and clothing. (Deuteronomy 10:17–18)

The church too may be called "strangers and sojourners" because it should not completely embrace the values of the world (1 Peter 2:11–12). And isn't it also true that sometimes women can still be strangers to political, economic, and social positions of power and influence?

Normally, feminists do not speak of themselves as "strangers," but they do speak of being "other."[16] One hopeful aspect of being the stranger or the "other" is to know that in due time things may change and one may be the agent of that change. To lift a weight one cannot stand squarely upon it, but must stand next to it. The marginalized stands next to a dominant culture and can find leverage to lift it to a higher plane. The stranger may be God's messenger. The one who is ignored and powerless may become elevated to a position of recognition and honor. Rosemary Radford Ruether summarizes: Jesus' story dramatizes that "those who are last in the present social order are the faithful ones who will be the first in the kingdom, the first to witness the resurrection and bear the good news to others."[17] Women such as Hannah and Mary eloquently voice this biblical theme of reversal of positions.[18] The lowly will become elevated, the high will be lowered in status and power when God's judgment arrives (Ezekiel 21:26; 17:24). Mary sang:

> My soul magnifies the Lord,
> and my spirit rejoices in God my Savior,
> for he has looked with favor on the lowliness of his servant, . . .
> [God] has brought down the powerful from their thrones,
> and lifted up the lowly;
> he has filled the hungry with good things,
> and sent the rich away empty (Luke 1:47–48, 52–53 New Revised Standard Version—henceforth NRSV).

Mary's reversal of positions is similar to Hannah's prayer:

> My heart rejoices in the Lord;
> in the Lord my horn is lifted high.
> My mouth boasts over my enemies,
> for I delight in your deliverance. . . .
> Do not keep talking so proudly
> or let your mouth speak such arrogance,
> for the Lord is a God who knows,
> and by him deeds are weighed.
> The bows of the warriors are broken,
> but those who stumbled are armed with strength.
> Those who were full hire themselves out for food,

but those who were hungry hunger no more.
She who was barren has borne seven children,
but she who has many sons pines away
(1 Samuel 2:1,3–5 New International Version henceforth NIV).

The strong and powerful and wealthy are contrasted with the weak and poor and hungry. Hannah and Mary were in very different contexts. Hannah was oppressed by the other wife, Peninnah, because Hannah had no children (1 Samuel 1:4–7). Mary and Hannah perceive life in terms of the incongruities that occur between appearances and reality. In this case, those who appear to be on top will be demoted to the bottom. Those who appear to be on the bottom will be elevated to the top. Jesus accentuates this theme of reversal of positions, for example, in the sermon on the plain:

Blessed are you who are poor,
for yours is the kingdom of God.
Blessed are you who are hungry now,
for you will be filled.
Blessed are you who weep now,
for you will laugh.
Blessed are you when people hate you, and when they exclude you, revile you, and defame you on account of the Son of Man. Rejoice in that day and leap for joy, for surely your reward is great in heaven; for that is what their ancestors did to the prophets.
But woe to you who are rich,
for you have received your consolation.
Woe to you who are full now,
for you will be hungry.
Woe to you who are laughing now,
for you will mourn and weep (Luke 6:20–25 NRSV).[19]

A number of feminists and Latin American scholars also note this "reversal of status," "social reversal," or "eschatological reversal."[20] The stranger too may be one of the lowly who will be elevated, as the psalmist sings:

The Lord lifts up those who are bowed down;
the Lord loves the righteous.
The Lord watches over the strangers;
he upholds the orphan and the widow,
but the way of the wicked he brings to ruin (Psalm 146:8–9 NRSV).

A second helpful perspective of Latin Americans is celebration or "la fiesta," the comestible experience or hospitality, family, generosity, and giving. Even in the midst of being a stranger, and being (or feeling) oppressed, one can celebrate. And who more than the stranger needs to be invited to the Messianic banquet? After collecting several essays from different Hispanic Christian perspectives (Catholic, Pentecostal, Methodist, and Baptist), Justo González summarizes that a key description of: "Latino worship is a fiesta. It is a celebration of the mighty deeds of God. It is a get-together of the family of God." He adds that "Our people need that sense of family in order to survive in an alien world; they need to celebrate God's future in the midst of an oppressive and alienating present."[21] Allan Figueroa Deck concurs: "Worship and prayer are concerned with the entire feast, the music, the party, the dance, and most certainly the food."[22]

This interest in hospitality goes even as far back as the Taino Indians. Christopher Columbus wrote in his journal that he and the soldiers gave the Taino Indians:

> Some red caps and some glass beads. . . . At this they were greatly pleased and became so entirely our friends that it was a wonder to see. Afterwards they came swimming to the ships' boats, where we were, and brought us parrots and cotton threads in balls, and spears and many other things, and we exchanged for them other things, such as small glass beads and hawks' bells, which we gave to them. In fact, they took all and gave all, such as they had, with good will.[23]

González explains that the most significant Latino *fiestas* are connected with a sense of family.[24] Jill Martínez agrees: "Understanding the community as family has been a way of life for the Hispanic."[25] Therefore, González in his "Hispanic Creed" can say:

> We believe in the Reign of God—the day of the Great Fiesta
> when all creation's colors will form a harmonious rainbow,
> when all peoples will join in joyful banquet,
> when all tongues of the universe will sing the same song.[26]

Focusing on the theme of the *fiesta* as part of the ministry of the redemptive community reminds the larger church of this biblical paradigm. It reminds us of the need to have experiences where we enrich one another through the commonplace practice of eating together. How many meals did the Gospels record where Jesus sat down for dinner! Jesus on the cross defined a Christian family as not being based on blood lines when he told Mary that John was her son and when he told John that Mary was his mother (John 19:26–27). She was not to be maintained by her relatives according to rabbinic tradition/law (*Mishnah* Ketub. 4:6). Like little children, Jesus' true disciples are to be childlike—innocent of evil, unconditionally loving, and fully ready to enjoy good fellowship (e.g., Luke 18:17). The Lord's Supper is after all a *supper* that looks forward to the messianic banquet: "I tell you, many will come from east and west and will eat with Abraham and Isaac and Jacob in the kingdom of heaven" (Matthew 8:11, NRSV; see also, Matthew 26:29; Isaiah 25:6; Luke 13:29). As God has been generous with us, we too are to be generous with others. Jesus' disciples are to welcome hospitality. Jesus said, "You received without payment; give without payment" (Matthew 10:8; Luke 6:30; 10:7–8).

Feminists in South and North America also highlight this theme of community. For example, the second common characteristic of the final statement of female Liberation Theologians in Argentina (in 1985) describes women's theological activity to be "Communitarian and relational, bringing together a vast number of experiences that express something lived and felt, in such a way that people recognize themselves in this reflection and feel challenged by it."[27] Community (*la comunidad* or *el pueblo*), according to Isasi-Díaz and Yolanda Tarango, is also:

> One of the most pervasive themes in Hispanic culture. . . . *La comunidad* is the immediate reality within which Hispanics find their personal identities and function. In concrete terms, the sense of community revolves around the *familia* (family) and the *barrio, barriada* (neighborhood).[28]

Isasi-Díaz defines herself as "a *mujerista*," "a Hispanic woman who struggles to liberate herself not as an individual but as a member of a Hispanic community."[29] Eldin Villafañe credits the Hispanic emphasis on community to the Amerindian. "Person-in-Community" defines the reality of the Hispanic.[30] Elisabeth Schüssler Fiorenza confirms that "a feminist Christian spirituality is rooted in the *ekklēsia* of women as the 'body of Christ.' "[31] María Pilar Aquino agrees that an emphasis on community unites Latin Americans and feminists but Latin Americans generally focus on mixed gender while feminists focus more on women-only groups.[32]

  A third helpful perspective of Latin Americans is an emphasis on the arts. After all, the *fiesta* includes singing and dancing. But the arts are more than celebration. They are an aspect of creative communication. They remind us that God is a Creator, thus we too should create.[33] Ana María Pineda explains that mural art and poetry are an important part of "the diverse Hispanic/Latino neighborhoods in the United States."[34] Whenever we would worship at the Presbyterian Church in Caparra Heights, when we lived in Puerto Rico, the church poet would always write and recite a poem for every special occasion. Ana María Díaz-Stevens observes that "Christian values related to the individual, family or community are exalted in [Hispanic] music and poetry."[35] Samuel Solivan points out how Hispanic Pentecostals have restored traditional musical genres of Puerto Rico (*la danza, el bolero, el le-lo-lai*) to their expressions of praise and worship.[36] Isasi-Díaz and Tarango include "liturgizing" as one of the four steps in the process used in doing Hispanic Women's Liberation Theology: "Liturgy has to do with the aesthetic side of our humanity . . . Hispanic culture, and Hispanic people in general" may be called "highly aesthetic. The Hispanic culture places a high value on feelings and emotions and the consequent ease of showing and sharing them."[37] Jill Martínez explains why the arts are important to Hispanics: "The Hispanic understands and lives the deep emotions of the heart."[38]

  Villafañe credits the Hispanic "passion" or "fervor" to the heritage from Spain, and "a style of life based on a network of personal relationships.[39] Ana María Bidegain credits the Hispanic interest in the arts to Amerindian artistic material creativity, "still very much alive today, in our practices and customs, in our culinary arts, in our handicraft."[40] Indians preserved their history in the form of pictures. Ana María Pineda posits that the oral tradition of the Mesoamerican world "lives on in narrative and symbolic form and is used today by teachers, artists, poets, and theologians in U.S. Hispanic communities."[41] Jeanette Rodríguez reminds us of pre-Columbian Nahuatt philosophical thought, "flower and song" (*flor y canto*). "Flower and song" connotes a "complementary union of two words or symbols to express one meaning . . . Truth intuited through poetry derives from a particular kind of knowledge that is the consequence of being in touch with one's own inner experience as lived out communally."[42] Villafañe also credits the African heritage as significant in Spanish "music, dance, folklore, religion, and language." For Hispanics, *la fiesta* connotes celebration, affirming that life is a gift and worth living.[43]

Tereza Cavalcanti reminds us of the close association of women prophets with "songs and hymns": Miriam, along with other women, plays the tambourine and dances (Exodus 15:20–21), Deborah sings a song of victory (Judges 5:1–31), and Hannah and Mary pray messianic songs of hope for the poor (1 Samuel 2:1–10; Luke 1:46–55).[44]

Artistic expression is an important aspect of feminist practice. For example, Fiorenza's hermeneutics of "creative actualization" utilizes "artistic imagination— literary creativity, music, and dance."[45] Therefore, the arts are a place in our paradigm where Latin Americans and feminists intersect quite closely.

A fourth helpful perspective of Latin Americans relates to time. Latin Americans are a bridge between cultures of time and event. Is time primarily a commodity to be spent, one to which people accommodate as we do to less or more money or is it primarily a process or a container for events of quality to be accommodated to people?[46] "Redeeming the time" for many Anglo Americans means "*arriving* on time" (so as not to *waste* a moment of it). But the Letter to the Ephesians is not talking about arriving exactly on time (Ephesians 5:16). As a matter of fact, the ancient Jews had no minute or second hands to their sun clocks, water-clocks, or rooster crowings. They were attentive to months, seven days, and hours but not minutes and seconds.[47] Rather, Paul's metaphor has to do with living as wise persons who understand and do God's will (Ephesians 5:15–17), that is, occupying the space of our times with furthering positive relationships with God our Creator and our peers. Unlike some *fiestas*, a wise use of time does *not* include over-indulgence of intoxicating substances (5:18). Nevertheless, for the Latino culture, using time to be more person-oriented is very important.

In addition, many Hispanics, especially devout Hispanics, are sympathetic to God's sovereignty over life happenings that then results in a more relaxed sense of timelines—*Si Dios quiere*. The New Testament agrees: "You ought to say, 'If the Lord might will, then we will live and we will do this or that'" (James 4:15). "If the Lord wills" is a necessary attachment to any Spanish plan. For most American Christians, attaching "if the Lord wills" to one's plans are a sign of lack of commitment, lack of planned effort, that is, being a slackard. Yet, for James it is a reminder of one's humble existence: "What is your life? For you are a mist for a little while appearing and then vanishing." (James 4:14). God is sovereign.

Villafañe concludes: "The Hispanic American is a 'homo religiosus.' There is no area of life, no matter how trivial, that is not 'transmuted' by the religious sentiment."[48] Ana María Díaz-Stevens also highlights how vernacular and oral Spanish tradition is "replete with references to God and divine intervention."[49] *Mañana*, according to González, is "a time of a new reality. . . . The world will not always be as it is. . . . God who created the world in the first place is about to do a new thing . . . For Hispanics, the church is a pilgrim people, but a people whose pilgrimage is no uncertain wandering. It is a pilgrimage to a *mañana* made possible by the death and resurrection of Jesus Christ, made present by the Spirit, and made certain by the power and the promise of none other than God Almighty."[50] González's view of time is reminiscent of the biblical reversal of positions.

Some feminists consider that women also have this more relaxed (or process) sense of time.[51] In my own experience, Anglo women compared to Anglo men may be more relationship- and process-oriented than task- or product-oriented, but I do not find the women necessarily more event oriented than men. However, a counterpart to being event- or process-oriented is an emphasis by both Anglo and Latin women on the importance of experience, especially the present. Experience helps in biblical interpretation and in interpretation of life. Honesty with oneself and others is the key. Consequently, God's nearness or immanence is often highlighted.[52]

For instance, Elisabeth Schüssler Fiorenza summarizes that "feminist biblical interpretation must place at the center of its attention everywoman's struggles to transform patriarchal structures."[53] Isasi-Díaz and Tarango credit the "feminist perspective" for bringing to "Hispanic Women's Liberation Theology the insistence on personal experience as the starting point in the process of liberation and, therefore, in the doing of theology."[54] Brazilian feminist Ivone Gebara agrees: "Feminist theological expression always starts from what has been lived, from what is experienced in the present."[55] María Pilar Aquino also sees an important feature of "Latina American feminist theology" as "the relevance and importance given to *daily life* . . . Daily life is where real transformations take place."[56] Isasi-Díaz explains that "the source of *mujerista* theology" is "the lived-experience of Hispanic women.". . . "In *mujerista* theology, lived-experience identifies those experiences in our lives about which we are intentional. It is the sum of our experience which we examine, reflect upon, deal with specifically."[57] Thus, she and Tarango conclude: "The method used by Hispanic Women's Liberation Theology is dialogic. Dialogue is a horizontal relationship that involves communication and intercommunication."[58]

Conclusion: The Ways These Themes Assist Transformation

How do these four similar themes assist our task in global Christian transformation as feminist New Testament scholars? To keep up the organization of four, let me conclude with four applications.

The Importance of God's Word

Many feminists, like many Latin Americans, are somewhat countercultural, like strangers in an alien environment. The danger though of being a stranger is having anomie, no law. That is why global Christian transformation done by feminists must be rooted in the Word, God's revelation. González agrees:

> When one is a member of a minority, and the entire establishment is trying to convince one that one is wrong, it is a necessity, for sheer psychological and political survival, to find an authority that goes beyond the hostile environment.[59]

Isasi-Díaz and Tarango explain that for Hispanic women, "Scripture and Christian tradition are not rejected but rather seen through the lens of Hispanic women's experience."[60] A 1986 conference of women theologians from the Third World in Mexico reaffirmed that "the Bible plays a vital role in the lives of women and in our struggle for liberation."[61] Rigoberta Menchú of Guatemala declared: "The Bible is our main weapon."[62] Toinette Eugene wrote: "Womanist theology relies on the Bible as a principal resource because of its vision and promise of a world where the humanity of everyone will be fully valued."[63] For me, feminism is an outgrowth of the Bible, not a competing authority.[64] Community helps one interpret, but it is not the ultimate authority. Relying on the Bible for one's rich insights gives one the freedom to learn from a variety of cultures. That is the thesis of *The Global God*, which I edited. What insights into God's nature does your cultural background provide and what does it miss?

Maintain Comestible Collective Experiences

Academia has historically been an individual, single, serious pursuit. A lot of this perspective that infiltrates academia similarly pervades the corporate world. In contrast, as feminists become more mainstream they need to make a place for emphasis on celebration, the family, the arts, and hospitality. Creativity is not "frivolous," neither is hospitality. I appreciated Scripps College for including my husband in their welcome. The means is as important as the ends. Anorexia is a serious concern for young women today. Loneliness is a serious concern for all North Americans.[65] In contrast, as global women we should be emphasizing the comestible collective experience as a potential means of God's grace.

Unite Justice for Women with Justice for Others

Justice for women needs to be related, as it often has been, to justice for others.[66] In the United States concern to speak out against slavery led women to seek the right to vote.[67] So too today, no ethnic group can be *reduced* to feminist concerns, yet, we all need one another mutually to enrich and encourage one another and to join in similar pursuits. Isasi-Díaz also reminds us that for herself and for many Hispanics personal liberation is not contrasted with structural change. Justice has to do not only with personal conduct but also the way social institutions are organized.[68] As Cesar Chavez said when he was asked what he wanted the church to do, "We ask for its presence with us, beside us, as Christ among us."[69]

Importance of Humility and God's Sovereignty

Sometimes considering oneself to be oppressed can lead to a type of reverse superiority: I, in my oppression, because I am oppressed, am made superior to you, my oppressor, in every way. Rather, we need to remember both that God is near but also that God alone is sovereign. We are all humble, fallen human beings who can easily move from being the oppressed to the oppressor. Therefore, we need to rely on God as we venture out into future global transformation. Only God can be impartial enough to avenge (Romans 12:17–19).

When I was young, in Santo Domingo, I used to step out onto our second story balcony. As I stood there at the edge of the wall, I could almost touch the orange Flamboyan trees that reached out to me. Their branches formed a canvas over the yard. And when I felt the gentle tradewinds, I felt enticed to float out with arms outstretched over the orange blossoms to look out over the garden, if only I could. Now the Spirit of God can help us, while standing at our perspective, to take that larger view, that more godly perspective, of the world around us.

Yes, I am Latin American. I am also a woman. What helps me sift through both perspectives is relying on God's revelation, enlightened by the Spirit, transformed by the Savior.

Notes

1. Robert W. Pazmiño, "Double Dutch: Reflections of an Hispanic North American on Multicultural Religious Education," *Voces: Voices from the Hispanic Church*, ed. Justo L. González (Nashville: Abingdon, 1992) 137.

2. Samuel Solivan, "Sources of a Hispanic/Latino American Theology: A Pentecostal Perspective," *Hispanic/Latino Theology: Challenge and Promise*, ed. Ada María Isasi-Díaz and Fernando F. Segovia (Minneapolis: Fortress, 1996) 137.

3. Patty Lane, *A Beginner's Guide to Crossing Cultures: Making Friends in a Multi-Cultural World* (Downers Grove: InterVarsity, 2002) 23.

4. Daniel R. Rodríguez-Díaz, "Hidden Stories," in *Hidden Stories: Unveiling the History of the Latino Church*, ed. David R. Rodríguez-Díaz and David Cortés-Fuentes (Decatur: A.E.T.H., 1994) 3.

5. Noah Webster, *Webster's New Universal Unabridged Dictionary*, 2nd ed. (Cleveland: Dorset and Baker, 1979) 674. Elisabeth Schüssler Fiorenza also defines "feminism" as "a women's liberation movement for social and ecclesiastical change" in *Bread Not Stone: The Challenge of Feminist Biblical Interpretation* (Boston: Beacon, 1984) 5. María Pilar Aquino voices similar concerns, "The Collective 'Dis-covery' of Our Own Power: Latina American Feminist Theology," in Isasi-Díaz and Segovia, ed., *Latino Theology*, 252.

6. Aída Besançon Spencer, "Eve at Ephesus: Should Women Be Ordained as Pastors according to the First Letter of Timothy 2:11–15?" *Journal of the Evangelical Theological Society* 17 (Fall 1974): 215–222. This article was adapted as a chapter in *Beyond the Curse: Women Called to Ministry* (Peabody: Hendrickson, 1985).

7. "Won't Get Fooled Again," *Ultimme Umana/La Voz Oculta* 2:3 (December 7, 1973): 3; "No te deje cojer de bobo," *La Llave* Trenton State Prison News VII: 1 (Enero 1974): 11–14.

8. Ada María Isasi-Díaz, "A Hispanic Garden in a Foreign Land," in *Inheriting Our Mother's Gardens: Feminist Theology in Third World Perspective*, ed. Letty M. Russell *et al.* (Philadelphia: Westminster, 1988) 92.

9. Justo L. González, *The Theological Education of Hispanics* (New York: Fund for Theological Education, 1988) 33–34. See also his *Mañana: Christian Theology From a Hispanic Perspective* (Nashville: Abingdon, 1990) 41–42.

10. Ada María Isasi-Díaz, *En la Lucha/In the Struggle: A Hispanic Women's Liberation Theology* (Minneapolis: Fortress, 1993) vii.

11. Allan Figueroa Deck, "At the Crossroads: North American and Hispanic," *We Are a People!: Initiative in Hispanic Theology*, ed. Roberto S. Goizueta (Minneapolis: Fortress, 1992) 3.

12. Justo González, "Hispanic Worship: An Introduction," *¡Alabadle!: Hispanic Christian Worship*, ed. Justo L. González (Nashville: Abingdon, 1996) 19. See also Orlando E. Costas, *Christ Outside the Gate: A New Place of Salvation* (MaryKnoll: Orbis, 1982).

13. Fernando F. Segovia, "Toward Intercultural Criticism: A Reading Strategy from the Diaspora," *Reading from This Place*, ed. Fernando F. Segovia and Mary Ann Tolbert (Minneapolis: Fortress, 1995) 2, 308, 319, 322. See also "In the World but Not of It: Exile as Locus for a Theology of the Diaspora," in Isasi-Díaz and Segovia, ed., *Latino Theology*, 199.

14. Isasi-Díaz, "Strangers No Longer," in Isasi-Díaz and Segovia, ed., *Latino Theology*, 367.

15. See further, Aída Besançon Spencer, "Being a Stranger in a Time of Xenophobia," *Theology Today* 54:4 (January 1998): 464–469; "God the Stranger: An Intercultural Hispanic American Perspective," in *The Global God: Multicultural Evangelical Views of God*, ed. Aída Besançon Spencer and William David Spencer (Grand Rapids: Baker, 1998) ch. 4.

16. Fiorenza, *Bread Not Stone*, 5.

17. Rosemary Radford Ruether, "The Liberation of Christology from Patriarchy," *Feminist Theology: A Reader*, ed. Ann Loades (Louisville: Westminster, 1990) 142.

18. María Pilar Aquino states how important Mary is for Latin American women: "Mary is the paradigm of faith, prayer, and solidarity with all the oppressed and all women on earth." *Our Cry for Life: Feminist Theology from Latin America*, trans. Dinah Livingstone (MaryKnoll: Orbis, 1993) 159.

19. See also Luke 4:18; 7:22; 10:21; 14:11; 18:14; Matthew 23:1–12; 6:1,6; James 1:9–11; 2:1–4; 4:6,10.

20. Pedrito Maynard-Reid, *Poverty and Wealth in James* (MaryKnoll: Orbis, 1987) 38; Fiorenza, *In Memory of Her: A Feminist Theological Reconstruction of Christian Origins* (New York: Crossroad, 1983) 122; David M. Scholer, "The Magnificat (Luke 1:46–55): Reflections on its Hermeneutical History," in *Conflict and Context: Hermeneutics in the Americas*, ed. Mark Lau Branson and C. René Padilla (Grand Rapids: Eerdmans, 1986) 218; Richard Bauckham, *Gospel Women: Studies of the Named Women in the Gospels* (Grand Rapids: Eerdmans, 2002) 64, 275.

21. González, "Hispanic Worship," *¡Alabadle!*, 20, 22.

22. Deck, "Hispanic Catholic Prayer and Worship," *¡Alabadle!*, 39.

23. *The Journal of Christopher Columbus*, trans. Cecil Jane (London: Anthony Blond, 1945) 23.

24. González, *¡Alabadle!*, 22.

25. "In Search of an Inclusive Community," *Voces*, 62–63. Jill Martínez agrees that commitment to family is important to Latin American culture. *The Liberating Spirit: Toward an Hispanic American Pentecostal Social Ethic*, ed. Eldin Villafañe (Lanham: University Press of America, 1992) 13, 118.

26. González, *¡Alabadle!*, 115.

27. "Theology from the Perspective of Women," *Through Her Eyes: Women's Theology from Latin America*, ed. Elsa Tamez (New York: Orbis, 1989) 151.

28. Isasi-Díaz and Yolanda Tarango, *Hispanic Women: Prophetic Voice in the Church* (Minneapolis: Fortress, 1988) 6–7, 11. See also pp. 102, 104–109, 113.

29. Isasi-Díaz, *La Lucha*, 4.

30. Martinez, *Liberating Spirit*, 8, 115, 134.

31. Fiorenza, *Memory*, 350. See also Rosemary Skinner Keller and Rosemary Radford Ruether, eds., *In Our Own Voices: Four Centuries of American Women's Religious Writing* (San Fransisco: Harper, 1995) 59–60, 441–445; Tamez, *Eyes*, 47–48, 144; Isasi-Díaz, "The Task of Hispanic Women's Liberation Theology," *Feminist Theology from the Third*

World: A Reader, ed. Ursula King (New York: Orbis, 1994) 90–91; Díaz and Tarango, *Hispanic Women*, ix, xvii, xx, 6.

32. Aquino, *Cry*, 195. See also pp. 121, 169, 174. Stephanie Y. Mitchem also notes the importance of "personal truths and communal networking." *Introducing Womanist Theology* (MaryKnoll: Orbis, 2002) 23.

33. See Aída Besançon Spencer and others, *God through the Looking Glass: Glimpses from the Arts* (Grand Rapids: Baker, 1998) ch. 1.

34. Ana María Pineda, "The Oral Tradition of a People: *Forjadora de rostro y corazón*," in Isasi-Díaz and Segovia, eds., *Latino Theology*, 112–113, 115.

35. Ana María Díaz-Stevens, "In the Image and Likeness of God: Literature as Theological Reflection," in Isasi-Díaz and Segovia, ed., *Latino Theology*, 91.

36. Isasi-Díaz and Segovia, *Latino Theology*, 143.

37. Díaz and Tarango, *Hispanic Women*, 97, 100.

38. Martínez, *Voces*, 66.

39. Martínez, *Liberating Spirit*, 5–6, 112.

40. Ana María Bidegain, "Women and the Theology of Liberation," in Tamez, ed., *Eyes*, 17.

41. Isasi-Díaz and Segovia, *Latino Theology*, 105–108.

42. Jeanette Rodríguez, "Latina Activists: Toward an Inclusive Spirituality of Being in the World," *A Reader in Latina Feminist Theology: Religion and Justice*, ed. María Pilar Aquino, Daisy L. Machado, and Jeanette Rodríguez (Austin: University of Texas, 2002) 127.

43. Martínez, *Liberating Spirit*, 10, 15, 117. See also Raquel Gutiérrez-Archón, "An Introduction to Hispanic Hymnody," *¡Alabadle!*, 108–109.

44. "The Prophetic Ministry of Women in the Hebrew Bible," Tamez, ed., *Eyes*, 134–135.

45. Schüssler Fiorenza, *Bread*, 21.

46. Sherwood G. Lingenfelter and Marvin K. Mayers, *Ministering Cross-Culturally: An Incarnational Model for Personal Relationships* (Grand Rapids: Baker, 1986) 38–43.

47. Henri Daniel-Rops observes: "As to the division of the hour into minutes and seconds, known to the mathematics of Egypt and Chaldea from far earlier times, the ordinary people had either never heard of it, or took no notice if they had" *Daily Life in the Times of Jesus*, trans. P. O'Brian (New York: Hawthorn, 1962) 216.

48. Martínez, *Liberating Spirit*, 41.

49. Isasi-Díaz and Segovia, *Latino Theology*, 91–92.

50. González, *Mañana*, 164, 166–167.

51. For example, Anne Wilson Schaef, *Women's Reality: An Emerging Female System in White Male Society* (Minneapolis: Winston, 1985) 100–101, 108, 132.

52. Aída Besançon Spencer and others, *The Goddess Revival* (Grand Rapids: Baker, 1995) 133–140.

53. Fiorenza, *But She Said: Feminist Practices of Biblical Interpretation* (Boston: Beacon, 1992) 8.

54. Díaz and Tarango, *Hispanic Women*, xiii, xiv.

55. "Women Doing Theology in Latin America," Tamez, ed., *Eyes*, 45. See also pp. 50, 100–101.

56. Isasi-Díaz and Segovia, *Latino Theology*, 256.

57. Isasi-Díaz, *La Lucha*, 12, 173–176.

58. Isasi-Díaz and Tarango, *Hispanic Women*, 95. Ivone Gebara also concludes that women do theology starting with "shared experience," "sharing life," "from what is experienced in the present." "Women Doing Theology in Latin America," *Feminist Theology from the Third World*, 49, 55.

59. González, *Mañana*, 22. See also Solivan, "Pentecostal Perspective," in Isasi-Díaz and Segovia, ed., *Latino Theology*, 137, 143.

60. Isasi-Díaz and Tarango, *Hispanic Women*, xiv.

61. "Mexico Conference," *Theology from the Third World*, 38. The Bible "belongs to the people of God, the poor and oppressed, and therefore also to women." "Jesus' whole life speaks of a God who is not indifferent to the unjust misfortunes of the poor and oppressed." Aquino, *Cry*, 121, 147.

62. "The Bible and Self-Defense," *Theology from the Third World*, 186.

63. "Document," *Own Voices*, 447.

64. See Spencer, *Beyond the Curse*.

65. Aída Besançon Spencer and William David Spencer, *Joy through the Night: Biblical Resources for Suffering People* (Downers Grove: InterVarsity, 1994) 42.

66. Elsa Tamez agrees: "The goal of women's discourse is the search for justice." "Introduction: The Power of the Naked," *Eyes*, 6. See also *Latino Theology*, 253, 326. Ismael Garcia describes Hispanic inequality in social and cultural spheres, "A Theological-Ethical Analysis of Hispanic Struggles for Community Building in the United States," Isasi-Díaz and Segovia, ed., *Latino Theology*, 293–302.

67. Spencer, *The Goddess Revival*, 181.

68. Isasi-Díaz, *La Lucha*, 37, 41. See also Isasi-Díaz and Segovia, *Latino Theology*, 327–332.

69. Martínez, *Liberating Spirit*, 42.

Chapter 9

Response: A Framework Toward Solidarity and Justice

Elizabeth Conde-Frazier

I am responding from the perspective of a Latina feminist practical theologian. My approach to a response is not to deconstruct or dismantle the arguments of my colleague, exposing the gaps she may have left in the interest of a rigorous inquiry of truth. This places our engagement in a competitive win/lose situation where one's power is enhanced and the opponent's minimized. When this is the focus, it limits our possibilities of understanding to either/or dichotomies and polarizations. Instead, I believe that we can be just as academically rigorous if we co-construct with one another. This is to affirm the strong points of my colleague's presentation and to explore creative alternatives and ways of building upon these. The focus is placed on the inventive collaboration of a new vision. The emphasis is on joint participation, ownership, and decision making. It invites collaborative change rather than defensive behavior. Change requires relationship. By responding in this manner, we model the community building necessary for transformation. As Latinas, we honor our framework of community.

Besançon Spencer has presented to us four well-articulated points that characterize a Latin American feminist perspective in the United States. These are: God as stranger, fiesta or hospitality, the emphasis on the arts, and a new understanding of time. These, I believe, are congruent with some of the central points in Hispanic/Latina theology—both Catholic and Protestant. They have been offered as the gifts of the Latino community in the United States and as the construction of a praxis that leads to justice and the overcoming of oppression. More needs to be said about role reversal and how it is part of global Christian transformation. I begin this response by affirming the gifts of each one of the themes Besançon Spencer has explored by using them to construct a framework that might help us reach out across our differences; a beginning toward solidarity and justice. In this way I construct upon her foundations so that we might participate in creating a model of a community or collaborative effort.

Aída ends by asserting that the Bible, the revealed word, is central to us as Latina feminists in the United States. I agree and would add that in the Latina context, scripture is not read to conform to scientific truths, but because it mirrors our experience of the transcendent in the immanent or of our everyday experiences more commonly named *lo cotidiano*. Her own journey is an example of this. "*Lo cotidiano* allows the voiceless to tell their stories and to cry out to the heavens for justice and peace. It allows us to see how God's grace, justice, presence and love manifest themselves in everyday occurrences." When we come closer to our daily experiences we take them seriously and we read the biblical text so that we approach it with questions that come from our lives.[1] To be rooted in God's revelation is to come to an understanding of an enfleshed word.

It is the idea of this enfleshed word that I want to explore for a bit. I believe that in this millennium we have heard so many counterfeit words that it is characterized by a spiritual hunger so great that nothing less than an enfleshed or living word will have the power to bring the transformation of persons and communities. An enfleshed word is needed to release the word of God from the rhetoric in which we have imprisoned it both as scholars and as preachers.

Such a word begins with hospitality where the breath of God enters the word and enlivens it. Hospitality is a place where we are connected to one another, to God as the stranger and to each other as strangers. We make this initial connection with the hope that we might not remain as strangers to one another. It is a space that is safe, personal, and comfortable. It is a place of respect, acceptance, and friendship. It is a space where we offer each other a life-sustaining network of relations. Hospitality offers attentive listening and a mutual sharing of lives and life stories. It calls us to enlarge our hearts by offering the generosity of our time and personal resources.

Hospitality leads to encounter, where we connect with each other's lives more deeply. This is the redeeming or restorative word. Encounter is where we risk. It is a place for the collusion of two worlds—for the multiplicity of views. It is where various streams meet. It is the bringing together of a variety of sources that might not often be placed together. It is conjunctive places where we hold together what might be seen as opposite. This is the borderland. In these spaces hybrid significations are created requiring the practice of cultural translations and negotiations. It is here that we transcend dualistic modes of thinking of either/or and we come to understand how opposing ideas and knowledge can interact with each other. This place is called mestizo/a consciousness. Gloria Anzaldúa describes this term as a continual walking out of one culture and into another.[2] It is the transfer of the cultural and spiritual values of one group to another. It is straddling cultures. It is a consciousness of the struggle of the border.

Encounter is not only the place where we can find God but also where the "other" becomes neighbor. "Other," is a term that already expresses alienation but neighbor connects us with the duties and obligations of justice toward one another. In our encounters, the telling and listening of stories leads us to deeper relationship. To share the stories of our daily pain and hope is to make new meaning, which results in both deeper ethnic and Christian identities. Encounter is the place for shared experience. This means letting the silenced stories be heard. This exercise repositions our perspectives by allowing other perspectives to be heard first. It begins with the act of appreciation of our neighbor. It is the place for the emotions or feelings that you spoke of and their expression through the arts.

Feelings are important because they mediate relationships not only between persons but between subjects. Relationships between subjects are essential because when we separate everyday reality from theory we create possibilities for oppressing others. This is how unjust policies are fashioned. Feelings, on the other hand, ask why we do what we do and help us grasp how we learn behavior. Feelings lead to the knowledge of the *corazón*. *Corazón* or heart from the Latin American perspective is the "biological symbolic site of wisdom and knowledge. It is a metaphor for the whole of one's conscious, intelligent and free personality. The heart integrates and informs aspects of a person including the mind, will and emotions. This is close to the biblical understanding of heart which refers to the core and center of a person and the source of ultimate understanding."[3] Ultimately encounters cause us to ask, "What is missing from the reality of our lives? Whose voices are we not used to listening to?" This fosters a consciousness of the existence of those who are cast outside of our reality because of their sex, age, color, culture, religion, or class. It causes us to read the text from a neighbor consciousness. This knowledge leads us to compassion.

Compassion is the word as the movement of the womb of God. This word reveals God's intimate and powerful emotion for those who are plundered. Compassion comes from the words *cum patior* that mean to suffer with, to undergo with. It connotes solidarity. Compassion therefore works from a place of the strength of mutuality. It is participating in the sufferings of another from a strength born of awareness of shared weakness.[4] It is this sense of shared weakness that distinguishes compassion from pity. Pity takes more distance from the one suffering and sees her/him as weak or inferior. In pity, there is less participation in the suffering of the other person. Pity allows for a sense of superiority in relation to the one we pity. Compassion however, does not strip others of their dignity and power to act on their own behalf but partners with them, complementing their gifts and efforts toward humanization. In compassion as well as in celebration or *fiesta*, it is the togetherness that is empowering. We share our sufferings and our joys. Compassion is the process whereby we connect to others allowing them to pervade us until they become significant in our lives. As these connections take place we learn empathy. Empathy makes us aware of the world of our neighbor in the way that our neighbor experiences it. It can then take the form of doing justice. Compassion transforms us and our apathy turns to passion.

Passion is the witness of the living word. Latinas speak of the word as a guide to truth, a truth that takes form in us. This form is devotion. Devotion is the act or condition of giving oneself up for another person, purpose, or service. Devotion is a sacred and reverent expression of the totality of our person. The fruit of such worship is solidarity.[5]

The empathy stirs our souls and in this stirring the spirit impassions us. The passion comes from reflection upon and participation in the divine pathos where God is involved in the life of the community. Passion is intimacy and sympathy with God and with humanity. It is divine consciousness and neighbor consciousness engaging each other. This borderland existence enables us to be soaked in God's tears that locate places in need of the spirit's gift of wholeness, faith, hope, and love.

This empowers us to bring life-giving fruits and wisdom to the struggles of our communities. When our love for those who suffer, and the love of the heart of God for those who are in need of justice comes together in us, this now becomes a borderland between God and humanity; a prophetic space and a place of covenant with one another. Our initial connection with one another has now matured and it facilitates the building of *shalom* or *salaam* together.[6]

Salaam is the empowering word of God. *Salaam* is a concept that cannot be captured by a single word for it includes many dimensions: love, loyalty, truth, grace, salvation, justice, blessing, and righteousness. *Shalom* is a biblical vision of world history where all of creation is one, every creature in community with every other, living in harmony and security toward the joy and well-being of every other creature.

When speaking about time, Besançon Spencer spoke of Justo González's notion of *mañana* as a time of new reality where the world will not always be as it is. This is not only a promise of the hereafter. She has made it clear that it is made present by the Spirit in the here and now. I would suggest that the form it takes is the form of *salaam/shalom*.

Aída's themes allow us to see how there are two sacred texts; the biblical text and the text of the everyday, *lo cotidiano*, which is the testimony of where God has entered our lives. Both are an account of God's activity in the world. The two texts mutually release the power of God in each other. It is in this dialectic that the Spirit gives illumination and we are then able to appropriate these texts in ways that previous generations had not. Now they have come to us in a new fullness. This has implications for expanding and deepening the tradition in ways that make it relevant to new places and people. It also has implications for displacing the tradition and its full power from the hands of the powerful to the hands of the powerless. This is in keeping with Jesus' teaching, himself the word that became flesh. The incarnational power of this word subverts all other powers and is indeed transforming. Those suffering from an identity crisis due to power over and others from subjugation are transformed by humility. Humility is to know who we are and who we are not. This keeps us from usurping the place of another and brings equal value to both so that we can each be free to bring our gifts to bear toward the work of transformation.

Notes

1. See Elsa Tamez, "Women's Rereading of the Bible," in *Feminist Theology from the Third World: A Reader*, ed. Ursula King (London and Maryknoll, NY: SPCK and Orbis Books, 1994) 190–200.
2. Gloria Anzaldúa, *Borderlands/La Frontera: The New Mestizo* (San Francisco: Aunt Lute Books, 1999) 99.
3. Daniel G. Groody, *Border of Death, Valley of Life: An Immigrant Journey of Heart and Spirit* (Lanham, Maryland: Rowman & Littlefield, 2002) 8.
4. Matthew Fox, *A Spirituality Named Compassion and the Healing of the Global Village, Humpty Dumpty and Us* (Minneapolis: Winston Press, 1979) 2.
5. Solidarity is a term derived from the Latin *solidare*, which means to join together firmly. Michael A. Kelly traces the origin of the term. He shows how it is shaped by the

changes brought about by the Enlightenment and the Industrial and French Revolutions. Although the deconstruction of the old regimes brought a popular spirit of freedom, a vision was needed to carry out the systemic realization of equality. The French and the Germans made significant contributions to the exploration of such a vision and in so doing, gave shape to the theme of solidarity. Each attempt at the vision sought to give shape to a global basis of the common good or to the Christian idea of love realized in the sociopolitical sphere where people would live for others in the service of all humanity. Philosophical, sociological, and religious expressions were explored in this endeavor. For further discussion see Michael A. Kelly, "Solidarity: A Foundational Educational Concern," *Religious Education* 93 (Winter 1998): 44–64.

6. Originally, I used the Hebrew term *shalom*. During our conference, one of the participants suggested to me that given the Israeli nation's break with the principle of *shalom* through their present oppression of the Palestinians, that I might use the word *salaam*, which has the same meaning in the Arabic. In so doing, she pointed out, I might lift up the need that the Palestinians have for *salaam*. I am grateful to her insight and therefore honor it.

Chapter 10

Biblical Studies in the Twenty-First Century: A Japanese/Asian Feminist Glimpse

Hisako Kinukawa

If as feminist New Testament scholars we would like to say we are still eligible to keep doing our studies of the scriptures or keep talking about the good news of our God, what are some significant ideas that we are to keep in mind? And what practices are we urged to commit ourselves to? There must surely be multiple ways to answer these questions. In this chapter, I would like to focus my attention on the "perspectives." The perspectives I need to have when I do my studies and praxis as a Japanese, feminist, and Christian. Needless to say when I describe myself as Japanese, feminist, and Christian, those three identities are inseparably related to each other and intertwined with my involvements with Japan, Asia, and the world.

This chapter consists of two parts. First, on what I mean by perspectives, and second, on reading the scriptural texts using these perspectives. I talk about the perspectives in three ways: (1) a political perspective, (2) a perspective given by the peculiar position of Japan in Asia and the world, and (3) a perspective given as a woman in Asia. Then I read some scriptural texts using these perspectives.

Perspectives

Political Perspective

Looking at the recent situations of the conflicts and turbulence across the globe, especially the conflict between the United States and Iraq, the United States and North Korea, or the one between the Bush government and the UN, we cannot turn our

eyes and minds away from the reality of our life. The reality in which so many innocent lives are in danger. Not only in the possible wars, but also through poverty,
famine, fatal diseases; in these situations of violence so many lives are in danger.
Almost all the conflicts or strife we observe have their basic causes in the global web
of economic or political relations. Furthermore when we realize that the current
political, economic, or social conflicts are quite often related to the religious affiliations of the people or the ethnicities connected with religious affiliations, we are
made to know that the problems are more complicated and entangled.

On the one hand, we could watch a live telecast of the collapse of the World Trade
Center buildings on TV, but on the other we have very little vivid information on the
people—the civilians, women and children, and "Others," for example, living in Iraq
or North Korea. The reality of our life may be hidden, censored, undercut, or ignored
from the sight of other people. It is actually a great challenge for us to be able to gain
a fair understanding of what is actually happening on the globe. Though it is said that
the globe has become borderless in many ways, it is also true that higher borders have
been produced as the result of breaking down the traditional borders. I am most
concerned about the invisible walls that have been built among different religions or
between our minds. I am most worried about those invisible walls that are one of the
main causes for ethnic strife.

Since the writings recorded in the scriptures are contextual, they reflect the situations of the world of that day, the idiosyncrasies of the regions at the time of the writing, and they also reflect the community/ies of faith to which the writings were
related. If we want to converse with the texts in the scriptures, we are naturally
required to expose ourselves to the political, social, economic, cultural, and religious
situations of the ancient world where the writings were born. Furthermore, if we
want to read the texts in a way that they speak to our contemporary situations,
we need to know what kind of political, social, economic, cultural, and religious
situations we are currently facing.

Peculiar Position of Japan in Asia and the World

In Asia, Japan has been in a very peculiar position. It is said that most of the Asian
countries belong to the so-called Two-Thirds World or the Third World, but Japan
has been exempted from the group because of its economic power that connects it to
the First World. I notice advertisements and products of Sony, Toshiba, Canon, Seiko,
Panasonic, Toyota, Mitsubishi, Nissan, and so on wherever I travel.

I have experienced being excluded from an Asian women's group at a theological
meeting in Asia for this reason. Japan has never been invited to be a member of
EATWOT, the Ecumenical Association of Third World Theologians, which is a
powerful theological group worldwide. In addition, when the women's committee of
EATWOT held its dialogue with the women of the First World, none of us women
from Japan were invited, either. I ended up inviting myself to the meeting. Quite
often I have been embarrassed about not finding any place in the circle of the ecumenical or theological world.

I am currently participating in a ground-breaking project of producing a "Global Bible Commentary," in which a variety of theologians from different parts of the world are invited to write "contextual commentaries" on the books in the scriptures. Each book is interpreted by a person or two from a certain part of the world with the concrete interest of "What is the teaching of this text for believers in my specific social, economic, cultural, and religious context?" I quoted this phrase from the invitation letter written by the chief editor of the commentary, Dr. Daniel Patte. It is an exciting project in the sense that the commentary will be dealing with contemporary issues on our globe in relation to the messages written more than 2,000 years ago in their own political, social, economic, cultural, and religious contexts. It can also be said it is a very big challenge to revive the good news for this contemporary, confused, and complicated world. I am writing a commentary on the Gospel according to Mark from my context. I see the commentary as bearing an important mission for the global future of biblical studies in the twenty-first century.

Daniel Patte continues to write, "the commentators will include a majority of scholars from the two-thirds world [40], a few scholars from the first world (North-America and Europe) [15], and scholars from the second world (Eastern Europe, including from the Orthodox tradition) [5]." It is wonderful to see so many writers invited from the Two-Thirds World, whose voices have been suppressed. However, when I received this invitation letter and read the above sentence, I had to wonder to which group I belonged. I could not find my place. Of course, Daniel recognized the problem as soon as I pointed it out and corrected the sentence and I have no intention to put any blame on his understanding, but this instance again shows our peculiar position. I must admit that there are reasons for such misunderstanding.

The first reason is that, even though Japan has been identified as belonging to the First World as far as economy and technology is concerned, Christians are the minority of the minority in this country. Japan has a long history as a non-Christian, but multireligious, country. In Japan the ratio of Christians has never been more than 1 percent of the total population since 1549 when Francis Xavier, a Portuguese priest, first arrived. Current statistics puts the figure at 0.9 percent. This means you may not meet another Christian if you are among 100 people in the general public. Actually you will feel very much a minority and hidden if you come to visit Japan as a Christian, where, on its small islands, a little smaller than the state of California in the United States, live more than 120 million souls, half of the U.S. population. What is distinctive about Japan (in its relationship with Judeo-Christian scriptures) when its people encounter different faiths their whole lives long?

The voice of Christians may be respected, but this voice is not always heard as very powerful. If you ask the other 100 people what their "family" religions are, you may get more than 100 answers because they may identify themselves with more than one religion—such as Buddhism, Shintoism, Confucianism, to name only a few. It is not unusual for the average Japanese to have their weddings at Shinto shrines or at Christian churches and to have their funerals at Buddhist temples. The younger generation may claim themselves nonreligious, even though they follow quite a few religious conventions that take place in their daily lives. It seems that the Japanese people have adapted what is most convenient from each religious tradition and lived with these modifications so long that it has become almost meaningless to tell which custom comes from which religion. We may say in such circumstances as this that the Japanese Christians have not impressed their existence strongly enough to be forgotten both domestically and globally.[1]

The second reason is related to the language. There is no common language among Asian countries. Each country has its own language. Therefore when we communicate with Asians, we cannot help but choose to use English. This fact reflects the heritage many Asian countries share of being colonized by English-speaking countries. In our country, English has never been a language of daily use. Therefore the Japanese tend to be silent in the international setting regardless of whether they have voices to raise or not. It may be noted here that very old Koreans and Taiwanese can also speak Japanese because their countries suffered from the Japanese imperial control of colonialism.

This fact, then, leads us to the third reason why Japan is excluded. Japan is peculiar among Asian countries because of its colonial invasion of other Asian countries before and during World War II. There are many Japanese who struggle with the unsolved issues that have continued since the defeat of the war until now, but a true reconciliation with the colonized countries by the Japanese government has not yet been realized. One of the big issues is the so-called comfort women's issue, which symbolizes the guilt of war and the crimes against humanity. Thus it is very difficult for me as a Japanese to speak for Asia. I must limit myself to speak on Japan in Asia and its relationships to Asian countries.

At the same time, Japan, being under the big umbrella of its ally, the United States, has recently been in danger of losing its autonomy. After the incident of 9/11, the congress of Japan has been trying to change the most important article of our constitution, Article 9, which declares Japan would never fight another war. Even a new law, the War Law is about to pass the congress. We may say that Japan, being invisibly colonized by the power of the United States, has been both a colonizer and a colonized nation. Thus as a Christian, feminist, and Japanese, I am not necessarily in a comfortable position to make a speech here.

I cannot practice my feminist theology without painfully acknowledging the "relational" history of Japan with other Asian countries. To look at history from a politically relational perspective means that I must understand the victimization, pain, and suffering of other Asians and acknowledge the guilt of my country. Thus if I dare search for a general or typical Asian methodology, I am afraid I risk setting Asians as a counterpart to the so-called Westernism and end up with another regionalism. I hope to search for a spirituality that will create solidarity beyond the differences in political, economic, and cultural contexts. Following Ched Myers, I would also like to say "My point here is simply that diversity is our reality; the challenge is how to build a *just* society around it."[2]

Women Living in Asia

As women living in different parts of Asia, however, it should be said that we share some common experiences in theology. Almost all the women of Asia have their theological backgrounds immersed in a "God" who is defined by male perspectives and experiences. Asian feminist theologies have had a strong motivation to move from being passive in defining God, Christ, and discipleship to finding God as being among women, working with them, supporting, befriending, and empowering them. We have declared that male-oriented absolutism in theology must be rejected, and the definition of discipleship that emphasizes women's sacrifice and devotion to men must be transformed. To overcome the sexist interpretation of the scriptural texts has been a major agenda in Asia.

Furthermore, I cannot practice my feminist theology without a critical analysis of my own cultural and social contexts in their relationship to Asian countries that Japan has invaded and colonized: in the past in the form of wars, and in the present as one of the economic powers. To be politically critical of my own government is directly related to another serious question, namely for whom do I advocate and for whose human rights do I commit myself? One of our engaging experiences as women and men is to have held the International Women's Court in December 2000.

Maybe it is now appropriate to talk about some of my own personal heritage of faith. I have lived as a Christian for more than 40 years, but I have my primary religious foundation or orientation in a traditional religious heritage and praxis that cannot be named as belonging to just one religion. Rather it is a mixture of all the religions that have existed in Japan for more than 1,500 years, while Christianity has figured in but a little more than 200 years of that history. It is almost impossible to distinguish which part of my existence or praxis is based on which religion. My life itself consists of spirituality nurtured by those multireligions of Buddhism, Shintoism, Confucianism, and others. When I found Jesus having grown up in a multireligious soil, I was amazed by this fact and more convinced that multireligious experiences have enriched my spirituality. Having multi-logues with other religions or religionists does not mean becoming syncretic, but being enriched by their spirituality.

When I was 18 years old I committed myself to the Christian faith and affiliated myself with a Christian church. I do not mean I changed my religion or I converted to Christianity. It was my faith commitment. The church is called *Mu-Kyoukai*. Its literal meaning is "nonchurch," but it can imply a community of faith without borders. It was originated by a Japanese man who was deeply influenced by a missionary from the United States, who eventually went there for further studies. When he came back home to Japan, he chose to be independent and to enculturate the Gospel into the soil of Japan. He did a great amount of scriptural interpretation, which has become a distinctive tradition of the nonchurch. Influenced by that tradition, I started studying Greek, Hebrew, and Latin during the first year of college at the International Christian University in Tokyo so that I might read the scriptures in their original languages.

Later I found the nonchurch interpretations of scriptural texts were quite patriarchal as well as hierarchical, despite its spirit that can be very liberated and open. The discovery motivated me to stride onto a new journey toward feminist interpretation of the scriptural texts. It was a lonely and painful struggle until I acquired access to the writings of feminist theologians in Europe and the United States. Finally I was convinced that what I had been doing on my own was not wrong.

Reading the Scriptures

So far, I have pointed out that there are three perspectives that I am aware of when I do my scriptural studies, especially when I do scriptural interpretation. To review, these are (1) political analysis of personal context and its relationship with global contexts; (2) awareness of the peculiar position of Japan in Asia; and (3) struggles of women in Asia for survival and liberation.

Now I would like to give some examples of how I read scriptural texts from these three perspectives. First, a reading from a multi-faith or interfaith perspective, second, a reading from a social–locational perspective, which means placing and defining myself as a colonized woman in a colonizing country, Japan. And third, a reading from a postcolonial perspective, which means seeing myself as becoming a postcolonial subject in the world.

Multi-faith or Interfaith Readings of the Texts

It may be appropriate to give a brief overview of Christianity in multireligious countries in Asia. A distribution map of world religions says the Christian population is greater than that of other religions of the world. However, when it comes to regional distributions, the ratio varies. In Asia only 7.9 percent of the populace belongs to Christian churches; in Latin America the figure is 97 percent, while in Europe it is 75 percent, in Oceania 65 percent, and in North America 54 percent. In Africa, where Islam has had a powerful influence, Christians amount to little more than 30 percent of the population.[3]

It can easily be explained why Asia has the smallest number of Christians in comparison with other regions, as Asia is known as the birthplace of all the major world religions. Asian countries that have been exposed to religions besides their indigenous religions have become multireligious in the course of their long histories.

Even Christianity was born in the west end of Asia, but what was unusual about Christianity was its way of spreading. Other religions such as Buddhism, Hinduism, and even Islam spread primarily toward the east from their birthplaces. Christianity was the one exception that moved from the west end of Asia further westward, though there were a few anomalies. For instance, we find Christian churches in India which trace back to the Apostle Thomas, and Nestorian missionaries promulgating the gospel in Persia, in Afghanistan, and finally reaching into China in the seventh century.[4]

When Christianity arrived back in Asia through Western missionaries, it was already Westernized. By then the scriptures had become the norm for judging other cultures and Christian converts were asked to abandon their traditional cultures and indigenous religions. An interesting speculation would be what difference would have been brought to the history of Christianity if Paul had taken the gospel in the other direction, toward the east, instead of to Rome. What then would have happened to Christianity as it moved into the multireligious countries of Asia?

Westernized Christianity, with its highly cultivated monotheistic conception of religion met an unexpectedly strong resistance in Asia where other religions had had their histories for a long time. Asia, consisting of so many countries, is not mono-lithic. The historical backgrounds of each country offer clues to how Christianity has been accepted. In the Philippines, almost 90 percent of the populace are Christians following the hardship of several centuries of Spanish colonization. The Christian faith supported the people as they went through the struggle to be free from Spanish rule and the subsequent control of the United States. In Korea, the number of Christians increased remarkably during and after the colonization by Japan. Almost 50 percent of the population there is said to be Christian. In other countries, Buddhism, Hinduism, and Islam have gained most of the population. Therefore, the ratio of Christians is very low: Hong Kong 10 percent, India 2.4 percent, Indonesia 8 percent, Sri Lanka 8 percent, Thailand 0.5 percent, and so on.[5]

Japan, which is located at the east end of Asia, has been a kind of terminal for various religions expanding eastward. As each religion was inculturated and indige-nized in the course of passing through different countries and being accepted by the people, it could not avoid being transformed once again when the Japanese accepted it. Culture, history, social structure, and even economic status affect people's spiritu-ality and their understanding of a particular religion. How do the Japanese people experience religions that exist around them in the form of social conventions as well as the faiths they have experienced since they were born?[6]

As an example of the multi-faith reading of texts, I would interpret a faith expression spoken by Ruth that is recorded in the Hebrew scripture. My interest in reading this particular text is in the question of how we can nurture openness to those of other faiths. One particular phrase in Ruth inspires my mind to a long pon-dering. It is spoken in her statements when she gives her determined response against the last plea given by her mother-in-law, Naomi to her to go back to her mother's house. Ruth says, "Do not press me to leave you or to turn back from following you! Where you go, I will go; where you lodge, I will lodge; your people shall be my peo-ple, and your God my God." The phrase that has struck me is her confession ". . . and your God is my God." Naomi is from Israel and Ruth and her sister-in-law, Orpah, are from Moab, a neighboring country of Israel.

Naomi, mother-in-law of Ruth and Orpah, tries hard to persuade them to remain in their home country when she made up her mind to leave Moab after losing her husband and two sons. Naomi's family migrated from Israel to Moab when the seri-ous famine attacked Israel. One of the daughters-in-law, Orpah, decides to go back home after Naomi's continuous persuasion, but Ruth does not and clings to Naomi.

Seeing off Orpah, Naomi utters to Ruth her last and final plea by referring to the Gods of Moab for the first time. She has kept trying to persuade them to stay and find socially stable places for themselves. She says Orpah has gone back to her people and her Gods, and urges Ruth to follow her. Until the last moment, Naomi does not refer to the Gods of Moab in whom Ruth must believe. We only learn from what Ruth says that Naomi has kept her faith in Israel's God, Yahweh, while she has stayed in the land of Moab. Ruth replies to Naomi saying "Your people shall be my people, and your God my God." It is amazing to hear her say that Naomi's God is her own God. How could it happen?

Until Ruth and Orpah married the two sons of Naomi, they were apparently nurtured by the traditional culture of Moab and disciplined in the ways and customs their people built up throughout their history. They most probably worshipped the main God Chemosh and other Gods of Moab with their families and people. Their religion might be termed polytheistic. It is natural to understand their basic worldview is founded on their faith regardless of whether they are serious believers or not. This spirituality is the air both Ruth and Orpah have breathed since they were born. This spirituality has permeated the environment in which their lives have developed.

By living with Naomi's family, Ruth has encountered Naomi's God, Yahweh. However, the commitment of marriage is not strong enough to abolish all that Ruth has nurtured in herself and experienced before the marriage. Through the daily routines of the family, the two religions have met, taken part in one another, and accepted one another. This illustrates the interfaith dialogue or encounter.

A reader can identify many encounters in this episode such as personal, ethnic, cultural, social, and religious. Through the personal experiences of sharing their lives on various levels of daily as well as social life, they have learned to know more about how each of these individuals experience their faith in Yahweh or the Gods of Chemosh. They must experience what I call multireligious spirituality by accepting each other as they are and understanding what they believe.

Thus behind the confession of Ruth, ". . . your God is my God," one sees more than a simple devotion of Ruth for the companionship of Naomi. Perhaps the reason Naomi stays away from touching the issue of faith until the end is that she might think Ruth would stay with the Gods of Chemosh in Moab, which would be the last blow and result in Naomi being left all alone. Yet contrary to her expectation, Naomi hears Ruth's commitment to her God Yahweh, and the confession makes Naomi stop persuading Ruth to return to her people.

Ruth confesses that "your God is my God" and commits herself to Naomi's God. To her, it means to commit herself to a hope without a concrete future in her prospect. Ruth's commitment implies transgressing the boundaries of cross-families, cross-races, cross-religions, cross-ethnic groups, and nations. What is it, then, that leads Ruth to make such a decision?

Looking at her commitment of faith, it seems to be that the Gods of Moab and her worldview play the most important role in her decision. In her confession, Ruth chooses to identify herself with Naomi's God. This action of faith reveals the borderlessness of her faith. Ruth does not just stick to the world of Gods in which she has been brought up. On the contrary, the horizon of her faith is broad to the extent she can confess Naomi's God as her own.

Where, then, in concrete, is the sensitivity of Ruth's faith found? It is revealed in her ability to focus herself on finding out who is the most powerless and helpless around her at the moment of decision making? Ruth knows that Naomi is such. Her decision is made on the edge of almost losing her own faith identity. She shows her answer through this "faith action" to the question of for whom she should advocate and whose human rights should be protected.

So far, I have not used the term "conversion" to explain Ruth's confession. Ruth does not mean to be converted. She chooses to commit herself to Naomi's God. I believe that all the Moabite Gods do not disappear from Ruth's mind and life. Her Gods certainly support her along with Naomi's God. The words of Ruth are the evidence of God's endless flexibility and broadness. It shows the reader, in concrete terms, what it means to accept people of other faiths and to understand ourselves as each coming from different parts of the world with different social locations.

When I do my work of interpretation from the interfaith or multireligious perspective, I can see Ruth inspire contemporary readers with her openness to other faiths and her courage to cross the borders. As readers are we also challenged to cross the borders that may lie ahead? What are the borders that we are challenged to deal with?[7]

Social Locational Reading/Praxis of the Texts

When I read the scriptural texts from the perspective of my social location, I am led to a very practical but serious question: how am I committed to social, political, and cultural issues in my society or our world? The message of the scriptural texts asks the reader in concrete ways how s/he advocates for the marginalized, the survivor, and the subjugated as "others" in their daily life. In that sense reading and praxis of the texts are not separable. As a woman, I have been involved with the issues of violence against women. As a Japanese, I have not been able to avoid relating myself to the comfort women's issue, which I think reflects violence against women in its most intense way.[8]

It is saddening to know that there is hardly any Asian woman who can tell her story without referring to the invasion by the Japanese military during World War II, the Japanese economic forces since the 1970s, or Japanese tourists since the 1980s. Their stories remind me of Japan's long history of infringing on the human rights of people in Asia and other countries.

Christian women in my country have eagerly worked with women of other faiths and of nonreligious positions in various forms of grassroots movements. It has been easier for those in different faiths to form coalitions on social and political issues and work together. One of the remarkable movements carried out the people's court entitled, Women's International War Crimes Tribunal in December 2000, which was originally proposed by a group of Japanese women, VAWW-NET, Japan: Violence Against Women in War Network, and which was supported by the International Advisory Committee, women's groups in Asia, and international human rights organizations. The leading woman of the executive committee of VAWW-NET, Japan was Yayori Matsui, a Christian, who lost her life very recently. She said, "The Women's International War Crimes Tribunal 2000 showed that women have power not only to rewrite history but also to create a new history." The tribunal was held in Tokyo for five days after two long years of rigorous preparation.

The main purpose of the tribunal was to pass verdicts upon the perpetrators of the war crimes against women in Asian countries committed by the Japanese imperial government and military power during the Asia–Pacific War (1931–1945). But the most important part of the tribunal was to listen to the witnessing stories told by the comfort women survivors. There were 64 such women who represented nine countries. The voices of the surviving women suppressed and silenced for almost 50 years were finally heard and acknowledged publicly.

Most of the comfort women were 16 to 20 years of age at the time of their abduction. They were forced to receive 10 to 50 soldiers per day. Under tight military surveillance, they could rarely succeed in escaping from the "comfort stations" to which they were drafted without their knowledge. Physical abuse and harassment were daily routines.

Although the four judges, Gabrielle Kirk McDonald (United States, presiding), Carmen Argibay (United Kingdom), Christine Chinkin (Argentina), and Willy Mutunga (Kenya) announced the final judgment in the Hague nearly a year later, at the end of the Tribunal in Tokyo, ten Japanese individuals, including Emperor Hirohito, all of whom are now dead, were sentenced as guilty. When the sentence was announced by the chief judge, McDonald, all the survivors burst into an emotional explosion, expressing their joy and relief through tears and cries, which was followed by stepping up to the stage and sharing their happiness with the judges. Seeing their faces and actions, the audience gave an extended standing ovation. It would seem from their expression that the survivors felt their dignity as human beings regained and assured.

It is the task of Christian women to keep pressing the government to carry out its obligation to the survivors: disclose the truth, acknowledge it, record it, express full apology, compensate them, teach children the history, and so on. My personal participation in the preparation of the court and my seeing the process of the court on site has taken me back to do my theological reflection on the issue and given me a new vantage point for reading the scriptural texts. Action and reflection go side by side, influencing each other in the form of a spiral.

The text of the history did not see the comfort women's issue worth recording. The dominant powers silenced the voices of these women. The same incidents can easily be traced in the texts of the scriptures.

Reading the Texts as a Postcolonial Subject

While reading any scriptural text, a reader should carefully observe the power relationships under which the particular texts were written or edited. As long as the texts were written or edited in particular social, political, economic, cultural, and religious locations, they could not be free from the biases operated or influenced by the powers that were at work. Readers need to liberate the texts from being colonized by the powers that be.

Feminist theologians struggling in countries colonized politically, economically, and technologically by dominant countries have claimed that women of the Two-Thirds World have suffered under the pain, frustration, and anger of "double colonization." It means "they are oppressed by two structural systems: imperialism and patriarchy."[9] Readers can detect various forms of colonialism or imperialism going around even in the current world. How can the world be free from their fetters? How can the world/readers be free from imperial and patriarchal readings of the texts?

Musa W. Dube from Botswana problematized the fact that white middle-class women have paid attention only to patriarchy. She proposes that scriptural feminist discourses also "need to adopt de-colonizing feminist practices, given the pervasiveness of imperial biblical oppression in the global structures of the past and present."[10] She challenges all readers to become postcolonial subjects when they do the reading of the texts, regardless of whether they belong to First or Two-Thirds World countries. Unless such praxis takes place, readers will not be able to do the reading of the texts for the purpose of breaking down the borders between the powerful and the powerless and practicing the interdependence as the community of faith.

Now I would like to introduce an example of a postcolonial reading of the Syro-Phoenician woman recorded in the Gospel of Mark (7:24–30). My main interest is to locate the power relationships at work because they are the cause for producing dominant and subordinate relationships between the protagonists in the story.[11]

The story begins with the plea of a mother, introduced as "a Greek, of Syro-Phoenician origin." She, a foreigner, comes out and falls down at the feet of Jesus asking for a favor. Her plea is made for healing of her little daughter who has an unclean spirit. It takes place in "the region of Tyre," the rural territory surrounding the center city of Tyre, which is the island off the coast of the Mediterranean Sea. The villages inhabited by the Jews exist right next to the villages inhabited by Syrians and Phoenicians in the hinterland of Tyre where there are no clear borders.

It has often been wondered why Mark puts in Jesus' mouth such a bitter response to the woman's plea. Jesus says "Let the children be fed first, for it is not fair to take the children's food and throw it to the dogs" (7:27). The children represent the Jews and the dogs imply foreigners, including this woman and her child. The expression is therefore Jesus' overt rejection of accepting her plea. In addition the reader wonders why Jesus responds to her by using the bread language, even though he knows her main concern is in the healing of her sick child.

In order to address these two questions, we inquire into the social location of the story. The research on the cultural context and historical situation of the regions of Tyre and Galilee given by Gerd Theissen[12] and the recent archaeological research done by Jonathan L. Reed[13] are very helpful.

The city of Tyre, on an island, was well known for "its wealth based on metal work, the production of purple dye (cf. Pliny Nat. Hist. 5.17.76; Strabo Geogr. 16.2.23), and an extensive trade with the whole Mediterranean region. Its money was one of the most stable currencies in circulation at this period; it survived for decades without significant devaluation. This was certainly one reason why the temple treasury was kept in Tyrian coin, even though this meant accepting the fact that the coins of Tyre depicted the god Melkart."[14] Because the city of Tyre had very little space for farming, it depended on importing agricultural products from Galilee and other places. "The Galilean hinterland and the rural territory belonging to the city (partly settled by Jews) were the 'breadbasket' of the metropolis of Tyre."[15] Most of the products were bought out by the rich dwellers of the city and the peasants in the hinterlands were always in want.[16] Peasants were in constant shortage of food and money, even though they labored from dawn to dusk all through the year. The Galilean peasants were deprived of their stable life under the threefold exploitation by the colonial control of the Roman Empire, the Herodian monarchy that fawned on Rome, and the local religious power of the Temple politics in Judea. In addition, Tyre, the rival colony of the Roman Empire deprived them of food. Agricultural crops they produced did not come around their daily table to satisfy their own basic needs.

If the Syro-Phoenician woman in this story is from one of the villages in the hinterland of Tyre, which is very plausible, the village is surely peripheral as seen from the urban center of the city of Tyre. Then she might not be so rich and so privileged in comparison with those in the urban part of the city.

If we take the bitter relationship of economy between affluent Tyre and exploited Galilee into consideration, we can see that Jesus' bitter words in Mark 7:27 have a powerful impact. The saying, which is so offensive to the woman, would reflect the humiliating relationship of power that Galileans have to endure with the urban Tyrians. Then the words could mean: First let the mouths of the poor people in the Jewish rural areas be satisfied. For it is not good to take poor people's food and throw it to the rich Tyrians in the city. The words overtly express the destitute reality of the Galilean peasants and show their resistance against the power exercised by the urban people of Tyre. Then why is she not knocked down by Jesus' words? It is because she does not identify herself with those to whom Jesus' bitter words are thrown and criticize. It is because she is from a village in the vicinity of Galilee where the life may not be so different from that of the Galilean peasants.

She returns with her strong counter-assertion, "Yes, it is so, but, sir, even the dogs under the table eat the children's crumbs" (7:28; literal translation of the original by this author). She acknowledges the primacy that the Galilean peasants ought to have. But at the same time, she reminds Jesus of the fact that there are the other kinds of dogs (people of Tyre destitute like her and her child) that also need to be fed. In this expression, we may see her raising a serious question—can Jesus totally ignore a sick child while talking about feeding the "children" of Israel? If Jesus protects the children of Israel, the woman insists, then she and her sick child should also be protected. She insists that Jesus' harsh words do not apply to her and her child. To the contrary, she and her child will be exploited by Jesus, if he will not feed them, as they are also suffering. Therefore she does not give up.

Jesus responds to her with words that fully accept her request, "For your words, you may go. . . ." Jesus affirms her, as if he has learned a new lesson from her. In the first part of the encounter between the two, the equilibrium of the power is apparently in favor of Jesus, but toward the end it becomes reversed. "So she went home, found the child lying on the bed, and the demon gone."

Thus we may conclude that Jesus decolonized the relationship between those within the Tyrian power base and the Galilean peasants. The woman decolonized Jesus' primacy that was limited to the Jews. By reading the text with a postcolonial perspective, we see the powers at work and can disentangle their control over it.

Conclusion

From my observation, analyses, and experiences, what has become clear is that the praxes of reading texts and practicing theology in daily life are intertwined and inseparable. In other words, the perspectives I took up in the first half cannot be gained without knowing where we stand or with and for whom we advocate. If we lose sight of our social locations and the reality of the world, our praxis of reading texts will also tend to be lifeless because we also lose sight of the social locations and the reality of the world of the texts. This is the first type of multi-logue we are challenged to keep.

Multi-logue, as I use it here, implies practicing our multiple dialogues with the social locations of the texts and our contemporary world in my case, and in general practicing our multiple dialogues with diverse people or thoughts or texts through activating our plural feelers of communication. Then the second multi-logue comes around by asking us to keep our minds as open as possible to other faiths or religionists so that we may learn from them as well so we may work with them collaboratively for our enterprise to pursue a world of justice and peace. Lastly, the most difficult but most urgent need is to continue our multi-logue with women and men in other countries so that we may keep decolonizing ourselves and keep becoming postcolonial subjects as we read the texts. I hope the praxis of doing feminist liberation theology in such a way as I have proposed in this chapter may help real peace to advance in this confused world.

Notes

1. For more discussion on the theme, see my article, "Feminist Perspectives: Ecumenical Theological Education in Japan," *Ministerial Formation*, 90 (WCC, July 2000): 40–49.
2. Ched Meyers, *Who Will Roll Away the Stone?* (New York: Orbis Books, 1994) 314.
3. *Christian Year Book 2000*, Editorial Department Kirisuto Shinbun (Tokyo: Kirisuto Shinbun Sha, 2000) 110–111.
4. Kwok Pui-lan, *Discovering the Bible in the Non-Biblical World* (New York: Orbis Books, 1995) 1–4. Some more discussion on the issue can be found in my article, "Feminist Perspectives."
5. Internet Home page: www.odci.gov/cia/publicaltvis/factbook/rn.html: Country Listing.
6. For more detailed discussion, see my article, "Looking at the Web: A Political Analysis of Personal Context and Its Relationship to Global Context," *Journal of Asian and Asian-American Theologies*, II/1 (1997): 51–63.
7. For more discussion on Ruth, see my article, " '. . . and your God my God': How We Can Nurture Openness to Other Faiths (Ruth 1:1–19 Read From a Feminist Perspective of a Multi-Faith Community)," in *Scripture, Community, and Mission*, ed. Philip L. Wickeri (Hong Kong: CCA, 2003) 198–208.
8. For more detailed discussion and theological reflection on the issue, see my article, "Re-covering the History of 'Comfort Women': Re-membering and Re-conciling," to be published in a book by WCC.
9. Musa W. Dube, *Postcolonial Feminist Interpretation of the Bible* (St. Louis: Chalice Press, 2000) 113.
10. Dube, *Postcolonial Feminist Interpretation*, 115.
11. More detailed discussion will be found in my article, "De-colonizing Ourselves as Readers: The Story of the Syro-Phoenician Woman as a Text," in *Distant Voices Drawing Near: Essays in Honor of Antoinette Clark Wire*, ed. Holly E. Hearon (Minnesota: Liturgical Press, 2004) 131–144.
12. Gerd Theissen, *The Gospels in Context: Social and Political History in the Synoptic Tradition*, tr. Linda Maloney (Minneapolis: Fortress Press, 1991) 61–80.
13. Jonathan L. Reed, *Archaeology and the Galilean Jesus: A Re-examination of the Evidence* (Harrisburg: Trinity Press International, 2000) 163–164, 185–186.
14. Theissen, *Gospels in Context*, 72–73.

15. Theissen, *Gospels in Context*, 73.

16. Theissen, *Gospels in Context*, 72–75. Pointing out that popular coins used in Israel were with Tyrian imprint, Reed says they "were a daily reminder of Tyre's economic influence to Galilean commerce." (Reed, *Archaeology and the Galilean Jesus*, 186). Paula Fredriksen, in her book, *Jesus of Nazareth, King of the Jews: A Jewish Life and the Emergence of Christianity* (New York: Alfred A. Knopf, 1999) also points out that the Temple in Jerusalem relied on the Tyrian coins and so there were money changers that converted the various currencies of pilgrims from various places to this standard coinage (208).

Chapter 11

Response: An Asian Buddhist Response to a Japanese Feminist Glimpse of Biblical Studies in the Twenty-First Century

Zhiru

I would like to emphasize at the outset what a pleasure and learning experience it has been for me to read and respond to Hisako Kinukawa's chapter. For that, I have to thank the conference organizers for their kind inclusion of my participation on a subject that I have no claim of expertise. Since I have no formal training in either women studies or Christian theology, I regard myself more as an interloper who has been invited to savor the exciting riches of this religio-intellectual exchange. Given my lack of expertise in the areas, I can only comment on the chapter as an Asian scholar-practitioner interested in the study of religion. As a woman, I am naturally interested in the search of religious expression that fully acknowledges the gender and ethnic identities of the practitioner.

As I read Kinukawa's chapter, I was struck by the wealth of perspectives that she has so ably integrated into her discussion: on the one hand, she applies an array of approaches to the study of religious texts, ranging from cultural, economic, gender, and sociopolitical issues, to the development of what she calls "multi-logue"; and on the other hand, she has creatively juxtaposed the various strands of her identity as a Japanese, feminist, and Christian theologian. Underscoring her entire presentation is a commendable insistence on connecting the past with the present, introducing an urgency to contextualize scriptures within larger historical realities, in order to better apply the text to contemporary situations. As she points out, readers necessarily bring to the reading of texts particular perspectives that are conditioned by individual and sociocultural experiences. The art of reading scripture, for her, becomes integrally intertwined with the practice of theology in daily life. In her reading, the study of biblical scripture becomes an opportunity to bring to life the various dimensions of past historical conditions that are invoked precisely for their instructive lessons on the urgent questions, which we, as scholars and practitioners of religion, face today. In short, Kinukawa offers a nuanced model of reading scripture that enables us to arrive at a historically more useful interpretation of religious texts, which accounts for the socioeconomic, political, and gender realities of text and reader. However, the task of the theologian does not stop there for her; instead the theologian needs to apply the understanding to the present historical reality that one faces.

Emerging from this act of reading religious text is a "multi-logue" in three senses of the word: first, a multi-logue with the historical realities encapsulated in the texts, as well as present in the contemporary world; second, a multi-logue that converses with other religions allowing the building of a world of justice and peace; and third, a multi-logue that transcends the contraposition of the empowered against the weak, so that we may break free from the inhibiting societal power structures that we inadvertently perpetuate. In Kinukawa's treatment, religious texts of the past become the very vehicle for social transformation that would undercut political, economic, ethnic, and gender disparities. Her goal, as she points out, is to "search for a spirituality that will create solidarity beyond the differences in political, economic, and cultural contexts." She models herself after Ched Myers, reiterating that "diversity is our reality; the challenge is how to build a *just* society around it."

Kinukawa's chapter has several rich implications that I cannot discuss fully here; instead I restrict my comments to two points: (1) her advocacy of a "multi-faith" perspective for reading scriptures; and (2), her contribution as an Asian feminist voice in the interpretation of religious texts.

Multi-Faith Conversation and the Problem of Religious Categories

For Kinukawa, her realization of the urgency for multi-faith arises from her personal experiences. Throughout her chapter, she identifies herself as a Japanese with sociocultural experiences that definitively shape her religious experience. She describes her experience as follows:

> I have lived as a Christian for more than 40 years, but I have my primary religious foundation or orientation in a traditional religious heritage and praxis which cannot be named as belonging to just one religion. Rather it is a mixture of all the religions that have existed in Japan for more than 1500 years, while Christianity has figured in but a little more than 200 years of that history. It is almost impossible to distinguish which part of my existence or praxis is based on which religion. My life consists of spirituality nurtured by those multi-religions of Buddhism, Shintoism, Confucianism, and other religions.

Kinukawa concludes that "having multi-logues with other religions or religionists does not mean to become syncretic, but to be enriched by their spirituality." This constitutes a crucial point that she contributes to the ongoing interfaith dialogues. She reads the biblical story of Ruth's acceptance of Naomi's God as offering a scriptural model for what she advocates.

Kinukawa's call for the need of an open attitude to other religions is especially timely in the politically charged environment that we live in today. We need only to recall September 11 and the current war situation to realize the urgent necessity for honest attempts to reach out to understand other faiths and religions on their own terms, without superimposing prior cultural and truth claims. Kinukawa astutely observes that because the world has become increasingly global in many ways, this has often been mistaken for open communication. However, global access does not always imply real understanding, and there exist those "invisible walls that are one of the main causes for ethnic strife." Given the ways political and economic realities are integrally related to religion, Kinukawa suggests that open conversations with other religions would be a crucial step in the effort to build a better society. She introduces the concept of "faith commitment" that allows one to commit to a particular religious tradition, while exposing oneself to other religio-cultural influences. For Kinukawa, exchange with other religious traditions should ultimately enable the participant to return with new eyes to the texts of one's own tradition. It is precisely her identity and experience as a Japanese that allows her to grasp the advantages of a pluralistic religious ecumene.

Mutual learning across different religions indeed has proven to be fruitful in the past. In the case of Buddhism, revivalist or reformist movements, which have sprung up in Chinese and Southeast Asian communities over the last century, quite often have drawn inspiration from contact with the West, and in particular Christianity. For example, at the turn of the twentieth century, the movement in modern Chinese Buddhism that came to be known as "Humanistic Buddhism" (*rensheng fojiao* or *renjian fojiao*) was in part a Buddhist response to the influx of Western ideas, especially Marxist ideology, into the intellectual circles of pre-Communist China.[1] Condemning the "age-old" association of Buddhism with funerary rites and afterlife practices, Chinese Buddhist leaders propounded a vision of Buddhism that rejected the otherworldly emphasis in favor of a this-worldly engagement with society in an effort to "modernize" Buddhism as China moved away from the feudal structure of traditional societies. Although Humanistic Buddhism never quite took roots in Mainland China, it has flourished in Taiwan and become the hallmark of contemporary Taiwanese Buddhism.[2] In the latter part of the twentieth century, Buddhist leaders in contemporary Taiwan have developed Humanistic Buddhist teachings so as to accommodate Buddhist practices of social engagement, often in response to Western influence or Christian challenge.[3] In this regard, the foremost spokesperson is the nun Zhengyan (1937–), who founded the charity movement known as Buddhist Compassion Relief Meritorious Association (*Fojiao ciji gongdehui*), which over the last four decades had evolved from a group of nuns and housewives to a multi-dollar transnational foundation that has the ability to mobilize large-scale economic and human resources.[4] In her biography, Zhengyan traced the founding of the Buddhist Compassion Relief to a few incidents, including a conversation she had with Catholic leaders, who questioned her as to what Buddhists have contributed to society.[5]

For some time now, there has been a tradition of Buddhist–Christian Dialogues in the United States, a forum of exchange that meets at certain academic venues (e.g., AAR), which brings together scholars and practitioners of the two faiths. Catholic leaders have also implemented interfaith dialogues; as a recent example, in May 2003, the Monastic Interfaith Dialogues has sponsored a retreat for Buddhist Nuns and Catholic Nuns that allowed the two groups of women to engage in conversation and exchange religious experiences.[6] Given the turn of world events, the model that Kinukawa proposes is especially applicable, and we can envision the forum of Buddhist–Christian dialogues expanding to include Islam, Judaism, and other religions, and become truly a multi-logue.

Having said that, I would still have to voice a nagging reservation that interfaith multi-logues may still wind up privileging the Christian tradition. Much of the study of religion is defined by Judeo-Christian tradition(s), so much so that Asian religions have simply adopted key categories set by the Judeo-Christian tradition, translated them into their own languages, and applied them almost uncritically onto Asian cultures and religions. This has sometimes led to misleading representations of the religion or culture in question. The classic example is Japanese use of the term *shūkyō*, coined to translate the English word "religion." Since the Japanese understood *shūkyō* largely in terms of the Western model of a system of beliefs, Japanese tend to see themselves as not particularly religious and refer to their daily ritual practices as "cultural customs," to be distinguished from "real religion." Ian Reader explains the situation:

> The Japanese word generally used in surveys and elsewhere to denote "religion" is *shūkyō*, a word made up of two ideograms, *shū*, meaning sect or denomination, and *kyō*, teaching or doctrine. It is a derived word that came into prominence in the nineteenth century as a result of Japanese encounters with the West and particularly with Christian missionaries, to denote a concept and view of religion commonplace in the realms of nineteenth-century Christian theology but at that time not found in Japan, of religion as a specific belief-framed entity. The term *shūkyō* thus, in origin at least, implies a separation of that which is religious from other aspects of society and culture, and contains implications of belief and commitment to one order or movement—something that has not been traditionally a common factor in Japanese religious behavior and something that tends to exclude many of the phenomena involved in the Japanese religious process. When tied to questions of belief it does conjure up notions of narrow commitment to a particular teaching to the implicit exclusion and denial of others—something which goes against the general complementary nature of the Japanese religious tradition.[7]

In a similar vein, Winston King has cautioned that what the West calls "religion" is for many societies so integral a part of the total way of life that it is hardly experienced or thought of as something separable or something that can be narrowed to this or that definition.[8] Jonathan Z. Smith too has concluded that the term "religion" is a scholarly category and a modern Western invention, which really has no independent existence outside of the academy.[9]

It seems to me that any endeavor to engage in interfaith multi-logue must develop and emphasize sensitivity to religious categories in order to arrive at some kind of real understanding of the "Other." This would imply that in addition to the array of perspectives highlighted by Kinukawa, we need also to be self-conscious of the ways we structure reality with language. Whose language are we using to describe whom?

What terms of discourse are employed for the multi-logue and who is defining these terms, and for whom? In other words, in addition to the various perspectives that Kinukawa has highlighted, we must be aware of the linguistic implications that are integrally tied to political, religious, and social conditions.[10] Above all, any dialogue with other religions must grapple honestly with differences before hastening to subsume the other tradition(s) in perceived common grounds. The act of reading scripture should not become another form of colonization, where the religion and culture that possesses the economic and political means to initiate the multi-logue ends up dominating the forum of religious exchange through the terms of discourse.

The Search for an Asian Feminist Reading

Next, I will address Kinukawa's contribution as an Asian feminist voice in the interpretation of religious texts. A major contribution of this conference is its recognition of the multicultural expressions of feminist voices in the interpretation of religion, in this case, New Testament studies. In her chapter, Kinukawa recollects her feminist journey:

> When I was 18 years old I committed myself to the Christian faith and affiliated myself with a Christian church. . . . The church is called *Mu-Kyoukai*. Its literal meaning is "nonchurch," but it can imply a community of faith without borders. . . . Later I found the nonchurch interpretations of scriptural texts were quite patriarchal as well as hierarchical, despite its spirit that can be very liberated and open. The discovery motivated me to stride onto a new journey toward feminist interpretation of the scriptural texts. It was a lonely and painful struggle until I acquired access to the writings of feminist theologians in Europe and United States. Finally I was convinced that what I have been doing on my own was not wrong.

For Kinukawa, the feminist approach to the reading of scripture must go hand in hand with the practice of reading texts as a postcolonial subject, arguing that patriarchy and imperialism are related and need to be undermined simultaneously. She offers an example of a "postcolonial reading" of the Syro-Phoenician woman in the Gospel of Mark. Not an expert in this field, I cannot assess her reading of the passage, but I certainly found her interpretation fascinating, to say the least. In my minimal reading of the New Testament, this passage has always struck me as baffling. Hence, her exposition clarifies the passage for me, revealing the inherent socioeconomic power structures that underline the text. She reads the passage as undermining the reigning colonial structure of that time, offering an example of liberation from inhibitive social structures. For Kinukawa, the interpretation of a text through the postcolonial perspective allows one to recognize and ultimately decentralize the powers at work. This perspective allows her participation in the legal proceedings on behalf of the comfort women, the otherwise unacknowledged victims of the Japanese World War II.

While I find her proposal of a synthesis of feminist and postcolonial perspectives intellectually stimulating, I am still unclear how this reading could be distinctively characterized as *Asian* feminist. It would have been helpful for me if Kinukawa had addressed more explicitly how an Asian feminist reading of religious text may differ from a Western feminist reading.[11] This question calls up again my previous point—that Western categories have dominated and defined the study of religion and religious experience. With roots deeply entrenched in the West, the history of feminism has been defined largely in the Western context. Asian women have identified with the feminist cause and have joined in the enterprise to uncover the voices of women in history, religion, and society. Kinukawa's biographical account of her spiritual journey illustrates this development. However, the challenge remains for Asian women to find ways of interpreting religion that will preserve their cultural and historical identities while affirming their rights as women. A key question is thus how and what can an Asian woman draw from her ethnic identity and cultural history to enhance her reading of scripture. In other words, what can the Asian experience, or more accurately Asian experiences, contribute to feminist reading of scripture?

Historical studies have shown that the image of the Chinese woman as the eternally oppressed victim of a patriarchal society was a myth, and that Chinese women had assumed agency in society even as they had endured one of the atrocities in human history, the plight of foot binding. The history of Chinese religions holds up local cults of female divinities centered on a model of the woman who rebels against the prevailing patriarchy and refuses to be domesticated into the prescribed social roles of woman as wife and mother.[12] In Chinese Buddhism today, nuns far outnumber monks, and they enjoy economic and sometimes institutional independence to a degree not found in most religions.[13] We will recall that in Taiwanese Buddhism, it is a woman, the nun Zhengyan, who initiates and heads the previously mentioned charity group known as Buddhist Compassion Relief, a multi-dollar transnational foundation. Adhering to and exalting the female virtues prescribed by a Confucian society, Zhengyan assumes leadership over and commands the respect of an overwhelming following that includes men.[14] She is but one of numerous examples of Asian women who successfully articulate their voices through the very social structures and moral frameworks that have been designed to subvert them as women. This style of female expression would be frowned on by many Western societies, just as many Asian women would be uncomfortable with the liberalist and modernist discourse that characterizes Western expressions of feminism. I am not offering any assessment or resolution; I am simply pointing out that the search for an Asian feminist reading of religious text should be cognizant to the nuances of Asian women's experiences, identities, and histories.

In conclusion, I like to reiterate how much I have enjoyed reading Kinukawa's chapter. Her identity as a Japanese Christian woman allows her to approach the biblical texts through a combination of perspectives. In doing so, she brought to life the act of reading a religious text, so that the historical realities of the text and the reader are integrally bound to provide inspiration for how to lead one's life. She brings to the forefront of discourse the need to develop a female spirituality, a topic that for too long has been marginalized by society, religion, and culture.

Notes

1. For a study of this fermenting period in modern Chinese Buddhism, see Don A. Pittman, *Toward a Modern Chinese Buddhism: Taixu's Reforms* (Honolulu: University of Hawai'i, 2001). For Marxist influence, see Charles B. Jones, "Buddhism and Marxism in Taiwan: Lin Qiuwu's Religious Socialism and its Legacy in Modern Times," *Journal of Global Buddhism* 1 (2000): 82–111.

2. Chinese Buddhist leaders usually traced the beginnings of Humanistic Buddhism in Taiwan to the Mainland Chinese reformist monk Taixu (1890–1947); see n. 1. Another major figure who helped to lay the intellectual framework for Humanistic Buddhism in Taiwan is the scholar-monk, Yinshun (1906–), regarded by the tradition as the foremost thinker in modern Chinese Buddhism. For works in English on Yinshun, see Zhiru, "Chinese Master Yinshun's Study of Indian Buddhism: Significance of Historical (Re)construction for a Contemporary Buddhist Thinker," MA Thesis, University of Michigan, Ann Arbor, 1993; Tien Po-Yao, "A Modern Buddhist Monk—Reformer in China: The Life and Thought of Yinshun," PhD Dissertation, California Institute of Integral Studies, 1995; and Scott Christopher Hurley, "A Study of Master Yinshun's Hermeneutics: An Interpretation of the Tathāgatagarbha Doctrine," PhD Dissertation, University of Arizona, Tucson, 2001.

3. The undertaking of social welfare is not unprecedented in Buddhist history. There are certainly Buddhist antecedents in the history of Asian religions, although I have here limited my discussion to Western influence and Christian challenge, which in the twentieth century were important catalysts for such Buddhist undertakings.

4. For a detailed study of the Compassion Relief Movement, see Chien-yu Julia Huang, "Recapturing Charisma: Emotion and Rationalization in a Globalizing Buddhist Movement from Taiwan," PhD Dissertation, Boston University, 2001.

5. The foundation's official website recounts its own history by invoking events in Zhengyan's life: "Many past incidents shaped her vision and she felt a higher calling. When her father had died of a heart attack, she felt guilty. In his passing, she felt that she had erred in caring for him. Later, at a hospital, she witnessed a penniless, aborigine woman being denied medical attention while bleeding on the floor. Another time, a Catholic missionary said to her, 'You Buddhists are a passive group and ignore the needs of others.' Master Zhengyan was determined to serve all humanity. She envisioned a world of kindness, compassion, joy and equality." See http://www.tzuchi.org/global/about/founder/master.html.

6. This weekend retreat was held at a Chinese Buddhist temple, the Hsi Lai Temple, at Hacienda Heights.

7. Ian Reader, *Religion in Contemporary Japan* (Honolulu: University of Hawai'i, 1991) 13–14.

8. Winston King, "Religion," in *The Encyclopedia of Religion*, vol. 12, ed. Mircea Eliade (New York: Macmillan, 1987) 282.

9. Jonathan Z. Smith, "Religion, Religions, Religious," in *Critical Terms for Religious Studies*, ed. Mark Taylor (Chicago: University of Chicago, 1998) 281–282.

10. In this regard, it should be noted that Kinukawa does discuss the problem of language in terms of the use of English as the *lingua franca* for global communication, as well as communication among Asian nations. Her point is to highlight how Japanese are somehow excluded from cross-cultural conversations because English is not their language.

11. On the necessity of a feminist discourse that recognizes colonizing tendencies, see the introduction to Laura E. Donaldson and Kwok Pui Lan, eds., *Postcolonialism, Feminism,*

and Religious Discourse (New York: Routledge, 2002) 1–38. Also see Kwok Pui Lan, "Unbinding Our Feet: Saving Brown Women and Feminist Religious Discourse," in the same volume.

12. A prominent example is the legend of Princess Miaoshan, who refused marriage and entered a Buddhist monastery for religious training. Her father, the king, tried to burn down the monastery, but the legend concluded with Miaoshan performing the ultimate act of filial piety, using her own flesh and eyes to heal her father. She was subsequently recognized as an incarnation of the Bodhisattva Guanyin, a popular deity in Chinese religion. On the legend of Miaoshan, see Glen Dudbridge, *The Legend of Miaoshan* (London: Oxford University Press, 1978); Chun-fang Yü, *Kuan-yin: The Chinese Transformation of Avalokiteshvara* (New York: Columbia University Press, 2001) 293–351.

13. For a discussion on Buddhist nuns and the feminist movement in Taiwan, see Wei-yi Cheng, "Luminary Buddhist Nuns in Contemporary Taiwan: A Quiet Feminist Movement," *Journal of Buddhist Ethics* 10 (2003): 39–56.

14. See Chien-yu Julia Huang and Robert P. Weller, "Merit and Mothering: Women and Social Welfare in Taiwanese Buddhism," *Journal of Asian Studies* 57 (1998): 379–396. On the teachings of Zhengyan, see Yu-ing Ching, *Master of Love and Mercy: Cheng Yen* (Nevada City: Blue Dolphin Publishing, 1995).

Chapter 12

Feminist Theologies in Latin America

Rosemary Radford Ruether

Feminist theologies arising in the Latin American context have generally developed in relation to the liberation theologies of their regions. Latin American liberation theology was pioneered by priest-theologians, such as Peruvian Gustavo Gutierrez[1], in the mid-1960s in response to the crisis of poverty and revolutionary violence in their regions, and the failure of the capitalist developmental model promulgated by North American and Western European corporations and governments to promote social justice.

In 1976, in the wake of the rise and destruction of the socialist reform government of Salvador Allende in Chile, Latin Americans, such as Sergio Torres, reached out to Asian and African theologians to found the Ecumenical Association of Third World Theologians (EATWOT). Latin American liberation theology focused on questions of poverty and economic oppression within their countries and particularly between Latin America and the "First World." They were challenged by Asian and African theologians to be more sensitive to questions of race and culture as well.

However, questions of sexism and gender were virtually ignored by these male theologians from all three regions. By the late 1970s a growing cadre of women theologians were attending the international meetings of EATWOT: Mercy Oduyoye from Ghana, Virginia Fabella and Mary John Mananzan from the Philippines, Marianne Katoppo from Indonesia, Sun Ai Park from Korea, and Ivone Gebara and Elza Tamez from Latin America. They began to challenge the lack of attention to gender in Third World theologies. The issue surfaced at the 1978 assembly in New Delhi when the plea of Marianne Katoppo for inclusive language brought jokes and trivializing comments from the men.[2]

In 1983 an international dialogue between Third World and First World theologians was convened in Geneva, with a mandate to make the delegations from Asia, Africa, Latin America, North America, and Western Europe gender-inclusive.

The result was a considerable number of women theologians from the five regions who gravitated toward each other to discuss feminist issues in theology and social analysis. This brought further resistance from some of the male Third World theologians who wanted "their women" to stay "in their place," that is, behind the agenda of the men of their area.

This resistance took the form of claims of the priority of race, class, and cultural issues. It was said that white women were beneficiaries of white racism along with white men, and so there was no reason for Third World women to trust them. Further, feminism was a First World movement, and its intrusion in the Third World was an expression of cultural imperialism. From a more Marxist orientation, class or economic hierarchy was said to be the major contradiction that needed to be dealt with, and gender was of secondary importance.[3]

At the end of the conference the women theologians from Asia, Africa, and Latin America rose together and demanded a Women's Commission within EATWOT that would meet separately in order to allow Third World women to establish a dialogue and develop their own feminist theology in their own contexts. "We have to decide for ourselves what feminist theology means for us", they said. "It is not for First World women to tell us how to do it, nor is it for Third World men to tell us it is not our issue."[4]

This proposal was accepted by the EATWOT leaders and a four-stage process was planned; national, regional, and intercontinental meetings of Third World feminists. These took place in 1985 and 1986. The papers from these conferences made their way into major publications.[5] These were to be followed by a world consultation that would bring the Third World women theologians into a new stage of dialogue with First World feminist theologians. This was delayed as women in each region began to intensify their own regional organizing for meetings and publications. The world consultation finally took place in December of 1994 in Costa Rica, bringing together 45 theologians from 14 countries.[6]

By 1994 some of the definitions of First and Third World were themselves in question. The paradigm of the dialogue expanded somewhat to add an Eastern European woman, an Arab woman, and a delegation of women theologians of both European and indigenous ancestry from the Pacific. The boundaries of the two "worlds" were further complicated by the presence of a white South African and a Japanese feminist theologian, both seen as "First World" within the "Third World." (The term Third World for the three regions has been retained in this chapter because the theologians from these areas have not, so far, seen it as necessary to rename themselves[7].)

This process of developing Third World feminist theology led by the Women's Commission of EATWOT is of great importance. Without this it would have been much for difficult for women theologians of these regions to develop and publish their thought. Thanks to this support, Asian, African, and Latin American women were able to gather, regionally and internationally, to organize regional networks of communications, to develop a sense of their own identities as women theologians from Asia, Africa, and Latin America, and to receive the stimulation of South–South dialogue.

It should not be supposed that the EATWOT process was the only impetus for the development of Latin American feminist theologies. There were already secular feminist movements in many of the countries of these regions by the 1970s. In some countries in Latin America there had been women's movements at the turn of the century working for women's legal and property rights and access to higher education. In the 1970s a new wave of feminist movements began in Latin American and other Third World countries. As in North America and Western Europe, this "second wave" of feminism has often focused on questions of rape, domestic violence, and reproductive rights. The issues have taken distinct forms in different countries. For example, in India the feminist movement has played the major role in exposing the practices of female feticide and dowry murders.[8]

The interconnection of the secular feminist movements and the rise of feminist theology among women in the churches has varied regionally.[9] Latin American feminism's militant anticlericalism and focus on sexual and reproductive issues taboo for Catholics kept Catholic feminist theologians leery of ties to these movements in their countries.[10] The secular feminists were perceived as "middle class" even though they often were engaged in services to poor women on issues of violence and reproductive rights. In Latin America in the wake of growing unemployment and cut back on basic food, health, and educational services from the state, popular women's movements arose to create neighborhood kitchens, and to serve other survival needs. Women in religious orders were involved in supporting these popular women's projects. Feminists working in the churches in liberation theology often felt more comfortable supporting these popular women's movements than in the circles of secular feminists.

The ecclesial base for doing feminist theology has also varied. Protestant women whose churches began to ordain them had a claim to education in their denominational seminaries, but only a few of these seminaries, such as the Seminario Biblico (now Universidad Biblio) in Costa Rica and the Lutheran Seminary in Sao Leopoldo, Brazil, have made themselves centers for feminist theology. Catholic women had less access to seminary theological education. However, some Catholic universities, as well as Protestant colleges, have developed women's studies or religious studies departments open to feminist theology.[11] Catholic women have also founded their own feminist organizations for grassroots ministry, publications, and conferences, such as Talitha Cumi in Lima, Peru and the Conspirando Collective in Santiago, Chile.[12] Women in Catholic religious orders play a role in supporting both these initiatives.[13]

In an interview in 1993, Brazilian theologian Ivone Gebara traced the development of feminist theology in Latin America over the previous 20 years.[14] In the 1970s Latin American women, stimulated by the new secular women's movement and the translation of feminist theology from Germany and the United States, began to recognize that "we are oppressed as historical subjects. We discovered our oppression in the Bible, in theology, in our churches". The first phase of response to this discovery was the search for positive female role models in the Bible: prophetesses and matriarchs; Mary Magdalene, and other women disciples.

The second phase of feminist theology began a "feminization of theological concepts. We began to discover the submerged feminine expressions for God in the Bible. We discovered God's maternal face in texts such as Isaiah 49."[15] There was also an expansion of women's teaching and ministering roles in the churches, as academics, catechists, and leaders of base communities on the grassroots level. Male liberation theologians began to include a few women in their conferences and publications, to give the "woman's perspective" (typically confined to topics, such as family, anthropology, and Mary, not the "big" topics like Trinity and Christology).[16]

For Gebara, both of these stages of feminist theology were still "patriarchal feminism," which did not challenge the hierarchical paradigm of humanity, God, and the cosmos, but simply added women to it. Women were thought of as having distinct (even morally superior) moral insights and ways of being than men. One needed to add the "feminine dimension" to theology and pastoral life. Gebara sees herself and others engaged in a third and more radical step in feminist theology that is not simply adding the women's perspective, but dismantling the basic patriarchal paradigm that has shaped all relations, of humans to each other, to nature, and to God.

These first stages of Latin American feminist theology also were much dominated by the patronage (and limits) of male liberation theologians. More radical gender critiques of society, the church, and theology were muted to stay within the limits of the "woman's voice" that male liberation theologians were willing to hear. But by 1990, however, there was a sense that the older liberation theology paradigm was in crisis. The Sandinista defeat in Nicaragua and the fall of Eastern European communist states gave the sense that all the struggles and sacrifices that had been made by Latin American people for revolutionary change over the past 30 years were for naught. Poverty was worse that ever, while the ability to even imagine an alternative economic order to triumphal global capitalism was being declared impossible.[17]

This sense of crisis of the old hope of socialist revolution and its theological reflection led to a recognition of a need for a new more inclusive paradigm of liberation that would recognize multiple aspects of oppression and sites of struggle. Critiques from feminists and theologians from other regions of lack of sufficient attention to gender, race, and culture in theology brought some Latin American male theologians, such as Leonardo Boff and Pablo Richard, to focus more on these topics.[18]

The 1992 observance of the "500 years of Resistance" as an alternative to the celebration of "Columbus's discovery of America" gave a forum to the Indigenous peoples to voice their experiences of genocidal oppression and cultural suppression during the years since the Spanish "invasion." Afro-Caribbean and Afro-Brazilian peoples also began to gain a voice to tell their story and to denounce the racism of Latin American white and mestizo culture and society.[19] The ecological movement began to be taken more seriously as a Latin American problem, not seen just as a pseudo-problem imposed by the wealthy nations. In fact, impoverishment of the people and of the land had gone hand in hand in Latin America since the Spanish and Portuguese invasion, although this crisis was now more aggravated by modern industrialism.[20]

Elsa Tamez, a Mexican Protestant biblical scholar and dean of the Universidad Biblico in San Jose, Costa Rica, has taken the question of cultural oppression in relation to the Indigenous peoples of the Americas as a central preoccupation. Her quest to vindicate the Indigenous voice, not just as victims of social oppression, but as people with a legitimate religious tradition that needs to be heard and integrated into Christian theology, breached the walls between Christian exclusivism and other religions, particularly toward Indigenous "pagan" peoples, that had been foundational to Christian evangelization of the Americas, as much for Protestants as Catholics.

Tamez' pamphlet, *Quetzalcoatl y el Dios Cristiano*[21] was based on the theme of the "conflict between the Gods" that had been explored by theologians such as

Pablo Richard.[22] Richard had argued that the "God problem" of contemporary Christianity was not between atheism and belief in God (as liberal Christianity assumed) but between the true God and the idols. The true God is the God of Life, the God of the prophets and of Jesus, who calls us to preferential option for the poor. Idolatry is not primarily a question of "false gods" of other religions, but rather the corruption of biblical faith so that the biblical God is converted into a tool of the rich and powerful to sacralize their wealth and power, to call for submission to this unjust regime of military, economic, and political dominance in the name of submission to the "will of God." Liberation theology must be about denouncing this false God of death and announcing the true God of life.

Tamez used this theme to analyze the relationship between the Christianity of the Spanish conquerors and the defeated Aztec and Nahuatl peoples of Mexico. Eschewing any simple dualism between Christianity and the indigenous religion in which one is good and the other bad, even in reversed form, Tamez seeks to show that the God of Life was already known in pre-Aztec Nahuatl religion in the form of Quetzalcoatl, but this figure had been corrupted in later militarized Nahuatl society, culminating with the Aztecs who imposed their war God, Huitzilopochtli, upon the traditions from the earlier God. Traditions of self-sacrifice in the interests of the well-being of the people were perverted into a violent practice of human sacrifice of war captives.

When the Spanish arrived, justifying their conquest in the name of bringing salvation from the "true God" to the "Indians," they were repelled by these practices of human sacrifice and used them to reinforce their view of Indigenous religion as totally demonic, but they failed to recognize that their own version of Christianity was just as much a perversion of Christianity into a religion of war, violence, and human sacrifice. Tamez draws on sixteenth-century documents to show that the Indians submitted to Christianity out of powerlessness, with full recognition that it spelled "bad news" for themselves. Yet they also were able to glimpse positive elements of the biblical God of life and justice behind the swords of the Spanish, similar to their own faith.[23]

It is time, Tamez believes, for Christians, in turn, to recognize the valid religious principles in Indigenous religions. A liberating theology must be based on a mutual respect for the liberating elements in both traditions, and a struggle against the death-dealing aspects of both traditions, rather than an assumption of essential superiority of Christianity to Indigenous religions. In her talk for the 1994 global dialogue of feminist theology in Costa Rica: "Cultural Violence against Women in Latin America,"[24] Tamez lays out a complex analysis of Latin American culture. She says that Latin Americans need to claim all the layers of their traditions as Mestizo people of both Indigenous and European ancestry. This does not mean romanticizing Indigenous cultures as totally egalitarian toward women against Spanish patriarchy, or seeing Latin Americans just as innocent victims vis-à-vis Northern aggression. Rather there must be a frank appraisal of the themes that mandated violence against women in the Indigenous cultures. These were overlaid by Spanish patterns that were violent toward their own women, and doubly so toward Indigenous women, victims of triple oppression of impoverishment and racial and sexual contempt.

Tamez wants to develop a Latin American feminist "hermeneutic of culture" that can differentiate what is oppressive and what is liberating in both Indigenous and

Christian cultures. She also calls for a relation to feminists of the North that must be based on mutual respect for each other's differences of culture. Only on this basis can there be alliances between feminists internationally to fight against the violence of oppressive foreign cultures coming from the powerful nations. Latin American Christians need to develop a nondiscriminatory discourse that honors true elements in other religions, and to work toward egalitarian relations between men and women in their own churches and societies.

While Elsa Tamez has focused on cultural critique, Mexican theologian Maria Pilar Aquino has sought a more expanded analysis of economic injustice. She analyzes gender oppression in the context of the multidimensional aspects of racial, class, cultural, and ecological violence wrought by neoliberal global economy, as the framework for her feminist liberation theology. In her 1992 book, *Nuestro Clamor por la Vida* (*Our Cry for Life*)[25] Aquino sought to sketch the foundations for a Latin American feminist theology. In this book she uses liberation theology methodology as a foundation, deepening it by situating Latin American women's oppression and praxis of liberation as its central optic.

For Aquino, an adequate shaping of a Latin American praxis of liberation must be situated in a comprehensive analysis of the historical, ideological, and socioeconomic forces that have determined woman's oppression. This means reclaiming the many layers of Latin American women's history: not only indigenous women's spirituality and her subjugation, but also resistance to Spanish colonialism; not only the shaping of divisions between women, Indigenous, black, mestizo, and white, but also breaking across these divisions in praxes of solidarity. It also means overcoming the split of public and private of modern ideology that falsely naturalizes women's oppression in the household and informal economies and fails to recognize these patterns of women's work as an integral part of the total system of socioeconomic exploitation.

Oppression is cultural as well as social. Feminist liberation theologians must analyze the logocentric modes of discourse that silence women's voice and experience. They should shape a new mode of "sentient intelligence" to allow women to articulate their resistance to oppression and their hope for well-being. Ideological critique includes critique of the androcentrism of the Bible and theology. Women must uncover the oppressive content of biblical stories and theological symbols and shape alternative readings of scripture.

For Aquino the possibility for this lies in Jesus' liberating praxis for all, women equally with men. Jesus' announcement of "good news to the poor" points to God's recreative "liberating purpose for creation, history, the world and humanity."[26] Redemption is an ongoing praxis to realize this fullness of life, overcoming all oppressive hierarchies. Latin American feminism is about reading this critique and hope from the optic of the multiple dimensions of oppression of Latin American women. At the end of her book, Aquino sketches unfinished tasks to deepen this work of reflection on liberating praxis for Latin American women: less dependency on male liberation theologians, more critical feminist theory and social analysis, deepening critique of the patriarchal elements of the Bible, closer collaboration with the Latin American feminist movements, more interclass and race collaboration, more reclaiming of Indigenous spirituality and Latin American women's history.[27]

In her most recent writings Aquino has done more work "across the border" in the circles developing a North American Hispanic theology.[28] She has also been concerned with the development of a fuller critique of the neoliberal global market economy, with its privileging of an economic elite, mostly white and male, and its deepening poverty for all others, female, black, or brown, Third World, and the earth itself. In her 1996 essay "Economic Violence in Latin American Perspective" she shows that this neo-Liberal market economy that claims to have triumphed as the only possible economy and way of life, in the wake of the fall of socialist alternatives, is not only creating poverty and violence for most humans outside this elite, but also rests on an idolatrous claim to universal truth and normative ethics for human fulfillment.[29]

For neoliberal ideology the competitive individual seeking to maximize "his" profits and consumer reach is the only model of human activity and fulfillment. The market is good, just, and "democratic" because it not only automatically rewards all who adopt this way of life, but also punishes all those who stand outside it. The false claim of neoliberalism is that *all* can win in this system, concealing the obvious reality that the system works by only a small minority winning at the expense of all others. By refusing to admit this, it conceals its true elitist (racist, sexist, classist) face, and makes poverty the individual failings of the poor for which they alone are responsible.

Aquino calls for a feminist liberation theology in which women (and men) from Latin America would join hands with those from other areas of South and North to critique this system and expose its true face of violence for most humans and to the earth. This critique must also entail creating an alternative universalism, not based on the false universalizing of the power claims of one elite group, but on the aspirations of all humans within the planet earth to shared life and well-being.

This means dismantling the claims of neoliberalism to be the only possible economy, showing that it is in fact ultimately impossible and destructive for all, for the system that presently impoverishes almost all must itself end in general destruction. Revolt against its false claims to promote prosperous democratic societies must recreate a new imagination about what could be a livable future that would be inclusive of all living beings on earth. A feminist liberation theology speaks on behalf of this alternative livable future, against the false system that points to general death.

While Elsa Tamez breaks across the Christian–Indigenous cultural division to shape a new liberating theology of life, and Aquino seeks a broader and deeper analysis of the multilayered system of oppression as the context for inclusive liberating praxis, Brazilian theologian Ivone Gebara has focused in her recent writings on dismantling the patriarchal cosmovision of dualistic hierarchy that sustains ideologies and social systems of domination of some (Christian white male ruling class humans) over others (non-Christians, nonwhites, women, the poor, and the earth).

Gebara too sees all theology, including feminist theologies, as arising in distinct contexts and needing to own those contexts, speaking both within and out of their particularity, and yet also seeking to point from that context to what interconnects us all, as humans, as earth creatures, as parts of the whole cosmos. She speaks as a privileged Brazilian woman (white, middle class, educated) but one who has chosen to identify with the poorest Black and Indigenous Brazilians of the northeast of her country both as an option for the poor and as the context from which the oppressive system can be more truthfully discerned from its underside.[30]

The northeast of Brazil where Gebara has chosen to live and work is a region of violent contrasts of wealth and poverty that has been shaped by colonialism and capitalism; a few with great power, the majority powerless; a few with vast landholding and most landless. As a context for doing theology it does not afford monastic or ivory tower solitude and quiet that has been the traditional Christian "place" for cultivating spirituality and theological reflection. Rather it is a place of noise and garbage. The noise is both the noise pollution of a disfunctional modern industrialism and the noisy responses of the poor who live in this world. Garbage is the waste discarded disproportionately by the wealthy that scarcely touches their own pristine precincts, but this is the garbage in which the poor must live. To live one's spirituality, to do one's theology, in the midst of such noise and garbage is to do them in the midst of oppression, but also with consciousness of the vitality of the poor who somewhat manage to survive and even celebrate in it and despite of it.[31]

For Gebara, women are coming to theological voice at a unique time, at a time when history is irrupting in their lives and they are becoming aware of becoming historical agents. It is also a time when the historical systems of domination built by humans over millennia, and their religious ratifications, are coming apart and revealing themselves as unviable. Women theologians must dare to see through the successive layers of distortion that justify this dominant system in our theology and to reflect on our inherited symbols from the context of our real questions, the questions of defense of life in the midst of violence. They must overcome their timidity in approaching these monumental theological constructs that claim such authority and respect and to ask the questions of daily life, shaping new ways of speaking, even if they are halting and less than systematic.

For Gebara this daring to ask questions in the face of great systems of authority begins with a deconstruction of theology, revealing its reality as anthropology. We must constantly reclaim our own theological projections and recognize that all theology, including the Bible, is a human cultural construct. Christian theology, the Christian Scriptures, are one such construct[32] among others. There is no God "out there" revealing "His Nature" and "His Plan" to us. It is we ourselves, the thinking part of the cosmos, who are thinking, imagining, and constructing systems of interpretation. Christian theology must be done ecumenically in relation to the many other human religions, recognizing ours is one human construct among others. We must deconstruct our traditions to see how our ways of structuring our stories validates violent power of some over others, and find ways to retell them that can be mutually life-giving.

Gebara has particularly focused on the symbol of God as Trinity in her work of deconstruction and reconstruction.[33] For Gebara, the Trinity is not a distant separate God living some place else, controlling it from outside creation. Rather the Trinity is a symbolic expression of the basic dynamic of life itself as a process of vital interrelational creativity. Life as interrelational creativity exists on every level of reality. As cosmos it reveals the whole process of cosmic unfolding and interrelation of planets and galaxies. As earth it shows us the dynamic interrelational process of life unfolding in the biosphere.

Each species ramifies into many differences, including human beings with their many races and cultures. We must celebrate this diversity of human plurality of races and cultures, and affirm their interrelation with one another in one human community on earth. Likewise interpersonal society and finally the person herself exists as a dynamic of plurality, interdependency, and creativity, of unity and diversity in interaction. While she sees this dynamic of life in vital interrelationality as the real meaning of the Trinity, for Gebara this also raises the question of the origin and reproduction of evil.

For Gebara, the reality of the life process is by its very nature fragile, limited, and threatened, reproducing itself in a dynamic of pain and joy, birth and death, and birth again.[34] In this sense evil (tragedy) is a natural part of life and inseparable from it. But humans are threatened by this fragility, this relation of life and death, diversity, and connection. There is a constant urge to secure life permanently against death, to secure power as control to ward off vulnerability, to ward off difference by subjugating the "other" to our uniformity. Women, other races and cultures, and the earth itself have all been victims of this urge to control and secure life, to assert power and uniformity against death, vulnerability, and difference. Women have been victimized especially because they represent the vulnerability of the life process, its threatening power and otherness to men.

Out of this urge to control and secure life and power, powerful groups of people, particularly males of those groups, have arisen to shape systems of domination, attempting to secure a monopoly of power over life for themselves, and reducing women, other races and, the earth to subjugation, thereby distorting the dynamic of interrelation into extreme unbalances of power and powerlessness, dominance and violation, wealth and poverty. We live at a time when this system of distortion has reached its nadir, threatening to destroy the whole planetary life system. These systems of unbalanced power are what evil means in the second sense of sin, of unnatural evil, unnecessary and finally destructive evil, the evil that humans have constructed, but which humans cannot and should not accept, but can and must seek to overcome, both for justice and for the defense of life itself.

Religion plays an ambivalent role in this construction of system of sin, or unnatural evil, for Gebara. Most religions have been a projection of this urge for control and domination by the powerful. We create a powerful, patriarchal, invulnerable God who reflects the desire of men for control of life without death. The powerless, in turn, imagine countermyths of great Messiahs who will defeat the evildoers by violence and bring in a permanent state of bliss without death. Messianic countermyths, including much of the hopes of liberation generated by Liberation theology, tend simply to reproduce the system of violence.

The Jews produced Messianic hopes to counteract the oppression they suffered at the hands of great empires, but they did so in a way that assumed counterviolence. Jesus, however, for Gebara, was a very different prophetic figure. Far from reproducing the cycle of violence, he sought to break through it. Taking the side of the victims of oppression, he also called us to a new community of mutual service. The dominant system could not tolerate his message and killed him to silence his message. But his followers also betrayed him by turning his new vision of shared love into a new warrior, imperial Savior who would secure the new Christian system of dominating power.[35]

For Gebara, a feminist theology must not project either a paradise of the beginning or a paradise of the future that reproduce the flight from finitude and difference.

Rather we need to withdraw all these projections and seek to dismantle the systems of violence and domination, not to create a future paradise secured from pain, limits, vulnerability, and death, but to learn to share with one another our fragile goods, our vulnerable joys and sorrows in a way that is truly mutual. We need to overcome domination and exploitation of each other in order to learn to embrace each other and celebrate our joys in the midst of sorrows, birth in the midst of pain, and the resurgence of life in the midst of death.

We must, as Gebara put it, "take the side of the serpent," (of the Genesis story), refusing the orders of the patriarchal God that keep us in a state of childish dependency.[36] We can then recognize that the fragile fruit of the Tree of Life is indeed lovely and good for discernment, and eat with relish, making it a part of our bodies. This is the possible redemption of life on earth. But it is possible only when we put aside the impossible redemptions of final conquest of limits in a realm of immortal life untouched by sorrow, vulnerability, and finitude.

Notes

1. Gustavo Gutierrez, *Liberation Theology*, Fifteenth anniversary edition (Maryknoll, NY: Orbis Press, 1988).
2. See Prologue by Mary John Mananzan, in *Women Resisting Violence: Spirituality for Life*, ed. Mary John Mananzan et al. (Maryknoll, NY: Orbis Press, 1996) 1.
3. This account is taken from my personal remembrance of these events as a delegate to this conference.
4. For this history of the EATWOT process and the emergence of Third World feminist theology within it to 1993 from her experience, see Virginia Fabella, *Beyond Bonding: A Third World Women's Theological Journey* (Manila: Institute of Women's Studies, 1993).
5. Major papers and statements from the intercontinental conference, as well as continental conferences, are found in *With Passion and Compassion: Third World Women Doing Theology*, ed. Virginia Fabella and Mercy Amba Oduyoye (Maryknoll, NY: Orbis Press, 1988).
6. Major papers that emerged from this conference are found in Mananzan et al. eds., *Women Resisting Violence*.
7. White Western people tend to assume the term "Third World" is a putdown that implies a "third-down" on some hierarchical scale. However, in her book, *Beyond Bonding*, Virginia Fabella recalls that this term had a different meaning for the EATWOT movement, suggesting a parallel to the French revolutionary term "third estate," meaning a whole new group that is emerging beyond the dominant hierarchy and reshaping a new majority (see 3–4).
8. See issues of the Indian women's journal, *Manushi*, C1 1202, Lajpat Nagar, New Delhi, 110024.
9. For the Asian parallel, see Gabriele Dietrich, "South Asian Feminist Theory and its Significance for Feminist Theology," in *The Power of Naming: Concilium Reader in Feminist Theology*, ed. Elizabeth S. Fiorenza (Maryknoll, NY: Orbis Press, 1996) 45–59.
10. These remarks are drawn from my personal experience during a 1994 lecture trip to Brazil, Argentina, and Chile. My agenda was to interconnect the secular women's movement in those countries and feminist theologians, particularly in relation to issues of reproductive rights. The extent to which Catholic feminist theologians particularly were concerned about censure from the church if they ventured into those topics was evident.

See Maria Jose F. Rosado Nunes, "Women's Voices in Latin American Theology," in *The Power of Naming*, 14–26.

11. Maria Clara Bingemer, Tereza Cavalcanti and Ana Maria Tepedino are Catholic laywomen who teach at the Catholic University of Rio de Janeiro. In Sao Paulo the Methodist College has a lively program of graduate women's studies that includes religious issues and women. This information comes from my own trips and personal experience giving lectures at these universities in these two cities.

12. Information comes from personal trips to Santiago de Chile and Lima, Peru, and extended association with leaders of these two groups. The Conspirando collective and its publications can be contacted through Judy Ress, Casilla 371–11, Correo Nunoa, Santiago, Chile, and Talitha Cumi, through Rosa Dominga Trapasso, Republica de Portugal 492, Lima 5, Peru.

13. The Maryknoll sisters and lay missionaries have played a key role in these Catholic feminist networks.

14. "Ecofeminism and Panentheism," Interview by Mary Judy Ress, *Creation Spirituality* (Nov/Dec, 1993): 9–11.

15. Ress, "Ecofeminism and Panentheism," 9–11.

16. The major publication of liberation theology edited by Ignacio Ellacuria and Jon Sobrino, *Mysterium Liberationis: Conceptos fundamentales de la teologia de la liberacion*, 2 vol. (Madrid: Editorial Trotta, 1990), contained two essays by women, both with explicitly female themes: "Teologia de la Mujer," by Ana Maria Tepedino and Margarida L. Ribeiro Brandao and "Maria," by Ivone Gebara and Maria Clara Bingemer, a total of 30 pages out of 622 pages, 287–298 and 601–618. In the English abridged edition, published by Orbis Press, 1993, these are 222–231 and 482–495.

17. See especially Franz Hinkelkammert, *The Ideological Weapons of Death: A Theological Critique of Capitalism* (Maryknoll, NY: Orbis Press, 1986).

18. See Leonardo Boff, *Ecology and Liberation: A New Paradigm* (Maryknoll, NY: Orbis Press, 1995). Also the interview of Pablo Richard in Elsa Tamez, *Against MacHismo* (Oak Park, Illinois: Meyer-Stone Books, 1987).

19. Numerous publications erupted from the observance of the Five Hundred Years of Resistance in the Americas. See, e.g., Michael McConnell et al. *Dangerous Memories: Invasion and Resistance since 1492* (Chicago: Chicago Religious Taskforce on Central America, 1991).

20. Boff, *Ecology and Liberation*, 123–130.

21. Elsa Tamez, *Quetzalcoatl y el Dios Cristiano in Cuadernos de Teologia y Cultura*, 6 (1992), San Jose, C.R.

22. *The Idols of Death and the God of Life*, ed. Pablo Richard (Maryknoll, NY: Orbis Press, 1983).

23. Tamez, *Quetzalcoatl y Dios*, 24–25.

24. In Mananzan et al., eds., *Women Resisting Violence*, 11–19.

25. Maria Pilar Aquino, *Nuestro Clamor por la Vida: Teologia latinoamericana desde la perspectiva de la mujer* (San Jose, Costa Rica: DEI, 1992); English: *Our Cry for Life* (Maryknoll, NY: Orbis Press, 1993).

26. See Aquino's "Perspectives on a Latina's Feminist Liberation Theology," in *Frontiers of Hispanic Theology in the U.S.*, ed. Allan F. Deck (Maryknoll, NY: Orbis Press, 1992) 24.

27. Aquino, *Our Cry for Life*, 178–190.

28. See her "Directions and Foundations of Hispanic/Latino Theology: Toward a Mestiza Theology of Liberation," in *Mestizo Christianity: Theology from the Latino Perspective* Arturo J. Bañuelas (Maryknoll, NY: Orbis Press, 1995) 192–208.

29. Mananzan et al., ed., *Women Resisting Violence*, 100–108.

30. Ivone Gebara, "Women Doing Theology in Latin America," in *Through Her Eyes: Women's Theology from Latin America*, ed. Elsa Tamez (Maryknoll, NY: Orbis Press, 1987) 38; see also her book, *Teologia a Ritmo de Mujer* (Madrid: San Pablo, 1995) 12.

31. Gebara, "A Cry for Life from Latin America," in *Spirituality of the Third World: A Cry for Life*, eds. K.C. Abraham and Bernadette Mbuy-Beya (Maryknoll, NY: Orbis Press, 1994) 109–118.

32. See her chapter "La Biblia y la Mujer: una hermeneutica feminista," in *Teologia a Ritmo de Mujer*, 27–38.

33. Gebara, "La Biblia y la Mujer," 109–156; condensed English translation in Rosemary R. Ruether, *Women Healing Earth: Third World Women on Ecology, Feminism and Religion* (Maryknoll, NY: Orbis Press, 1996) 13–23.

34. See her "En los origenes del Mal," and "Cuerpo de Mujer," in *Teologia a Ritmo de Mujer*, 39–52 and 71–88. See also Gebara's recent books: *Out of the Depths: Women's Experience of Evil and Salvation* (Minnesota: Fortress, 2002) and *La Sed de Sentido: Busquedas ecofem-inistas en prosa poetica* (Montevideo: Doble Clic, 2002).

35. See Gebara, "Critologia fundamental," in *Teologia a Ritmo de Mujer*, 53–70.

36. See her "The Face of Transcendence as a Challenge to Reading the Bible in Latin America," in *Searching the Scriptures*, vol.1, ed. Elisabeth Schüssler Fiorenza (New York: Crossroad, 1993) 178.

Chapter 13

Reflections on Conversation Two

Holly Hight and Lydia Sohn

Part two of the tripartite Conversation on the global future of feminist New Testament studies addresses a wide-range of issues facing feminist New Testament scholars in Latin America and Asia. Presenters Aída Besançon Spencer and Hisako Kinukawa are informed by an ethic of scholarship particular to their positionality, and their ethic is problemtized in their praxis of feminist New Testament studies (henceforth FNTS). Rosemary Ruether sheds light on the contributions of three Latin American feminists: Elsa Tamez, Maria Pilar Aquino, and Ivone Gebara—each contributing to the life and vitality of FNTS but specifically to Latin American feminist liberation theology. A multitude of questions emerge from these chapters: How can specific communities influence the praxis of FNTS? How does the social location and the specific experiences of each scholar influence her engagement in FNTS? What is sacred text? Where is the center of power? Where should feminist New Testament scholars place themselves in relationship to this power? How does their work influence the future of FNTS?

Besançon Spencer begins with a summary of her journey as a feminist New Testament scholar and proceeds to reconcile her feminism with her identity as a Latin American Christian. As an intercultural person and a feminist Christian, Besançon Spencer weaves four comparable themes within each of these identities into her scholarship and engagement with scripture. Her interpretation of the scripture reaffirms her identity and experience as a Latin American Christian feminist.

Kinukawa creates a methodology of FNTS that engages her identity as a feminist Japanese Christian living in a multireligious society and as "a colonized woman from a colonizing nation." Her multidimensional approach to interpreting scriptures establishes her work as relevant to contemporary national and global issues. She applies her perspectives to FNTS by performing a multi-faith reading of scripture. In her analysis in the book of Ruth, she identifies herself with Ruth—especially because Ruth is a foreigner urging Naomi to make her God, Ruth's God. Kinukawa underlines the commitment that Ruth has made to Naomi's God as relevant to Kinukawa's own social location in a multireligious society. In a country where less than 1 percent of the people claim Christianity, Kinukawa understands the importance of cultural practices influenced by Shintoism, Buddhism, and Confucianism. Kinukawa's commitment to Christianity does not require her abandonment of the cultural practices influenced by these religions. Ruth is an inspiring figure, because she crosses cultural and religious boundaries to love and commit to Naomi.

Zhiru responds to Kinukawa from her own context as a Buddhist nun. Zhiru's background and experience complements Kinukawa's methodology. She comments on the influence of Judeo-Christian concepts upon Asian religions and problematizes its authority in Asian contexts. She also calls for FNTS and religious studies around the globe to be involved in an interfaith multi-logue, where sensitivity and understanding become vital for connecting across the many differences.

Finally, Rosemary Ruether presents the contribution of three Latin American feminist theologians: Elsa Tamez, Maria Pilar Aquino, and Ivone Gebara. Elsa Tamez' position as a Mexican Protestan biblical scholar, has uniquely influenced her work with cultural studies. She examines the relationship between the Indigenous peoples of the Americas and Christianity. Tamez calls into question the labels that Christianity has placed upon Indigenous religious traditions, and hopes to reclaim the God of Life present in both traditions. Maria Pilar Aquino, a Mexican theologian, calls for a reclaiming of the layers of Latin American women's history, in order to critically analyze and challenge the multidimensionality of oppression. Brazilian theologian Ivone Gebara intimately identifies herself with the "poorest Black and Indigenous Brazilians of the Northeast of her country." In the midst of this pain and suffering, Gebara is inspired to engage herself and her work with the lives of these people. She is confronted with many questions about the interconnectedness of oppressions and how FNTS can relevantly respond to such realities.

All of these women create for themselves an ethic of scholarship that critically engages their scholarly work with their particular experience. Elizabeth Conde-Frazier, the respondent to Besançon Spencer, desires to see FNTS build upon the positive themes within the discourse in order to create a communal praxis focused on an ethic of justice. She stresses the importance of co-construction guided by an ethic of compassion and a desire for justice.

Hisako Kinukawa's ethic of scholarship is exhibited in her engagement with the reality of women hurt by Japanese imperialism—specifically the Korean comfort women. Kinukawa openly urges Japanese women to "keep pressing the government to carry out its obligations to the survivors: disclose the truth, acknowledge it, record it, express full apology, compensate the survivors [and] teach the children the history." Ultimately, Kinukawa advocates the "search for a spirituality that will create solidarity beyond the differences in political, economic, and cultural contexts."

Ruether presented Elsa Tamez' suggestion of a feminist "hermeneutic of culture" that will reclaim a biblical faith centered on a God of Life rather than the idolatrous, corrupted God that justifies the rich and powerful. Tamez specifically addresses the demonization of indigenous religious practices by Christianity. She calls for a liberation theology based on mutual respect for the life-giving qualities of both religious traditions, rather than the assumed superiority of Christianity. Maria Pilar Aquino opens the practice of feminist New Testament scholarship to an analysis of the multitude of oppressions. Her focus upon economic injustice calls for a multidimensional analysis of the systems of power promoting violence and oppression. She uses her New Testament scholarship to critically analyze and call for a radical change of the neoliberal global economy, which she views as the root of many oppressions. Gebara seeks "to dismantle the patriarchal cosmovision of dualistic hierarchy," which she views as maintaining the domination and power of certain systems over others.

Conversation Three: Africa and the Diaspora

Chapter 14

Rahab is Hanging Out a Red Ribbon: One African Woman's Perspective on the Future of Feminist New Testament Scholarship

Musa W. Dube

Introduction: Waking Up From a Nightmare

I never felt closer to her than now. I mean Rahab the sex worker of Jericho. I have been (and I am still) in her house. I have thought her thoughts. I have laughed with Rahab's laughter. I have cried with Rahab's tears, until I realized that maybe I will just have to hang my tears to dry.[1] I have walked her walk to the window of her home, which was built in the wall of the great city of Jericho—a city about to be pulled down, destroyed together with its inhabitants, by those with physical might and divine claims. Together with thousands of other inhabitants of the city, they are counting days to the dreadful day of their destruction. The enemy is gathering around to besiege the city. The sin of Jericho, and its inhabitants, is that they are different and, perhaps, less powerful. As Rahab walks to the window, she stops to glance at the bed by the far end—the bed where she made love with the two spies from the enemy camp. She walks on toward the window and begins to hang the red ribbon. It hangs loosely down the wall so that her enemies must see it and save her, when they destroy the city of Jericho and all its inhabitants.

As she walks away from the window, I realize that I am her. I am Rahab. I am also leaning on a small window, stuck in a world divided by great walls—walls that too easily pretend that we have not touched and made love to one another and felt the passion of our humanness. Like Rahab, I am also standing at the window by a great wall that divides the powerful and the less powerful. I am standing in the shadow of death, where the powerful threaten to wipe out cities and they do. I am a witness: war invades the screens of our TV sets and comes straight into our homes, while we sit and watch. It makes us and our children consumers of violence, and perhaps even collaborators for many of us sit and watch silently.

Like Rahab, I am also tying a red ribbon in a world rocked by another silent war, the war against HIV/AIDS. It has killed and still kills millions. It has infected and still infects millions. It has affected all of us, or so I want to believe. I tie out a red ribbon, inviting the world to stand in solidarity with Africa and all other people living with HIV/AIDS, to save life. I tie the red ribbon to say, "Lets own up. We have already made love." Will the world see this red ribbon hanging and hasten to stop violence, to address the social injustice that fuels the spread of HIV/AIDS?

This is not the first time that I walk with Rahab, the sex worker of Jericho.[2] I have read her story in Joshua chapter two, as a story written by the powerful about their victims.[3] In the eve of the invasion of Jericho by the Israelites, she becomes the host of two spies, sent to explore the land and report to Joshua. They enter Rahab's house and never explore any other land, save, I presume, the sex worker's own body.[4] When the king of Jericho learns that she has received such visitors, he sends investigators. Instead of Rahab taking sides with her people, she hides the spies in her house and misdirects the investigators. She is a traitor. Thereafter, she releases the spies and sends them safely away. She saves their lives. Rahab releases them to escape, but not before she speaks and bargains with them. She says,

> I know that the Lord has given you the land, and that dread of you has fallen on us, and that all the inhabitants of the land melt in fear before you. For we have heard how the Lord dried up the water of the Red Sea before you when you came out of Egypt, and what you did to the two kings of the Amorites that were beyond the Jordan, to Sihon and Og, whom you utterly destroyed. As soon as we heard it, our hearts melted, and there was no courage left in us because of you. The Lord your God is indeed God in heaven above and on earth below. Now then, since I have dealt kindly with you, swear to me by the Lord that you in turn will deal kindly with my family. . . . The men said to her, "Our life for yours!" (2:9–14)

When the spies get back to the camp they report to Joshua, using words that are almost a replica of Rahab's words. They say, "Truly, the Lord has given all land in our hands; moreover all the inhabitants of the land melt in fear before us" (Joshua 2:24). The reader knows four things: First, that far from melting in fear the people of Jericho came bravely in search of the spies when they heard the enemy spies were in town, and even followed them out of the city. They were ready to fight in defense of their city. Second, the reader knows that the spies hardly explored the city or gathered stories from people. As the story tersely tells us, "they went, and entered the house of a prostitute whose name was Rahab, and spent the night there" (Joshua 2:1). From her house they went back to the camp. So the land and the people they describe are no other than Rahab herself. The words of Rahab are presented as the words of Jericho. Rahab is Jericho. Knowing Rahab is knowing Jericho. Third, Israelites have been repeatedly warned against the daughters of Canaan who purposely prostitute themselves to their Gods (Exodus 34:15–16). Lastly, privileged readers know that Rahab herself sounds more like she has been reading Deuteronomy and Exodus.

As a Two-Thirds World woman reading this story, I am struck by the ideology of employing gender in narratives that legitimate the domination of one nation by another. I note how Jericho itself has been portrayed as the body of a sex worker, which easily changes hands from one master to another. The story tells us that Jericho must be entered and taken and indeed Jericho is entered and taken. Jericho is portrayed, through the words of Rahab as in total awe of the invader, as having no courage in her own capacity to protect herself—but as begging to be taken and protected by the invader. Rahab stands in the long line of a literary motif that tends to equate invaded or entered lands with women who fall in love with or strongly desire the enemy. "This pattern is evident in *The Odyssey* and *The Aeneid*, where imperial traveling heroes, Odysseus and Aeneas, are constantly detained by women and goddesses of foreign lands who want them to stay in their lands."[5] The pattern is also evident in the story of Pocahontas.[6] Rahab's story belongs here.

Hence some biblical scholars have rightfully noted that in this passage Rahab sounds like she has been reading Deuteronomy and Exodus. That is, Rahab's words are almost a replica of the words, agenda, and ideology of her invaders. So who is quoting whom? It is easy to see why Rahab appears in the literature of her subjugators. Her story is written by them, projecting their own desires and agendas on her. She tells their story. Rahab is therefore,

> a literary creation of the colonizer's pen, she is the mouth piece of their agendas. The colonizer's ideal dream is that the colonized will proclaim the colonizer's superiority, pledge loyalty, and surrender their rights voluntarily. . . . Rahab's story contains the somewhat hidden agenda of the colonizer that proceeds by characterizing the colonized as people "who require and beseech to be dominated."[7]

For many of us, the Two-Thirds World women who read the Bible, Rahab embodies both colonial and patriarchal domination. We read her with a keen sense of how Rahab's double oppression works together with other systems of oppression such as racism, ethnicity, class, culture, military arrogance, and religious and sexual differences. But what if we do allow Rahab to tell her own story, to speak with her own words, instead of just reproducing the words of her dominators? This is the story I try to hear from Rahab and one I wish to tell. And hence I have adopted the story of Rahab as my model of a feminist reading—a paradigm that does not only resist patriarchal oppression and all its hierarchical dualism, but also seeks to decolonize the text and the world. Reading through Rahab's prism means that I underline our inevitable hybrid identities, our contact zones, our yearning for life—regardless of our differences we all do want to live peacefully and in justice. Reading through Rahab's prism means that I make efforts to look through the little window of hope, past the thick walls of division, and try to hang a red ribbon to some powerful aggressors—calling all to respect life and justice for all members of the earth community. As my postcolonial feminist reading model, Rahab is therefore not just a parroting Rahab. Rather, she challenges the powerful, through her words and acts. She asks them to read her text of life and brings them to commit themselves to her, when they are forced to say, "Our life for yours!"

The reader may well say, "Well, Rahab sure did hang a red ribbon, but the city still fell, after all! All the inhabitants of the city save for Rahab and her family, died."

They sure did. I cannot deny this.[8] In this chapter, I seek to push the boundaries of her act, from a selfish saving act to an act that bears a communal strategy of saving life. My position, therefore, is that the city fell because, there were not enough people, who are willing to take the place of Rahab, to look through a small window of hope, to plead for life, to hang a red ribbon. Second, my position is that there were not enough spies from the oppressor's camp, who were willing to shelf the mission to kill and begin to bond with the less powerful—those marked for death—and to pledge their commitment to them by saying "our lives for yours!" Suppose the whole army gave up on their national mission to kill?[9] The story would be very different. The city of Jericho and many other cities of the world fall because there are not enough of us who are willing to make love rather than to make war. When we take our places and acknowledge our interaction, our hybrid identities, we would have taken a step in the right direction toward being servants of life and love, rather than servants of death, oppression, and exploitation.

The success of Rahab's act is therefore as important as that of the spies. As they say, it takes two (and more) to tango! The spies, as Israelites, have been repeatedly warned against the daughters of Canaan, for they were supposedly reputed "to prostitute themselves to their gods." Yet lo and behold, when the spies enter Jericho, "they went and entered the house of a prostitute . . . and spent the night there" (Joshua 2:1). The reader can rightfully presume they did business that night. There is no indication that Joshua, their leader, had instructed them to make any concession with anybody in Jericho. They make these decisions for themselves, having touched Rahab and having been touched by Rahab. There is a sense in which both Rahab and the spies, therefore, betrayed their own people and cultures in the service of life. In short, the business of serving life and justice will only be possible, when both the powerful and the less powerful, the oppressed and the oppressors are willing to skip walls of division/violence/patriarchy/imperialism, to make love rather than war, to look through windows of hope, to betray forces of death and bond for the sake of serving life and justice.

Reading through Rahab's reading prism, therefore, means that I keenly seek to understand the construction of men and women; of international relations of the past and present; of black and white differences, ethnicity and sexual orientation, indeed, of how our identities are constructed and the power relations they produce and perpetuate. Reading through Rahab's prism also means that I underline our inevitable hybrid identities, our contact zones, even as they are still characterized by unjust power relations. It means looking through a window and seeing through a seemingly thick dividing wall. As my reading model, Rahab is, therefore, not just a parroting Rahab, who sounds like she has been reading Deuteronomy and Exodus or the master's text—that is one who is presented as being one with the enemy. Rather, Rahab challenges the powerful. She adds a twist to the master's texts, when she turns around and says, "Swear to me by the Lord you will in turn deal kindly with my family" (Joshua 2:12). She asks them to begin to measure their relationship on the basis of their meeting and knowing the very humanness and vulnerability of each person. The Rahab that I highlight here thus also challenges the powerful—she brings them to commit themselves to her well-being when they say, "Our life for yours!" (Joshua 2:14). She challenges them to read her text, the red ribbon that she hangs out, a text that calls them against their mission of killing and destroying lives, to a mission of saving life. When I read through Rahab's prism, I read for justice: justice for women of various backgrounds; justice against historical and contemporary imperialism and justice for all people who are subjected to various forms of oppression. I read for life.[10]

Yet I cannot deny that, as I read this ancient biblical story of the invasion of Jericho by Israelites, and the candidness with which the book of Joshua describes violence as sanctioned by God; and how this violence is systematically unleashed on those who are seemingly powerless for their differences, I realize just what little progress we have made. Violence and merciless killing, the crushing of other human beings in the twenty-first century is still our daily bread. The powerful name the evil of the less powerful and crush them. Multinational media corporations, in turn, generously serve this violence to us in our houses for breakfast, lunch, dinner, and for continuous snacking. The First, Second, and Two-Thirds World display and demonstrate the use of a range of sophisticated weapons of mass destruction to crude outdated and Stone Age weapons on each other—they are all deadly. It seems the current world would have liked to characterize itself as not only scientifically advanced, but also sensitive to human rights, human development, and earth rights. I am no longer so sure. It seems the so called "civilized" nations are no less barbaric than the ancient histories that are described in narratives such as the book of Joshua. In this our day, in this new millennium, children's rights are still violated, women's rights remain groaning for their full realization, racism and ethnic violence and discrimination abound. Imperialism proclaims its salvation as progress, civilization, development, democracy, and freedom to the oppressed who need to be saved from their own savage/evil systems, even if it takes invading and killing them. Discrimination on the basis of sexuality, age, and health status continues. In the Two-Thirds World regions, it seemed that we had successfully fought for liberation from colonization, but we know that neocolonization and globalization quickly followed. The struggle continues.

As feminist scholars thinking about the future of global feminist New Testament studies (henceforth FNTS) the current global context of increasing violence and suffering must be taken into consideration. We must ask how and what can the future of FNTS do to become active midwives of justice and peace in the world. What and how can FNTS do in a world rocked by violence, environmental degradation, increasing poverty, HIV/AIDS epidemic, wars, globalization, racism, anti-Semitism, ethnic, disability, sexual and age related discrimination? How do these situations affect women in different contexts of the world? How does the New Testament text and its interpretations contribute to these situations? How can FNTS bring healing to the earth communities? How can FNTS strive to address these in their interpretations of the text, teaching methods, research, writing, and their engagement with their communities and the world? While I do not attempt to address all these issues, I believe they are some of the questions that will need to be addressed by contemporary and future FNTS.

Remembering Feminist New Testament Dreams: Where I Have Been!

They say to go forward you must look back; to see the future you must see the past. So where has the FNTS been and where can it go? Can Rahab's reading prism offer us any sign posts? When we speak of modern FNTS, we are thinking of a range of 150 years. We are thinking of the time beginning in the nineteenth century when Elizabeth Cady Stanton[11] together with other women activists produced *The Women's Bible* in protest against the use of the biblical text to authorize social marginalization. The story of *The Women's Bible* has been told and retold many times.[12] What I wish to underline is that the beginning and writing of the *Women's Bible*, rose from a context of confronting social injustice that denied women and slaves their human rights. This was, therefore, a socially engaged feminist biblical interpretation, that read the text for social transformation and justice. In fact, this feminist *Women's Bible* was informed by the findings of its social activism on what needs to be changed in biblical interpretation. FNTS needs to constantly remember these beginnings in its practice. To avoid an ever-increasing temptation of being theory-driven (when theory sophistication becomes an end in itself) and academically confined scholars, who hardly interact with the most burning issues of our communities and world, we need to remember and work with these beginnings.

Although these early beginnings were suppressed for decades, until the late 1960s when feminist biblical studies resumed again, we note also that it was in a context of the civil rights movement and times for wars of liberation in the Two-Thirds World. The seeds of contemporary FNTS of the past 30 years, therefore, began to germinate and thrive, once more, in a context of social engagement in search for justice. As we reflect again on the future of global FNTS in the twenty-first century and in a new millennium, one cannot overemphasize the obvious: *the need for feminist practice to remain a socially engaged activist practice*, one that is committed to the establishment of justice and peace for women of various contexts and all people who are oppressed in the society. It is not far fetched to say, "Where and how FNTS must proceed should be informed by its social activism as agents of social justice."

Since the early 1970s Feminist New Testament (FNT) scholarship has seen much growth. It involves women (and men) from various backgrounds: white, black, yellow, brown; Jewish, Asian, African, African Americans, Asian Americans, Hispanic, Latin American, Europeans, North Americans, Native Americans, and other indigenous people. It is practiced by heterosexual, bisexual, and homosexual women and women identified feminist men. It is practiced by women from various religions such as Judaism, Islam, Hindusm, Buddhism, African indigenous religions, Native American Religions, Christianity, among others. Feminist readers also take different ideological angles in their reading of the New Testament (NT). We have reformists, conservatives, liberationists, survivalists, revolutionists, rejectionists and so on.[13]

Of late, FNT scholars are categorized according to the methods and theories that they apply, since the latter also influence the outcome. With the approach getting more interdisciplinary, most feminist scholars use a number of methods and theories all at once, making it more difficult to categorize FNT practice. Obviously, with this diversity, the future of global feminist studies must and will be different in and for different contexts according to where women live and read the New Testament for their own empowerment and for the establishment of justice in general. The diversity of its practitioners underlines the challenge; namely, the need to listen to one another and to empathize with situations that are outside one's immediate context. But, perhaps more importantly, we will also need the skill to know the histories of colonialism, imperialism, and current world forces of globalization that bind us together in our seemingly different economic, ethnic, racial, geographical, and cultural contexts. As FNTS feminists of different backgrounds we are divided (and also, ironically, bound) by class, race, age, dis/ability, ethnicities, history, religion, colonialism, sexual orientation, and all that makes us different. Our relationships, even as we are involved in reading for the liberation and empowerment of women and all the oppressed groups, are characterized by various power struggles that characterize our worlds.[14] One thing that characterizes the FNTS power struggles is that the discipline is still largely dominated by Western feminist scholars, who tend to focus on class, race, and gender, with a very limited accountability to international histories and structures.

I have had a first-hand experience of these power struggles. In 1989 when I first undertook my graduate NT studies, Western FNT scholarship was seemingly calling for the voices of Two-Thirds World women. I thus entered graduate school believing in the saying, "Sisterhood is powerful." As I have said elsewhere,[15] I entered with the euphoria of those days that held that, "until every woman is free, no woman is free!"[16] I was drawn by such statements as "Whatever diminishes or denies the full humanity of women must be presumed not to reflect the divine or an authentic relation to the divine."[17] So sweet was the call of her song of liberation on the alleys of a justice starved world—the song of feminist biblical scholarship. Which woman who is interested in women's empowerment, liberation, and justice in general would not say, "Count me in?" And so I enlisted to this great theological call for international gender justice. I repeat these statements not only because I am being nostalgic, but because they remain burning in my memory as words of great expectations, which encoded, for me, enormous revolutionary energy. These words said we will stand with and for the liberation of every woman regardless of our differences and our religions. They underlined that every woman's liberation was in the top drawer, at the top of the agenda. Our different religions, cultures, classes, races, ethnicities would not take priority over any woman's liberation. It was a beautiful dream. And so I stood to be counted.

Having responded and registered for graduate studies, my actual experiences, however, have sometimes been to the opposite. While sweet was the call of the feminist liberation agenda to and for all women, along the way I became aware that my questions as a Two-Thirds World woman were not addressed. In particular, I found FNTS excellent and vigorously committed to exposing and counteracting the various forms of systematic patriarchal oppression and their networks of oppression, but I did not find equal, if any, commitment toward various forms of systematic imperialism, colonialism, neocolonialism, globalization, and how it affects women and men; how it employs texts in its agenda; how it is structurally reproduced and maintained in our institutions. I am not saying that there was a lack of FNT scholars who often listed colonialism together with other social evils such as racism, classism, anti-Semitism, ethnicity, and compulsory heterosexuality. Rather, there was lack of any elaborate method of how to read and to identify a colonizing text, its ideology, its strategies of domination, and how it is maintained, even in the production of knowledge in the academia. I found very little elaboration on decolonizing feminist methods of resistance. Coming from a background of modern colonialism, neocolonialism, and the current globalization, I felt that it was important that FNT readers should not only seek to be committed "resisting readers" of gender oppression, but also to be decolonizing resisting readers, whose analysis seeks to understand how these forms of oppression overlap and differ; how they function with other social categories such as gender, class, race, disability, age, ethnicity, sexual and religious identity.[18] Without an equal attention to international relations of the past and present, my liberation as a Two-Thirds World woman was incomplete. Without factoring international injustice and its impact on the lives of women, injustice was in fact maintained.

And so for my PhD dissertation proposal, I sought to explore postcolonial feminist interpretations of the Bible. I had only one FNT scholar in my committee. When she read my proposal, she was adamant for the rest of the year that, "I had no thesis." I paid many visits to her office, we had many discussions and I decided to audit more of her classes, in attempt to build a bridge. My efforts to create a bridge of understanding were in vain. She continued to evaluate my work and its perspective with one summary sentence: "You have no thesis." The day of defending my dissertation proposal finally came. I passed, but she made it clear that were it not for the views of other members of my examination committee, that if she had her way, I would not pass. After a whole year of this painful experience, I did not see any need to have the only feminist NT scholar on my dissertation committee any more, so I dropped her after a year.[19] But this was not the end of the story.

I wrote my dissertation, seeking to articulate postcolonial feminist interpretations of the Bible. As I said, I was seeking for a feminist biblical agenda that was both depatriarchalizing and decolonizing. Toward the end of my dissertation, news had gone out about my dissertation, so a number of publishers asked for the manuscript even as I was still writing it. But to my surprise, they returned the manuscript, with the comment "excellent but sorry it is not publishable." One editor sent a full-paged memorable letter of praise, one that I have nicely filed away, but still at the end, it was "I am so sorry. . . ." Fortunately, one of the former graduate students of my school was working for a publisher, he said to me. "I am dying to publish your work. Submit it." And that is how I got published. I knew that the people who were reviewing my manuscript and rejecting it were FNT scholars.[20]

Through these experiences, I came to realize that although Western feminists said they were looking for and encouraging Two-Thirds World women to bring in their voices, they were in fact expected to come in as "parroting Rahabs"—women who reproduce the words and perspectives of their colonizers, the Western guild. These experiences make it clear that FNT scholars are actively involved in power struggles that characterize their worlds, even as they purportedly labor for justice of all women and all the oppressed of the earth. For me, these experiences also indicate that many feminists are yet to become decolonizing critical readers of their countries' colonial discourse and agenda in the production of knowledge. Perhaps, this is underlined by Carolyn Osiek, who points out that "minority women have learned from their experience that 'all women' do not necessarily stand in solidarity against the oppression of women, but that racism and classism have determined the relationship of the rich and poor, slave and free women."[21]

Further, while FNTS is characterized by women from diverse backgrounds, the majority of these are white middle-class women from North America and Europe.

In the whole of Africa, a land that is purportedly three times the size of the United States, I know only four women New Testament scholars. One is still writing her dissertation. In Asia and Latin America, the situation is not any better. Indeed, even among the North American minority groups, the number of trained FNT scholars is only a handful. This situation speaks for itself; the future of FNTS must strive to train women from Two-Thirds World, since the locus of the Christian religion has shifted to these places, particularly Latin America and Africa. Further, globalization itself brings multicultural communities and students to Western metropolitan institutions and neighborhoods. In making this effort, however, Two-Thirds World women must not be muzzled, or modeled after parroting Rahabs. Rather they should have the space to tell their own stories, to resurrect from the colonial and patriarchal graves of oppression and death; to thrive in peace and justice.

This lack of trained academic FNT scholars in Two-Thirds World, however, should not blind us to the fact that NT is read by many millions of women who are not in the academy. How do church women read and use the NT?[22] What feminist methods of reading arise from these women and how can the academy know these methods and teach them?[23] What happens when academic readers divorce themselves from the readings of their faith communities? I would say they become participants in maintaining that which they ignore. These questions call for future feminist studies that will seek to be in touch with the grassroots NT readers, as well as use methods that are not only propounded from academic halls, but also from implementing institutions and individuals.[24] Such methods will be better suited and more applicable to bring the necessary change, given that they rise from the communities that implement the text in their lives and institutions. More importantly, such an approach will be informed by the fact that feminist biblical practice does not only seek to understand the world, but also to change it.[25]

Concerning the success of FNTS and feminist theology to inaugurate systematic change, some raise doubts. In her article, "Feminist Theologies and the Possibility of God Talk," Millicent C. Feske contends that:

> As they enter the twenty-first-century, mainstream feminist theologians are compelled to recognize *the significant but relatively small gains made* in the inclusion of new images for God in contemporary church language and practice. They must recognize the *failure of reason* to convince the broader church of the importance of their claims, regardless of the retrieval of ancient traditions of female imagery and women's leadership in the early churches, despite appeals to justice and egalitarianism at the heart of Christian teaching. And they confront an impasse represented by their own unpronounceable names G'd and God/dess—that in their silence announce with utter clarity the complexity of the web of spiritual, historical, social, political and personal relationships of freedom and oppression embedded in human attempts to speak of the divine in Christian tradition. (emphasis added)[26]

Feske further contends that,

> At the end of 150 years of noteworthy feminist scholarship on gender and God talk, feminist theologians find themselves asking: Are we crazy to keep talking about God in a church that is almost wholly resistant to change and thoroughly patriarchal? Are we blind and in denial about the possibility of real and lasting transformation?[27]

Feske's evaluation may be too harsh, for numerous achievements can be tabled,[28] but it serves to underline that while a lot has been done and achieved in feminist program of liberation and FNTS, a lot more still needs to be done. Moreover, her evaluation presents us with the ghastly reality of the big gap between academic scholars and their communities of faith, hence underlying the need for a socially engaged and community-oriented scholarship as an imperative in the future of FNTS. Fortunately, major examples have now been presented to us, demonstrating that working with and within our communities of faith do not necessarily yield a less intense scholarship.[29] Feske also challenges feminist scholars to rethink their major reliance on "reason" to address spiritual matters.[30] Given the FNTS ongoing commitment to the program of justice and liberation, I wish to contribute some ideas to the question of the future of global FNTS by focusing on three major points, with several subdivisions. These consist of; first, taking up many feminist proposals and ideas to new levels. Second, taking the voices of Two-Thirds World women seriously and, last, pointing toward some new directions.

The Future of Global Feminist New Testament Studies

Taking Proposed Ideas to New Levels

Many excellent ideas have been put forward in FNTS, but have not been sufficiently followed up and implemented. Here I just want to highlight five of them for the future of global FNTS. These are:

1. *Reconnecting with communities of faith;*
2. *Continuing the reconstruction and reimagining of Christian histories, texts and interpretation;*
3. *Improving on our feminist commentary style;*
4. *Building capacity;* and
5. *Setting up a Society of FNTS.*

1. FNT scholars must strive to operate within the communities of faith that read the NT and apply it to their lives if its scholarship seeks to empower women and to liberate them from patriarchal worldviews and structures.[31] Early feminist studies (second wave) began with a focus on conscietizing groups, but, that stage has been largely left behind without any obvious alternative. So far, excellent liberating interpretations and resources have been put forth in the past 40 years, but it seems to be largely between the academic scholars themselves and their students, who may or may not have the courage and commitment to deliver these ideas to their congregations and in the classroom. While the academy is, no doubt, more of a space for research, writing, and developing ideas, FNTS must not lose sight of the fact that the larger community must be the place where these ideas are implemented—and yes,

indeed, where they must also be generated! But given that FNTS hermeneutics of liberation holds to the "goal of changing consciousness and transforming reality," it would seem social engagement is imperative.[32]

While FNTS has been quite critical of mainstream academic assumptions, it has nonetheless inherited the stance of historical critical male scholarship, which sought to read in a scientific, neutral, and objective way—a stance that put a deep wedge between the communities of faith and the academy. It is also a stance that Feske criticizes for its reliance on reason. Consequently, there is a gap between the academic FNTS, its excellent ideas, and the resources that it has proposed and produced for the promotion of the empowerment of women and the reality in the New Testament contemporary communities of faith. But since the FNTS has openly declared that theirs is "an interested scholarship," one that takes an option for women and the oppressed, advocating their rights, FNTS needs a more deliberate connection with the communities of faith, who are, by far, the biggest readers and implementers of the New Testament. FNT scholarship should also seek a "spiritual language" to address spiritual things especially since women remain the majority of consumers of religious texts.[33] Such a reconnection is important to avoid what Feske characterizes as bordering on madness. That is, a situation where feminists "keep on talking about God in a church that is wholly resistant to change and thoroughly patriarchal" and the "failure of reason to convince the broader church of the importance of their claims."[34]

This supposedly negligent impact of FNTS on communities of faith needs to be thoroughly examined; new strategies and new languages need to be developed and adopted. It is, therefore, imperative for the future of FNTS to also explore ways of doing NT studies with and from contemporary faith communities.[35] If FNTS cannot reach and change and be changed by the structures, institutions, and communities that consume the NT text, then its scholarship is still a long way from changing the world and empowering women in the Christian communities and societies. The task of working with and within NT faith communities will indeed be difficult. One may rightfully ask how academic freedom would be protected. Would the feminist voice be co-opted and compromised? Such concerns and difficulties are real and will be encountered.[36] But it will only be by working through such a strategy that a space of liberation will be carved out. It would also be helpful for all FNTS to remind themselves, that despite the difficulty and the need to maintain academic freedom, academic research is meant to help the world and its society to be a better place to live in—that is, if we are involved in a justice-seeking and socially engaged scholarship.

2. FNTS need to continue its strategy of reconstructing and reimagining NT texts, histories and interpretations and striving for gender inclusive translations. FNTS has shown that the authors, selectors of the canon, and their subsequent interpreters and translators were patriarchal.[37] While women were there and at the center of the Jesus Movement and early church, their presence is deliberately omitted, their role is minimized. In many different ways, the NT gives us what has been rightfully described as "the tip of the iceberg." FNTS scholars have indeed undertaken many ground-breaking reconstructions and reimagination of its texts and early Christian history. But in my opinion, this area remains largely unattended. I would suggest that the future of global FNTS should fully enter the *Semoya* space, the creative oral-Spirit place, to hear anew God speaking to them about the well-being of women and all the

oppressed.[38] I would suggest that the future of FNTS should see books and commentaries with such titles as *Feminist Reconstruction/Reimagining of Matthew, Mark, Luke, John, Acts*—virtually of every book of the New Testament, by different scholars and using many different methods. In these reimaginings, we would have the words of the likes of prophetess Anna (Luke 2:37) and the prophesies of the four daughters of Phillip in Acts fully recorded for us. In fact, we need volumes that reconstruct the words of such women as Prophet Anna, who reportedly spent many years prophesying in the temple (Luke 2:36–38). It would seem, however, that current FNTS scholarship has greatly suffered from the male academic space and its standards to live out its agendas, creativity, and visions. Hence feminist reimaginings are openly recommended but remain largely unattended. As I said elsewhere,

> Creativity in feminist circles has long been suggested. Yet it is only too true that such a method has lacked the courage of application. To this day we cannot boast of elaborate feminist re/writings of sacred texts from Africa, Asia, Australia, Europe and the Americas. The various feminist theological discourses have largely remained content with re-reading ancient patriarchal and colonizing scriptures.[39]

Perhaps, this is because FNT scholars and other feminist religious scholars are afraid that their work will be held to be less academic, or they fear to be expelled from their faith communities and academic positions in institutions that are still largely patriarchal and colonial. Again, I have already said elsewhere,

> In the feminist oral-Spirit space, responsible creativity; active prophecy that speaks against oppression and seeks liberation; intent praying that seeks partnership with the divine, can begin to hear, speak and write new words of life and justice. . . . I would suggest that the oral-Spirit framework needs to be employed to invite women from diverse cultures completely to rewrite, create, hear, speak, sense and feel new sacred words of life, wisdom, liberation and justice. The oral Spirit space needs to be employed to seek and to articulate life-affirming words which speak justice with, from and for all oppressed people. This, I would argue, is a necessary feminist theological step that will take patriarchy, imperialism and other forms of oppression seriously in the scriptures of the world as well as to allow women to speak their own sacred words.[40]

Coming to translations, early biblical feminists, in the nineteenth and twentieth century alike, showed great concerns on this area. Feminists of the past 40 years have made a visible contribution. Now we have a number of gender-inclusive and sensitive biblical versions. But many versions remain unshaken battalions of patriarchy, reproducing gender exclusive colonizing translations, and remaining insensitive to other forms of social exclusion that perpetuate the oppression of many.[41] Obviously, the FNTS agenda on gender and liberation sensitive translations need to be pursued. More gender and liberation sensitive theories/theology and translators need to be propounded and trained, respectively. More boards and directors of translating houses need to be lobbied to change their policies. Current translators need to be regularly retrained on translating for the liberation of God's people and creation as a whole. Faith communities need to be engaged. But, given that exclusive male translations sparked the 1885 *Women's Bible* and given the persistence of male-oriented translation, this is the century in which FNTS should set up its own translation projects and run translation and distributing houses that will uphold gender justice and justice for all.

3. On a similar, but slightly different note, FNTS needs to improve on its century and a half commentary style. This style that was first practiced in the 1895 *Women's Bible*, focuses primarily on biblical passages that feature women. *The Women's Bible Commentary of 1992*; *Searching the Scriptures Volume 2* of 1995; and Bonnie Thurston's *Women in the New Testament: Questions and Commentary* of 1998, while methodologically are theoretically more sophisticated than the Elizabeth Cady Stanton's volume, but contemporary feminist commentaries still largely focus on passages that feature women. This approach seems to suggest that patriarchy, its gender constructions, and the various other forms of oppression only function where women characters are specifically featured. If, however, we regard gender as a social construction that pervades all aspects of life, then feminist commentaries should focus on any passage of the Bible.

4. FNTS of the future needs to build its capacity. It has long been recognized that we need to train more feminist scholars from different backgrounds and to mentor those who have started. A lot has been done and achieved in this regard, but a lot more still needs to be done. In particular, the training of women from Two-Thirds World populations, where the Christian center is now located, is urgent. So far, FNTS' training and production of scholars from Africa, Asia, Latin America, and all other minority groups remain too small and too slow. Part of this has to do with the fact that graduate biblical studies as a whole are a long and expensive process, which has many language prerequisites. NTS thus easily becomes a classy discipline. The performance and contribution of many minority and Two-Thirds World students, who enter biblical studies is compromised by the amount of time they spend trying to finish their PhDs due to lack of scholarship funds. I, for example, only managed to do my graduate studies because the University of Botswana assumed full responsibility for all my graduate education to its very end. A crucial part of building capacity must, therefore, include setting up a scholarship fund to support women who wish to undertake FNTS. Without such a deliberate effort, I foresee a future where the locus of Christianity will continue to shift toward Two-Thirds World populations, while scholars or academic specialists in the field will continue to be based in Germany, UK, and the United States. Setting up a training fund is, therefore, imperative for the global future of the FNTS. Part of building capacity in FNTS must also be accompanied by a deliberate effort to increase and create FNTS journals that not only carry the necessary academic attraction, but also seek to serve the many different levels of FNTS agendas.

Further, the content of the curriculum and the methods of teaching will need to be revisited to ensure that they are designed to address the concerns/contexts of our various feminists students. Indeed feminist scholarship has been marked by admirable attempts to develop feminist pedagogy. Yet many of Two-Thirds World students have suffered from academic exclusion, irrelevance, and intellectual death, where training programs colonize us further.[42] It is often assumed that Western ways of teaching and theorizing are familiar, meaningful, acceptable, and relevant for all. The Western historical, cultural, political, and mythological worldview is thus predominantly used for biblical studies, an approach that not only suppresses other histories of the biblical text in the world, but one that is also colonial and colonizing. Feminist pedagogical efforts of liberation need to be pushed further. To develop a FNTS liberating pedagogy, one that is sensitive to both patriarchal and colonial ways of silencing and of dominating as well as various other categories of oppression, global feminist ways of teaching FNTS need to be explored and tried by various FNT scholars.[43] These pedagogical challenges are imperative for a justice-seeking discourse.

5. For all these issues to be systematically addressed and maintained, I would propose that, it would be helpful to have a Society of FNTS, that meets regularly to discuss its concerns, exchange research ideas and draw its short and long term program of action. In many ways, feminist biblical scholarship is to be congratulated for having been able to permeate Society of Biblical Literature (SBL) meetings and structures. But apart from just meeting at the hectic, crowded, and often impersonal SBL meetings, FNT scholarship needs a space of its own to hew the way forward. So far, FNTS is characterized by pockets of different groups who are either connected by method and theories, ethnicity, race, books of interest or those who quote each other. This is good, but not good enough to release the revolutionary energy of FNTS. If FNTS conceives itself as a movement for change, it also needs an organizational forum and a strategy, where a systematic approach to dislodging forces of oppression and the empowerment of women will have goals and objectives that are specific, measurable, attainable, and reasonable and set within defined time frames. If FNTS is serious with its activism, then it will need a plan of action with identified role players to implement the objectives and to periodically evaluate its program. It will need to raise funds to finance its vision and agenda. FNTS, therefore, need to establish ways that will foster dynamic coalitions of resistance; coalitions that will respect our differences and yet keep the struggle for justice uncompromised by our differences. Establishing a society of FNTS would go a long way in coordinating this effort. A society of FNTS could well serve as a forum for FNTS to meet with faith communities, filmmakers, and other stakeholders who market the NT to the wider society.

Once more, working models are already available to us. I am thinking here of the Circle of Concerned African Women Theologians, which was formed in 1989 under the leadership of Mercy Amba Oduyoye. The Circle now has a membership of about 300 African women in and outside the continent. The Circle functions as a space for motivating the production of action-oriented African feminist theologies. Its structures organize women at continental, regional, and country levels to work together, to study, research, write, teach, and preach religion/s in such a way that faith/s liberates/empowers women and all the oppressed. Within and through the Circle, a number of admirable feminist strategies are achieved: an interreligious and ecumenical forum is made available; academic and church women leaders work together; young potential scholars are identified, mentored, and helped to undertake further training. But above all, the women sit together and identify major issues of concern and decide to give them the necessary attention through research, writing, publishing, organizing workshops, and by drawing a plan of action with well-identified implementers. FNTS of the future will greatly benefit from adopting such a systematic organizational approach if it seeks to sharpen its revolutionary impact.

Taking Up the Voices of Two-Thirds World Women

Now turning to the second point, the future of global FNTS need to seriously take up the voices of Two-Thirds World women. As Carolyn Osiek points out, one of the major issues confronting feminist biblical scholarship is "the full incorporation of minority women's voices and experiences into what has been until very recently a dominant-culture of women's experience."[44] I deliberate on this point by subdividing it into three points; namely,

1. *Recognizing our overlapping histories of imperialism and colonialism;*
2. *Searching the world scriptures;*
3. *Taking Two-Thirds Worlds methods and scholars seriously.*

1. The global Future of FNTS needs to recognize and mainstream into their scholarship the fact that we may be women from First, Second, and Two-Thirds Worlds, living as we do in very different geographical, economic, and cultural spaces, yet we must not lose sight of the fact that we are bound together by our overlapping histories of modern imperialism, colonialism, neocolonialism, globalization and its accompanying race, class, ethnic, and religious divisions. The very fact that we are women of diverse cultural and religious backgrounds who read the New Testament is closely linked to modern imperialism, which worked with and through its Christian readers to establish cultural, economic, and political domination over 85 percent of the geographical spaces of the earth.[45] Those of us who come from non-Christian traditions, who are now Christians, are best seen for what we are: Rahabs, who bear the wounds of collaborating with the enemy, making love with the enemy, hanging out red ribbons to be identified and saved from the invader's might, crossing over to the enemy camp and betraying our people, cultures, and economies—I, for one, am still trying to discover how this adoption of the master's tools can subvert the master's house, if at all.[46] Or shall it only dent it, shake it, but keep it intact. Signs taken for wonders! Indeed, our acts of betrayal challenge the spies (in this case northern feminist readers) from the dominant side to also betray the oppressive forces of their nations and cultures for the sake of justice and liberation.

A crucial point here is that Two-Thirds World women need to be seen and recognized for their hybrid identities and scriptures.[47] But in fact a history of hybridity belongs to all of us. Two-Thirds World Women embody this history and cannot pretend that they are liberated by FNTS that do not fully take on the fact that imperialism, colonialism, neocolonialism and, now, globalization, have not only happened but they are often reproduced in academic frameworks and institutions.[48] FNT scholarship cannot liberate Two-Thirds World women or facilitate strategic coalitions, unless it interrogates how international domination and oppression is propounded and maintained, how it affects women, and what strategies of feminist resistance and decolonization can be adopted in FNT research, writing, teaching, and the empowerment of women to facilitate global justice with and for all members of the earth community. Although we, the Two-Thirds World women, dare to make love with the enemy and to hang a red ribbon for the sake of serving life and justice, we equally need spies who will transgress their own boundaries of being enemies, messengers of oppression and death and to say to us, "Our life for yours." We need, to use Mary Ann Tolbert's words, First World feminist readers who are prepared to commit the necessary "cultural treason"[49] for the sake of justice and liberation. North American FNT scholars will need to factor that they are the current empire. The work of Judith E. McKinlay, *Reframing Her: Biblical Women in Postcolonial Focus*, sets a notable example for all biblical feminists of current and past colonial powers on how this history needs to be fully owned in the liberatory discourse of feminist research, writing, and teaching. As I have argued elsewhere, our hybrid identity needs to be owned by all of us—for we have already touched and made love.[50]

2. Accordingly, the global future of FNTS need not just undertake a project of "Searching the Scriptures" but also that of searching the world scriptures.[51] I must narrate how I first received *Searching the Scriptures Volume Two*. It was a huge book with a cover that I mistook for a Chinese/Asian face. Putting that together with its title, I thought the volume was searching all the world scriptures for the course of justice and the empowerment of all women of the world. Upon realizing that it focused on NT books and its noncanonical counterparts, I was quite disappointed. Mainstream male scholarship has always studied the Bible together with its extra-canonical counterparts, although not for feminist agendas. So the contents of the scriptures covered by this volume were indeed radical, but they were not radical enough for a postcolonial world. The New Testament, as a Christian text, now exists with many other world scriptures and cultures as a direct consequence of modern imperialism. This coexistence happened under a history of domination and suppression, namely colonialism. To invite women from around the world to bring their expertise to focus on NT, excluding their own texts, which the NT was used to annihilate, is tantamount to inviting them to come as parroting Rahabs, who sound like they have been reading the master's text rather than their own. We need spies from the enemy camp to hear Rahab's negotiation and to read her red ribbon as a text that calls out to a different course: the course to defend life and justice despite our differences.

As we ponder on the future of FNTS, we need to undertake another "Searching of the Scriptures," where, in addition to integrating the crimes of patriarchy, the context of modern imperialism, colonialism, and globalization will be taken into consideration;[52] where hybridity will characterize global FNTS.[53] No longer shall Rahab be the only one to read and reproduce Deuteronomy and Exodus. Nor will Rahab seek to be saved alone, while her whole nation dies, for such salvation is not salvation, rather the rest of her people should also be saved from death-dealing forces. Thus, the enemy spies will also hear her voice of challenge—they shall also read her red ribbon as a call to defend life and justice, hence challenging the powerful to abandon their agenda of invasion, domination, and killing—challenging them to choose life and love. Rahab defies the great wall of division by highlighting the presence of a window of hope—the hope of saving and serving life and justice. Moreover, this searching of the world scriptures will need to disavow the colonialist model of comparative literature that sought to subject all other cultural/religious narratives to the literary corpus of the empire. Rather, the future of global FNTS must search all the world scriptures to empower women and for the sake of establishing justice around the world and building relationships of liberating interdependence.[54]

3. Similarly, the future of global FNTS must shake off the imperial framework and begin to take methods and theories propounded by Two-Thirds scholars seriously. The ideology of modern imperialism and colonialism can be crudely defined as "nothing good can come from the colonized centers, and everything good comes from the colonizers' centers." The colonized were constructed as savages and infants and to this day they are still called "developing nations," who need to depend on the "developed nations." This means that the religions, theories and methods of Two-Thirds World are seen as "developing." In fact, they get assigned marginal status in the academic halls and they tend to serve as optional and less serious scholarship, by virtue of their status as "developing nations." Hence culture, economic, and political structures of the so-called First World are held to be the standard that can be and should be transported to and must be acceptable and usable in all other parts of the world. The Western version of democracy is one case in point. This unequal, dualistic, and hierarchical framework that was established during colonial times still continues in the academy today, even among feminist scholars. One finds that textbooks, methods, and theories of reading and research expounded in the West are held to be the required and standard methods of FNT scholarship worldwide. What emanates from Two-Thirds World may be read as some form of academic tourism, but it is most of the time ignored or left just where it belongs—on the periphery.[55] Some of us, who studied in the West, therefore, experience the anomaly of reading exclusively Western books, historical settings, articles, theories, and methods. I dare say even in our African departments, the discourse is Western based, established as they were by colonial masters and in many cases sponsored or accredited by the same. It's a one-way traffic. Talk of being colonized, here is a perfect space! I do not, however, believe that FNTS as a liberation and justice-seeking practice wants to be a colonizing instrument or to work within the colonial framework. Further, given that the faith communities of the New Testament texts are shifting toward the Two-Thirds World, their textbooks, methods, and theories of reading need to become part of the future of global FNTS—if FNTS does not want to be a colonizing practice. In the book, *Other Ways of Reading: African Women and the Bible*, we made efforts to propose methods of reading from African cultural perspectives and many other minority scholars have also made such efforts.[56] It remains to be seen how these methods will be received and used in the FNTS and biblical studies in general.

New Directions for FNTS

My last point on the future of global FNTS is that the scholarship must also explore new directions and connections in its practice. Taking seriously the history and importance of operating as a socially engaged scholarship, I believe that some of the new directions that need to be explored are as follows:

1. *Undertaking human-rights-based and human developmental approach to FNTS;*
2. *Reading the text within the context of globalization;*
3. *Reading the NT within the context of violence;*
4. *Reading the text within the HIV/AIDS context.*

I shall now briefly elaborate on these in their given order.

1. The future of global FNTS must strive to embark on teaching, research, writing, and implementation that assumes a human-rights-based approach. Of course, feminist discourse has been influenced by the human rights movement and the UN-initiated women's empowerments assemblies that set a worldwide agenda for the realization of women's rights as human rights and the empowerment of women in all aspects of life. The last such meeting was held in Beijing in 1995. In Beijing the various global feminist and women's movements/NGOs/government departments, and ministries who gathered there identified 12 critical areas of concern, which would become the main focus in the global struggle for the empowerment of women for a decade.[57] We are in the end of this decade, but how much has FNTS contributed toward these 12 critical areas? I do not think I will be wrong to say that one hears very little, if at all, on how/what FNTS is deliberately doing its scholarship within the identified 12 critical areas.

In the year 2000, a Beijing +5 follow up meeting was held in New York. It was attended by 10,000 women from all over the world. They came to reevaluate their progress and to sharpen their way forward. I happened to be there, working with a small group called Religion Counts. What was shockingly evident at the preassembly and during these meetings were two things: First, the conservative Christian movements had sent many of their members to lobby against policies that empower women to take control of their lives. Inside, the meeting, where the worldwide policy paper was being drafted to set a global framework for the empowerment of women, the Vatican, the Christian right, and some conservative Islamic country representatives were putting aside their religious differences and working together to defend their patriarchal beliefs. The same stance was evident in the 1994 Cairo UN meeting on population. One thing that is evident in the UN forums is that, more often than not, religion stands for opposing, most strongly, the empowerment of women, or women's rights.[58]

When I attended the 1995 Beijing +5 UN meeting, I observed that the work of feminist religious scholars with all its wonderful proposals and resources hardly had a voice there. It was unknown, unfelt. The drafters of the document knew only the opposing and frustrating voices of the Vatican, some Conservative Christian groups and some conservative Moslem country representatives. As a FNT scholar, I had much time to reflect on what and where exactly is the impact of our work in the global forums. I wanted to know why four decades of feminist research in religion had no voice or impact in such a forum.

For me, it suggests that FNTS and other feminist religious studies are not only disconnected from their faith communities, they are also disconnected from the human developmental world that is trying to concretely empower women. It suggests that we are possibly doing a scholarship that is largely ancient, theoretically based, academically detached, rather than socially engaged and action-oriented toward executing real changes in the communities and structures of the world. Of course, FNTS holds that its discourse must be a public, political, and justice-seeking discourse. But just like our negligible impact on faith communities, we are seemingly not working within the UN articulated agenda, which is drawn by women activists, NGOs, and organizers from all over the world. I believe the future of global FNTS stands to benefit, to contribute from assuming a more deliberate and direct effort of undertaking a human rights, activist, and human developmental approach to their practice by working with various women groups, NGOs, women's departments/government ministries, and agencies that are laboring for women's rights and working for the empowerment of women in all aspects of life.

Further, I think the informal yet evident UN collaboration of the Vatican, conservative Christian Right and some Moslem countries against the global move to empower women and to recognize women's rights as human rights, underlines my earlier point. Namely, that FNTS must move toward an interreligious approach, or what I have called, "searching the world scriptures" approach. It also underlines the point that FNTS, together with feminists of other religions, need a society of their own, where they will work together to put up a coordinated plan of action on rereading the world scriptures, the written and unwritten ones, for the empowerment of women in the world and for a just world.

2. The global future of FNTS needs to have a full understanding of its own age/era; namely, globalization.[59] This term is everywhere. Globalization is defined as "the compression of the world,"[60] or "the absorption of all countries and systems into one,"[61] or a "process which has led to the creation of a single, international (global) financial or capital market," which "happened in stages over the last twenty or thirty years" and "its effects" we are told, "are nothing less than short of revolutionary."[62] The assessment of the impact of globalization holds that the "market now has control over social, economic and cultural relationships of people. All other social forces, including the state, which regulated people's needs and priorities, have ceased to operate."[63] How does globalization affect women of different races, ethnicities, nations, and religions and all the marginalized people in general?[64] What is the role of the NT in this process? How is and how should FNTS function within the context of globalization? A much more direct link and exploration is needed here. If, as the above definitions tells us, globalization and its effects are revolutionary, that the market has taken priority over life in globalization, how does FNTS engage globalization in its work? Has FNTS, so far, shown any serious engagement of this context? Once more, if assessed, FNTS will demonstrate very little engagement with the prevailing context of globalization. As I have argued elsewhere, it is important that our work should ask:

> What is the impact of globalization on the lives of women and men? Does globalization empower women and men equally? How can feminist/womanist inculturation hermeneutics maintain an oppositional stance that enhances the lives of women in their struggles for liberation in the era of globalization.[65]

3. The future of FNTS needs to explore new directions in involving their students and communities of faith in reading NT texts against violence. Our world has always been violent but it is also becoming more violent and resorting to violence as a source of resolving differences. Violence is served under claims of freedom and democracy. Moreover, it would seem that the link to religion is evident. The question can be asked on how violence affects women. I believe much has been done on the latter, but for FNTS, it is critical that its practice should explore how it can read for both justice and peace between women and men of different cultures, religions,

ethnicities, races, and nations. A hybridity and searching the world scriptures approach should be one way of contributing toward learning to live peacefully with one another in our multicultural world. We need to enlist many Rahabs and spies that are willing to transgress the walls of their own people, identities, agendas, and institutions to serve and save life and justice. Moreover, when such are at work, the whole city and its entire people must be and will be saved, from death, oppression, and exploitation.

4. If FNTS is also theological (reads the scriptures within and for the present social context and needs), then the future of FNTS must explore new directions on reading the text within the HIV/AIDS context. The world has lost at least 22 million people since HIV/AIDS was medically discovered in 1981. HIV/AIDS kills more people than war. At least 40 million people are currently infected and 14 million children are orphaned.[66] HIV/AIDS works within prevailing networks of social injustice, attacking the less privileged members of the society, the poor, women, children, homosexuals, displaced people, immigrants, discriminated races and ethnic groups, and so on who have no power to protect themselves from infection or to get quality care.[67] Women and other socially marginalized groups are, therefore, at the center of this epidemic, which is rightfully described as a global catastrophe. With a disease of such magnitude, those who are not infected are affected. The disease dehumanizes and impoverishes those who suffer from it, before they finally die. And, worse, the disease is accompanied by another epidemic; namely, HIV/AIDS stigma and discrimination. The latter is more rampant than the virus itself making the world unlivable for those who are infected. Stigma is manifested in silence and indifference. Biblical interpretations that linked HIV/AIDS with God's punishment and curse for the immoral contributed to the stigma.[68]

Due to its impact on all aspects of our lives; due to its spread through prevailing social injustice, HIV/AIDS is no longer just a health issue or an issue of individual morality.[69] Rather, HIV/AIDS' impact calls for a multi-sectoral approach. That is, all of us, wherever we are, and whatever disciplines and departments and institutions we serve, need to use our space to contribute toward the struggle against HIV/AIDS, its stigma, its impact and for the provision of quality care to the infected. This strategy has been adopted to fight HIV/AIDS as a disease of social injustice.

Twenty-two years into the HIV/AIDS epidemic, how has FNTS responded? Perhaps, more importantly, how can FNTS respond in order to be part of the solution?[70] Does or can the FNTS say anything about HIV/AIDS prevention, stigma, provision of quality care, and mitigation of impact? If FNTS scholarship does not have anything concrete to show, when 22 million people have died in 22 years and 40 million more are infected and when it is clear that women are at the center of this epidemic, can we still claim that FNTS is "not a neutral and disinterested scholarship?" Has FNTS noticed and responded—if our research, our writing, our teaching, our SBL sessions have nothing to show—then I believe there is something drastically amiss in our practice. This gap should make it imperative for us to explore these new directions in our practice. Namely, how can FNTS become a socially engaged scholarship, which can let its research and writing[71] practically enrich communities of faith, Women's NGOs, human development program officers, human rights activists, and others in fashioning a world of justice, peace, and healing for and with all people. The future of FNTS must seriously interrogate its position and implementation capacities and be able to fashion itself in such a way that it engages major issues of our world such as environmental degradation, globalization, poverty, violence, HIV/AIDS, anti-Semitism, racism, ethnic, and sexual discrimination, which have drastic impact in the lives of earth communities and of women in particular.

In so far as HIV/AIDS, and all other social evils that sponsor it, are concerned, I am happy to display myself as a Rahab. I am happy to peep through this small window that is stuck in a huge wall that seemingly divides us. I am happy to tie my red ribbon for your reading. I understand that the reader may rightfully insist that, "Rahab tied the red ribbon, but the city still fell, after all." Well, yes. Tragically, many cities are still falling right now even as some Rahabs are trying to hang out red ribbons. But I would say that Jericho fell because there was only one Rahab and only two unfaithful spies. What could be the impact, if all of us wore Rahab's shoes and walked her walk to the window and tied the red ribbon before the forces of death? What if more spies, all spies, all members of the enemy camp, chose to save and serve life and justice, rather than to destroy the lives of their targets? Perhaps this would be the "cultural treason" against hegemonic structures that Mary Ann Tolbert[72] says we all need to commit to bring liberation through transformation rather than reforming oppressive structures. Undoubtedly, the story would be very different. Similarly, I know that some readers belong to nations and institutions that have the power to bomb any wall down, in whatever way, to the utter destruction of its citizens. Nonetheless, I am still tying this red ribbon before the reader, to invite FNTS readers, to use their powers for saving and serving life and justice;[73] to join in the struggle against neocolonialism, globalization, poverty, violence, HIV/AIDS, abuse of children, earth degradation, violence, and discrimination of the bases of dis/ability and sexual orientation in their scholarly practices—not only theoretically, but also practically. FNTS, in other words, must also endeavor to carry out its liberation project within contemporary contexts and concerns. Let those who have eyes read this red ribbon that I have hung before their eyes. Let those who have ears hear the tap of Rahab's feet calling for attention. And those who have feelings and any memory must remember, we are not so far apart—we have made love already. We have bonded and we are lovers.

Notes

1. The tone of lamentation that pervades this chapter is the HIV/AIDS text that cries to be heard and for justice. I have maintained this tone to reflect the context of my writing the chapter, which was during the time when I worked as an HIV/AIDS activist, but also to underline that HIV/AIDS remains a global catastrophe. Millions are still suffering and dying, more children are still being orphaned, and many more women bear the burden of care than this chapter could ever tell.

2. See also my article, "Rahab Says Hello to Judith: Postcolonial Feminist Hermeneutics of Liberation," in *Toward a New Heaven and a New Earth: Essays in Honor of Elisabeth*

Schüssler Fiorenza, ed. Fernando F. Segovia (New York: Orbis Press, 2003) 54–72. And "Jumping the Fire with Judith: Postcolonial Feminist Hermeneutics," in *Feminist Interpretation of the Bible and Hermeneutics of Liberation*, ed. Silvia Schroer and Sophia Bitenhard (New York: Continuum, 2003) 60–76.

3. See Musa W. Dube, *Postcolonial Feminist Interpretation of the Bible* (St. Louis: Chalice Press, 2000) 69–80.

4. Dube, *Postcolonial Feminist*, 76–80.

5. Dube, *Postcolonial Feminist*, 78.

6. See Laura Donaldson, "The Sign of Orpah: Reading Ruth Through Native Eyes," in *Ruth and Esther: A Feminist Companion to the Bible*, ed. Athaya Brenner (Sheffield: Sheffield Academic Press, 1999) 130–144, for an analysis that problematizes the ideology of the Pocahontas and Ruth characters.

7. Dube, *Postcolonial Feminist*, 78.

8. I am not a very firm believer in "using the master's tools to bring his house down"; I am often unconvinced about its transformative power. I find it frustrating that biblical feminism seems stuck in rereading of very oppressive texts, instead of creating new sacred texts. So I am treading on a very shaky ground here in daring to reread Rahab's act for liberation.

9. See Mary Ann Tolbert, "Reading For Liberation," in *Reading From This Place Volume 1: Social Location and Biblical Interpretation in the United States*, ed. Fernando F. Segovia and Mary Ann Tolbert (Minneapolis: Fortress Press, 1995) 263–276, argues that the agenda of liberation fails because too many proponents are more interested in protesting their pain than privilege; they are too faithful to their faith and traditions. Consequently, the impact is, more often than not, that of reformation than transformation. Tolbert thus challenges liberationists to be willing to commit "cultural treason" in order to bring about the demise than reform of oppressive social structures.

10. For the call to read the Bible for life see Teresa Okure, "First Was the Life, Not the Book," in *To Cast Fire Upon the Earth: Bible and Mission Collaborating in Today's Multicultural Global Context*, ed. Teresa Okure (Pietermaritzburg: Cluster Publications, 2000) 194–214.

11. For African Christian women theologians, our historical model is Kimba Vita, the Congolese woman who was baptized Dona Beatrice, who rebelled against the colonial Christianity in 1706, asserting that Jesus and his disciples were black and that the kingdom of Congo would be restored. She was martyred for her politically subversive theology, but her approach marked the beginning of African Independent churches, which resist both colonialism and patriarchy. See Musa W. Dube, "Readings of *Semoya*: Batswana Women's Interpretations of Matt. 15:21–28," *Semeia* 73 (1996): 111–129, reference at 112–114.

12. See Carol Newsom and Sharon Ringe, "Introduction," in *The Women's Bible Commentary*, eds. C. Newsom and S. Ringe (Knoxville: John Knox Press, 1992) xiii–xix and *Searching the Scriptures Volume II*, ed. Elisabeth Schüssler Fiorenza (London: SCM Press, 1994) 1–14.

13. I must say that such terms no longer describe the contemporary feminist biblical practice partly because, unlike the early second wave feminism, the current one has largely become content with reading and rereading the masters' texts, than being brave enough to say the option to choose/create other reality is viable for the liberation search.

14. Much has been written about these power struggles and how they have positively contributed by bringing the feminist scholarship to take cognizance of race, class, ethnicity, sexual identity, or just about all that makes us different.

15. See Musa W. Dube, "Go therefore and Make Disciples of All Nations (Matt 28: 19A): A Postcolonial Perspective on Biblical Criticism and Pedagogy," in *Teaching the Bible: The*

Discourses and Politics of Biblical Pedagogy, ed. Fernando F. Segovia and Mary Ann Tolbert (New York: Orbis, 1998) 224–246, quotation at 241.

16. Quoted in Elizabeth Schüssler Fiorenza, "The Will to Choose and to Reject," in *Feminist Interpretation of the Bible*, ed. Letty Russell (Philadelphia: Westminster Press, 1985) 125–138, quotation at 127.

17. Rosemary Radford Ruether, *Sexism and God Talk: Towards a Feminist Theology* (Boston: Beacon, 1983) 19.

18. See Dube, *Postcolonial Feminist*, 23–84.

19. A few years ago (1999), a women's breakfast session was held in SBL on mentoring. Young women who were writing or had just finished writing their dissertation under the supervision of feminist scholars were asked to deliberate on their experiences. Feminist scholars and deans were also featured on the panel. One participant gave a testimony that closely matched my experiences. This is not to say that feminist scholars must play mothers to women students or suspend their critical faculties when dealing with feminist students. Rather my point is that the power relations that are sometimes at play are outrightly meant to suppress and silence younger women scholars whose voices are critical to the mainstream discourse/perspectives. For Two-Thirds World women the experience can border on being silenced and colonized.

20. Recently, one African student, who has found my book quite helpful, was told she should not be too proud of the book, for they (feminist biblical scholars) had completely closed the doors for its publication, until I was redeemed by a Vanderbilt graduate.

21. See Carolyn Osiek, "Reading the Bible as Women," in *The New Interpreter's Bible: A Commentary in Twelve Volumes* (Nashville: Abingdon, 1994) 181–187, and quotation at 186.

22. Mercy Oduyoye, "Biblical Interpretation and the Social Location of the Interpreter: African Women's Reading of the Bible," in *Reading From This Place Volume 2: Social Location and Biblical Interpretation in Global Perspectives*, ed. Fernando F. Segovia and M.A. Tolbert (Minneapolis: Fortress, 1995) 33–51.

23. Dube, *Postcolonial Feminist*, 111–129.

24. See Musa W. Dube, "Readings of *Semoya*," in *Semeia* 73 in which we went to read with women from the African Independent Churches, stating that "We have come to learn from you," 115. In this process, "I was searching for modes of reading that are subversive to imperialistic and patriarchal domination, and I was suspicious of my own training," 115.

25. See Mary Ann Tolbert, "Protestant Feminist and the Bible: On the Horns of Dilemma," in *The Pleasure of Her Text: Feminist Readings of Biblical and Historical Texts* Alice Bach, ed. (Philadelphia: Trinity Press International, 1990) 6.

26. See Millicent C. Feske, "Feminist Theologies and the Possibility of God-talk," *Quarterly Review: A Journal For Theological Resources for Ministry* Summer (2000): 138–151, quotation at 144–145.

27. Feske, "Feminist Theologies," 145.

28. Among many others, one can outline here the number of women in theological studies, churches that ordain women, the use of inclusive languages in worship and translations, feminist and gender studies in theological and biblical studies.

29. Vincent Wimbush, ed., *African Americans and the Bible: Sacred Texts and Social Textures* (New York: Continuum, 2000). This illustrous collection is a testimony that critical biblical readings go beyond the academic practices and that academic biblical interpretations are just a drop in the ocean in so far as different methods and context of biblical interpretation are concerned.

30. Indeed, in my field work research based paper, "Readings of *Semoya*," where we sought the biblical interpretations from church women, it was striking how they underlined that, "*Kana re bua ka dilo tsa Semoya*," i.e., "remember we are discussing issues of the Spirit," 116.

31. For a good example, see my article, "Readings of *Semoya*," 111–129, where we sought to read with nonacademic women in search for subversive feminist and decolonizing methods of reading that arise from these church women. See also Gloria K. Plaatjie, "Towards a Post-Apartheid Black Feminist Reading of the Bible: A Case of Luke 2:36–38," in Musa W. Dube, ed. *Other Ways of Reading*, 114–144.

32. Renita Weems, "Response to 'Reading With': An Exploration of the Interface Between Critical and Ordinary Readings of the Bible," *Semeia* 73 (2003): 257–261, quotation at 25.

33. Perhaps the work of Renita Weems, its focus on academic as well as spiritual departments, offers feminist biblical program of liberation a much needed model in this area.

34. Feske, "Feminist Theologies," 144–145.

35. Dube, "Readings of *Semoya*," 111–129. See also Barbara Holridge, "Beyond the Guild: Liberating Biblical Studies," in *African Americans and the Bible*, 138–159.

36. See Renita Weems, "Response to 'Reading With,'" where we proposed "reading with" nonacademic readers. Weems asks, "One can only wonder what would happen if North American biblical scholars, e.g., were to follow the lead of their Southern African colleagues and read with ordinary readers? What would happen if scholars of this learned journal read with religious right wing, conservatives in this country? What would happen if North American biblical scholars took it upon themselves to seek out the Bible study groups with militant millenialist sects scattered throughout its borders? What would happen if we actively pursued conversations with demagogues of hate, inviting them to join us in reading the Bible, listening intently to their strategies and rationalizations for interpretations and offering them new lens through which to view the Bible and themselves? These can be admittedly odious tasks to take on. One can hardly imagine anything fruitful to be gained on the part of scholars from such a dialogue," 261. Nonetheless, Weems underlines that withdrawal and silence of the scholarship only amounts to collaboration with these "pockets of apartheid hate and violence."

37. See Elizabeth Schüssler Fiorenza, ed., *Searching the Scriptures II: A Feminist Commentary* (New York: Crossroads, 1983).

38. Musa W. Dube, "Scripture, Feminism and Postcolonial Contexts," *Concillium* 4 (1998): 45–53, where I suggest that feminist readers must creatively and prayerfully enter the *semoya* space or, the space of the oral-Spirit "to articulate their own sacred, life-affirming and liberating words of wisdom," 53. A further discussion on the oral-Spirit is taken up by Nyambura Njoroge, "The Bible and African Christianity: A Curse or a Blessing?" in *Other Ways of Reading: African Women and the Bible*, ed. Musa W. Dube (Atlanta: SBL, 2001b) 218–224.

39. Ibid., 53.

40. Dube, "Scripture, Feminism and Postcolonialism," 53.

41. One example is the prevalence of colonizing translations in many missionary produced translations. In the Setswana Bible, e.g., demons were translated as *Badimo*, i.e., Ancestors, in a context where the latter were intermediaries between God and the people! For further exploration of this translation see my "Consuming the Colonial Cultural Bomb: Translating Badimo into Demons in Setswana Bible," in *JNST* 73 (1999): 33–59. Se also my response to a translator who defended this translation, "What I have Written, I have Written," in *Interpreting the New Testament in Africa*, ed. M. Getui and T.S. Maluleke (Nairobi: Acton Publishers, 2002) 145–163.

42. I describe some of my experiences in the following articles, Gerald West and Musa W. Dube, "An Introduction: How We Come to Read With," *Semeia* 73 (1996): 7–17 and "Go Therefore," 240–241.

43. Following on storytelling as a major method of sharing and imparting information as well as analyzing issues among African women, I try to utilize this mode of communication in

a number of my works, including the framework of this chapter. Other examples include such articles as, "Fifty Years of Bleeding: A Storytelling Feminist Reading of Mark 5:21–43," in *Other Ways of Reading*, 50–62 and "John 4: 1–42: Five Husbands at the Well of Living Waters," in *Talitha Cum! Theologies of African Women*, ed. Nyambura J. Njoroge and Musa W. Dube (Pietermaritzburg: Cluster, 2001) 40–65; "Villagizing, Globalization and Biblical Studies," in *Reading the Bible in the Global Village: Cape Town*, ed., J. Ukpong et al. (Atlanta: SBL, 2001) 41–63.

44. Carolyn Osiek, "Reading the Bible as Women," 181–187, quotation at 186.

45. See Edward Said, *Culture and Imperialism* (New York: Knopf, 1993) 8–11.

46. For me, this remains a long journey that involves a lot self-interrogation and self-suspicion, as I am often not sure if what I do as a biblical scholar does not in fact reinscribe the master's/colonialist intention. See, e.g., the opening of my book, *Postcolonial Feminist*, where I say that, "Those of us who grew up professing the Christian faith in the age of the armed struggle for liberation, from World War II to South African Independence in 1994, were never left to occupy our places comfortably. Debating societies in high schools and colleges passed one motion after another and constantly summoned us to debating floors. We were called upon to explain the ethics of our religion; to justify its practice, its practitioners, and its institutions. Debating societies demanded to know why the biblical text and its Western readers were instruments of imperialism and how we, as black Africans, justify our faith in a religion that has betrayed us—a religion of the enemy, so to speak," 4. I constantly problematize both my Christian faith, my Western academic training, and my work as a biblical scholar—see "Savior of the World, but Not of this World: A Postcolonial Reading of Spatial Construction in John," in *The Postcolonial Bible*, ed., R.S. Sugirtharajah (Sheffield: Sheffield Academic Press, 1998) 118–135, quotation at 119 and "Readings of *Semoya*," 115.

47. On several occasions I have taken this position, see "Towards a Postcolonial Feminist Interpretation of the Bible," *Semeia* 78 (1997): 11–26 and *Postcolonial Feminist*, 31–34.

48. See the classical article of Fernando F. Segovia, "And They Began to Speak in Other Tongues: Competing Modes of Discourse in Contemporary Biblical Criticism," in *Reading From this Place Volume 1*, 1–34.

49. See Mary Ann Tolbert, "Reading for Liberation," 270.

50. See Musa W. Dube, "Reading for Decolonization: John 4:1–42," in *Semeia* 75 (1996): 37–59, quotation at 56.

51. For more detailed discussions, see Dube, "Go therefore," 242–243 and Dube, *Postcolonial Feminist*, 38–39.

52. I have made several attempts to take seriously both the colonial/neocolonial/globalization history of our lives as well as to make attempts at interreligious reading of the New Testament, see Musa W. Dube, "Fifty Years of Bleeding: A Storytelling Feminist Reading of Mark 5:21–43," in *Other Ways of Reading: African Women and the Bible*, 50–62 and "John 4:1–42: The Five Husbands at the Well of Living Waters: The Samaritan Woman and African Women in, " in *Talitha Cum!*, 40–65.

53. For a good example, see Madipoane Masenya, "Esther and the Northern Sotho Stories: An African South African Woman's Commentary," in *Other Ways of Reading*, 27–49.

54. For a contribution by African women see Musa W. Dube, ed., *Other Ways of Reading*. In this volume we advanced a number of African feminist methods of reading the bible such as storytelling, divination, reading with and revisiting colonizing and patriarchal translations.

55. I address this issue at length in relation to African methods of biblical reading in my article, "Villagizing, Globalizing and Biblical Studies," 60–61.

56. Some good examples include, the work of R.S. Sugirtharajah; Fernando F. Segovia; Kwok Pui Lan; V. Wimbush, ed., *African American and the Bible*; Benny Liew, *The Bible in Asian*

America, Semeia 90/91 (Atlanta: SBL, 2002); Randall Bailey, ed., *Yet With a Steady Beat: Contemporary Afrocentric Biblical Interpretation: Semeia Studies 42* (Atlanta: SBL, 2003) and Gerald West and Musa W. Dube, *The Bible in Africa* (Leiden: Brill, 2000).

57. These include (1) Women and poverty; (2) Women education and training of women; (3) Women and health; (4) Violence against women; (5) Women in armed conflict, (6) Women and the economy; (7) Women in power and decision making; (8) Institutional mechanisms for the advancement of women; (9) Human rights of women; (10) Women and media; (11) Women and the environment and (12) The girl child.

58. See Religion Counts Report, *Religion and Public Policy at the UN* (Catholics for Free Choice: Park Ridge Center, April 2002).

59. See Musa W. Dube, "Villagizing, Globalization and Biblical Studies," 41–64, for some of my efforts on taking globalization seriously in biblical hermeneutics.

60. Roland Robertson, "Globalization and Future of Traditional Religion," in *God and Globalization Volume 1: Religion and the Powers of Common Life*, ed., Max Stackhouse and Peter J. Paris (Harrisburg: Trinity Press International, 2000) 53–68, quotation at 53–54.

61. Peter Tolluch, "Globalization: Blessing or Curse? Buzzword or Swear Word," in *Sustainability and Globalization*, ed., Julio de Santa Ana (Geneva: WCC, 1995) 99–106, quotation at 101.

62. See Christopher Lind, *Something is Wrong Somewhere: Globalization, Community and Moral Economy of the Farm Crisis* (Halifax: Fernwood Publishing, 1995) 31.

63. Asian Theological Conference 2000, "Thou Shall Not Worship Other Gods: Towards a Decolonizing Theology," *Voices From the Third World (EATWOT)* XXIII/2 (2000): 213–231, quotation at 218–219.

64. Yassine Fall, ed., *Africa: Gender, Globalization and Resistance* (New York: AAWord, 2000) 86.

65. Dube, "Villagizing, Globalizing and Biblical Studies," 57.

66. UNAIDS, *The Report on the Global HIV/AIDS Epidemic* (Geneva: UNAIDS, 2002) 8.

67. WCC, *Facing AIDS: The Challenge and the Churches' Response* (Geneva: WCC, 1997) 14–15.

68. WCC, *HIV/AIDS Curriculum for Theological Institutions in Africa* (Geneva: WCC, 2001) 6–8.

69. See UNDP and UNAIDS, *Fact Sheet: United Nations Special Session on AIDS* (New York: UNAIDS, 2001).

70. For some of my efforts, see "Preaching to the Converted: Unsettling the Christian Church," *Ministerial Formation*, 93 (2001): 38–50; "Theological Challenges: Proclaiming the Fullness of Life in the HIV/AIDS and Global Economic Era," *International Review of Mission XCI*/363 (2002): 535–549; "Healing Where There is No Healing: Reading The Miracles of Healing in AIDS Context," in *Reading Communities Reading Scriptures: Essays in Honor of Daniel Patte* ed. Gary Phillips and Nicole Wilkinson Duran (Harrisburg: Trinity Press International, 2002) 121–133 and *Missionalia* 29/2 (2001): 121–133, a special issue focusing on HIV/AIDS, which I coedited with Tinyiko S. Maluleke.

71. For African women's efforts toward this end, see Musa W. Dube and Musimbi Kanyoro, ed., *Grant Me Justice: HIV/AIDS & Gender Readings of the Bible* (Peitermaritzburg: Cluster Publications, 2004).

72. Mary Ann Tolbert, "Reading for Liberation," 270.

73. In her article, "Reading From This Place: Some Prospects and Problems," in *Reading From This Place Volume 2*, 52–69, Teresa Okure insists on a life-centered biblical interpretation, holding that, "any interpretation that fails to do this . . . becomes suspect and should be regarded as inauthentic," for it would have failed to "be in tune with this universal intention of God to liberate, save, give and sustain life," 57. I think that this life-centered hermeneutic that Okure proposes has a powerful ethical potential if its depth is grasped and applied.

Chapter 15

Response: A Perilous Passage From Scarlet Cord to Red Ribbon

Isabel Balseiro

I would like to start by quoting a poem by South African Luvuyo Mkangelwa entitled "The Women Sing."[1] Hopefully, during the course of my discussion, I will be able to persuade you of the connections between the women depicted in the poem by Mkangelwa and those Musa Dube so eloquently has referred us to in her chapter.[2]

> The women sing
> songs of worship
> to make their journey
> only a step away
>
> The women sing
> banging carriage walls
> and whacking their bibles
> with their strong hands
> for drum-like sounds
>
> The women sing
> to conquer the thoughts
> of the day's orders
> The women sing
> the women sing
> to be free!
>
> The women sing
> to possess themselves
> for a moment
> at least!

The women in this poem are en route to work. It may take them one to two hours to travel from their township homes to the suburbs where many find employment as child minders, domestic workers, cooks, perhaps nurses. Despite the fact that during their working day they will be at the beck and call of demanding bosses (in most instances women of a different race and class), and notwithstanding the fact that this type of labor inhibits their freedom, these women with strong hands and commanding voices are empowered by embracing songs of worship that will sustain them through the hardships of the economic apartheid still entrenched in many parts of the world, not only Southern Africa. They sing "to possess themselves," "to conquer the thoughts of the day's orders," and "to be free." It is thus through their religious practice that solace is to be found. And this practice extends well beyond the confines of the Church. For these women carve a place for their faith in the everyday. I think it is about the pivotal role of women like these that Musa Dube's chapter reminds us.

A striking image opens the chapter: that of Dube's identification with Rahab, the sex worker of Jericho. By embracing Christianity, Dube identifies herself with the treason committed by that Old Testament figure. Yet in accepting that act of betrayal she asserts herself as champion of women's rights and, more specifically, of the right of all Two-Thirds World women to express their voices in both the praxis and theorizing of Christianity. Her chapter, hence, is a call to action to not only ground New Testament scholarship in grassroots organization among communities of faith that profess Christian and, as discussed later, non-Christian beliefs, but also to decolonize New Testament scholarship in order to make room for Two-Thirds World women's full vocalization of their socially engaged, activist, and interpretational practices. This is no small task.

Here I propose to trace that idea of complicity and identification between Dube and the historical Rahab. In probing this relationship we might find the kernel of progressive thought the chapter holds. While a traitor to her people, Rahab was a survivor—not unlike La Malinche in sixteenth-century Mexico, or Krotoa in seventeenth-century South Africa. As a feminist New Testament (FNT) scholar, Dube defends the right of women in Africa and the Two-Thirds World, the right of the oppressed, to strategize not merely to save themselves but to struggle for greater social justice. Religion, that impenitent ally of the world's invading armies, must be transformed into a tool of liberation by the very same peoples it once oppressed.

In following the tracks that bring their paths together, perhaps the most vivid image the chapter sketches out is that of Two-Thirds World women, like Rahab and Dube herself, "tying red ribbons in a world rocked by [a] silent war, the war of HIV/AIDS." Reading the New Testament within the context of the HIV/AIDS pandemic in Africa seems to me as particularly fitting to a discussion of Christianity in the twenty-first century. Yet because the chapter makes only passing reference to this war, the initial promise remains unfulfilled.

Rahab's scarlet cord is a sign that will alert the enemy: the house where it is hung is to be spared as those inside are accomplices of the invading army. But, what are the implications of this identification? Both Rahab and Dube are witnesses to a war. Rahab and her family were spared by the invading Israelites, but what is in it for contemporary African women who sleep with the enemy? The red ribbon of AIDS is emblematic of empathy and solidarity; not a secret message, it is a form of communication meant to be understood by all. The scarlet cord of Rahab, on the other hand, was a secretive code, a tool of survival—survival, in this case, not of her community or her people, only of herself and her family. Rahab's scarlet cord saved her own skin but it left the people of Jericho under the control of an invading army. What about Two-Thirds World women who sleep with the enemy? Millions of African women who exchange sex for money, or food, or favors, or sleep with soldiers or truck drivers or mine workers or merely with the fathers of their children are being rewarded with a lethal disease. The implications of the AIDS ribbon and scarlet cord would seem to lead us in very different directions.

In bringing up the literary motif of invaded lands equated with women who espouse the invader's ideology, a narrative shift occurs in the chapter: we move from Rahab to the personal pronoun "I," and finally to "we." It is this process of transformation, I sense, that Dube is most keen to reveal for us. For Rahab is the model she proposes for the fight against patriarchy and colonialism because, beyond the HIV/AIDS pandemic, the ribbon is also calling attention to the need to "stop the violence, to address the social injustice." And Dube strives to read for justice. For this reason she denounces that in the twenty-first century, little progress has been made. War continues. And she asks how does "the New Testament and its interpretations contribute to this situation?" She then poses a great challenge: feminist New Testament Studies (FNTS) must "become a midwife of justice in the world." Her chapter then guides us through an outline of just how this might be done.

Dube acknowledges that since its inception 150 years ago, FNTS has been a "protest against the use of the Bible to authorize social marginalization." And she insists that feminist practice must remain socially engaged in order to create "an egalitarian society for all."[3] In an autobiographical note, Dube positions herself as having been victimized by FNTS: neither sisterhood nor mentoring was offered her in her first years of study. Instead, she found that there was no "commitment toward [fighting] various forms of systematic imperialism, colonialism, neo-colonialism, globalization and how it affects women and men." Furthermore, during her graduate student days, she was dismayed to learn that Western women, instead of encouraging independent thought, expected Two-Thirds World women to "reproduce the words and perspectives of their colonizers." Like Rahab. And it is precisely this mimicking Dube proposes to undo. Instead of complying with expectations, she wants to increase the presence of New Testament scholars among Two-Thirds World women. In terms of numbers, Dube identifies four in Africa, and she believes the situation is not much better in Asia and Latin America.[4]

Her objective, then, is that FNTS must take up in earnest the training of Two-Third World women because the "locus of the Christian religion has shifted to these places, particularly Latin America and Africa." Thus, the future for feminist studies in New Testament must be rooted there.

In a brief literature review of FNTS, Dube recognizes that while a few African women have been participating since the last decade of the twentieth century much more remains to be done. Why is this important? She offers many reasons, among them one relating to language I find especially promising: the gender-inclusive translations of the Bible. Translations of gender-specific images of God seem to continue undermining feminist readings. But what happens in the case of translation into African languages? Dube explains that in some of those languages the names for God are gender neutral, or even androgynous. Research on this topic is certainly an important contribution African FNT scholars could make to the field.

Another major contribution African FNT scholars could bring to the field in these times of globalization is an interfaith understanding. Dube calls this "searching the world scriptures" as she invites us to consider the New Testament in relation to other world religions. Identifying herself as coming from a non-Christian tradition but now being a practicing Christian, she urges us to "search all the world scriptures to empower women, for the sake of establishing justice around the world and building relationships of interdependence." Searching the world scriptures would demand an exploration and candid discussion of hybrid religious practices where Christianity may be on the menu but where it is by no means the only course, accompanied as it is by many other spiritual practices. I find this to be in synchrony with African and Latin American reality, and Dube must be credited for bringing this point into focus.

Since most Christians now live in the Two-Thirds World, it is indeed important to reconnect scholarship with the communities of faith—that is, to match theory to praxis, for it is in the larger community that ideas have to be generated. Instead of a reliance on reason, a new spiritual language should be found to address spiritual practice, for only a reconnection of biblical interpretation to those who live the faith will make FNTS advance. While I fully agree with Dube's position on this subject, I feel there is some room for elaboration on just what steps must be followed in order to create this space of re-approximation she calls for. In other words, how does academic research (including that of Dube) "help the world and its society to be a better place to live in"? How does FNTS become involved in socially relevant scholarship?

And yet, she is suggesting some venues that one should not overlook: the reconstruction and reimagining of New Testament texts, histories, and interpretations. Scholarship must expand to include books and commentaries on feminist reconstruction of Matthew, Mark, Luke, John, and Acts, she writes. It is just that, given the collusion between imperialism and religion in the past, this reconstruction can no longer be left in the hands of so-called experts on the Two-Thirds World. This reimagining must emerge from the Two-Thirds World itself, namely, from New Testament feminist scholars and activists such as Dube.

But contributions by Two-Thirds World women will not happen spontaneously without a concerted effort by FNT scholars to become truly inclusive. In order for these contributions not to be squandered, a number of steps need be taken such as:

1. the training of more feminist scholars in the Two-Thirds World requires funding scholarships;
2. the opening up of the curriculum and the methods of teaching to ensure that they address the concerns of a diverse group of students; and
3. the founding of a society of FNTS that should meet annually to discuss issues like the ones already mentioned and program a plan of action. As a model for that society, Dube proposes the Circle of Concerned African Women Theologians (formed in 1989 and with membership of 300).

To conclude, I would like to raise a few questions about the policy recommendations Dube includes in the final section of her chapter under the heading "New Directions for FNTS." While she divides them into four categories I focus on two of them: the first, through which she calls for a human-rights-based approach to FNTS, and last, which takes us back to the HIV/AIDS pandemic.

I would be curious to know how Dube would respond to the consideration that many Two-Thirds World activists and scholars remain skeptical of the validity of human-rights approaches to Two-Thirds World problems. Assuming that a human rights discourse presents an ideal conceptual "model" through which the world and its multiple social entities should be mapped against raises thorny issues. Complex ideological and political concerns are indeed evoked by this position. The UNs model Dube herself discusses is actually confirmation of how troubling the claim of universality can, and often does, become. How can FNT scholars counter the stance of conservative religious groups that oppose women's rights in these UN forums? How, ultimately, can the action-oriented scholarship she so vigorously proposes begin to execute real changes not only in the communities of faith but on world structures?

I end with the last category. After presenting some sobering statistics on HIV/AIDS and emphasizing the prominent role of women in this world catastrophe, Dube writes that, along with the poor, children, and the discriminated races, women "have no power to protect themselves from infection or to get quality care." This may be true generally speaking but I fear statements like this usher in a defeatist note that could be read as robbing agency from those most in need of preserving their human dignity—people with HIV/AIDS. In the South African context, for example, where the pandemic has reached tragic proportions, it is largely unemployed women living with HIV/AIDS who are organizing themselves in alternative movements like the Treatment Action Campaign (TAC) to fight the African National Congress government for proper health care.[5] Although I agree with Dube that FNTS may not have responded to the HIV/AIDS pandemic with the vigor and timeliness required, I am afraid at the end of her chapter we are left with a troubling image.

Just how Dube, a self-identified twenty-first-century Rahab, and all who "have made love [to the enemy] already" join the struggle against this global pandemic will indeed determine how one bears witness through the hanging of red ribbons. In that gesture of solidarity, when it surpasses the purpose of saving oneself, and through reestablishing an organic connection with the singing women from the poem with which I opened this response, lies the kernel of progressive thinking Dube embraces as the future of FNTS.

Notes

1. Luvuyo Mkangelwa, "The Women Sing," in *Running towards Us: New Writing from South Africa*, ed. Isabel Balseiro (New Portsmouth, NH: Heinemann, 2000) 15.
2. All references to Musa Dube are to her chapter included in this volume.
3. Osiek, quoted in Dube, this volume.

4. While I cannot speak about numbers in Asia, more than a handful of women, mostly feminist, biblical scholars are currently engaging with these matters in Brazil alone. Perhaps what Dube is reflecting is the fact that seldom does the work of Latin American scholars finds translation into English—though there are exceptions, such as publications by Elsa Tamez, Ana Maria Bingemer, and Yvonne Gebara among others.

5. Steven Robins, "Mbeki, Nationalism and Aids in South Africa," *The Sunday Independent* (2002): 7 July.

Chapter 16

Lucy Bailey Meets the Feminists

Althea Spencer Miller

Who is Lucy Bailey? One might say that her alluring mystique and anonymity is metonymic of Caribbean biblical hermeneutics and compels a deconstructive effort. Questions about Lucy Bailey's identity and writings receive similar answers as to questions about specific sources for Caribbean biblical hermeneutics. Someone once sought access to her writings. Lucy's heritage is not in print. It is only in the memories of those who knew her personally. Questions about articles and books on Caribbean biblical hermeneutics evoked a similar consternation.

Lucy did not give permission to use her name in this chapter, nor to memorialize her life in this way. This causes some pause over the ethics of using her name and person in this way. I wondered, "Would I be using Lucy as a clay pigeon?" Lucy as a metonym for Caribbean (feminist) biblical hermeneutics lays bare any pretension on my part to envisage a prospective role for the Caribbean in future feminist New Testament studies as being merely embryonic. There is warrant for apprehension in the decision to proceed with this project. There is a rider. If the consequence of my daring is that Lucy or the Caribbean falls like a clay pigeon, then it is my failure, not theirs. This chapter, then, is a libation for my ancestress in the faith, Lucy Bailey. To her I say, "My intent is good and I desire to do honor." I also ask her to allow me, when we meet where the ancestors commune, to talk with her about this too. My Caribbean colleagues may take me to task sooner.

Lucy's age is indeterminate though she may have been in her eighties when she died. She was small in physique but great in stature. The standard canons of greatness will not describe Lucy. She was quite poor, quite undereducated, quite "black,"[1] quite small, and quite old in an era when each of these attributes was sub-status quo. To the best of my knowledge, Lucy Bailey earned her livelihood primarily, perhaps solely, as a household helper. In the era of Lucy's working life, household helpers were called, scornfully, "Girl" or "Maid." Undereducated in letters, Lucy excelled in lived learning. She was wise, kind, very caring, diligent, faithful, articulate, knowing, giving, trustworthy, willing, seeking, and very courageous. Any weaknesses, failings, fears, or doubts that she might have harbored were quite secreted or decorated by age and wisdom. For every attribute named, there is a Lucy anecdote. My association with Lucy began and developed in the context of a Christian congregation located in a neighborhood that was out of bounds for *sensible* and *respectable* people. This was Lucy's kind of neighborhood and she had much to teach the *sensible* and *respectable* ones.

Lucy Bailey was pivotal in teaching me the importance of perspective in biblical interpretation. In many Jamaican congregations, worship services include a time of spontaneous testimony sharing.[2] Lucy always had a testimony. She tended to open her testimony by quoting Psalm 37:25 from the KJV, "I have been young, and now am old; Yet I have not seen the righteous forsaken, nor his seed begging bread." I cannot pretend to know what Lucy Bailey had in mind when she claimed this verse her own. I only understood that, in her old age, Lucy received beneficence and experienced a peacefulness that dignified her survival of long and rigorous working years. When in a Hebrew Bible class at Columbia Seminary, in Atlanta, I heard a corpulent, white male, in a white polo shirt, a finely pleated dark pant, and a large buckled belt intone the Lucy verse, with the smug confidence of humble wealth, my sense of perspective in biblical hermeneutics developed another layer. Nationality, class, education, wealth, age, and gender provided the material for perspective and signaled the battleground for supreme interpretative legitimacy. Lucy versus polo shirt? How could she win? In such a scenario, what was the most important question?

The question may be, "Whose progeny begs bread?" There is every reason to think that the composer of the Psalm was an educated person with access to the king's court. The NRSV (New Revised Standard Version) actually attributes the Psalm to King David. On the surface then the Psalm rightly belonged to this man at Columbia. He was well on the way to being old, he was attesting God's blessings in his life, and it was hardly likely that his children begged for bread, not from desperation, at any rate. Can Lucy match this? To be poor is to bear a curse. To be insufficiently educated is to bear fetters. To be colored "black," in her times, was to invite scorn. All these were burdens that Lucy bore. The Lord's righteous were clearly the very opposite of these. Either Lucy did not know this or she did not acknowledge it. Her experience was that the main theme of this Psalm, that God would vindicate the righteous, rang true in her own life. Biologically childless, there were, nonetheless children of many ages who nestled in the warmth of her lap and her dress folds. She was poor but she always had something extra to give. This socially lowly woman knew that God was with her. Her seed, she knew, would not suffer. I believe that if Lucy heard this man quoting her Psalm she would be undaunted. She would quote it in his very presence. Every time that Lucy quoted that Psalm, she challenged the religiously sanctioned social stigmata of her day. She used the words of the powerful to subvert their very power. I do not know to what extent Lucy understood this. I know she fervently believed that she was counted among the Lord's righteous. In the contest for interpretative legitimacy, this is subversive knowledge.

Academic feminist biblical scholars of North America and Europe could substitute for the man in the story above. In between "Lucy Bailey" and such "Feminists" are chasms of education, culture, politics, time, social location, availability of opportunity, and disadvantages. Lucy Bailey, a figure of the past, is also the face of the Caribbean future that academic feminist biblical scholars must meet. How is

Lucy Bailey the future face of Caribbean Christianity? Who are the constituents of this meeting? Of what will they speak? Lucy Bailey, as representative of Caribbean anonymity, needs further explication.

Lucy Bailey: The Future Face of Caribbean Christianity?

We may regard Lucy Bailey as an icon. As a Caribbean woman, she stands in for Jenkins's portrayal of the future face of Christianity. In *The Next Christendom: The Coming of Global Christianity*, Philip Jenkins suggests the portraiture of future Christianity. He postulates, "If we want to visualize a 'typical' contemporary Christian, we should think of a woman living in a village in Nigeria or in a Brazilian *favela*."[3] Lucy is the Caribbean counterpart of the women in the Brazilian *favela* and the village in Nigeria. Based on Jenkins's postulate she is the icon that opens the discussion with feminist biblical critics. Paradoxically, she critiques Jenkins's portrayal. Jenkins is correct insofar as his iconic representation presents a numerically dominant face. His icons, however, are densely packed, comprehensive, impressionistic, representations of complex realities. These realities defy facile statistical predictability because they present more variables than Jenkins considers.[4] As an icon Lucy represents the invisible, idealized, homogenized, sometimes pasteurized persons whom feminist/liberation hermeneutics intends to liberate. As a bible reader, she is iconic of that nexus of Caribbean biblical interpretation, a nexus formed by the preacher/interpreter and the lay interpreter. This cluster of groupings represents the complex relationships that feminist biblical hermeneutics is involved with as it portends the future. Within each group of the cluster are people from every level of society. Some treat others as invisible, others resist invisibility and yet all share in this common Caribbean invisibility. Lucy Bailey is also iconoclastic because as an icon she disrupts the tidiness of Jenkins's portrait.

There is great value in Jenkins's study of the implications of the emergence of Christianity in the Two-Thirds World. However, he did not pay sufficient attention to interfaith relations, education, and culture and their impact on religious hospitality in a globalized world. These would have implications particularly for his predictions on theological developments and ethical trends in the Caribbean. The Two-Thirds World is not a homogeneous repository of fundamentalist or conservative theology, the diversity of which is marked only by disagreements within a conservative camp. Multiple contextual movements will impact the future in ways that are not yet predictable. Much of his analysis is interesting and disturbing. When he says, "A generation ago, [American and European Christian] liberals saw their own views reflected by the rising masses of the Third World, marching toward socialism and liberation. Today, conservatives have the rosier view"[5] he reinscribes the power relationships between Europe and America, on the one hand and the Two-Thirds World on the other. To imagine the Two-Thirds World as a product over which developed theologies may haggle like apples in an apple eating competition is a grave misjudgment.

For the Caribbean, the historical complexities of class, race, religion, gender, sexual orientation, age, Christian denomination, family, marital status, require a far more nuanced picture of Christianity and interreligious relationships. The development of indigenous theologies in relation to national aspirations and circumstances remains an urgent commitment. Our people of Christian persuasion are Pentecostals, Roman Catholics, Protestants, Orthodox Christians, Seventh Day Adventists, Jehovah Witnesses, Christian Scientists, Mormons, and members of the World Wide Church of God. There are also Rastafarians, meaning that they belong to the Twelve Tribes, Bobo Dreads, Coptic or Ethiopian Rastafari denominations of Rastafarianism. Some dance to the beat of the Kumina drums, some are priestesses of Myal. Some whirl and twist under the influence of the spirit of Pocomania, others rank in the practices of Santeria and other Yoruba related religions. The presence of African religious survivals, their varied adaptations of Christianity, and emergent relationships with established religious practices increase the density of the picture, and consequently, its analysis. Similarly, it would be quite inadequate to suggest that any singular iconic representation can adequately represent this religious mix. How can Lucy, as icon, accomplish such a task?

There are many Lucy Baileys throughout the Caribbean. The other Lucy Baileys have identifiers in addition to class and religion. They are Spanish, French, Dutch, and/or English speakers. They also speak variations of those colonizing languages based on their island or territorial location. They are farmers, factory workers, household helpers, cane workers, banana growers, hagglers on the streets, market women, custodial workers (or as some would say "sanitation engineers"), hustlers, bus drivers, professionals, or simply, unemployed. Their ancestors are Africans, English, French, Portuguese, Spaniards, East Indians, Chinese, Jews, Dutch, and Caribs among others. One of my favorite stories is that of a social revolution generated by female higglers who became international traders, undercutting the local formal retail market through sidewalk sales. Their sales locations were known as "bend down plazas." There were sufficient numbers of them to become a new kind of middle class that retained inner city mores. The great achievement of these women is their emergence as an economic force in the island. This development was unforeseeable at the turn of the nineteenth century.

In a tiered, social system, the residue of colonialism, there are other categories of people who have great visibility within Caribbean society but share in the region's invisibility. The roll call of these notables have been women such as, Nanny, Jamaican military leader in the First Maroon War (1720–1739), Mary Seacole, 1805–1881, adventuress and author. "Mary was an avid traveller, skilled nurse, writer and healer. During her extensive travels to inhospitable environments in Nassau, Panama, Haiti and Cuba, she learnt to care for people with many tropical diseases, updating her medical skills and developing her own remedies of healing herbs and local plants."[6] Dare we say that this black, nineteenth-century Caribbean woman should receive historical honor as the paradigmatic Florence Nightingale.[7] She is the author of a book published in 1857, republished in 1984, *Wonderful Adventures of Mrs. Seacole in Many Lands*. This book contains the record of her famed hospitality and nursing work during the Crimean War, (1854–1856). Mrs. Gwendolyn Omphroy-Spencer, founding member and president emeritus of the Jamaica Midwives Association, a pioneer in the development of midwifery in Jamaica, and contributor to its development in other parts of the world. Honorable Barbara Gloudon, who played a significant role on the Intergovernmental Council of the International Programme for the Development of Communications, Dame Eugenia Charles, prime minister of Dominica from 1980–1995, first Caribbean woman to become a premier and one of the few women in the world to hold such office. Dr. Lucille Mair, Special Adviser to UNICEF on Women's Development, was the first woman to hold the title of under-secretary-general of the United Nations (1983). Her task was to serve as secretary-general of the United Nations Conference on the Question of Palestine, held in Geneva.

Significant international leaders include Sir Eric Williams, 1911–1981, a former prime minister of Trinidad and Tobago and writer of the earliest revisionist histories of the Caribbean, *From Columbus to Castro: History of the Caribbean 1492–1969*. The Honorable Michael Manley, a former prime minister of Jamaica, 1978 recipient of a gold medal for distinguished service in the struggle against apartheid, and in the 1970s a leader in advocacy for a New International Economic Order. We also contributed to international religious institutions. There is Ms. Carmen Lusan, former general secretary of the World Young Women's Christian Association. Sir Hugh Sherlock served the World Council of Churches with distinction. Dr. Philip Potter of Dominica served as general secretary to the World Council of Churches during some of its most controversial years in the 1970s. (The athletes of the Caribbean, netballers, cricketers, bobsledders, sprinters, medium distance runners are unnamed here along with our popular musicians because they perform in public sports and are usually visible.)

This roll call of Caribbean leaders conveys but an idea of the caliber of the leadership capacity of the Caribbean. There is a pluckiness that evinces a will to overcome adversity while producing people and leaders who excel—despite. An amnesia for the Two-Thirds World as a repository of potential realized and *in potentia* tends to accompany the developed world's focus on the plight of the Two-Thirds World. It seems, too often, to be a focus intuitively informed by the idea that sustained international economic and political power is the major criterion for determining the successful person/nation. The poor and developing citizens judged by that criterion are innately and circumstantially students and not teachers. Lucy defies this and represents the unseen pluck that Caribbean people share.

Lucy, herself, occupied multiple categories of invisibility within her contemporaneous Caribbean society. The multitiered nature of Lucy's invisibility legitimizes her representation of Caribbean persons whose tremendous international achievements, high regional visibility, and personal courage could not dispel the opacity occluding the Caribbean's intellectual potential. Lucy is the paradoxical icon of the invisibility of a social class within the Caribbean and the generally underappreciated capacity of the region to contribute meaningfully to international intellectual religious endeavors.

Lucy Bailey can be the icon of Caribbean peoples and their religions because despite her difficulties she lived with courage, tenacity, and dignity. Across classes, creeds, and ethnicities these are characteristics shared by a vast number of Caribbean people. It is important to acknowledge the role of the Bible and her religious practice in her self-understanding. The pursuit of regional identity is perhaps the most pervasive social quest of the Caribbean since the mid-1960s. Issues of religion and received theologies are most pertinent to this quest. We can note here that Caribbean biblical hermeneutics falls within the purview of these broadly labeled issues. Cradled within the still incipient stages of this pursuit the Caribbean woman reads her Bible. From this cradle, she enjoins the conversation with other women of the Two-Thirds World and elsewhere. A popular, axiomatic, descriptor used to describe the Jamaican character is "likkle but tallawah." It means "small but strong, effective, and great." We might even say that it means, "we are bigger than our size." It is certainly applicable in general and true ways to the Caribbean character. It is the character of Lucy. Therefore, we name the Caribbean's peoples greatest and least. Our "likkle" people can live with courage and dignity. Our "likkle" region has made huge contributions to the world. "Likkle but tallawah" sets the tone and pitch of the character of Caribbean peoples. We certainly bring this to our religious experience as to this feminist conversation on biblical hermeneutics.

The Likkle and the Tallawah

Hemispheric power relationships form the framework for North/South relationships. When speaking of the Two-Thirds World in contrast to the developed world there are associations along the axis of North/South polarities: North/wealthy/oppressive/strong—South/poor/oppressed/weak. These categories are very useful in clarifying the imbalance of power relationships between the North and South and for demarcating clusters for assessing the impact of socioeconomic and political trends such as globalization. However, these designators reinscribe unhelpful characteristics that oversimplify the realities so categorized. Therefore, the Two-Thirds World woman should understand herself as belonging to the poor, oppressed, and weak: the *likkle*. The One-Third World woman might uncritically subscribe to those attributes while assuming the mantle of the tallawah in relation to the Two-Thirds World woman. There are two concerns here. One is that, within religious discourse the categories of marginalization and disempowerment tend to dominate North/South relationships. It attracts, with compelling force, the idea that the subjects of oppression live completely in accordance with the mind-set of the perpetual victim. The other concern is the establishment of competitive relationships at the South/South pole where Two-Thirds World groups jostle for the largely commodity-oriented attention of their American/European counterparts.[8]

Political and economic power relationships and perceptions also determine the distribution of intellectual commerce. The particular interests of providers of intellectual conference funding are the major determinants of the agendas of conferences. This in turn has impact on the diversity of participants. Take for example the Caribbean region. The most significant issue faced there is the economic and social development. Religions, especially Christianity, have critical roles in these areas of Caribbean development. There is significant funding (never sufficient) for this aspect of the Church's role. When the agenda of funding organizations aims at socioeconomic development with little surplus for intellectual development the choice is not only clear, but also necessary. The ongoing experience is that scarce Caribbean conference capital more often supports developing the income generating capacities of our peoples while the formal theological enterprise struggles.[9] It means then that the Caribbean contribution to religious academia is either dependent on its diaspora academics, remains in a Caribbean academic ghetto, or awaits the beneficence of the dominant centers of academic dissemination to create opportunities for participation. Our relationship to the dominant centers for the propagation of intellectual discourse is then necessarily one of dependence. In such a relationship, the subjugation of regional agendas to the various agendas of Northern academic interests is the only variety of strategy available. Someone else, somewhere else, has the power to determine both our presence and the issues at the conference table. This, one may daresay, contributes to that anomaly in international theological understanding that occurs where a regional epistemology is absent.

The lingua franca for negotiating presence at the conference table is that of marginalization and disempowerment. The language of marginalization and disempowerment requires that the Two-Thirds World theologian finds his/her point of need and declares it. Then she can say, "Look at me! I am hungry, naked, unsheltered, sick and in want. But my spirit is strong." Those are the terms by which the strong/powerful/oppressive/wealthy/militaristic/North will pay attention to the weak/powerless/oppressed/poor/bedraggled/South. The competition is won by those whose weakness makes their case most compelling. On the South/South axis an awareness that there is not enough room for all vanquishes our need to converse on that plain, without the attendance of our patrons. We subtly compete with each other for the scarce beneficences. Who then can attract the necessary attention? Obviously, the hungriest, the most naked, the most exposed, the sickest, the most poor. These are the conditions of engagement that sustain dysfunctional hemispheric relationships: often stultifying the reach for conceptual equity across regions.

Perhaps the Caribbean theologian should join the chorus, saying "We are the hungriest, the most naked, the most exposed, the sickest, the most poor." Except for Haiti, that would not be true. Though the Caribbean experience includes extremes of any of those conditions, there is not a sufficiency of their presence to make our case direly compelling. Our spirits do not have the most extreme of human conditions against which to fight. Our governments are democratic, mostly, if we overlook Cuba and a turbulent Haiti. We have a strong history of the development of democracy and in most instances, we did not need a formal civil war or a revolution. We have difficulty attracting funding for theological development certainly because of our developing socioeconomic condition. However, those conditions, in the extreme, do function as magnets for attention. Those who cannot completely own the language of marginalization and disempowerment, despite the many present conditions to which it applies, are lesser magnets. If the axiomatic, polarizing descriptors and their attendant attributes were to be dismantled, would the funding situation change? It might not but our presence at the table may contribute to a subtle alteration in the impact of hemispheric political and economic power imbalances on the sharing of intellectual capital, certainly, as it relates to biblical interpretation that is based on a hermeneutic of liberation and prophetic notions of justice. Can Lucy's subversive knowledge provide some impetus toward such an end?

Peregrinating the "Likkle and the Tallawah"

The oxymoronic *likkle and tallawah* are mutually contradictory, strange bedfellows. Paradoxically, their conjoining, rather than effecting a reciprocal denial of their individual qualities, conversely effects their growth and establishment. Effectively, they constitute a symbiotic relationship. The following story involves two of those for whom Lucy stands. Years ago, when I was a young minister, fresh out of seminary, I was the second minister in the largest circuit in Jamaica. It was my morning to preach at the chief congregation. At the time, the first family of Jamaica worshipped there. It could at times be a heady experience and this particular Sunday morning was one of them. I was, therefore, *tallawah*. On that Sunday, I preached on "Touching the Untouchables and Loving the Unlovable." Leaving the church premises later in the day, I reversed into a very narrow lane. Through the car's rearview mirror I spotted one of the denizens of the inner city sleeping on the sidewalk. He was filthy and I was filled with the wonder of my sermon. I immediately recognized an untouchable. Challenged by my own sermon I determined to leave him some money. To secure the money on him necessitated tucking it into some fold in his clothing or skin. One look, one whiff and *tallawah*, I, feared the tactile approach.

The alternative solution I devised backfired and I had to do the daring deed myself. I drew my car up as close as was safely possible. From behind the door I eyed him for the fold in which to insert the now carefully rolled and elongated paper currency. Some sixth sense must have conspired with him against my carefully elongated paper money and me. As my hand hovered over him while I looked for the crease in his rags, he suddenly awakened. In one glance, he understood the situation, stretched up a hand and grasped my fingers as he took the money from me. His exceedingly grimy fingers had scooped my hand. An untouchable had touched me and my arrogance was exposed. It took me years to understand the nature of that sidewalk dweller's ignorance. He did not share my assured knowledge that he was "untouchable." By his simple act, the *tallawah* became *likkle* and the presumed *likkle* showed that the *tallawah* was in him. This is the knowledge that resists the impulse to regard the South as oppressed because the desire to act out of alien designators is weaker than the urge to act from self-understanding. Lucy Bailey's Psalm citation signified her authentic self-identifiers even though she was surrounded by and immersed in imposed designators that clamored a repeated denial.

How then does the Lucy Bailey icon function to signify the future of Caribbean Christianity? This section of the conversation bears the designation, "The African diaspora." Lucy was certainly of the diaspora, African in her appearance. Although the majority of the Caribbean is of African ancestry, there is a significant diversity, especially in Trinidad, Guyana, and in Jamaica. We cannot exclude the other ethnicities from our Caribbean musings. Her ethnicity cannot be the foundational significant component. Neither can the sole foundational signifier be her religious experience as a Caribbean Christian when there are religions other than Christianity in the Caribbean. Her poverty is also significant but, again, not the uniquely signifying mark. In different religious arenas, the international, regional, national, and local these characteristics vary in the degree of marginality, invisibility, centrality, and visibility. It is her social invisibility within her own country that signifies the multi-tiered invisibility of the Caribbean peoples and their religions in Northern religious academic departments. Invisibility cloaks the other characteristics. Additionally, Lucy allows us to see the indomitability of the Caribbean spirit. The roll call of Caribbean leaders reveals the fecundity of that spirit. This invisible, indomitable, fecundity is the spirit that Caribbean female biblical scholars bring to the conversation. This spirit can effect the subtle perceptual transformation that alters the terms of the conversation just ever so slightly. In the spirit of Lucy, we can use the displacing designators South/resource-owning/resourceful/resistant/tallawah. This is when the conversation can really begin.

The Conversation

There was never a time in the history of North American feminist biblical hermeneutics that there was homogeneity of hermeneutic, methodology, and goals. The selection of conversation partners is therefore large. Elisabeth Schüssler Fiorenza coined the term "kyriarchy," meaning "multiplicative systems of oppression," recognized the tension in relationship between the universal and the particular, and most importantly affirms the goal that:

> feminist and liberationist movements and theologies . . . keep the knowledge of liberation and the vision of radical equality alive before the eyes of the disenfranchised and disempowered whose radical democratic dreams have been subverted.[10]

It seems most comprehensively useful and productive that Schüssler Fiorenza, a paradigmatic feminist biblical scholar, should be the feminist that Lucy Bailey meets. The *kyriarchical* notion coupled with the association of feminist and liberationist movements in a common vision propels white, privileged, and feminism into that complex vortex where multiple arenas of oppression are in constant kinetic competition, sometimes with centrifugal, sometimes with centripetal impact, always in a systemic relatedness, for nuclear attachment to the center. Systems comprise a framework that regulates and controls complex relationships, seeking to sustain and nurture that symbiotic/parasitic harmony that produces the envisioned systemic purpose: a purpose that may or may not have had democratic determination. Mega governing systems are economic, political, national, and social. Systems and arenas are similar but distinguishable and separable entities for purposes of analysis. Arenas, for example, class, age, sexuality, education, ethnicity, nationality, and culture can be systems too but are determinative only in relationship to and under the influence of mega-systems. Their systemic relationships are subordinate to the mega-systems that sustain inter- and intra-arena hierarchies. The arenas are present at every level but always subservient to the interests of the mega-system they are meant to serve.

Kyriarchy encapsulates and conceptualizes the density and complexity of the oppressive and resistant structures that women confront. It compels a confrontation with the network of subjugating relationships that demands women's loyalties and commitments, and diverts our focus from our common oppression. This capsulizing concept is, perhaps, most amicable to persons whose colonization has occurred in a distant geographical separateness from that of the colonizing powers. It is pertinent to the Caribbean as an epitomizing term representative of our own complex experience of emerging from the colonial. Should the Caribbean not adopt this term, the term offers something to each of the diverse emphases that feminism in an international arena might hold. It is the "corn with an ear for most, perhaps, all" and readily available as the term that can bridge the gap in understanding between Two-Thirds World and One-Third World women.

In his book, *The Marginalization of the Caribbean Male*, a Jamaican educator, Errol Miller, argues that the education system in Jamaica did not sufficiently accommodate the needs of the Jamaican male. The consequence over time was that the percentage increase of registered female students at the University of the West Indies, Mona Campus, and Jamaica resulted in a predominantly female student body. He cited other statistics that showed men to be abdicating higher education for jobs and occupations that required limited skills training and personal development but which paid well, quickly. By these choices, men were eliminating themselves from the decision-making cadres of the society. Many of these men were from the lower economic strata of the nation and their choice was a response to a system that seemed to have no place for them. Therefore, via the education system and the demands of culture capital the "glass ceiling" also existed for the lower-class Jamaica male. Errol Miller recognized this as the class component in patriarchy that negatively affected the socioeconomic prospects of the Jamaican male. Errol Miller's concerns about education led him to a discussion that accentuated the collusion between patriarchy and class: an accentuation that is lost in the focus on patriarchal sexism. For him the systemic arenas of patriarchy also functioned to keep classes of peoples in their socially designated places, possibly of servility in relation to the upper classes and to those, who by dint of personal good fortune, broke through the "glass ceiling."

Miller's insightful portrayal of male marginalization and the juxtaposition with class issues aligns his discussion with Schüssler Fiorenza's at certain points. Unfortunately, Errol Miller does not discuss the place of women of the lower economic classes in his understanding of the function of patriarchy. Indeed, he sees male restoration as requiring a higher priority. He avoids the greater complexities of gender, a construct of culturally determined, culturally valorized, intersexual relationships, as an all-pervasive arena of patriarchy. Adoption of *kyriarchy* focuses the conceptualization of the problem in a way that compels the complexity of the inter/intra-structure of all arenas of oppression.

Class is an arena of systemic oppression that the Caribbean shares with many postcolonial and post-neocolonial nations.[11] Yet there are particularities within all the arenas that remain sufficiently sensitive and urgent as to require a response to one of the warnings or challenges of Schüssler Fiorenza. A substantive tenet of feminist biblical criticism is the parochialism of the Eurocentric masculinist interpretation that arrogates a monopoly on universal applicability. Moreover, Schüssler Fiorenza declares that,

. . . the proliferation of "new" Jesus books does not undermine and undo the literalist masculinist desire of christological fundamentalism for an "accurate" and reliable Christology. Rather it tends to re-inscribe such a Christology in terms of positivism.[12]

It is in the context of these concerns that her warning that Christological "regionalism," professed as ethnic or local perspectives, plied in positivist terms, plays "into the hands of . . . authoritarian fundamentalism," and tends "to serve the interests of liberal pluralism."[13] The consequence is a reinforcing of the divisions "articulated by Western colonial political powers."[14] Her recommendations to counter these risks may be put thus:

1. Claim the universal validity of regionalist and local critique.
2. Disentangle feminist Christologies[15] and their validity claims from colonialist frameworks.
3. ". . . Reflect critically on feminist methods of analysis and on theories of interpretation that provide the discursive frame of feminist Christological (re)construction."[16]

We honor the integrity of the work of Schüssler Fiorenza by assuming that in the clamor that regional and local faith claims are universally valid there will be an avoidance of the mind-set that has led to egregious intellectual hegemony by "malestream"[17] critics. The claim for universal validity, it seems, should evolve from critical, pluralistic processes, maintain categories that include possible limits of applicability and authority and possess the capacity to acknowledge and adapt to contrary universal viewpoints. With this challenge/warning, Schüssler Fiorenza identifies the problem of a strong trend toward particularistic biblical readings: the tension between the universal and the particular.

Lucy Bailey and Everywoman: Particularity and Universality

Kyriarchy, then, is a term that makes accessible sense of the impact of the colonial system. If it is to be used more meaningfully by the Two-Thirds woman, it must include the arena of culture, as a site of imposition and oppression. In Jamaica, the road to full emancipation runs through the English culture back to our African ancestry. Globalization compounds the issue. Along with its economic impact, globalization includes, among other things, an efficient method for the mass exportation of one culture and the suppression of another. With an intensity that overshadows the phenotypical cultural hybridization of colonialism, the cultures of lesser-developed countries are experiencing severe cultural upheavals. Globalization does not permit a mutual exchange of cultural behavior and attitudes between the Two-Thirds and the One-Third Worlds. The cosmetic assimilation and exportation of cultural products such as craftwork, music, dance, and food involve the aspects of "exotic" culture that are easily distilled within the dominant consumer populace of the power countries. Language, history, philosophies, ideologies, community organization and assumptions, property roles, and meaning are the more deeply ingrained traditions to which music, dance, and the like provide clues. These traditions, more deeply rooted, are the main cultural sensibilities that will inform how Bible readings are done and provide the soil of indigenous hermeneutics. These are the elements thoroughly raped by globalization. For the Caribbean, this transgressing cultural infusion comes at a most delicate time. It is also the time in which developed world academia is critically interested in voices from the margin. What does it mean to make particularity-based universally valid claims when your own particularity is but a fragile stake in the marketplace of plurality? The Caribbean feminist must not separate herself from her fragile ground of particularity, which is the commonness of all that it means to be a Caribbean person and a woman in it. In a conversation with One-Third World feminists there has to be an appreciation of the inseparability of cultural factors that makes the Caribbean participation in the biblical *polylogue* one of hermeneutical self-hood/subjectivity.

The Caribbean theologian is still in that process. Michael Miller pinpoints our stage in that process. In an unpublished paper, "Impulses in Caribbean Theology,"[18] Miller surveyed and examined the contributions of various Caribbean theologians beginning with the founders such as William Watty and Horace Russell, later writers Lewin Williams, Ofelia Ortega, Horace Russell, and referencing the younger Burton Sankeralli. Included in Miller's survey are the contributions of Teresa Lowe Ching and Althea Spencer Miller, women who focus in different ways on the role of the Bible in Caribbean theology. Miller identifies "a specific area of conflict that gives some concrete indication of the future of Caribbean theology."[19] The conflict exists because a younger generation is willing to explore beyond the traditional formulations as for example, Sankeralli's cosmotheistic discourse: a combination of East Indian (Hindu and Muslim), Amerindian, and African cosmologies and spiritualities that dismantle traditional christocentrism and trinitarian formulations. Early theologians have founded the legitimacy of the task of developing a Caribbean theology. Miller recognizes that the newer thinking engages a trajectory that moves beyond the Afrocentric, class-focused thinking of the earlier efforts to include historical differences, pluralistic cultural sensibilities, multiple ethnicities, and religious pluralism. The new agenda must confront the task of identifying and analyzing hermeneutical particularities and uncovering indigenous reading and methodologies that, in some way, reference the elements he mentions. The Caribbean scholar, therefore, enters a conversation in which some participants' theological reflection and biblical criticism have enjoyed a longer history and may be at a more mature stage of coalescence. Nonetheless, we cannot abbreviate our processes. We know that "force ripe fruit not so sweet." The participation of some Two-Thirds World peoples may require a deceleration in the process of claiming universals. Alternatively, on the other hand, it may indicate the contextualized, parochial, and transitional nature of any universal claims.

The troubling relationship between international power and claims of universal validity requires pertinacious commentary. The claim that one particularity has some universal validity intones differently when declared by North American and European women. When American and European women make universal claims they have decades and centuries, respectively, of domination for which to atone. Their spirit should perhaps be careful. The Caribbean feminist making her claims has centuries of culturally oppressive religious leadership and impositionist thinkers to dethrone. Theirs are the very claim-sources that the Caribbean theologian must identify and critique while traversing toward her own universal contributions. We have lived for centuries with the idea that European formulations are universal truth. The American claims to ownership of universals, universal democracy, universal supremacy, universal mighty right, universal humanity, universal pluralism, is but another layer to the burdens of history's parochial, pretentiously universal bequests. Miller quotes Watty's denunciation of that heritage:

> One of the commonest ways in which theology has and still becomes prone to unreality is by the spurious claim to universality and finality. If it is true that we know only in part and see through a glass darkly, then every brand of theological formulation is *partial and provisional*. In other words, there is no theology so far formulated which has not been contextual, parochial and historically conditioned.[20]

Nonetheless, Schüssler Fiorenza is quite correct to sound the warning that emphasizing particularity could lead to an exclusion from the formulation of insightful and valid universals. It seems, though, that such a concern nestles most comfortably, where particularities have already received the validation that may be associated with the practice of dominance. Rightly or wrongly, when a culture or political group presently or historically enjoyed sway in the world there is a tendency to employ the subtext that says, "*We've got it babe! We are it! We've got what everybody wants!*" The Caribbean woman will need to deliver her universal claims with a "despite clause" because she delivers it to a world of academics that is unaccustomed to seeing or hearing her. The issue of cultural identity is especially critical for Caribbean peoples. We are formerly displaced peoples, with a heritage that includes the suppression of many significant aspects of our patrilineage (especially the African ancestral culture), their expressions displaced and replaced.[21] The healing of the psychic schism is vital. In such a context, particularity is essential to the development of a mature community of peoples. In such a spirit and with such a memory Schüssler Fiorenza's caution must be heeded.

For the Caribbean Feminist Biblical Student (CFBS)[22] heeding the caution is attended by the challenges that (1) Caribbean biblical study is predominantly a faith exercise; (2) the need to present our own efforts in a way that can be taken seriously while remaining authentic; and (3) our own entrenched orthodoxy. Practitioners of the Christian faith do most biblical study. Some are ordained, full-time church workers, the vast majority are laypersons of the faith. There is the occasional observer of religion who may not be a practitioner but who has a very lively interest in biblical matters. Even biblical academicians are usually, themselves, pastors or church workers. Therefore, biblical study is not a disinterested academic study subject primarily to the idiosyncrasy of the particular scholar. Interested biblical study is rarely guided by a need to seek justice or liberation. It is fair to say that "interested" biblical study is done within the context of denominational agendas. This in itself restricts the agenda of the academic enterprise. The CFBS works within and on behalf of faith communities. How can her subjectivity help this dogma-driven, interested scholarship contribute to a universalism that is radical, transformative, counter-colonial, and open-ended?

It is worth taking a special moment to discuss the tensions between universals and particulars. These concepts bring Christian feminists to the heart of a religion that declares its faith system to constitute universal truth. However, what truth can be universal when its declarants are a hegemonic cluster of ghettoized investigators, such as biblical scholars in the North have been? Insufficient work has been done on this conclusion-affecting element of research. It remains true that the argumentative and declarative tone of biblical scholarship continues to haggle for monopolistic accuracy of those conclusions: at the very least, this represents the will to universalize. Although the question of owning subjectivity might raise challenges for many biblical scholars, who only in recent years have begun to recognize the impact of their cultural particularities, it has relevance for all of us who claim our particularities. How can any declarant claim a truth for all people of all times?

Universals are useful for establishing commonalities. All visible creation needs oxygen. Not all creation needs oxygen in the same way: look at the fish in the sea. All creation needs families. Not all need the same kind of family. Commonalities must perforce be accompanied by exclusion clauses. The one set of all-inclusive commonalties is at best elusive. I might borrow the mathematical language of the "least common multiple." It is a relational principle and though used for purposes of division it is only common because of an even relationship to a certain set of numbers. Therefore, any number can function as a least common multiple if it has that set of numbers to which it can relate with evenness. Note that it does not end up with the same result for all the numbers in its set. This moves toward the observation by Schüssler Fiorenza that,

> . . . equality or egalitarian structures are characterized by what sociologists call role-interchangeability. Organizational equality is sustained by shifting and alternating authority and leadership among members of a group, all of whom—in principle—have equal access to authority, leadership, and power.[23]

I suggest, therefore, the construal of universals in terms of sets of variables. The universal is not singular. Multiple sets of pluralities represent the universal: sets of subjectivities, mutatis mutandis, ever changing and constantly in motion. The CFBS cannot imagine herself as finding space for a fixed chair at a fixed table. Neither can she participate in a quest for a fixed universal of which she too is a fixture. Mutatis mutandis must also be our possibility. The global future that demands change requires it of both the developed world and the CFBS. The effort of envisaging is futile if the Two-Thirds World is a fixed social entity that will grow from its past in a fixed trajectory.

It is certainly not adequate for Two-Thirds World theologians, feminist or otherwise, to stand around posturing like a display case. Engagement with the other is also important. One of the challenges that we must bring to the conversation, which is also a rebounding challenge to us is the deconstruction of the concept of universals. We must acknowledge our complicity in the retentions of orthodoxies bequeathed to us by the colonial past that we so rightly assail. We assail that past but not its doctrinal orthodoxies. It is often these doctrinal orthodoxies that undergird the misappropriation of universality by male-stream thinkers. In Jamaica *mi granny use to seh*, *"Finga neva seh*, *"look ya,"* *it always seh*, *"Look deh."* Fingers do not accuse their own hand; they always accuse the hands of others. We are quite contrary in this bifurcated approach. With the inclusion of Two-Thirds World peoples in the conversation, the need for reconstruction of the concept of universality becomes apparent both for us and against received impositions.

This affects, then, the approach of the CFBS to global future of FNTS. We must decenter the picture of the globe. For Jenkins the globe consists of the other, that is, the Two-Thirds World outside of his center. Lucy is his other and I, too, am his other. However, we are only "Other" to those who are not of us. From the viewpoint of the supposed "Other," such as I am, the Caribbean is the center and the developed world is the other. Yet Otherness is an unsustainable viewpoint. The Caribbean has for so long been the Other listening to the Other. Although we have listened to the One-Third World for too long we still need to listen, study, but contribute while we shape our own voices. This decentering of the picture highlights an entrenchment on our own part. We must avoid being so particular and contextual that we can only read certain parts of the Bible because those are the parts that relate to our sociopolitical and economic realities. We might develop strategies for reading the scriptures that reflect indigenous methodologies. My preference is narrative criticism, because it has some cultural resonance. Also, its outgrowth from and relationship to the philosophical movement of deconstruction has political and counter-colonial effectiveness. The philosophical and epistemological groundings of our indigenous reading methodologies become the pervasive, subverting knowledge that guides our reading of any pericope. They are our subjective hermeneutic.

One of the gifts of colonialism is that we can be functionally multicultural people. While we persistently and insistently offer our methods and insights to the larger world, we must be unhesitant about using methods and insights that are of the Other so that otherness can transform into the one another-ness of multiple communicative moments. In other words, we, too, must be prepared to undertake the vulnerability of engagement. It cannot be that only people of faith and poverty can elicit viable interpretations. We must not forget that our Bible readings have led us to partial emancipation. We have desired economic, and political, justice. It is easy and justifiable to read the Bible for these. Our faith communities have only inadequately addressed the issues of class. Additionally we have utterly failed to address theological and biblical relationships to inherited gender, family structural, sexual, and cultural biases that parade under the guise of virtue and righteousness. We cannot pretend that our difficulties perfected us. We share in a very human enterprise, this study of religion. Our faith communities need to be prepared to learn from multiple others, including those who do not have faith and those with whom we differ in faith. If we cannot, then what is the faith of which we speak?

Additionally, we must be self-conscious in our awareness that our particular readings are capable of constructing exportable life-applicable realizations for people other than ourselves. We must expect that the Other will see herself, himself, and their future generations in us. Our particular understandings can be normative but not fixtures. In the words of the Honorable Robert (Bob) Nesta Marley, "Emancipate yourself from mental slavery! None but ourselves can free our minds." In this conversation, we must be more than museum pieces to ourselves. It is important that Caribbean feminist New Testament scholars introduce ourselves to our feminist sisters so that their perceptions of us may be better informed. We also need to consider how we self-identify as participants in the conversation. There is a way of envisaging the future that leads us all to speak about the destabilizing impact of the Two-Thirds World upon the developed world. Oftentimes the tacit understanding of that desta- bilization, in which we are complicit, is that it is the consequential impact of our happenstance. This is a new version of the naive savage, capable only of benign response and simplistic idealism. We would be devoid of any intentionality, and pur- posefulness should we capitulate to that notion. We have yet insufficient access to those places where we might declare, "This is our vision!" A reasonable, upstart of a goal for our participation, in addition to the Other adjusting their understanding of us, would be that they make adjustments to their life understandings in the light of ours, that our vision too has universal meaning. This is "Likkle thinking tallawah." As a Jamaican might put it, *"Is a Lucy t'ing dat,"*—This is Lucy's way.

Who is Lucy?

Who will be the Caribbean feminist New Testament scholar? The Caribbean has special family issues. There has never been a "Father Knows Best"[24] family model operative in popular family structure.[25] On the contrary, a strong residual issue of the colonial years (seventeenth to twentieth century) is that of the absent male, that is, fathers are absent from the home. (Consider also Miller's concern for the underde- velopment of the Caribbean male.) Given these factors and with a rapid and ongoing increase in crime and violence the male is endangered species. There has to be sensi- tive consideration given to the role of the male in the society. Some of the issues that generated the feminist movement in the North were either absent or less important for our women. The thrust of Caribbean women must include the Caribbean man. This does not require the surrender of women's particular reading. It does mean that the CFBS must exercise sensitivities to the place of gender in the colonial history. North American and European women in conversation with the Caribbean woman will need to be aware of the sensitivities involved, where the men of our lands share in a history of subjugation to dominant Eurocentric women. Caribbean women involved in this conversation flirt with the perception of betrayal. We cannot over- look the implicit conundrum in such an approach and the tensions it generates.

Subject though the Caribbean man is to kyriarchy he is not an innocent victim in the situation. He is fully capable of exerting the values of patriarchy even as he rails against the impact of colonialism upon himself. His perceptions of traditional gender roles also need critical analysis. Nonetheless the future portent is that the Two-Thirds World male will be a participant in the conversation, perhaps overtly, perhaps hover- ing in the background, certainly one of its subjects.

The representatives of the academic CFB scholar will bring the Caribbean reality already described in this chapter. The network will include persons who will never be academics. They must be careful lest external training does not lead to peculiar detachments. Our confidence that we are of our people may be misplaced if we allow ourselves to forget to bring the people, the air, the mountains, the aridity, the rainy seasons, the fruits, the harvest, the animals, the hurricanes, the trade winds, the music, the dance, as well as the hardships, the poverty, the unemployment, the geopolitical power structure with us as we read. CFB scholars will need to remember that which Lucy represents. Undoubtedly, the CFBS need to be *tallawah*. Fortunately, they are not the only element in the process.

Reading Biblical Texts with Lucy: The Widow's Mi(gh)te

The power relationships that both integrate and disrupt systems is of interest to the postcolonial biblical scholar. Geopolitical realities constantly impose restrictions upon nationalistic thrusts for self-governance and economic independence. Caribbean peoples live on small islands, except for those on the Central and South American mainland. The region is a small one that consists of small islands. To the northeast is the huge, powerful United States of America. The Caribbean Community and Common Market (CARICOM) must compete against larger regional bodies such as the European Common Market. The urge to create and pre-serve our own posterity marks every aspect of Caribbean life, including our theology. How does our *likkle* negotiate this labyrinth of power relationships? In the arena of biblical criticism, what difference would a feminist reading make?

Lucy lived in a violent neighborhood. She frequented neighboring areas where children learn how to play "dodge bullet" early. Some of these neighborhoods were dangerous for strangers. Often in the act of pastoral work Lucy's various pastors had to enter these areas and would think many times before entering some of these areas. Lucy, who was a familiar presence to the residents and gangsters in these areas, was the guarantor of safe passage. There was no need for police presence or bulletproof vests. She was known and respected by residents and the dons.[26] They would not harm anyone who was in her company. Little Lucy, physical diminutive, had the power to still the weapons and malevolent intentions of the most hardened of human hearts. Lucy's mite was the protection that effected the temporary cessation of even that kind of power. This was Lucy, *tallawah* in mi(gh)te.

Lucy brings to mind the story of the widow in Luke 21:1–4 who gave her two, small copper coins while the rich gave their gifts. About her giving Jesus said, "Truly I tell you, this poor widow has put in more than all of them, for all of them have con-tributed out of their abundance, but she out of her poverty has put all she had to live on."[27] Read in isolation "The Widow's Mite" does not appear to be a story about authority. If we contextualize it beginning at Luke 19:45 we see a transformation of the notion of power throughout ending with the widow's stamp. Space does not per-mit an equal analysis of each passage in this pericope. Except in one instance, I do not attempt to address the historicity of the episodes. I treat each passage in its narrativ-ity, with general historical references where necessary, but without presuming one way or the other for (facticity of sequence). Luke 19:45–48; 20:1–8, 18–19, 20–26, 27–40, 41–44, and 45–47 receive cursory attention and Luke 20:9–17 and 21:1–4, a fuller analysis.

St. Luke 19:45–48—The Cleansing of the Temple

This is a brief tale filled with significant details. Jesus enters the temple after his parade into Jerusalem. Presumably, there were buyers in the temple but the sellers, rather than the buyers, bear the brunt of Jesus' anger. Thereby the buyers are placed outside the pale of judgment. The sellers are the front men. They receive the blame for converting the house of prayer into a den of thieves. Selling was the front end of a corrupt system that offered neither religious nor financial benefit for the ordinary buyers.[28] The sellers were complicit in a web of systemic exploitation, reaping bene-fits for its administrators and leaders. For this reasons Jesus expels them from the temple and clamors for the restoration of the temple as a place of prayer/worship.

The chief priests, the scribes, and an anonymous group labeled the "leaders of the people" reacted swiftly. The sellers were upset but the reaction came from the threat-ened group. "*T'row stone in a pig pen, de one whe squeal a 'im i'lick.*"[29] The leadership squealed. The affront was theirs. Clearly, the conflict is not between Jesus, on the one hand, with the buyers and the sellers on the other: it is with the holders of power. Jesus continues to teach daily in the temple. In that immediate time, he escapes any punishment of this "nefarious" deed because of the people. The stage is set then for ongoing confrontation between the leadership and Jesus. By an act of rebellion staged within the symbol of Israel and transacted at the point where the temple's economic system has immediate impact on the people Jesus challenges that which the system supports. The leaders are angry.

St. Luke 20:1–8—Jesus' Authority Questioned

The setting remains the temple but now Jesus is teaching there. The identity of the third element in the leadership group changes from "leaders of the people" to "the elders."[30] They question Jesus about the source of authority for his actions. Is this a retrospective reference to the ejection of the sellers? They do not ask about his teach-ing. They specifically make a reference his action so it might be a reference to both the manner of his entry into Jerusalem and the ejection of the sellers. Jesus responds with a counter question about the source of John's baptism. The implicit corollary is that the judgment on John is by extension a judgment on Jesus' source. Contemplating their response the trio of leaders restricts their choices to either a heavenly or a human source. The reader overhears the ruminations of the troubled leaders who are very sensitive to the judgment of the people whom they perceive as opposed to themselves. They know the people think John is a prophet: hence the quandary that makes it inex-pedient for the scribes, chief priests and elders to answer this question forthrightly. To say that John's authority is prophetic, therefore heavenly, would validate Jesus. To say otherwise is to invite a stoning to death by the people.

The leaders' dilemma is reminiscent of an ancient rabbi's words, "Should the stone fall on the crock, woe to the crock. Should the crock fall on the stone, woe to the crock. In either case, woe to the crock."[31] The leaders develop an immediate case of neutralizing ignorance because of the dilemma. Jesus reciprocates with a refusal to answer their question about his authority. The question of *authority* is now explicitly introduced to the pericope with a choice between earth and heaven as the source of authority. It is also present because Jesus' counter question and refusal to answer is another clear flouting of the leaders' responsibility as guardians of Jewish life. Authority, expressed in terms of the exercise of power, pervades the pericope as a theme. The stakes are high. Life and death are in the balance.

St. Luke 20:9–19—The Parable of the Vineyard and the Tenants

The interpretation of this parable by the scribes and chief priests is a pivotal element in identifying how the confrontation with powers unfolds. In the parable of the tenants, the owner of the vineyard goes away. At the appropriate season, he sent two slaves in turn to collect his share of the harvest. Each returns empty-handed having been severely ill-treated by the tenants. Finally, the master sends his beloved son whom the tenants kill. Jesus predicts that the owner of the vineyard will eventually return to destroy the tenants and give the vineyard to others. Many scholars regard this parable as an allegory in which the tenants represent the scribes and chief priests, the beloved son is Jesus, himself,[32] and God is the landowner. If the scribes and chief priests used the same allegorical coding they would understand that the parable fore-tells their indictment and destruction by the allegorical God (landowner). So the parable functions as a warning of God's impending judgment against them. Is this a realistic and credible parable? Could such tenant rebellion really happen? Is it or is it not an allegory? Do answers to these questions lead to a plausible estimation of the chief priests' and scribes' understanding of the parable as told against them.

What would be the logic of the parable should the chief priests and scribes be put in the place of the landowner? It would be a parable about a socioeconomic situation in which the landowner has the power to determine the fate of the tenants. The landowner would be an absentee master who exploits the labor of the tenants to his own exponential benefit. There would be rebelliousness because the tenants wish to retain more of the fruit of their labor for themselves. The ill-treatment of his first two representatives and the murder of his beloved son would provoke the landowner to return to destroy the tenants and redistribute the land. This is a very troubling situa-tion with violence breeding more violence. There is no redemption in the parable itself and this reading permits the presence neither of God nor of a beloved son who is Jesus. Is this a plausible reading and where does it lead?

This reading takes seriously the land tenancy circumstance as a real situation and not only a useful allegorical backdrop. John Kloppenborg in a monograph, *Reading Ancient Viticulture: The Social Context of the Parable of the Tenants in Mark and Thomas*[33] thoroughly examines the tenant situation as it relates to Mark's Gospel and the Gospel of Thomas and concludes in favor of the realism of its arrangement and the possibility of the results indicated in Luke. Alan Culpepper also indicates the documentation of the system of tenancy dating back over 300 years.[34] The setting of this parable, arguably, represents a lived situation that elicited deep feelings. The attitude of the tenants is not dismissible. Were they reprobate ingrates or people living with a serious sense of outrage? In 1956 William Arndt wrote, "The abusive and unconscionable cruelty of the dishonest tenants and their disregard of undeniable obligations is remarkable, but something that can be observed now and then among *illiterate, emotional people* especially when a mob spirit flares up (emphasis mine)."[35] (Arndt should know that illiteracy is not a sign of unintelligence and that literacy is not a prerequisite for a serious recognition of oppression and injustice where it exists. Neither is an outraged response a sign of irrationality.) So the tenants are dismissed.

Closer to the historical times is Culpepper's recognition that raising grain resulted in a "grim struggle for subsistence, hard agrarian labor, heavy taxation, and recurring conflict between peasants and landlord."[36] This parable was credible in its contemporary setting.[37] Did such tenant rebellion did really happen? It is not likely that the chief priests, scribes, and elders were members of the Sicarii[38] and Zealots.[39] Discontent was in the air. It is very possible that many members of the audience inwardly resonated with the actions of the tenants.

Is the story a parable or an allegory? Scholars are divided on this issue.[40] The parable depends on allegorical identification for its effectiveness. Scholarly reading of its allegorizing details is replete with cross-references to the Hebrew Bible. Motifs of the vineyard, land ownership, the sending of messengers, a beloved son as an ideal redeemer figure are evocative of themes found in the Psalms and the Prophets. In all these motifs, God is owner, sender, and judge. The motif of the beloved son is certainly reminiscent of the voice at Jesus' baptism that declared him a beloved son. Retaining God as an invisible character in the story and these motifs compel the identification of the chief priests and scribes with the tenants and argues against my repositioning of the identity of the landowner. The motifs are certainly present. God's presence is not innate, necessary, or implied as an actor in the story. The identification that places God in the role of an exploitative landowner is problematic. It facilitates a sense of solidarity with those who are exploitative owners but does nothing for the improvement of those rendered invisible by this association, that is, the seething disenfranchised populace.

There is a similar parable in Gospel of Thomas 65 (GTh).[41] Here the owner is a good person who sends two servants to collect the profits. The third person he sends is his son, who is not a beloved son, just a son. The vineyard is present but lacks the divine evocation because GTh makes the financial arrangement clear. "The owner rented it to some farmers, that the farmers might work in it and the owner might collect the profits from them." The owner also does not go to a far off land as he does in Luke. Very significantly, GTh ends with the killing of the son and the saying, "Whoever has ears ought to listen." GTh lacks the Isaianic based quote of verses 17 and 18 in Luke that establishes a messianic connection. It is less likely that someone listening to the bare-boned parable in GTh would have associated the landowner with God. This parable circulated without that definitive association. It is possible then that in the Gospel, while the landowner can be representative of God, there is no need to be definitive in that association. Dissociating God from the landowner leaves room for another interpretation and I posit the Scribes and chief priests. If the parable is an allegory then how did the chief priests and scribes hear it?

My analysis does not exclude the possibility of allegory. However, in this story the literal representation of the economy of first-century viticulture reduces the allegorical potency. The reality is not benign and it is very near. In its immediate context, the parable has allusions to its immediate precedents and is antecedent to others. When the leaders questioned the authority of Jesus and he countered their question, their fear was of the people's response. The landowner luxuriated at the tenants' expense. The returns of their own labor were meager. It barely enabled a subsistence existence. The temple, the arena of religious fidelity, was also a place of exploitation. Here the chief priests and scribes colluded to exploit. In 20:6, they feared the people would kill them. Where leaders enjoy the approval of the people they lead, is it likely that they would fear death should they err in the execution of their appropriate duty?

This fear of the people is a refrain up to this point. It appears in 19:48; 20:6 and 19. The imagery of the rejected stone calls to mind the chief priests' and scribes' fear in 20:6 that they were at risk of being stoned to death by the people. The group that constantly fears harm up to this point in the pericope consists in various permutations of the chief priests, scribes, leaders, and elders. They fear most the people's anger against them. Why would they then be the angry people and not the exploitative property owner? In addition, it is the leaders who are punishment minded. Their profile fits the landowner well. It strains my postcolonial credulity to think that these leaders would traverse class and economic mind-sets to identify with the angry victims and not the owner.[42] That would be too unusual a consideration, especially given the excesses of the nobility at this time in the Roman Empire. Rather, they would be more likely to identify with the landowner.

We may agree that the parable contains allegorical elements. There remains the question of understanding the parable in Luke. My reading considerably alters the general understanding. With the landowner identified as the Jewish leaders we have a parable in which their collusion with oppression is challenged, their leadership rejected. The parable reflects on their disturbed relationship with the populace, portraying them as distant, out of touch, parasitic, and vindictive. They have the power to exert their vehemence to the destruction of others. They also have the power to distribute property. The problem is not that they owned property. The problem is that they exercised this ownership in a way that created hardship, generated hostility, and matched hostility with more hostility. No wonder that the people responded to the suggestion with the outcry, "Heaven forbid." Would their concern be for the fate of the landowner/leaders? It seems more probable that familiarity with rapidly executed punishment would lead them to resist Jesus' projected outcome, the destruction of the tenants. Today we might, in their place, say, "Enough already." The rejected stone would include the teller of the parable and also the tenants, Arndt's so-called *illiterate emotional* people.

The prediction against the leaders is that the stone (the tenants/people) that they reject will be their cornerstone. Robert Tannehill does not understand this scriptural reference to point primarily to the resurrection. Rather, "It proclaims a reversal of status. . . . which means that the rejection of the stone by the builders will produce the exact opposite of their intention."[43]The quote from Isaiah 8:14, which there represents God as the stone of stumbling, is transformed by the time of 1 Peter 2:7 and 8 to represent the followers of Christ. Was there a process in which this adopted metaphor was democratized so that its application became more populist? God may not be present in the Lucan parable but the choices of life and death, heaven and humankind/social ills hover in the background. The ill-treatment of the tenants is a choice for social ills. It is a choice against heaven. The agnostic stance on the source of John the Baptist's power is a choice neither for heaven nor for humankind. That choice is not yet evident.

This parable lays down the gauntlet. The leaders' response, the desire to apprehend Jesus right there and then, suggests their understanding of the parable. Fear of the people prevents them. The parable is then a forthright and trenchant critique of their exercise of power, not as tenants but as landowners. Their cruelty is exposed. The parable reminds them that they are disrespected and detested. Their constant fear of the people renders them temporarily powerless. If they understood that the parable points to God's impending punishment of them as tenders of God's vineyard, then their fear is misdirected unless they believe that the people are God's instrument for their punishment. Their authority is crumbling and they continue to fear the people. They know their vulnerability and they do not appear again in this pericope to challenge Jesus publicly. Others undertake the task.

St. Luke 20:20–44—Variations on the Theme

The next challenge in verses 20–26 brings the choice between heavenly (God) and human enterprises into clear relief. Is it lawful to pay taxes? Taxes, of course, were another instrument of oppression. Jesus' answer is precise and insightful. He navigates between the Scylla and Charybdis with dexterity and efficiency. Should he answer, "No," he would be guilty of treason. If he answers, "Yes," he would be an affront to the people, possibly losing his influence. His skillful navigation is only the beginning of his answer. Allusions to earlier portions of the pericope serve to illuminate his response. To give to Caesar and to God their proper due means: (1) restoring to the temple its proper role as a house of prayer—collusion with the things of Caesar is wrong; (2) acknowledging the divine source of both John the Baptist's power and his; and (3) ending the pervasive evils in which the poor Jews lived out their lives.

Jesus' response is devastating. The spies sent to ask this question are silent and impotent. The response takes the question out of the arena of political submission and places it in the arena of values. The choice between Caesar and God requires ethical and moral decision making. Between the poles are webs of sociopolitical, economic, and religious situations in which choices place individuals closer to or more distant from one or other end of this polarized value spectrum. The poles determine the judgment. Where will this pericope end: will it be with the values of the covenant or will it be with the values of the empire?

In verses 27–40, the question is doctrinaire and the Sadducees take their turn. It is not clear that they too are out to trap Jesus in the way that the chief priests and scribes were. It is not necessary to include them in that collusion at this point. As the chief priests and scribes do not send the Sadducees, as they previously sent the spies, it seems that the literary context rather than specific narration taints them. Tannehill suspects their sincerity in the conversation because "their question assumes as true what they deny."[44] On the other hand, Caird regards this question based on Levirate marriage (Deuteronomy 25:5–6) to be academic as the "law had fallen into abeyance."[45] Joseph Fitzmyer, too, thinks the "question posed concerns neither Jesus himself nor his relation to Jerusalem authorities. The problem is theoretic, possibly even a stock question customarily put by Sadducees to Pharisees."[46] If Tannehill, Caird, and Fitzmyer are correct then this passage does not fit, with power as hermeneutic. There is insufficient information from which to adduce the response of the populace in general. Additionally, there is insufficient evidence on which to adjudge the distribution of various beliefs in the resurrection. Is "power," as a hermeneutical concern, at all applicable to this passage? Did the Sadducean question have political implications? What is a reasonable surmise about their intention? Is it relevant to the preceding conflicts between authorities?

The Sadducees opposed the Hasmonean[47] rulers for their usurping of the High Priesthood. The High Priesthood previously belonged to the Zadokite dynasty of which the Sadducees were descendants. The Sadducees were a mixed group, generally recognized as belonging among the wealthy, inclusive of aristocratic Jews, high priests, and merchants. As members of the Sanhedrin and the temple hierarchy, Sadduceans would have more than a passing interest in events at the temple including Jesus' teaching. They would definitely have interest in Jesus and his answer to their question. A definitive statement about their intentions would be purely speculative though we may be reasonably sure that the question was not disinterested. Even if the Sadducees were not yet involved in any collusion, their question was, at least, a doctrinal conundrum and associated with contending leadership groups. At its most innocent, it was a doctrinal snare: one that could embarrass the upstart.

A subtle change does occur in this passage that is significant for the transformation of power and the Sadducees provide the pivot. The question of the resurrection is not only an area of conviction but it also represents a conflict among the Jewish leadership. In Acts 23:6–10 the apostle Paul manipulates Sadduceean and Pharisaic disagreement over this belief. We are aware then that the issue of resurrection could cause dissension between different groups of Jewish leaders. As posed the question conflates Deuteronomy 25:5 and Genesis 38:8. Jesus' answer is traceable to books excluded from the Tanak (Jewish scriptures)[48] as it contains allusions to 2 Maccabees 7:9 and 4 Maccabees 7:18–19 and combined with a reference to Exodus 3:2. In Luke, it is an architectonically constructed response in contrast to Mark 12:24–27 where Jesus charges them with ignorance of the scriptures they accept and relies on the Torah's Exodus 3:2 to explain their error.

Jesus' answer in Luke extracts statements from the writings that the Sadducees reject and combines them with statements from the Torah that they do accept. The allusions provide the basis for Jesus' reasoned answer in his imaginative depiction of the nature of the afterlife. As Fitzmyer writes, "Verses 34–36 contain Jesus' own answer, which is not an interpretation of Scripture; his pronouncement corrects the misconceived idea that the Sadducees have of the afterlife, and of Pharisaic teaching about the resurrection."[49] In so doing, Jesus asserts both the right of explanation and the right of creative positioning of texts to assist his explanation. Further, the texts referenced in the answer bring together the writings that are important for the contending groups. Perhaps such a response bore ameliorating force for the moment. More importantly, Luke's ending differs from Mark's and Matthew's.

Mark's ending in Mark 12:27 denounces the Sadducean understanding as wrong. Mark's Jesus appeals to the Torah for his explanation. Matthew's ending, Matthew 22:33 indicates that the crowds are amazed. Luke's story ends with a commendation of

Jesus by some of the Scribes, "Teacher, you have spoken well." Some of Jesus' challengers must now praise him. Moreover, no one (not scribe, chief priest, nor Sadducee) dares to venture any more questions against him. He finally defeats his challengers because of his imaginatively constructed answer. Henceforth in this pericope, this is the basis for calibrating Jesus: not by the authority of the traditional leadership but by his supersession of their capabilities. This is a transfer of power.

In verses 41–44 Jesus assumes the mantle of he questioners by raising a question himself. How can the Son of David also be the messiah? The quotation, "The Lord said to my Lord, 'Sit at my right hand, until I make your enemies your footstool' " comes from Psalm 110:2. Luke leaves his hearers and readers with a conundrum at the end of verse 44. Would they have heard a messianic self-proclamation? It is not difficult to imagine that first-century Jews would have memorized or been very familiar with various verses and passages of their scriptures. Would this psalm be one such? Even if the first-century Jew recognized the psalm, would she understand it as an allusion to Jesus' messianic status? Many scholars understand this passage as foundational for messianic claims about Jesus. Fitzmyer argues that this is a development that properly belongs to Stage III[50] of the developing Gospel tradition. At Stage I, the Stage III meaning is unhelpful. Fitzmyer argues that in the first century CE this enthronement psalm would not have been associated in the Jewish mind with the enthronement of the messiah. Its messianic interpretation did not appear in rabbinic literature before the second half of the third century CE.[51] Fitzmyer makes a salient point here and so it seems that any messianic claim for this passage must either be premature or acknowledge that it imports the later Christian belief in Jesus as messiah.

In a thorough discussion of the problem, Fitzmyer rejects ideas that Jesus was denying the Davidic genealogy of the messiah: it was too entrenched. The final form of Luke leaves many clues to Jesus' connection to the Davidic lineage. The genealogy in 3:23–38 traces his ancestry through David, who became king of the united kingdom. In Luke 2:59, Zechariah prophecies that his unborn son, John, would be "the prophet of the Most High for (he) will go before the Lord to prepare his ways." Moreover, the angelic announcement in 1:32 and 33 declares that Miriam's child is to be called, "Son of the Most High" and declares, "the Lord God will give to him the throne of his father, David." Undoubtedly, the author and compiler of Luke makes a strong association between Jesus and the lineage of David. Yet Fitzmyer is reluctant to suggest that at Stage I the messianic connection is anything more than a hint, an insinuation.[52]

What is a plausible alternative reading? In the first century CE, the Sadducees were thought to be of the lineage of Zadok, the chief of the priests in the Davidic and Solomonic reigns. Perhaps their presence as questioners might be the allusive springboard for the Davidic messiahship. Would a candidate for the messiah emerge from the peasantry? It seems more likely that the messiah, as David's descendant, should derive from the aristocracy. Contenders for the throne certainly include the progeny of the Sadducees, the Hasmonean pretenders, and the chief priests. Fitzmyer suggests that the best reading of the pronouncement implicit in the questions is that "it is not a matter of either/or, but of both/and: Yes, the Messiah is David's son, but he is more. . . . "[53] Fitzmyer asserts that the "more" is that the messiah is David's Lord.[54]

The immediate intertextual allusions may elucidate the "more." If we could allow the possibility that the Sadducean presence prompts the association with David, we may summarily align them with the potential to produce David's messiah and distance ourselves from requiring a messianic declaration in the passage. An overlooked clause of importance in the quotation is, "until I make your enemies your footstool." Enemies: may be a reference to those who hounded him throughout the pericope. Given the merit of Fitzmyer's both/and reading, the messiah is of David but is also something more than David is. It could mean then that those who claim only genealogical descent have insufficient ground to stand on. We may then conclude that the heirs apparent are dismissed. Consider the subtle transformation in the progression of the pericope from Jesus as an upstart, questioned, suspect man, pivoting on a word of approval to become the one who asks the question that no one but himself answers. The status quo changed. His answers played with his enemies' "card decks" and he "trumped" them. Literally and metaphorically, his "enemies are now his footstool." This assertion need not bear the weight of later Christological importations. The question of the resurrection in the previous passage does not necessarily reflect later Christian notions. The later Christological titles are absent in the Davidic passage. David's Lord then, may not be the messiah of Christology, but the one who, being of the lineage of David, experiences the transformation of enemies into footstools.

From a form critical perspective, Fitzmyer identifies this passage as an implicit pronouncement story.[55] The word "pronouncement" tends to resonate with grand solemnity but there may be humor in this passage. How might it be read: with a smile, a smirk, a hearty laugh, or with wryness? Laugh a little with the author and the star character. His conundrum is difficult to fathom unlike the simplicity of the Saducee's question. If we laugh with Jesus, then we glimpse the ridiculousness of all that happened while he was teaching in the temple: his enemies—despite pretensions and mumblings—are for a while, his footstools. They are temporarily routed. They must now contemplate the question with clues from throughout the pericope, "Who really is David's Lord? How big a threat is Jesus? Power is at stake. It is worth a smirk from the underling.

This chapter, though not the pericope, ends with an undiscriminating and stinging denunciation of the scribes who walk around in long robes, love salutations in the marketplaces, prominence in the synagogues, and places of honor at banquets (20:46). Jesus' main nemeses are again in focus. His severe denunciation against them immediately succeeds his intellectual rout of their parries throughout the pericope. Their love of honor and prominence is in sharp contrast to their parasitism, "They devour widows' houses and for the sake of appearance say long prayers" (20:47a). The pericope addresses authority and impact of the temple system and its proprietors by affective criticism rather than by revolt. The interweaving of piety and hypocrisy underscores the egregious and cynical nature of scribal practices in particular. The people among whom they walk with expectation of greetings are the people whose living they sap. With the earlier parable in mind, we may understand that though the scribes and their co-conspirators may dole punishment upon their resistors "They will receive the greater condemnation." (20:47b). This, as a commentary on the abuse and corruption of power, perhaps religious power especially, measures it as deserving the severest punishment possible.

Luke 21:1–4—The Widow's Mi(gh)te

The reference to the scribal consumption of widow's houses at the end of the last chapter connects it to the widow's incident at the beginning of chapter 21. Chapter 19:28–21:4 is part of a larger pre-passion pericope that ends at 21:37. The setting for Jesus' teaching continues to be in the temple but the content turns to insurrectional eschatology beginning in verse 5. Verse 4 in chapter 21 provides a natural pause within the larger pericope and the stopping point for this analysis. Appropriately, the widow incident also reconnects with 19:45–47 by focusing upon the relationship between the temple system and individual monetary offerings and payments. The passage revealed angry dissatisfaction with the operation of the system. It is hardly likely that there is any comfort derivative from participation in the financial aspect of giving. Fitzmyer insightfully writes, "In the preceding episode Jesus was displeased with what the Scribes were doing to widows' estates; here he is no more pleased with what he sees. He heaps no praise on the widow, but rather laments the tragedy of the day: She has been taught and encouraged by the religious leaders to donate as she does, and Jesus condemns the value system that motivates her action."[56]

Unlike Mark, from whom Luke derives these passages, Luke does not quantify the offerings of the rich and the widow. He weights them in terms of proportions and totalities. The rich give a portion of their wealth. The widow's two lepta become her all. The hyperbolic contrastive picture unveils the impact of the temple system on the disparate groups each represents. Without the widow and her offering, the harshness of the system remains hidden. Hers is the contrasting prism that clarifies the distortion in which the ordinary person lived her life. The widow's might is a product of her mite. This is not the might of faithful institutional devotion. This might is the product of uncomplicated, faithful living: a kind that by its simplicity unveils the complexities of insincerity and guile. Her mite is the column on which the pretentious base their ostentation. Jesus had to look up to see this woman. Based on his description of the scribes' walking and sitting they are unavoidably visible. The widow in this portrayal provides the criterion for the judgment against the scribes. She is very present and her odd presence will unsettle the status quo. The hyperbolic contrast elevates the situation of the widow. It points to the preference for covenantal values.

The widow's situation is emblematic of the need for an ethic of prophetic justice in the practice of power. The widow's allegiance to the system that exploits her reminds me of the institutional church's role in alleviating poverty while inadequately opposing or transforming systems that perpetuate kyriarchy. Reading this pericope with power as hermeneutic unveils the widow's plight. The ongoing conflict between Jesus and the powerbrokers, his lament of the people's plight through the scope of the widow clarifies intolerability. The widow's mi(gh)te like Lucy's lies in reading this passage in the wisdom of subversive knowledge. Silence in the face of abusive power is acquiescence, tantamount to agreement. The possession of enforceable power is frangible. Clarification, criticism, destabilization, and redefinition of power are the widow's mighty mite. This is why Lucy and she, these two women, remind me of each other.

Conclusion

The reading of the pericope with the hermeneutic of "power" was contextual. The location of the Caribbean in relation to geopolitical power and its colonial and neocolonial sensibilities provided the viewpoint on power. This meant reading the pericope with allegiance to the victimized rather than to the elite. Fortunately, this pericope begins with the central character taking a stand for the victimized. Historical and narrative criticism collaborated to provide realism and literariness without attempting to suggest that the pericope itself provides a true sequence of actual events. This is another prototypical model of reading the scripture in a way that converses with historical critical research while maintaining an alternative perspective. It also falls within the tradition of liberatory readings. Together, these are the primary reasons that make it one kind of feminist reading.

Destabilizing the conversation means that the global future of FNTS needs a different focus. Given the geopolitics of domination, we all need to decenter authority, Americans, Europeans, Africans, Mujeristas, Womanists, Minjung and other Asian theologians, Pacific Islanders, Caribbean feminist biblical students, Christians, Muslims, Buddhists, professionals, laypeople. When Two-Thirds feminists speak of our contexts, I dare suggest, we tend to point our comments at Americans and Europeans. Therefore, even when protesting, we reinscribe their power to include, exclude, and further empower them with the potential to save us. Feminist biblical interpreters in the future of this conversation will have to model ways of walking in strategic alliance with partners who are at different stages in our common task of envisioning a more just and participatory world. Let us all retreat to the periphery. Can we imagine spaces in which we are all speaking with each other, in which the begging ends, the competition for beneficence is disallowed, covert supremacist attitudes are exorcised, where the feminist academic becomes a student, the layperson becomes the teacher and where the universal is present because a new configuration of multiple sets of subjectivities and pluralities are in the conference room and each has equal voice and vote? These places may be in the academy, at the conference tables, salons, weekend retreats, in street advocacy, on the mountainside, or down by the river. I further dare to suggest that though these ideas evoke vulnerability they are very *tallawah*: so very Lucy.

Notes

1. I use the term "black" to indicate the languaging of race in the times of Lucy Bailey and to help set the background for a fuller understanding her forcefulness.
2. Testimony sharing is a period during a worship service when the floor is open for individuals to publicly declare those particular events in which they have experienced the work of God in their lives.
3. Philip Jenkins, *The Next Christendom: The Coming of Global Christianity* (Oxford University Press: New York, 2002) 2.

4. Jenkins, *The Next Christendom*, 220. This is not an assessment of Jenkins's use of statistics. Rather it is a general reference to the complexities that statistic-based projections represent and the mutability of statistics. He recognizes this himself when he indicates that predictions for 2100 or 2500 BCE would depend on inspired prophecy.

5. Jenkins, *The Next Christendom*, 209.

6. Author unknown, www.internurse.com/history/seacole/marymain.htm (accessed February 2003).

7. Florence Nightingale's dates are 1820–1910.

8. Canadian feminists are distinct from their North American counterpart. Canada seems closer to the South given its history of colonization and the nature of its uneasy relationship with the United States. Additionally, Canada's relationship with the countries on the Southern axis, tends more to kinship than to otherness.

9. The United Theological College of the West Indies is one exception as it receives significant funding from international partners.

10. Elisabeth Schüssler Fiorenza, *Jesus: Miriam's Child, Sophia's Prophet: Critical Issues in Feminist Christology* (Continuum Publishing Company: New York, 1995) 7.

11. This distinction between postcolonial and post-neocolonial socioeconomic situations is a critical recognition of the historical trajectory from colonialism to globalization. Globalization is the post-neocolonial context of formerly colonized countries. Uncritical use of the term "globalization" tends to obscure its historical relationship to the socioeconomic and cultural tripod of colonialism, postcolonialism, and neocolonialism upon which globalization depends for the susceptibilities and vulnerabilities of some of the world's weaker and weakest nations. In this way, globalization is simultaneously a revelatory and obscurantist concept.

12. Fiorenza, *Jesus*, 9.

13. Fiorenza, *Jesus*, 9.

14. Fiorenza, *Jesus*, 10.

15. The principles listed earlier in the chapter were enunciated in a book on Christology. To Christology we should add ethics, spirituality, pneumatology, psychology, practical theology, biblical criticism as more of the theological spheres to which these recommendations apply.

16. Culled from Schüssler Fiorenza, *Jesus*, 10.

17. Another Schüssler Fiorenza neologism.

18. Michael Miller, "Impulses in Caribbean Theology," http://www.cwmnote.org/papers/miller.htm (accessed March 2003).

19. Miller, "Impulses," 3.

20. Miller, quoting William Watty, *From Shore to Shore: Soundings in Caribbean Theology* (Golding Printing Services: Kingston, Jamaica, 1981) 3.

21. This history of suppression is not shared in the same way by Arabic, Chinese, English, Indian, Irish, Jewish, Spanish, and other nation-based ethnicities that arrived in the Caribbean as indentured servants, entrepreneurs, or as somewhat willing immigrants.

22. I use "student" instead of scholar in order to include persons who are not biblical specialists but retain a stake in the fruit of biblical reading.

23. Elisabeth Schüssler Fiorenza, *In Memory of Her: A Feminist Theological Reconstruction of Christian Origins*, Tenth Anniversary Edition (Crossroad Publishing Company: New York, 1994) 286.

24. "Father Knows Best" was a TV sitcom that was aired on various networks in the United States from October 1955–April 1963. The title has grown to represent the idealized nuclear family in which father was the main breadwinner and recognized head of the family, mother's work was in the home and for family (she was always dressed, demure, yet very attractive), having two children, an older son and a younger daughter.

25. However the Caribbean woman does experience forms of male chauvinism. Gendered relationships within the family have distinctively different features and elements. Some women's development issues in the Caribbean have had to focus on female economic empowerment—because the woman is often the main wage earner in the household—on the supply and administration of family planning methods, and on skills training to enable the woman to work.

26. "Don" is the title of the local gang lord.

27. Luke 21:3, 4.

28. For fuller discussions of the relationship between peasants and the temple hierarchy that address issue of corruption see K.C. Hanson and Douglas E. Oakman, *Palestine in the Time of Jesus: Social Structures and Social Conflicts* (Minneapolis: Fortress Press, 1988) 131–159 and Ched Myers, *Binding the Strong Man: A Political Reading of Mark's Story of Jesus* (Maryknoll, NY: Orbis Books, 1988) 302–303.

29. "Throw a stone into the sty, the pig that squeals was hit."

30. It is a fair assumption that the terms "Elders" and "Leaders of the People" are alternative labels for the High Council.

31. Quoted from Frederick W. Danker, *Jesus and the New Age: A Commentary on St. Luke's Gospel* (Fortress Press: Philadelphia, 1988) 319.

32. R. Allan Culpepper, "Parable as Commentary: The Twice-given Vineyard (Luke 20: 9–16)," *Perspectives in Religious Studies* 26 (Summer 1999): 158.

33. J.S. Kloppenborg, *Reading Ancient Viticulture: The Social Context of the Parable of the Tenants in Mark and Thomas*, ed. Leslie Hayes (Claremont: IAC, 2002).

34. Culpepper, "Parable as Commentary," 153.

35. William F. Arndt, *Bible Commentary: The Gospel According to St. Luke* (Concordia Publishing House: Saint Louis, Missouri, 1956) 404.

36. Culpepper, "Parable as Commentary," 154.

37. Danker comments that the historical correspondence is not precise. Danker, *Jesus and the New Age*, 317.

38. The Sicarii were the dagger bearers. They were bands of violent nationalists who campaigned to set Palestine free. They arose in protest against political rule. In their earlier years, they fought primarily in urban settings often committing murder in crowds. Later they participated in a futile stand against the Romans at the end of the 66–70 BCE war.

39. Zealot is a term applicable to some features of Intertestamental Judaism: (1) Certain persons with fervent devotion to God's law; (2) a general attitude and movement of violent, religious, revolution; and (3) Jewish revolutionary factions that emerged during the 66–70 BCE war under John of Gischala.

40. For a detailing of several scholars' positions, see Culpepper, "Parable as Commentary," 151–152.

41. Marvin W. Meyer, tr., "The Gospel of Thomas," *The Secret Teachings of Jesus: Four Gnostic Gospels* (Random House: United States, 1986) 31.

42. Though the portrayed class relationships strain my credulity they clearly do not strain that of the author of the Gospel. The redaction of this passage, beginning with the earlier parable in Mark, does compel the alignment of God with the landowner and the leaders with the tenants. This reading excludes Jesus' audience from the allegorical import of the texts although they are, in reality, very involved in the issues as stake in the parable. It also leaves unanswered the question of succession that it raises. It is possible that Mark may have known the GTh and redacted that periscope to reflect his messianic concerns, which would include the motif of the "Beloved Son." The imposed messianism does overshadow the class tensions that are present in the parable. My reading does not satisfactorily resolve this conflict but it is also so that the traditional reading leaves some questions unanswered.

43. Robert V. Tannehill, *The Narrative Unity of Luke-Acts: A Literary Interpretation: Volume One: The Gospel According to Luke* (Fortress Press: Philadelphia, 1986) 192.

44. Tannehill, *The Narrative Unity*, 190. The questioners themselves do not assume as true what they deny. They present as ridiculous a belief held in varied ways by the Pharisees and Essenes.

45. G.B. Caird, *The Gospel of St. Luke* (Penguin Books: Great Britain, 1963) 224.

46. Joseph Fitzmyer, *The Gospel According to Luke X–XXIV* (Doubleday & Company, Inc.: Garden City, New York, 1985) 1299.

47. The Hasmoneans were descendants of the rulers of the Maccabean revolt.

48. The Sadducees are often portrayed as sticklers for the written law of the Torah explained by their accepting only the written Torah as scriptural. This means that they would reject the oral law of the Pharisees: another contentious point.

49. Fitzmyer, *Gospel According to Luke*, 1300–1301.

50. Stage III readings would reflect the final redacted form of the text and a fully developed kerygmatic theology in which the Christological titles can be applied to this text. It would reflect the understanding of the later early church and not the understanding of the very early church.

51. Fitzmyer, *Gospel According to Luke*, 1311.

52. Fitzmyer, *Gospel According to Luke*, 1313.

53. Fitzmyer, *Gospel According to Luke*, 1310.

54. Fitzmyer, *Gospel According to Luke*, 1310.

55. Fitzmyer, *Gospel According to Luke*, 1309.

56. Fitzmyer, *Gospel According to Luke*, 1321.

Chapter 17

Response: Lucy Bailey, "Likkle but Tallawah"

Lincoln E. Galloway

In her chapter in this book on the global future of feminist New Testament studies, Althea Spencer Miller introduces us to Lucy Bailey, of Jamaican ancestry. Lucy Bailey offers the unique perspective of a Caribbean woman's voice to an assembly that explores feminist scholarship. We cannot tell whether Lucy Bailey would have willingly lent her voice to this gathering or whether she has been conscripted for this task.[1] No doubt Lucy Bailey would recoil from bearing the burden of a crushing cross that requires she offer herself as representative of Caribbean women's voices.

The Caribbean is a unique geopolitical sphere, with people of diverse languages and ethnic backgrounds telling stories that articulate a Caribbean consciousness, and reflect a common soul, history, and destiny. These unique stories often use images, metaphors, or characters that are drawn from biblical narratives to express understandings of enslavement and freedom, sacred spaces and religious experiences, resiliency, and creativity. These stories may emerge in the context of colonial control, brutality, and waste reflecting a quest for human dignity and freedom, exhibiting creativity, resourcefulness, and resiliency in a long struggle toward self-determination, and the shaping of a Caribbean identity with its own distinctive features.

Whether willing or conscripted, Lucy Bailey's presence at the table changes the configuration and dynamics of the conversation. Though she cannot bear the burden of telling the diverse stories of Caribbean women, Lucy Bailey represents one means of asking the scholarly world: How large is the table? How inclusive is the conversation? For whom is our scholarship relevant? Who are the persons excluded, and why? More specifically, Lucy Bailey's voice echoes the expressions and yearnings of Caribbean people for genuine conversation that is relevant to our hopes and aspirations.

Lucy Bailey's story may help scholars to shape and provide strategies for engaging voices from the Caribbean.[2] Scholars around the table have in her story an invitation to shape our conversations by reflecting on the contributions of our Caribbean ancestors.

As such, Caribbean history becomes a critical conversation partner for New Testament studies. Althea Spencer Miller demonstrates that approach by engaging in a roll call of ancestors. She recalls the contributions of persons in a variety of fields from notable women among the maroons of Jamaica, to Mary Seacole, adventuress and author, to political leaders such as Dame Eugenia Charles, former prime minister of Dominica. A roll call of women and a celebration of their accomplishments provide one strategy for engaging biblical texts and relating them to the life stories and aspirations of Caribbean people.

Lucy Bailey also points to our engagement of scripture. Althea Spencer Miller sees in Lucy Bailey's appropriation of scripture something she terms "subversive knowledge." Lucy Bailey understands herself in relation to scripture in ways that permit her to appropriate meanings and readings that are empowering to her, even though those readings are baffling to others. Along with such "subversive knowledge," are wisdom traditions, and "repositories of knowledge" that Caribbean people find meaningful in daily life that are resources for engaging scripture. In this regard, study of scripture can be broadened when attention is paid to popular expressions, aphorisms, and proverbs. Althea Spencer Miller shows how this is done when she employs Caribbean sayings to describe people who are "*likkle but tallawah.*" She employs other expressions such as: "*force ripe fruit is not so sweet.*" Finally, she says, "*me granny used to say: 'finga neva say, "look ya," it always say, "Look deh." '*"

Lucy Bailey recites the Psalm and it becomes her words and testimony: "I have been young, and now am old; yet have I not seen the righteous forsaken, nor his seed begging bread" (Psalm 37:25 KJV). At this nexus of faith, spirituality, and hermeneutics, feminist scholarship will be challenged to take seriously the voices of the forgotten and the invisible, and the reading practices of those for whom scriptural understandings are woven into the fabric of their daily lives, values, and worldview. Such readings may exhibit subversive knowledge, or may be conducted from the margins, as well as from places that sustain oppressive traditions and practices in expressions of faith and spirituality.

Lucy Bailey's affirmation of the Psalm also points in the direction of Caribbean Spirituality. Feminist New Testament studies in the Caribbean must strive to honor the significance and depth of spiritual experience: the myriad ways in which people have experienced divine presence and activity. This spirituality combines wisdom of the ages, deeply rooted convictions of justice and fairness, grace and providence, quest for freedom, dignity, resilience, and destiny. Out of this depth of spirituality comes a way of life that reflects the deep longings and yearnings of Caribbean people, and an openness to the possibility that emancipation is an ongoing divine work with eschatological implications.[3]

Lucy Bailey points to our sense of place, belonging, and connectedness as Caribbean people.[4] This dimension finds significant expression in our connection to the land popularized in slogans about sand, sea, and sun. Connection to the land is one means of addressing the sense of belonging that is critical for Caribbean self-understanding, identity, and destiny. This connection to the land has provided stability to people's lives and contributed to the nurturing of community. Such a sense of belonging in Caribbean consciousness changes the paradigm and language from exodus or exile, to home and paradise. For Feminist New Testament Studies in the Caribbean, attention must be given to this sense of belonging and the building of community. Caribbean people's connection to the land provides an opportunity to invite greater stewardship of our land and natural resources, and for advancing theological understandings that reflect care of the earth's resources, ecological concerns, and ultimately, resistance to, and avoidance of all acts of violence, degradation, and devaluing of creation and life.

Lucy Bailey also makes us very conscious of the multiplicity of stories that emerge across diverse life experiences, opportunities, and resources. We recognize the indomitability of the Caribbean spirit through the creative responses or choices that women have made. However, such stories must lift the veil of invisibility of social class to include persons who experience the struggle for survival, recognition, or affirmation in vastly different ways. For Althea Spencer Miller this socioeconomic analysis is critical. She notes also that the way forward cannot only be driven by the question of whose struggle has been more strenuous or heroic. Stories cannot be limited to those persons or groups who represent the most invisible of the invisible, or most untouchable of the untouchables. As such, Caribbean feminists cannot construct a complete picture from the story of Lucy Bailey. The task is to recognize the diverse historical trajectories of struggle, survival, creativity, and resourcefulness from across the entire socioeconomic spectrum. The stories will not only reflect dislocation and severe rupture from ancestral roots but also the inspirational work of those persons who sustained traditions, provided for religious experiences, community building, and spiritual formation. There are stories of women who work within existing hierarchies and those who create new structures, provide leadership, bring about reform, enable change, and empower others to aspire to new heights. Lucy Bailey's story must be an invitation to make room for the stories of Caribbean women that demonstrate the miracle of struggle, dignity, and survival as well as those that demonstrate visionary, entrepreneurial, liberated, and wholesome humanity.

Lucy Bailey has provided us with a means of recognizing the powerful impact of colonialism, or neocolonialism, the legacy of dependence and the struggle for people/ nationhood in the current context of globalization marked by militarism and violence. As Althea Spencer Miller has indicated, Caribbean people do not have the option, or luxury of refusing to engage the imperialistic and pervasive notions of "universal democracy" "universal supremacy" "universal mighty right." Lewin Williams has observed a similar development that he terms the twin pillars or neocolonialism accompanied by neo-pietistic evangelism packaged in North American culture proclaiming capitalism and rugged individualism as the Gospel of salvation for the Caribbean region and in effect asserting that good Christians live by the capitalist ethic.[5] Feminist New Testament interpretation must take seriously these analyses in order to honor the quest of Caribbean people to live authentically as persons of worth and dignity.

The search for a Caribbean identity brings into sharp focus the problems of constantly having to filter through language, or cultural assumptions imposed on the region. The Caribbean region experiences unrelenting cultural bombardment that is often antithetical to our own visions and aspirations.[6] This imposition of foreign values and practices is also a malignant cancer in the soul of the church. Through this church, God as presented to the Caribbean spirit, was often not the symbol of freedom, and certainly not a "belonger," but an extension of the European or North American experience. Idris Hamid observes: "God is really foreign to us. In the religious imagination of our people [God] is a . . . foreigner. . . . Even the categories of our religious experiences are imports which do not reflect our cultural and native experiences. We experience God as an outsider."[7]

What does it mean to Caribbean people to be socialized or indoctrinated to worship God through the experience of other people? The challenge is to identify and critique the role and impact of imports or impositions on Caribbean spirituality, culture, and consciousness. There must be profound recognition that when God is understood through the medium of other people's experiences, there is the danger of losing identity, particularly for people whose culture is constantly been eroded and threatened by dominant powers. Noel Erskine notes that from such a perspective, God will then be interpreted as a foreigner to the consciousness of oppressed people.[8]

The language of our prayers and liturgy has to be guarded with care. Do they reflect realities that are foreign to our own experiences or aspirations? In a context where colonial domination has also borne strong racial overtones, what does it mean for persons of African, Indian, or Asian descent to repeat prayers that invoke whiteness as the standard of purity? Needless to say, snow is not endemic to the Caribbean. However, media images of whiteness and blackness are pervasive and have led some to procure products to convert their skin tone from dark to light. These two terms (dark, light) are also critical to theological conversation. Given this cultural context, can Caribbean persons continue to pray: "Lord, wash me until I am whiter than snow . . ." or "Lighten our darkness we beseech thee, O Lord . . .?"

Our encounter with the story of Lucy Bailey points us to all the other forms of cultural expressions including music, dance, songs, and poetry that reflect the soul of Caribbean people. These cultural expressions intersect with the study of scripture and provide meaning, or resonate with people's lived experiences. One such example of popular exhortation is found in the words of international reggae singer Bob Marley: "Emancipate yourself from mental slavery." From this perspective, it is vital that efforts to develop new forms of social consciousness, to articulate faith contextually, to further spiritual formation do not rely entirely on, or be limited to written texts by trained theologians or biblical scholars. Such efforts must take account of Caribbean people's stories, sermons, testimonies, prayers, literature, rituals, songs, and music.

Finally, Lucy Bailey's encounter with the feminists invites movement toward a more inclusive community of scholars and greater collaborative enterprises with Caribbean people. These cannot be schemes that masquerade as collaboration but in effect are oppressive systems of imposition and negation that call forth responses of imitation, distance, and subversion. These cannot be enterprises that proclaim justice while participating in and benefiting from structures that justify atrocities and contribute to oppression. In collaborative efforts, it is Caribbean people who are vulnerable to being flooded with foreign symbols, ideas, and messages. These cannot be appropriated in an uncritical manner. A significant part of the task before us is reinterpretation and rejection of inappropriate forms. In telling her story, Lucy Bailey invites collaborative enterprises that seek to honor her humanity, story, wisdom, spirituality, culture, history, and the realities of her daily life, and her hopes and aspirations as a person within a broad and diverse Caribbean community.

Feminist New Testament studies in the Caribbean will require collaborative activities that will promote social analysis as well as critical engagement of Caribbean history, traditions of folk religion, and cultural expressions. Althea Spencer Miller has provided a valuable approach to biblical scholarship in lifting up Lucy Bailey's story. She is calling for more attention to be paid to biblical texts and their intersection with Caribbean history and culture, spirituality, music/hymns/songs, dance, literature, sermons, liturgy, poetry, proverbs, and traditions. Her methodology also includes social and cultural analyses to speak meaningfully about issues of identity, community, visions of hope, and eschatological transformation. Ultimately, Caribbean people will test and validate the role and significance of feminist New Testament studies as the stories of women are told and women are continually affirmed as persons of dignity and worth, and as leaders and partners within the Caribbean community.

Notes

Althea Spencer Miller and I share Caribbean roots (Jamaica and Montserrat respectively). We have served the Methodist Church in the Caribbean and Americas and as New Testament scholars living in the United States we seek to find ways to make our work relevant to the Caribbean. I am grateful for this collaborative effort and the opportunity to respond to her chapter, "Lucy Bailey meets the Feminists."

1. In using the term "conscript," I wish to evoke the image of Simon of Cyrene who was compelled to carry the cross of Jesus (Mark 15:21). Indeed, Lucy Bailey's plight would seem impossible and overwhelming if she felt compelled to speak for all Caribbean women.

2. The notion of shaping voices, critical engagement of scripture, or meaningful, liberating, or empowering reading strategies among women has been of great concern to scholars in others settings. See Gloria Kehilwe Plaatjie, "Toward a Post-Apartheid Black Feminist Reading of the Bible: A Case Study, Luke 2:36–38," in *Other Ways of Reading*, ed. Musa Dube (Atlanta: Society of Biblical Literature, 2001). The writer suggests that from a background of entrenched apartheid, patriarchal oppression, and marginalization of black women in South Africa, the bible as a sacred, authoritative, and analytical text for social consciousness and change is not enough. She suggests that the post-apartheid Constitution recognizes the rights of women. As such the constitution that empowers women should be read with the bible to enable women to reap the benefits of a new consciousness and promise.

3. See Kortright Davis, *Emancipation Still Comin'* (Maryknoll, NY: Orbis Books, 1990).

4. I will call this "Connection to the Land." Philip Curtin describes the situation in Jamaica in the latter half of the nineteenth century as the church began to recognize its social responsibility to formerly enslaved people. The Methodist Church, although hesitant to meddle in social issues, or political questions, or intervene in wage disputes unless there was consent from both parties did not think that buying land could be considered intervention but rather a social responsibility. So Methodists would occasionally buy a moderately large run of land for resale to its members. See Philip Curtin, *Two Jamaicas* (Cambridge: Harvard University Press, 1955) 115.

5. Lewin Williams, *Caribbean Theology* (New York: Peter Lang, 1994) 25.

6. Williams, *Caribbean Theology*, 31–53. The Caribbean church beginning with its role during years of slavery has been described as the Missionary church, the church of the planter class, the church of colonial and neocolonial values, the church that embodies European

(and later U.S.) cultural values. Williams claims that the Missionary church compromised the Christian faith and its prophetic role through (1) its nurturing of feelings of cultural superiority, and (2) its unholy alliance with colonial powers in the quest for geopolitical expansion and exploitation of the region's resources.

7. Idris Hamid, *In Search of New Perspectives*, Paper presented at the Caribbean Ecumenical Consultation for Development, Trinidad, November 15–20, 1971 (Barbados, Caribbean: CADEC, 1971) 8.

8. Noel Erskine, *Decolonizing Theology: A Caribbean Perspective* (Mary knoll, NY: Orbis, 1981), 69–86.

Chapter 18

Signifying on Scriptures: An African Diaspora Proposal for Radical Readings

Vincent L. Wimbush

. . . every mention of her past life hurt. Everything in it was painful or lost . . .
it was unspeakable . . . [like] working dough, working dough . . .
the serious work of beating back the past. . . .
Remembering seemed unwise. . . . It was not a story to pass on.

—Toni Morrison, Beloved[1]

On several occasions in recent years I had the honor of serving on American Academy of Religion/Society for Biblical Literature Annual Meeting review panels for publication projects of female feminist colleagues. On both occasions the books we reviewed were commentaries; they were, of course, most worthy of celebration. Although the rhetorics of praise generally and are always expected to mark such situations, in these particular situations all the comments were enthusiastic and certainly genuine, heartfelt, and serious; we knew we were celebrating significant historic accomplishments of women in the academic guilds in which women's voices and works have not always been heard and respected. I was pleased to be part of such events.

My pleasure and overwhelmingly felicitous comments notwithstanding, I must confess that I also recall that some of my comments seemed a bit out of step with those of the others with whom I shared the dais. Some comments seemed out of step in the sense that I somewhat sheepishly and quietly raised the question about why it was that the *feminist* interpretation of the Bible as represented by the collaborative publication projects felt it imperative, appropriate, or even reasonable to try to make its case within the dominant discursive/literary production in the field of biblical studies that is the commentary. Should *feminist* biblical criticism, I asked, merely contest here and there the content-meaning of the texts assumed important or the approaches and methods to the texts assumed to be important? Is this what the decades-long challenge of feminists has been about? About equal opportunity to hold forth in this way, the way of the male old guard? Where was the more radical challenge to the whole enterprise?

Such questioning and challenge seemed to have stunned some of my colleagues. To be sure, there can be no doubt that feminist criticism is diverse and much of it represents an important challenge to the interpretation of (dominant-) male-conceived, male-dominated socioreligious traditions, including the production and interpretation of religious texts. The extent to which the female presence and voice are recovered, to this extent male-construed interpretation is greatly qualified, and without a doubt immediately made to appear what it is, notwithstanding its differentiation. Yet it also seems to me that much of the creative and radical interpretive challenges of the feminist voice in such texts are, in the final analysis, carried on within the terms of the dominant discursive formation and field that is (white-) dominant-male-determined academic biblical interpretation.

From its liberal-secular to conservative and fundamentalist confessional representations, it is such interpretive practices and politics that elevate the commentary to near-canonical status. So even as it manipulates and changes the boundaries of center-dominant academic discourse, much feminist criticism, insofar as it invests in what the commentary represents, and notwithstanding efforts to influence or radicalize here and there content-meaning and some approaches and methods, it remains on the exegetical farm, remains within what I term, following Jonathan Z. Smith,[2] the tribal-theological circle, namely the circle not of interestedness in general, but religious-confessional investment and apologetics in particular, no matter how masked the positionality may be.

My point is not so much about the commentary per se, but about modeling and advancing a challenge about positionality in critical interpretation. The challenge I would like to advance in this chapter puts me outside this discursive tribal–exegetical–religio–theological circle. This is not so much because there is anything inherently illogical or wrong or sinister about such a circle; the latter certainly has its place, its purpose, historically (in almost every situation) the privileged place and purpose. The issue is whether at the beginning of the twenty-first century the inside of the circle is or should be the only position for all or most students of religion, across the various academic–ideological–political leanings. Should feminist scholars of religion who are also biblical scholars, then, not be challenged, notwithstanding their different and sometimes radical substantive academic–political argumentation/interpretation, to consider what the objects of their focused scholarly energies ultimately reflect about their politics and positionality?

I would like to proceed first by problematizing the other parts of the theme of this collection of chapters to which this particular chapter belongs. What I should like to offer has not to do so much with "Globalization" per se or "the New Testament" per se or the one often used highly charged but seldom unpacked abbreviation in relationship to the other. Given the international headlines that frame our lives, I am sure many of you share my uneasiness about any discourse about globalization and any initiative named as such. And the degree to which the highly packed abbreviation we call the "New Testament" or interpretation of such is said to be globalized, even a cursory history lesson teaches caution or the need for heavy qualification.

The breathy abbreviation "New Testament" is the veiling of a long history of different forms of co-optation and violence, literary, rhetorical–ideological, and otherwise. The categories are not going to disappear of fade away. But I certainly want and need always to render such language problematic. My way of rendering both these categories problematic is to make the linkage between globalization and "the New Testament" in terms of the center-dominant white-male discourses that represent the agenda and orientation of the North Atlantic historically "mainline"- academic interpretations of the Bible. The nexus is all too often denied or masked. But the situation has been there for such a long period of time in the Western world that we should assume the possibility of heavy self-obfuscation and delusion on the part of perpetrators as well as victims. The harsh reality is that there is no globaliza- tion of the New Testament except in terms of a history of forms of domination.

In the extent to which feminist discourses and practices in relationship to the Bible continue to be off-center-dominance, what I want to offer can and should be understood as complementary. But the extent to which feminist and minority discourses see their interests in terms of the imitation of the practices and agenda of the center-dominants, generally content with the little bit of difference that the addi- tive approach brings to the traditional framework, then what I shall offer here should be understood as a challenge and criticism.

I begin with a statement of authorization and social power. I have arrogated to myself the psychosocial and political–intellectual authorization as a biblical scholar and historian of religion to begin my intellectual probing not in an ancient moment or with ancient texts already declared special ("canonical"), but with myself and the most intimate circle and the larger enveloping social world most responsible for the shaping of myself. Then I orient myself outward toward those other enveloping cir- cles or social worlds that constitute the larger world I inhabit and negotiate. This beginning assumes my acceptance of what literary critic Satya Mohanty[3] calls the "epistemic status" of minority subordinated sociocultural positionality and identity, and my identification with what anthropologist Ann Lowenhaupt Tsing, referencing the margins, calls

> . . . zones of unpredictability at the edges of discursive stability, where contradictory discourses overlap, or where discrepant kinds of meaning-making converge . . . an ana- lytic placement that makes evident both the constraining, oppressive quality of cultural exclusion and the creative potential of rearticulating, enlivening, and rearranging the very social categories that peripheralize a group's existence.[4]

For a number of years—all of my professional life, even if at first somewhat furtively and haltingly on account of a justifiable amount of paranoia—I have thought seriously and deeply about the Bible in relationship to the world that shaped me, that mid-to-late-twentieth-century world of urban independent evangelical Black church protestants. It was a significant segment of this world that was/is still to a great degree rhetorically shaped by the Bible. This widely accepted recognition has thrown into sharp relief for me one of the major problems faced by all peoples- made-Christians as a result of having had to undergo slavery and/or colonization, that of determining how to come to terms with the perduring sociocultural and political–ideological legacies of such experiences. How should the Bible, that master narrative text of Western culture, the text that has figured so prominently in providing ideological justification for the wresting of the land called new from native peoples, in providing warrants for securing it and building it up on the backs of the forced labor of Africans—how should we think about the Bible, and about continuing relationships with it? What might we do about the Europeanization of the Bible? And what about the overdetermined European-white North Americanist interpretive agenda and approaches in relationship to it?

The dramatic conjuncture of the Bible and the Black presence in the North Atlantic worlds forces into critical consideration several issues, the least of which are issues having to do with content-meanings, whether those of white evangelical and fundamentalist dominants or white liberal-mainliner dominants. How could consideration of the conjuncture not cause disruption in the "normal" dominance—the normal use of the Bible in the socialization of clergy-to-be in the ideology of religious leadership as a type of civil service, with the training in exegetical interpretation as obfuscation and disorientation that secures the silence of such leadership regarding the biblical underpinnings of the modern nation-states and the violence that is slavery and its aftermath? How could critical consideration of the conjuncture not force us to come to terms first not with content but with power/authority that lies not *in* the text but in the very invention of the text as locus of social authority, in the appeal to and uses of it?

John Jea,[5] one of those eighteenth- and nineteenth-century "narrators" of slave experience, recalled being challenged by his owner about the legitimacy of his claim to be Christian and therefore deserving of freedom and human dignity. Although the story indicates that the larger mixed-race religious community to which he belonged held that the enslavement of a confessing Christian was problematic, his slave-owner nonetheless refused to give ground (or give up human property) altogether. Assuming that he could not possibly provide the needed evidence of conversion—being able to read and interpret scripture—Jea's owner challenged him to read and interpret a passage from the Bible. In a now famous and chilling account, Jea recalled the utter astonishment of the slave-owner to his (nonconventional) "reading" (or recitation from memory) of a passage from the Gospel of John. And his "reading" was not of just any passage, but the first chapter, in which the claim about having received the truth is strongly made. Understandably incredulous, the slave-owner dragged Jea before magistrates who gave Jea another opportunity to prove his ability to handle the words of God. Again, Jea "read" from the book.

Convincing the magistrates, continuing to confound his owner, when asked to account for his skills Jea declared, "The Lord learnt me to read!" With this bold declaration and claim, referring to visitations and revelations and instructions from divine figures, Jea was, in other words, and under the circumstances, claiming a radical self-authorization. He understood precisely what was at stake in the slave-owner's use of the Bible—a special claim, an arrogation of power in relationship to divinity and in relationship to Jea's body. Because he had located spirit-power not in the text but in revelations, sources that neither the slave-owner nor any other person could question or gainsay, Jea was able to undermine the slave-owner's claims to power in relationship to the Bible and so also in a certain respect in relationship to his body. This was signifying on scriptures.

Jea's orientation to—that is, his signifying upon—the Bible as medium and locus of divine power and authority was clearly Africanist insofar as it reflected comfort with the notion of divinity or spirit being fluid and everywhere, including being with and in him. Thus, he was confident of his own conversation with and legitimate authority in connection with spirit. His response makes clear that consideration of the conjuncture of the Bible and the Black presence in the North Atlantic worlds should always raise the issue of power. It should have to do not so much with the meaning *of* or *in* the Bible, but with the Bible *and* meaning, the phenomenology and politics and social psychology of the making and engagements and social functions of, and social practices in connection with, the Bible.

The Africanist recognition of the power dynamics that are part and parcel of the phenomenon of scripturalizing, namely reading/engaging and manipulating scriptures, begs certain questions and issues. That the power tripping agenda in connection with scriptures was recognized and signified upon may have suggested the end of the African engagement of scriptures. But that this was not the case is dramatically clear. Coming to terms with the perduring interest in scriptures among African diaspora communities, especially those communities forced to undergo slavery and its long aftermath, the varieties of European–American Protestant scripture-focused cultures, can shed much light on a number of areas of interest—on African orientations and sensibilities, as they can be known in relationship to European orientations and sensibilities; on European orientations and sensibilities, as they can be known in relationship to African orientations and sensibilities; on the general phenomenon and politics of scripturalizing itself.[6]

One of the most significant developments in the modern world European–American cultural and ideological hegemony was the co-optation, the Europeanization or whitening, of the Bible. So one of the most important cultural translational, interpretive-ideological challenges that the North Atlantic Black diaspora communities—communities that at the beginning of their history in the Americas were predominately slave communities—had to face in the relationship to the Bible had to do with making the Bible more color-ful, that is, less fundamentally alienating, less a weapon of their own sociocultural erasure, invisibility, silence. One of the ways the erasure took place was through the phenomenon of the politics of the past. The agenda never was and is not now simply a matter of historicization—whether the engagement of the Bible ought to begin with or be about the past, but on what terms. The issue was whether the Bible was to be engaged on the basis of a European- determined past, a European-invented antiquity, on the basis of European-determined ancient texts, interpreted through the lens of various European historical cultural experiences.

Given such (over) determinations, how could African diaspora communities read the Bible on meaningful terms? They could not, except to the extent that the Bible as the idealized/canonical past was recognized as a European–American construction so that it might then be displaced, that is, placed within their own—African American—frameworks of interpretation. Such frameworks represented spaces in which the interpreting African American enslaved or formerly enslaved self was not erased, was rendered visible, was allowed to speak, was enabled to orient itself outward and to itself through (re)construction of a "usable" past, a past for affirmation. Such interpretive and ideological work did not represent a tight, vicious circle;[7]

it was done somewhat playfully, elliptically, described by African American folk cul-ture as "hitting a lick with a crooked stick."[8]

It is the matter of the past and how to engage it that Toni Morrison has addressed so compellingly in many of her works, especially in her acclaimed novel *Beloved*. The excerpt quoted above speaks to the need on the part of the character Sethe to "beat back the past" that was haunting and traumatic. The character Beloved has been understood in several different ways by reviewers and critics. Among the different interpretations of Beloved, that of the strange ghost-like daughter slain in infancy at Sethe's hand now returned from the dead is most apt. The strange young woman forces the past into (the) present consciousness. And this forcing—Beloved's presence—greatly disturbs, unsettles, traumatizes. Morrison's story and its schema and patterning seem to invite, to beg, conversation and different interpretations and responses.

The story seems to me to be powerful commentary about the continuing trauma of enslavement. It is about slavery's ongoing power to disturb, to traumatize, and to paralyze the enslaved. It is about the unbounded destructive reach of slavocracy as system, the deep psychic wounds and infections, the social death it causes. It is about how slavery continues to render the victims most vulnerable in terms of the stain of memory. What a dilemma—for slaves and sons and daughters of slaves there seems to be only two possibilities: either there is no past to speak of; or there is only a past that cannot be spoken of. Or might there be something else?

Morrison's novel *Beloved* suggests the possibility of something else. Through the development of certain characters that represent different relationships to the past—different interpretive stances in relationship to the past—it suggests that those robbed of significant aspects of dignity and selfhood, including a past, may recover and be healed. The matter is rendered problematic and solutions are advanced through the novel's characters, their experiences, sentiments, and orientations.

Baby Suggs. The mother-in-law. Sixty years of being a slave had caused her to suf-fer much and lose much. She had been psychologically and physically abused—slave life had "busted her legs, back, head, eyes, hands, kidneys, womb, and tongue." She lost much of her dignity. She lost members of her family. She lost a significant part of her self, her voice. And she lost her past. But she was also strong. She was a sur-vivor. She represented the survivalist and healing impulses, sensibilities, and practices of Black folk culture. She was "holy." She had plenty of "heart." With it she sought to heal. She was a doctor of folk medicines, "an unchurched preacher," "uncalled, unrobed, unanointed." She nonetheless allowed her "great heart" to beat for others. She was speaker at many of the folk churches; and she was the convener of the meet-ings at the Clearing—a place that signified both the necessity of and site and method for psychic cleansing and refreshment for the folk, a metaphor suggesting "the process of bringing the unconscious memories into the conscious mind."[9]

As the convener of the gathering at the Clearing, Baby Suggs was a folk priestess, a conjurer and diviner, a reader/interpreter of the ways of the folk and of the spirits. Her interpretations and exhortations were typically delivered in the "heat of every Saturday afternoon," while the people "waited among the trees." Situating herself on a huge flat-sided rock, she would typically first bow her head and then pray silently. The resonance with the stories about Jesus and other wisdom/salvation figures can hardly be missed here. When she would put her stick down the crowd would then know that she was ready to speak.

> Let the children come! . . . Let your mothers hear you laugh. . . . Let the grown men come. . . . Let your wives and your children see you dance . . .

Finally to the women:

> Cry . . . For the living and the dead. Just cry . . .

And always they would do so. And then they would dance. The men would then sit down and cry, the children would then cry—all continuing with such activity until "exhausted and riven." The narrator's summary of Baby Suggs's exhortations marking the similarities as well as differences between the white Christian scriptural and Black folk (sub-Christian) religious sentiments and orientations are illuminating:

> She did not tell them to clean up their lives or go and sin no more. She did not tell them they were the blessed of the earth, its inheriting meek or its glorybound pure.
>   She told them that the only grace they could have was the grace they could imagine. That if they could not see it, they would not have it . . .

Her own biblical (johannine and anti-johannine) pronouncements from the rock were arresting:

> . . . in this here place we flesh; flesh that weeps, laughs; flesh that dances on bare feet in grass. Love it. Love it hard. Yonder they do not love your flesh. They despise it. They don't love your eyes; they'd just as soon pick em out. No more do they love the skin on your back. Yonder they flay it. And O my people they do not love your hands. Those they only use, tie, bind, chop off and leave empty. Love your hands! Love them. Raise them up and kiss them. Touch others with them, pat them together, stroke them on your face 'cause they don't love that either. *You* got to love it, *you*! And no they ain't in love with your mouth. Yonder, out there, they will see it broken and break it again. What you say out of it they will not heed. What you scream out of it they do not hear. What you put into it to nourish your body they will snatch away and give you leavins instead. No, they don't love your mouth. *You* got to love it. This is flesh I'm talking about here. Flesh that needs to be loved. . . . And O my people, out yonder, hear me, they do not love your neck unnoosed and straight. So love your neck; put a hand on it, grace it, stroke it and hold it up. And all your inside they'd just as soon slop for hogs, you got to love them. The dark, dark liver—love it, love it, and the beat and beating heart, love that too. More than eyes or feet. More than lungs that have yet to draw free air. More than your life-holding womb and your life-giving private parts, hear me now, love your heart. For this is the prize. (81–82)

But as arresting as were Baby Suggs's words and healing offices, they were from Morrison's point of view inadequate: they represented a concession and capitulation to the awful acute pain and trauma that slave existence had wrought. Her ritual performances, her folk rhetorics and orientation, as important as they were for addressing the desperation of the present moments, as important as they were as part of the arsenal for the survivalist agenda, they were from the larger perspective of the novel against the pain that was the past at best a stopgap defense. Baby Suggs could not envision much of a future. She gave up from fatigue and the weight of the pain; she died, almost without notice, having been reduced to a state of listless incoherence.

Sethe. Sethe is the character with whom Morrison most sharply problematizes the matter of the engagement/interpretation of the past. She is the mother who out of desperation took the life of her baby daughter. She is the one who throughout much of the novel seemed haunted, paralyzed, hardly able to cope in the company of the ghost-like daughter come back to life, the troubling, trickster-like past.

Upon first reading, what troubles Sethe is not so mysterious. She had to undergo the pain of slavery and its continuing aftermath. Having undergone the brutality, the awful dehumanization that was slavery—including beatings, rape, and being marked/described as property—Sethe went mad in the way that a Black person, especially a female Black person, in a white-dominated world could (does Morrison mean *should*?) go mad: she determined to free her children from having their lives taken by the white world by taking their lives first. Successful in killing only one daughter, she spends the rest of her life getting away from the "rememory" of it all. For her "the future was a matter of keeping the past at bay." (40) Every mention of [her] past life hurt . . . was painful or lost . . . it was unspeakable . . ." (55). Like her friend Paul D she tried to keep the past as pain buried in a tobacco tin cup (68). But of course the haunting, the neuroses, only worsened with such burying and hiding.

Having at first physically locked out the wider community of those who also experienced acute life-pain as a result of the legacy of slavery, having emotionally shut out remaining close family members, including her other daughter Denver, having locked herself in a small bubble in which Beloved taunted and tortured her, and drained her of energy and perspective, Sethe found it impossible to directly confront Beloved. She was rendered silent, mute, invisible to herself and to others.

It was in Part Two of the novel when Sethe was pulled out of the torture chamber that was the bubble in which Beloved had held her prisoner. The three females Sethe, Beloved, and Denver, over a period of time in the same space began to turn to one another and free one another through confrontation, talking to one another and about one another, about what had happened to each other, about the meaning of what happened to them, about how what happened felt. Through these intense experiences refreshment, release, salvation was set in motion. What made the difference was the turn into one another so that the past could be collectively constructed in safe, affirming space.

Near a point of being able to fully open up and "rememory" the events leading up to the slaughter of her baby, Sethe confessed to Beloved what she felt and what were her motives when she did the awful thing. Notice the shifts in the tenses: now the past is becoming the present; the past is embraced in the present:

> . . . There must have been some other way. Let schoolteacher haul us away, I guess, to measure your behind before he tore it up. I have felt what it felt like and nobody walking or stretched out is going to make you feel it too. Not you, not one of mine, and when I tell you you mine, I also mean I'm yours. I wouldn't draw breath without my

children. . . . My plan was to take us all to the other side where my own ma'am is. They stopped me from getting us there, but they didn't stop you from getting there . . . (193)

Sethe comes to terms with the deed; she faces it and the ghost-child:

> . . . When I put that headstone up I wanted to lay in there with you, put your head on my shoulder and keep you warm. . . . I couldn't lay down with you then. No matter how much I wanted to. I couldn't lay down nowhere in peace, back then. Now I can. I can sleep like the drowned, have mercy. She come back to me, my daughter, and she is mine. (194)

In their own private mother–sister–sister ritual, they are finally able to come into common language in confessional song—in what I identify as archaic revelatory language intended to function as a type of scriptural language. In such language the women begin to see one another differently; revelations come to them. They are able to reconcile with memories and with one another. Confessions blend into each other in representation of happy confusion (or reconciliation):

Beloved
You are my sister
You are my daughter
You are my face; you are me
I have found you again; you have come back to me
You are my Beloved
You are mine
You are mine
You are mine

. . . . .

You are my face; I am you. Why did you leave me?
I will never leave you again
Don't ever leave me again
You went into the water
I drank your blood
I brought your milk
You forgot to smile
I loved you
You hurt me
You came back to me
You left me

I waited for you
You are mine
You are mine
You are mine (206, 207)

The revelations from the mother–sister–sister circle facilitated the internal freeing for all. But Sethe is finally freed of the haunting of the ghost-like daughter when the community of women through the mixed-tradition rituals—African; western Christian; and African diaspora sub-Christian—help her exorcise the ghost. Again, the scriptural-like language should be noted:

> It was three in the afternoon on a Friday . . . [The women] stopped praying and took a
> step back to the beginning. In the beginning there were no words. In the beginning was
> the sound, and they all know what that sound sounded like. . . . For Sethe it was as
> though the Clearing had come to her with all its heat and simmering leaves, where the
> voices of women searched for the right combination, the key, the code, the sound that
> broke the back of words. Building voice upon voice they found it, and when they did it
> was a wave of sound wide enough to sound deep water and knock the pods off chestnut
> trees. It broke Sethe and she trembled like the baptized in its wash. . . . Now she is
> running into the faces of the people out there, joining them and leaving Beloved
> behind. Alone. Again . . . (244, 247–248)

This ritual did not so much make Beloved disappear as it brought closure (offered the
Amen) to the revelation that Sethe had regarding herself, the past, the present, and
the future.

Denver. She was the other daughter, the one who represented the future. On
account of her mother's paralysis—the direct result of the haunting by Beloved—she
had learned to protect herself by retreating into solitude and secretiveness. Because
Sethe had been silent about and fearful of the past, Denver learned at first not to care
about the past. But not only was she smart in the conventional sense, having learned
the white letters and books, she was also sensitive and caring, curious and wide-eyed,
aggressive and courageous. During the period of time spent only with Beloved and
her mother, time in which she devoted herself to her mother's care, she noted how
both she and her mother were being utterly drained by the three-sided dysfunctional
relationship—"beribboned, decked-out, limp and starving . . . locked in a love that
wore everybody out" (230).

Then at a dramatic point when her mother spit up some object she had not eaten,
Denver was jolted into another reality. She knew then "it was on her" to act, to change
the dynamics. She resolved to leave the dysfunctional mother–sister–sister bubble, to
negotiate the world and do something to help herself and her mother. Dressed and
ready to depart, standing on the porch of the house, she was petrified. All the challenges that were part of being open to and living in the world rushed through her
mind. She remembered that she had been warned again and again by her mother and
grandmother Suggs about the bad things in the world, the bad people—"white
people" ("people without skin")—who meant her harm, people against whom there
was little or no defense. Her grandmother's summary wisdom about the matter, about
whether negotiation with the white world should be attempted, rang in her ears:

> There is more of us they drowned than there is all of them ever lived from the start of
> time. Lay down your sword. This ain't a battle; it's a rout. (232)

These words spoken by her grandmother seemed to encourage paralysis, resigna-
tion. But Denver, still standing motionless, with itchy throat and palpitating heart,
remembered the final words spoken by her folk priestess grandmother:

> "You don't remember nothing about Carolina? About your daddy? You don't remember
> nothing about how come I walk the way I do and about your mother's feet, not to speak

of her back? I never told you that? Is that why you can't walk down the steps? My Jesus my."

But you said there was no defense.

"There ain't."

"Then what do I do?"

"Know it, and go on out the yard. Go on." (232)

Denver went out—into the world. She went out to engage, interpret, and negotiate the world. She took critical note of everything, the little things, the ordinary things, differences—in colors, tones, shapes and sizes and textures. She developed awareness of development; she could measure the effects of time. She learned to negotiate the letters—and thus significant aspects of the orientations—of the dominant world. Under the tutelage of Lady Jones she read voraciously ("book stuff") and developed aspirations to attend Oberlin College. She also learned a different—healthier—way of relating to her mother and to Beloved. She realized that "somebody had to be saved" (239). She decided to go find a job and leave mother and sister by day to their destructive behavior. Having approached the home of the Bodwins to request work, she had an important turning-point conversation there with the black maid:

... You Baby Suggs' kin, ain't you?
    ... I heard your mother took sick, that so?
    ... What's the trouble . . . ? (240)

Although fearful and vulnerable, Denver "told it—told all of it" (240). As a result, she won the trust and support of the maid and got the work she was looking for. The miracle was not just Denver's opening up to another person; it was in her finding strength to *narrate* her perspectives and feelings. This narrativity, this discursivity regarding the past was the way to the future. Denver represented the future. As such, she could in the future help construct a better past.

Conclusion

The story that is *Beloved* and the development of the major characters in it can be made to represent or address many different issues and problems. Multiplicity of meanings in reaction to her writings is what Morrison always seemed to invite. What is most striking for me about the story and its characterizations is not simply that it interprets some issue, but that it problematizes interpretation itself—its reach, its radical indeterminacy, its multiple shapes and structures, its intonations, its textuality and orality, its grounding and authorization, its focus, the politics involved, the challenges in the way of it, the psychosocial power it represents and effects, the psychosocial occlusion it effects. About the self and the world, about the self in the world, the past and the present, the past in the present, the novel's focus is about significant things, not at all about or limited to (in the words of Harriet Tubman) "such small stuff as letters."[10] Here is signifying "with a vengeance" on scriptures and on all scriptural traditions: interpretation should never be only or primarily about the "small stuff" of texts or left to exegetes as mere text-handlers/ writers of commentaries.

Contrary to the story that has been told, historical core African sensibilities and orientations (not the contemporary fall into fundamentalisms) are far away from if not in sharp criticism of the Pan-Western religious tradition of the heavy, sometimes fetishistic, sometimes also disingenuous, investment in texts as media of transcendence. Not only are texts deemed too much a narrowing of possibilities through which transcendence can be mediated, they are associated with the most scandalous power dynamics among human beings. In all sorts of ways Morrison's novels represent this historical African and African diasporan dis-ease with scriptures: in almost all of her novels major characters are given biblical names that seem inappropriate for their narrative situation or are in some poignant ways the opposite of the biblical types. And with few exceptions throughout her novels a relationship is set up between the negatives of formal—Western white-determined, white-dominant ideological— education and the Bible.[11]

Nevertheless, Morrison's works have powerful, profound implications for interpretation, for the translation of sociocultural readings into social power. And these implications in turn have implications for an understanding of the import of scriptures. While critical of the power play interests of Western scriptural traditions, Morrison is nonetheless very much invested in helping readers determine what can facilitate the needed radical readings for social power and social psychosocial salvation of the sort quested by the major characters of *Beloved*. Morrison has her characters discover that radical readings, empowering readings, are the necessary readings of the self that include that part of the self that must constitute the past. Whether involving slaves or ex-slaves or children of slaves or those with very different experiences, such readings of the self always involve coming to terms with the pain and trauma of human existence as well as the psychosocial default response that involves either forgetting the past or as in the case of Sethe being haunted by it.

With its indeterminacy, its circling movement, its open-endedness, and repetitiousness, its focus upon pain and trauma, *Beloved* the novel is a kind of anti-scripture, a replacement for the race-tainted overdetermined texts called scripture and the violent phenomenon of scripturalizing. That there might be other ways of construing "scriptures" is possible. But what Morrison's characters—and a large segment of Black peoples—seem to have had to experience is the type and usage of "scriptures" that has not often saved. Furthermore, in the ways in which the ancestor Baby Suggs, the mother–daughter–daughter conversation and the rituals of the community of women figure in the story, she suggests how interpretation should mean, and how media of the sacred should function as part of meaning-seeking.

To be fully human is to interpret. To interpret is to seek meaning. The truly free individual is the one who seeks meaning through radical readings—open-ended readings about the self in the world, necessarily including the past, readings that represent openness to other ways of knowing, readings that expand the boundaries and genres of scripturalizing. The future of radicalized readings, readings needed by all those yet off-center, lies in what Denver represents: Female. Feminist-womanist. Color-ful. Graduate of Spelman College. Cosmo-politan. Able to speak different languages, to enter into different discourses. Open to old and new ways of knowing. Critically oriented in a way that she can not only read master-texts but can signify upon them. This is the future of interpretation of the past for our common good.

*   *   *

Remembering . . . her grandmother's last and final words, Denver
   stood on the porch in the sun and couldn't leave it . . .
      But you said there was no defense.
         "There ain't."
         Then what do I do?
"Know it, and go on out the yard. Go on."

Notes

1. All quotations from pagination of this edition (New York: Penguin Books, 1987), Reprinted by permission of International Creative Management, Inc. ©1987 Toni Morrison.
2. See Jonathan Z. Smith, "Sacred Persistence: Toward a Redescription of Canon," in his collection of chapters, *Imagining Religion: From Babylon to Jonestown* (Chicago: University of Chicago, 1982) 52. I have leveled the same critique and challenge to my Society for Biblical Literature colleagues who are members of racial and ethnic minority groups, especially some African Americans, regarding the lack of critique of the investment in the commentary project—even one that is supposed to be for African Americans. I have declined the invitation to participate in such projects for the reasons I am giving here.
3. Satya Mohanty, *Literary Theory and the Claims of History: Postmodernity, Objectivity, Multicultural Politics* (Ithaca: Cornell University Press, 1997).
4. Anna Lowenhaupt Tsing, "From the Margins," *Cultural Anthropology* 9/3: 279.
5. See his autobiographical text in Graham Russell Hodges, ed., *Black Itinerants of the Gospel: The Narratives of John Jea and George White* (Madison: Madison House, 1993).
6. With their long histories of subjection to European political–economic–military colonial powers, including the overlapping and continuing aggressive and fateful ideological hegemony of European–American, especially American, religious missionary activities, the situations in African countries are somewhat different, but not by any measure happier. They are not the focus of this presentation.
7. As in the long-standing modern beginning of twentieth-century phenomenon—"fundamentalism"—traditionally associated with groups of white Protestants. But the rather recent phenomenon among African Americans that is the too-tightly drawn non-reflexive thinking begs critical analysis. See Nancy T. Ammerman, *Bible Believers: Fundamentalism in the Modern World* (New Brunswick: Rutgers University Press, 1988); George M. Marsden, *Understanding Fundamentalism and Evangelicalism* (Grand Rapids: Eerdmanns, 1991). And for the beginning of work on African Americans, see Albert G. Miller, "The Construction of a Black fundamentalism Worldview," in *African Americans and the Bible: Sacred Texts and Social Textures*, ed., Vincent L. Wimbush. (New York: Continuum International, 2000, 2003) 712–727.
8. See Zora Neale Hurston's *Mules and Men* (New York: HarperCollins, 1990 [1935]) 33, 218.
9. Linda Krumholz, "The Ghosts of Slavery: Historical Recovery in Toni Morrison's *Beloved*," *African American Review* 26/3 (Fall 1992): 397, 400.

10. See Theophus Smith, "I Don't Read Such Small Stuff as Letters," in *African Americans and the Bible*, 83–91, note 1.

11. The characterization of the white School Teacher in *Beloved* is illustrative: he is cold and formal, invested only in figures and in instruments for measuring and describing slaves' body parts. Also, it is worth noting that Paul D is made to say that there is "Nothing more dangerous than a white schoolteacher," meaning that the ideology of white educational socialization is destructive of Black existence. In other novels, black characters are also criticized for being such. Formal education is usually linked with Christianity. And Christianity and education usually means the Bible. Cf. "Morrison's Voices: Formal Education, the Work Ethic, and the Bible," *American Literature* 58/2 (May 1986).

Chapter 19

Reflections on Conversation Three

Noelle Champagne, Filiberto Nolasco Gomez,
and Katrina Van Heest

Part Three of the tripartite Conversation on Feminist New Testament Studies (FNTS) addresses the field in Africa and the diaspora. The speakers locate themselves differently with respect to the academy, geography, and religious affiliation, but each expresses concerns that speak to the heart of the conference. Musa Dube from Botswana critically assesses the field of FNTS up to the present and gives her vision for the future from a set of possible trajectories. Althea Spencer Miller from Jamaica draws the attention of FNTS toward the most disenfranchised members of her Caribbean community as symbolic of the directions the field should take. Vincent Wimbush speaks from an African American perspective, questioning the notion of the scriptural canon itself and challenging New Testament studies to become identifiable and relevant to diverse marginal communities.

All the participants are involved in a struggle to base FNTS scholarship in the lives of the people that the New Testament engages and affects. Their chapters pick up on themes that have pervaded the conference as a whole. They engage the topic of the title of the conference, issues related to power, position, and the tension between universal and particular language in the context of engaged scholarship. Each crafts a chapter using specialized narrative forms and attention to social location to engage the Bible in a voice that distinct communities recognize or identify with in contextualized ways. In other words, this conversation emphasizes working from the pulpit of the people as opposed to or in addition to the pulpit of exclusive academic and ecclesial institutions.

How the Presenters Identify with the Title of the Conference

The presenters in this third conversation approach the topic of the conference from perspectives distinct from and yet complementary to those of their discussion partners in the first two conversations. Here, the presenters have been asked to speak not only from the margins of the Western academy, but also with connection to the identity and cultural category of "blackness." Their task is necessarily peripheral to mainstream biblical studies because it involves connecting Two-Thirds World identities and the experience of blackness within the context of this era's superpower, the United States. Because they have been asked to make such penetrating contributions to the conference, each inspected the very structure of the conference, appropriately beginning with its title.

In her consideration of the conference's title, Dube engages FNTS by charting the past four decades of scholarship and using it to frame a concrete vision for the future of the field. Dube uses the title of the conference to construct her vision of a future in which the topic of FNTS can be brought to the women of the world for study. She proposes that a global future be formed by the creation of a society focused on feminist engagement with the New Testament. Parallel to such a society, Dube envisions a concerted effort to bring academic work to churches. On the other hand, Spencer Miller, co-convener of the conference, used the title as a fertile ground in which to root her contributions. She uses a figure from her community to embody the future that Dube constructs. By using the figure of Lucy Bailey, Spencer Miller is able to present a vision of how FNTS should be pursued. She advocates bringing the popular and specific experience to the text in order to find relevance in sacred scripture. Wimbush poses a challenge to the definition of New Testament and the construction of canon itself. He contests traditional notions of the New Testament as a self-contained literary entity that can speak for itself. By way of example, Wimbush uses the text *Beloved* by Toni Morrison as an example of a piece of literature with relevance to a community. He draws out the intersections between the novel and the biblical tradition, pointing toward methods of studying scriptures. By expanding the canon of the New Testament, Wimbush hopes to move toward a more layered reading of the text that accounts for its interplay with social issues.

All three presenters see the effects of globalization and predict a global future for FNTS. Dube reminds us that *global* is a loaded term, especially because it conjures the more political term *globalization*. In her lecture, she extrapolates on the idea that in the United States people are not conscious consumers of African products within the global market, while she is aware of the American cultural influence all around her in Botswana. As an African, Western ideas contribute to the way she views and examines the many contexts of her own life. Dube sees the urgent need for a future in FNTS that opposes a Western position of privilege where the focus of the population is not constant struggle for subsistence, and a vision of future solutions takes a backseat to a drive toward growth and progress. A Two-Thirds World perspective contrasts Western values and constantly looks for solutions to alleviate the pain of oppressive structures, so that a vision for the future is constantly visualized.

Spencer Miller comes from a Caribbean background where the population falls between the First and Two-Thirds World. The figure of Lucy Bailey encapsulates awareness of societal position, concern with her experiential world, and creating her own theology. The formation of culturally contextualized scholarship is something that Spencer Miller emphasizes throughout her chapter. She also emphasizes the need to share ideas between the First and Two-Thirds World societies and implies that the success of FNTS relies upon doing this effectively. Wimbush's approach begins this work, assuming a marginal First World perspective and including new literary texts within the study of FNTS. Wimbush proposes focusing on FNTS with a commitment to the disenfranchised by working to find relevance in sacred texts that have been claimed by majority cultures.

Centers and Margins

Over the course of the conference in whole, the issue of central and marginal locations has emerged again and again. Understanding the importance of access to power and relationships based on dominance and subordination has become key to the enterprise of imagining a global future for FNTS. Dube deals with issues of center and marginality by moving Two-Thirds World frameworks for biblical interpretation to the ideological center. Spencer Miller wants to introduce the voice of the margin to challenge the authority that language holds over people. Her chapter is an example of reorienting centers and margins and placing centers to margins. In his "biblical" interpretation of the novel *Beloved*, Wimbush challenges the biblical studies guild and FNTS in particular to expand the margins and incorporate non-Christian voices to present a more formidable challenge to power centers.

Furthermore, all three speakers use narrative examples to express the significance of subordinated voices in the global future of FNTS. Dube frames her chapter from the perspective of Rahab, the sex worker of Jericho. Spencer Miller focuses her interpretation on the person of Lucy Bailey as a metaphor for the disenfranchised voices of Jamaica. Wimbush uses Tony Morrison's novel *Beloved* as a wedge into a discussion of the interpretive strategy of "signifying." The marginal culture takes a different point of interpretation by embodying a marginal actor in the biblical stories or offering a new insight into a former interpretation.

In previous sessions of the conference, the center was thought of as an ideological center. This session featured the conference participants helping to define the terms as power positions; they spoke of "centers of power." Specifically, a central location has to be focal, privileged, and empowered. To be in the margin is to be abject, peripheral, and disempowered. Respondent Lincoln Galloway says that there is no one center, and that centers are fluid and flow with power. Therefore, any position can actually be a central one because centrality is almost synonymous with power and functions in the same ways. Dube agrees with Galloway that there are many centers, and by changing the focus we can change the centers. It is thus very powerful that through this process of interpretation and inclusion the marginalized are able to recognize their cultures within the authoritative text, the Bible. Spencer Miller suggests that a center of power can exist within a person and that authority needs to come from within instead of without. Through a process of inclusive interpretation comes recognition of marginalized cultures within the authoritative text.

These models allow people to connect with the text specifically by translating the stories into their own terminology and cultural models. This method is in direct opposition to a formal model that imposes Anglo-Christian models of biblical interpretations on outlying, marginal groups as a form of colonization and domination. The significance is, then, that marginal cultures represent different ways of interpretation by embodying a marginal actor in the biblical stories or offering a new insight into a former interpretation.

But culture is more than a point of aesthetic departure; it is in fact the common characteristic of groups of people that are acting for each other's benefit and interest. In this way, culture also has a dynamic of dominance and power. As groups of people choose to acknowledge one another's authority, they often build systems that justify frameworks that support and affirm oppressive models of dominance. Power groups seek ways to legitimize the frameworks by co-opting centers of common authority, such as the Bible. Marginality's claim to power, then, causes clashes with and resistance to the dominant culture because that claim to power tries to expand what the dominant cultures choose to observe.

Universality and Particulars

The discussion of centers and margins that has been such a meaningful presence in the conference has been accompanied by a related discussion of language choices. The third conversation's presenters approach the issue of universal and particular language in very different ways. Whereas Dube suggests that we use universal notions such as human rights to frame how we deal with social conditions in interpreting the New Testament, Spencer Miller brings to bear a critique of the universals dispensed by purveyors of international power and colonialism. Wimbush's work embraces the particulars, finding literary works that represent them. Wimbush asks us to recognize the particulars and then use documents to enhance our understanding of the interplay between text and society.

This topic gives the conference an identifiable relationship to postmodern theory, which has reacted against Enlightenment thinking that privileged universals over particulars. It is the privileging of universals—and the crushing of particularities—that has led to global crises where difference is washed over in the service of maintaining sameness. Spencer Miller speaks of universals and particulars as a balancing act. It is such because we need to identify commonalities in order to commune with others, but we must treat universalities with suspicion because they all too often espouse and condone the perspective of colonizers. She concedes, though, the utility of seeing universals and commonalities as lowest common denominators. The problem is that those who have the most take the responsibility for defining the lowest common denominators, the universals. This practice of universalizing creates what we have called "the margins" and robs them of systemic power/centrality. Universals are useful for establishing commonalities and should be considered broad and malleable guidelines rather than authoritative constraints. The concept of the postcolonial condition is one that includes colonizer and colonized not in a simple binary but in a complex web of economic dependence and exploitation. Dube's suggestion that the postcolonial condition links all members of the global community provides a commonality with which we can construct a future for FNTS.

Conclusion

Feminist New Testament studies scholarship attempts to expand authority over scripture to encompass new perspectives from disenfranchised communities based on their experiences of the text. Through this process of integration and broadening, the voices of the marginalized are able to exert authority and impact both their circles of experience and the global community. The conversation on Africa and the Diaspora calls FNTS to broaden meaning, disrupt boundaries, and encourage mutually beneficial growth. Using lay interpretation as the catalyst for the transformation of the discipline to experience and incorporate diverse perspectives, these presenters set lofty goals for the future of FNTS.

.

Index of Proper Names

Index of Ancient Sources

Ancient and Classical References

Classical Texts

Early Christian Literature

Rabbinic Literature